INDEPENDENT AGING

Family and Social Systems Perspectives

Contributors

Greg Arling
Vern L. Bengtson
Ellie Brubaker
Timothy H. Brubaker
Rodney Cate
Thomas R. Chibucos
Charles Lee Cole
Terri A. Eisler
Beth Emery
June Henton
David J. Hubler
Helen Q. Kivnick

Joseph A. Kuypers
Shirley A. Lockery
William J. McAuley
Jay A. Mancini
Carla Masciocchi
Tamerra Moeller
Karen A. Roberto
Robert L. Rubinstein
Jean Pearson Scott
Wayne C. Seelbach
E. Percil Stanford
Adria Thomas

INDEPENDENT AGING

Family and Social Systems Perspectives

Editors
William H. Quinn
Texas Tech University
Lubbock, Texas

George A. Hughston
Arizona State University
Tempe, Arizona

AN ASPEN PUBLICATION®
Aspen Systems Corporation
Rockville, Maryland
Royal Tunbridge Wells
1984

Library of Congress Cataloging in Publication Data

William H. Quinn.
Independent aging.

"An Aspen publication."
Includes bibliographies and index.
1. Aged—Family relationships—Addresses, essays, lectures. 2. Aged—Social
conditions—Addresses, essays, lectures. 3. Aged—Care and hygiene—
Addresses, essays, lectures. 4. Dependency (Psychology)—Addresses, essays,
lectures. I. Quinn, William H. II. Hughston, George A. [DNLM: 1. Aged.
2. Family 3. Social Work. WT 30 I38]
HQ1061.I49   1984   646.7'8   84-14445
ISBN: 0-89443-550-7

Publisher: John R. Marozsan
Associate Publisher: Jack W. Knowles, Jr.
Editorial Director: N. Darlene Como
Executive Managing Editor: Margot G. Raphael
Managing Editor: M. Eileen Higgins
Editorial Services: Ruth Bloom
Printing and Manufacturing: Debbie Collins

Library of Congress Catalog Card Number: 84-14445
ISBN: 0-89443-550-7

Printed in the United States of America

1 2 3 4 5

To Four Family Generations

Norma Jean Benson Quinn, Jared Benson Quinn,
Whitney Elizabeth Quinn, Leo Robert Quinn, Jr.,
Mary Elizabeth Walrath Quinn, William E. Walrath,
and Regina Ayres Fuller Walrath

Table of Contents

Introduction

Informal networks of support are the means by which families meet day to day needs and crises. . . . They are cooperative, reciprocal, natural and informal. They are often the roots that gave life. (Johnson Foundation, 1979)

There have always been old people, but never in history have there been greater numbers of elderly people comprising a greater proportion of the population than at this time. These vast numbers—but most of all the vast percentages—have aroused a greater awareness of the need for knowledge about psychosocial development in later life. Thus, concern for the family and social network has become acute. Four- and five-generational families are increasing and are adding, overall, a mixture of richness, burden, and complexity in families. Research during recent decades has concentrated on contact and exchange patterns in families across generations. If they have done nothing else, these past studies have repeatedly confirmed that contact is significant for most families, regardless of their geographical proximity, and that mutual aid and support are clearly exchanged and are of paramount importance to almost all families. It is recognized, however, that these patterns of reciprocity hinge upon circumstance and individual characteristics, which differ among and within individual families.

Intergenerational family relationships continue over the life cycle, whether they exist by obligation or by choice. Concurrently, the difficulties of aging in our society are great—even when one considers advances in medicine and social services. The burdens of providing for the elderly (by families and by the larger society) have become a major concern, perhaps partially because of economic pressures and limited resources. Population shifts further strain available social service mechanisms for promoting the development of services to the elderly. As one examines the need for governmental and formal support system resources and the need for utilization of substantial family resources, one recognizes that a tremendous challenge lies ahead in comprehending the family in the context of development of the aged and in the assistance and utilization of all available support mechanisms to meet the physical and the emotional needs of our perpetually aging population.

Philippe Villers, a computer wizard who fled Nazi-occupied France as a child during World War II, has returned some of his good fortune by building a $40 million foundation to help make a "profound change" in the role of older citizens in American society. His underlying assumption is that basically, people need the opportunity to feel a sense of worth and to feel that they are part of and contributing to society; this is increasingly denied to older people and they have been relegated to a passive role which does not make self-fulfillment possible.

A neglected area of focus in research and service-related programs for the aged has been the preservation of independent aging. Many opportunities for personal and social gain in society are lost because the wide range of myths surrounding the elderly in society has inhibited the contributions older people can make to community, regional, and national well-being. This neglect was documented by the recent action of the Organization of the World Assembly on Aging, meeting in Vienna during August 1982. This body proposed that society should recognize older people as a continuing resource and see their experience, insight, and energy as important to the well-being of both their families and the community. In addition, the Assembly noted that efforts must be made to find new roles and meaningful activities for elderly persons. U.N. Secretary General Javier Perez de Cuellar, in a final session of the Assembly, stated that "countries need to help the elderly lead independent lives in their own family and community for as long as possible" (1982).

The intent of this book is to promote this very idea. Economic, political, and social structures exist that, by their nature, keep older persons unjustifiably dependent. Many potential contributions of our older people remain untapped. The creative, innovative human resources of this age group, which could allow society to promote and sanction independence for all adults, are underutilized. Emerson reminded us: "It is one of the most beautiful compensations of this life that no man can sincerely try to help another without helping himself" (*Bits and Pieces*, 1984). We emphasize instead a "more-of-the-same" approach as we attempt to uncover or to create new resources to support the dependence of the elderly. This strategy fosters a set of attitudes that erodes the strengths and the abilities of an already massive and rapidly growing cohort group, and so becomes self-fulfilling prophecy because there is the temptation to equate physical and mental expectation with actual potential. Minimal expectations of performance and behavior by the family, by society, and sometimes by elderly people themselves, inhibit their functioning at full capacity. Inasmuch as people, to a large extent, live up to their own and others' expectations, low expectations lead to low performance or functioning levels. Further, a disregard for the importance of compensation and of adjustment to decreasing functional capacities stabilizes the problem. According to Sydney Smith, "It is the greatest of all mistakes to do nothing because you can do only a little. Do what you can" (*Bits and Pieces*, 1984). All of these factors indicate the necessity to understand these processes and make inevitable the urgent and efficient development of strategies designed to promote the independence of elderly people.

The concept of dependence can mistakenly imply a linear relationship of society, family, or individuals affecting the older person. Neglected, however, is the influence of older persons on others. Circular causation or reciprocal influence is accepted by the authors of this book as a demonstration of the interrelatedness of parts in the context in which the older person lives and operates.

In the chapters of this book, the authors offer both practical application and empirical validation for a consideration of later-life development within the context of the social system. Each chapter maintains a common theme in its discussion of the independence of elderly people: independence is associated with individual and family development and relates to psychosocial well-being. A similar conclusion, repeatedly presented, exemplifies dependency in later life, particularly when potential is restricted, as a source of low morale and family stress. Autonomy and a connectedness or sense of belonging to a social group, such as the family, comprise a major proportion of well-being as perceived by the elderly. Of all the concepts and findings presented in this book, two themes are of major significance: (1) independence for many older persons is a realistic idea that catalyses a wide range of possibilities in promoting quality of life; and (2) when independence is limited because of health, economic status, social situation, mental functioning, and the like, compensation to offset such liabilities is feasible. Because the family and the social network regularly and predictably play a part in the consideration of both themes, these concepts are emphasized throughout the book.

The initial chapter by Kuypers and Bengtson provides a framework in which competence in families of later life is viewed from interactional, developmental, phenomenological, and structural perspectives. Concepts are drawn from family systems and developmental frameworks that apply knowledge about the family to independent aging, including dimensions of social role performance, ability to cope, and a sense of mastery. A cycle of individual incompetence, which the authors label as the social breakdown syndrome, is described and shown. They identify not causes but "stimulants to breakdown," which can help the reader to understand the processes that can inhibit healthy family functioning in later life. A conceptual view of these processes is described and helps to set the stage for the chapters that follow. on aging-family relationships, treatment and care issues within informal support systems, cultural and social aspects of aging, and specific characteristics of the aged that are associated with independent lifestyles. Intervention that promotes competence is also discussed and evaluated.

Several chapters that focus on familial relationships follow. In Chapter 2, Quinn emphasizes the importance of examining the qualitative aspects of relationships between older parents and their adult children. Although much is known about quantitative aspects, such as contact and mutual aid, much less is understood about the nature of these relationships, including interaction styles, changes that occur over extended periods of time, and shifts in roles and power dimensions. Several concepts are presented that may contribute to the enhancement of relationship satisfaction and to clearly conceptualized intervention goals. Kivnick's chapter on grandparenthood and family relationships is a creative, realistic, and well-integrated discussion of behavior, roles, life stage, and meaning attributed to these relations. She gives attention to approaches that help us understand grandparenting. She remarks, "But how can we articulate and quantify what it is that lights up an old grandfather's eyes when he talks about his grandson?" Her proposed reciprocal model of influence and causality allows us to conceptualize these intergenerational relations as time-based and as creative shifts. Interaction patterns are viewed within the family life-cycle framework, with (as in the preceding chapter) a focus on qualitative aspects and a further examination of issues of loyalty, personal debt, interdependence, and adaptability.

Mancini, in the first of two contributions, describes the leisure lifestyle of elderly people in the family from a functional perspective. He proposes a map for viewing various functions of the leisure role, their benefits to independent living, and the personal sources of those benefits. In realistic fashion, the liabilities of these family leisure experiences are delineated as well. Recognition is given to the influence of communication, mutual feedback, individual perceptions, and role patterning on well-being. Leisure lifestyle is viewed as a framework for fostering family connectedness and continuity.

Cole examines marriage in later life within the framework of independence. He describes the research on marital quality over the family life cycle, tying concepts from human development, personal adjustment, and marital history to marriage in later life. Dimensions of later life (e.g., leisure, division of labor, role redefinition, and marital interaction) are addressed to describe differences in adjustment between child-focused and spouse-focused marriages.

The second section of this book presents treatment and care issues related to the aging family and, in some cases, their association with long-term care. One major issue, which has been discussed in the literature for some time, is filial responsibility in care-giving and support. Seelbach suggests that the concept of filial responsibility will become even more crucial in family involvement of the aged as governmental and other formal support mechanisms for the elderly are reduced to accommodate more pressing economic burdens. Several dimensions of intergenerational family relationships—particularly those of older parents and their adult children, which can be embedded in a framework of qualitative interaction—also apply to filial responsibility. These include notions of loyalty and obligation, developmental changes within individuals, reciprocity, and interdependence. The author proposes that the children further define the structure of these relationships by becoming coordinators of the family network: in their management of resources, in their utilization of the human support network, and by making connections to interventionists. Brubaker and Brubaker extend these ideas by applying them to the aggregate of long-term care practitioners. In their chapter, they urge these helpers to understand and to integrate family involvement in order to reinforce family ties for the elderly and to solicit their cooperation. They use a case illustration to demonstrate that the "family is the client." Recommendations with guidelines are provided to help practitioners form a link with aging families.

The next two chapters of the section are reports of empirical studies that sort out some issues related to family care-giving. Masciocchi, Thomas, and Moeller begin with the premise that the family provides the majority of services to impaired elderly. One very important issue addressed, and one that requires further examination in the future, is the assessment of the consequences to families of their acceptance of provider roles. The authors report the types and the sources of aid family and friends provide. Of value is the discussion of the effects of this role on families providing care—for example, including personal stress, family structural changes, role change, and lifestyle alterations. Finally, possible intervention strategies for formal helping networks that aid family care-givers are presented. Arling and McAuley follow with a description of their study of a needs assessment. Consistent with previous chapters, they accept the premise that long-term care-providers have been frequently inattentive to family networks of support and unknowing of how to integrate them in the care-giving system. The primary objective of the chapter is to describe the role of the family in long-term care of the impaired elderly. After discussing the extent of family care given and the factors that influence it, they suggest that nonfamily sources of care supplement, rather than displace, family care-giving. Findings indicate the impressive array of types of care given and include the role of nonfamily sources. In a clear presentation of public policy issues rarely addressed in such detail, the authors specify the conditional aspects of support system functioning. Attention is given to cost-benefit issues in care-giving, delineation of responsibilities among informal and formal support systems, and an efficient balance of roles.

This second section of the book is completed with a look at the presence, the meaning, and the pattern of family abuse of the elderly. Henton, Cate, and Emery bring evidence demonstrating the prevalence of such family behavior, which we are only beginning to recognize. Elderly dependence of many kinds generates a sense of need for and reliance on those persons with power and resources, which makes elders at risk for conflictual interactional patterns. The frequency and definition of abuse and the lack of protective mechanisms are addressed. Four types of abuse and the factors that influence them are discussed. Finally, recommendations for intervention and support provisions are developed to aid the practitioner or persons providing support to the abused elderly.

Cultural and social differences in later-life development have recently received attention, but they are far from being well-specified and integrated into conceptualization or practice. This third section of the book examines racial, three cultural, and gender differences. None of these chapters is intended to be a comprehensive presentation of the literature or the scope of the problem. Rather, the emphasis is on a perspective of the uniqueness and particular circumstances of older persons and the specific demands or challenges of these groups: the black, the rural, and the female and male elderly. Stanford and Lockery present a demographic profile and the family structural characteristics of the black elderly to demonstrate this differentness. They adopt the premise that these persons have strengths and limitations associated with certain cultural values that help to determine life's journey through adulthood. Two areas given attention are (1) a discussion of the black elderly as community volunteers, and (2) a call for more awareness in service delivery of the cultural and the socioeconomic history of these families. The chapter by Scott and Roberto is an empirical investigation of support and contact patterns in rural aging families. They present data that demonstrate the extensive flow of mutual aid and reciprocal influence in promoting independence in two generations—adult children and their parents. The variability in aging rural families and the nature of their intergenerational involvement is described and compared with that in urban families. Rubenstein reports on a study made of elderly men in which he utilizes a participant-observation method of regular intervals and uses a split-sample. The strength of this chapter lies in its method of uncovering the unique challenges of men who live alone. The author uses an exchange framework to examine network functioning and emphasizes the "contextualized" idea of support systems.

The final section of the book considers future directions about the scope of later-life development and preservation of independence. Each chapter identifies a territory that is only beginning to receive some interest and attention. Social networks of family, friends, and neighbors are considered to be valuable support systems in the chapter by Quinn, Hughston, and Hubler. The presence of energy and strength in these networks, the shortages of professionals trained to work with the elderly, the financial limitations of providing formal support, and the qualitative aspects of these networks contribute to the justification for considering the importance of nonformal support. Policy and intervention implications are derived from the discussion to engage family and social network support. Chibucos constructs a model for examining the role of children in the independence and the development of old people. He begins to provide direction in thinking about children and older persons related to socialization patterns and reciprocal influences around interdependence. He proposes that we must foster more interconnectedness among generations throughout the life span, with an emphasis on uniqueness and diversity. His developmental perspective includes a diagram depicting this conceptualization and specifically highlighting the placement of children within the context of the environment of the aged.

The present economic structure and our negative view of old age as a stage of declining physical and mental powers have minimized the opportunities available for older persons to participate in the world of work. Eisler considers the impact of career on independence and society by the identification of the intrinsic and the extrinsic rewards. She outlines the positive consequences of mid-life career change and calls for researchers, educators, and employers to consider and to encourage the opportunities of work in old age. Mancini discusses the frontiers of research on family life in old age. He identifies the myths that hold us back and the theoretical issues that may provoke productive questions. The quantitative-qualitative dialectic is addressed, as it has been throughout the book. He succinctly states: "Conventional research designs are insensitive to the 'ebb and flow' of life; they are typically oriented to capturing a momentary, perhaps transitory, slice of everyday life in the hope that something more stable is reflected." He remarks that case-study approaches are practically nonexistent and suggests that we continue with research, using qualitative research methods. He addresses the limitations of global measures, like well-being, which do not allow us to understand specific changes in family life and identifies important areas of research that have been overlooked. Overall, he calls for more than a "whimsical approach" to family gerontology and includes a summary table outlining direction for a serious approach to it. He enriches the discussion with a plethora of examples of relevant research questions.

We hope that this book will appeal to social workers, health administrators and practitioners, psychologists, therapists, policymakers, and other persons interested in the prolongation of independence during later life. Educators, researchers, and students of gerontology may also find help in gauging the social characteristics of older persons.

Some chapters contain an emphasis on advocacy, with explicit recommendations and program implications for practitioners. Other chapters represent research investigations addressing questions and theoretical ideas based on the literature. They present evidence to enable the reader to formulate answers (as well as new questions), to accumulate knowledge, and to draw conclusions.

The orientation of the book not only encompasses various aspects of support utilized by older people but also proposes creative and useful ideas related to the promotion of health (both physical and mental) and the preservation of independence. It is hoped that the researcher, the educator, and the practitioner will find this study helpful as they consider support mechanisms of older persons and as they recognize the interplay of individual development of the aged in a social context.

William H. Quinn
George A. Hughston
September 1984

REFERENCES

Aging assembly cites concerns. (1982, September 19). *Lubbock Avalanche-Journal*, p. A–9.

Bits and pieces. (March 1984). Fairfield, NJ: Economics Press.

The Johnson Foundation. (1979). *Strengthening families through informal support systems* (A Wing-spread Report). Racine, WI: The Johnson Foundation.

Part I

The Family and Relational Systems in Independent Aging

Chapter 1

Perspectives on the Older Family

Joseph A. Kuypers and Vern L. Bengtson

Exchange, socialization, developmental, systems, and structural are some of the many frames of reference used to describe the family's dynamics. Part of the fascination of family life lies in the incredibly diverse range of activities and issues families confront over the course of time. Families are not simple or straightforward or easily understood. Several perspectives are helpful in organizing thinking about the older family. Some perspectives address qualities of human behavior. For example, change, continuity, interaction, the creation of meaning and system complexity are key concepts. Any perspective on the family must also look at competence and its value as a central organizer in sorting out the ways in which families relate to challenge, change, and stress. Further, it must consider the older family as an evolving system that creates and recreates its own history. The social breakdown syndrome is a model that describes that process.

It must be emphasized at the outset, however, that none of the organizing perspectives are relevant exclusively to the older family. In fact, most come from the social psychology of individual development. An attempt is made to show their relevance for understanding older family life. Obviously, attention to any one perspective is incomplete insofar as it isolates some parts and ignores others.

THE WAYS WE UNDERSTAND FAMILY LIFE

Four perspectives on human behavior seem basic to the study of the family and are applicable to the older family. These perspectives are labelled *interactional, developmental, phenomenological,* and *systemic.* Combined, they present the following argument:

1. The roles, the expectations, the conflicts, the knots, and all other aspects of family life ultimately reduce to a question of the way members relate to each other.

2. The way in which members relate is multidetermined. Yet, in the study of the family as it ages, one important factor in any description of interaction has to do with the different developmental issues and tasks various members face.

3. The interactions are also formed by the meaning members give to an event or episode. These subjective constructions are hard to reveal and are inherently different for each family member.

4. Families are a pattern of relationships that cannot be adequately described individually. They combine in a higher order to form a system. That system is always in a state of tension, caught between forces that strive to maintain stability and forces that promote or demand change. Accommodations to this state of tension are never secure.

These perspectives cross many levels, from the ways people interact to the ways interactions combine. They also vary in focus, from personal meaning to social issues, which spring from age or sex differences. Although some traditions of social science inquiry may consider this mixture inelegant, it is nonetheless purposeful. The mixture seems necessary for any attempt to give order to the complexity of the family.

Interactional Perspective

The intellectual history of this perspective is quite diverse. Social psychologists and family sociologists clearly articulate the view that role and status are formed by the way people interact (Biddle & Thomas, 1966). A role does not exist by itself; it exists always in reference to another role. This relational quality identifies many features of interaction that cut across the description of a particular role: power, authority, reciprocity, and so forth. Theorists and clinicians who focus on human communication (Satir, 1972; Watzlawick et al., 1967) contend that the way people interact through language, tone, and posture defines and redefines the identities individuals eventually assume. Likewise, ego psychologists (Freud, 1964; Hartman, 1958) claim that, through the mechanism of projection, past relationships are carried forward to new relationships. We see and act toward persons not entirely on the basis of who they are but partially through our history of the way we have interacted in the past. This feature is critical in understanding how older families struggle to transform old patterns of interaction to meet current and, sometimes, emergency demands. Finally (but certainly not exhaustively), the behavioral school of thought is clearly focused on the immediate action and interaction of persons. In clinical behavioral family work, considerable attention is given to revealing, describing, and charting how people interact. In this perspective, the interaction chain of action and reaction is a fundamental element in analysis and treatment (Patterson, 1971).

This study borrows from all of these traditions and claims that being in a family is being a participant in a continuous series of interactions. These interactions are the experiential bases for growth. They define, redefine, and maintain the roles and positions persons take on in the family and in the outside world. They also form the basis for one's identity. According to Goffman (1967), this identity is never entirely secure but is ''on loan'' and subject to change when interactions do not support or validate it. In this line of thought, interaction is also an important basis for creating a person's sense of the world: as a place of predictable and positive response or as a place where individual action has little effect. One's sense of confidence, personal control, autonomy, and freedom all rest, in large part, on the continuous interchange of action and reaction.

The way interactions take on a history of their own is of particular interest for analysis of the aging family. Roles and expectations stabilize as time passes. They are created again and again. Sometimes they are dysfunctional when they meet other changing realities. It must be stressed that these interactional patterns were initially formed when the family was young and also that the dynamics of the young family—response to authority, autonomy, power, and reciprocity—must be transformed as the family ages (see Chapter 3). This transformation process is an essential, yet never-ending, source of struggle and pain. It is not easily done. Families continuously struggle as they try to let go of old patterns of interaction. Letting go involves loss and pain and a faith that what is lost will be replaced with something equally workable. In the light of the prior statement that one's identity is on loan, the stakes clearly are high when a family tries to transform its interactional style.

Another feature of this transformation process is that the tempo and the timing of change are likely to be different for members who interact. One participant may be eager for renegotiation; another may feel threatened as the process begins. Interaction apparently endures beyond the point at which individual members wish for a change in the rules. Perhaps individual change precedes interactional change. Hence, a unique feature of family life emerges in which all members feel (from their unique positions in the family) that the stabilized family patterns of interaction are outmoded and not based on current feelings of capacity and interest.

Children of all ages, for example, whether 14 or 44 years old, may feel that their parents see them as younger or less ''mature'' than they feel themselves to be. Parents may, from their vantage point, wish for their children to let go of earlier images of parents as heroic or invulnerable or always available. Each person may seek a change in the balance of interdependency and the ascription of rights and responsibilities; yet, each continues to act and to interact in old patterns. The case study in Exhibit 1–1 illustrates this pattern of conflict.

Exhibit 1–1 Case Study 1

Barbara, 44 years old, was preparing for her annual visit to her parents' house in the East. As a mother of two teenagers and as a career woman, she saw herself as an able person—independent, clear-headed, with interests developed over the years, and certainly grown-up. Yet, going home inevitably brought terror. Her mother still gave unsolicited advice, commented on manners and dress, and betrayed her suspicion that her daughter was close to failure. Barbara, in turn, always came away from her mother's house feeling immature and devious. Upon arrival, daughter and mother would find their initial politeness yielding to irritation and bickering. Barbara felt crowded and unseen. As much as she tried to prepare for this episode, Barbara could not change how she responded to her mother. She felt like a teenage daughter—rebellious, powerless, angry, and frustrated.

Developmental Perspective

Developmentalists have charted regular and episodic patterns of growth and stability in human life as it matures and ages. Periods of rapid change are followed by periods of relative quiet, and the focus of the change varies as the person matures. Furthermore, the source of change varies as the person ages; biological development takes a predominant place in early life, and socio-psychological forces assume greater importance later in life. (See Haan, 1977; Havighurst, 1973; Piaget, 1929.)

These principles of individual development are fundamental to the study of lives over an extended period of time. Their application to this study leads to a simple but profoundly complicated fact: persons follow their individual courses of development in a system (the family) in which other members are at very different points in the cycle. Therefore, the study of the development of the family requires an analysis of how cycles of individual development influence and interact with each other (Bross, 1982; Haley, 1971). Analysis of the family cycle reveals patterns in the tempo, the content, and the source of family change.

If all members of a family were the same age and changed at the same rate, family life would be dramatically less complex than it is. Certainly this is not the case. Age and sex differences determine that the important issues and concerns of each family member are different. A 40-year-old mother may feel the "quiet desperation" of middle life or an eagerness to reactivate certain career interests or a willingness to be freed of full-time parenting. Her 15-year-old daughter may be fully immersed in her peer culture. She may be seeking freedom and autonomy while expecting the usual availability of her mother's attentions when she needs them. The mother's mother may be seeking to cope with her recent widowhood by reestablishing a more intense intergenerational connection with daughter and granddaughter. Each may be dealing with the issue of freedom, but in very different ways.

In an earlier paper (Bengtson & Kuypers, 1971), the authors argued that the developmental issues of youth and middle age were inherently conflictual. The term *developmental stake* was coined to reflect such growth-related tension. Although members of the middle generation use their children as a means to address questions of meaning and continuity, members of the younger generation use their parents as a means to struggle for freedom. For members of the middle generation, in their position as parents and teachers, an important task is the achievement of a sense of continuity. Hence, threat—and ultimately conflict—arises when signs of difference (often interpreted as rebellion) emerge. Concerns for autonomy prompt members of the younger generation to perceive a difference between themselves and their parents; however, signs of similarity between generations may be perceived as challenges to autonomy. The meaning each generation gives to an event is bound to be different and yields a substantial disparity between real or perceived differences or similarities.

The older family's capacity to join together and to cope as a unit with the profound changes of age is dramatically affected by the different developmental positions of members. Starkly stated, family needs may not blend well with individual needs. Families, however, are often not prepared to understand this fact. Their confusion, guilt, or conflict may be a natural product of a natural dissonance between the developmental cycles of its members.

Phenomenological Perspective

In trying to understand why a given event prompts vastly different human responses, many authors have given central importance to the mediating influence of subjective processes. Jerome Frank (1961) speaks of a person's and a culture's "assumption world"—the meaning of context that lends order and selectively interprets the inherently neutral nature of existence. Wanda Bronson's research (1968) focuses on the emergence of these assumptions in early childhood. She describes "central organizers" that are formed early and serve to order experience throughout life. She claims that these organizers are persistent over a life course. Humanistic psychologists have consistently claimed that subjective experience is a crucial element in the creation and maintenance of health. Disease is rooted in a person's alienation from personal or subjective experience (Bugenthal, 1967). Likewise, a growing number of health scientists argue that faith and confidence in the future are essential elements in the creation and treatment of disease (Pelletier, 1977). Even reputably objective physical scientists acknowledge the ultimate subjectivity of inquiry and knowledge (Oppenheimer, 1954). In the area of family therapy, Laing (1971) and Watzlawick et al. (1967) have been most consistent, perhaps, in their analysis of the subjective foundation for personal and familial dysfunction.

The authors also place the subjective in a central position. Their understanding of the diverse intellectual traditions concerned with this aspect of human experience is that family members are certainly more than passive participants in family life. They are *interpreters* of family life: they continuously construct analyses of what family interactions mean, how these are consistent or inconsistent with previously constructed meanings, and what they imply by way of expectation, duty, loyalty, and individual rights. It is these personal interpretations of family action which bind together and lend order to the extreme range of feelings and behaviors of a family.

Constructed Meaning

Certain features of the "constructed meaning" help explain how families create binds and knots for themselves. First, subjective meaning is usually not seen for what it is: subjective. A person's "sense" of things is his or her reality. This reality appears "correct" and "universal." Interpretation and fact are often confused, which can lead to persistent conflict about the issue of whose view is "true." A corollary to this tendency to objectify one's subjective sense is that constructed meanings are hard to reveal—to the person holding the view and to an observer. Simply stated, persons do not usually notice that they are selecting or constructing a certain view of a situation rather than another view. The meaning seems to be in the situation, not in their hands. They simply "make sense" of the matter and continue, unaware that *they* have done it, that the meaning resides in the person and not inherently in the external world.

A second feature of constructed meaning is the natural pressure to maintain a stable interpretation. We conserve our views and hold them as permanent. In his introduction to *Loss and Change*, Peter Marris (1975) makes the following statement:

> The book begins with a discussion of conservatism, because the argument as a whole depends on the assumption that the impulse to defend the predictability of life is a fundamental and universal principle of human psychology. Conservatism, in this sense, is an aspect of our ability to survive in any situation: for without continuity we cannot interpret what events mean to us, nor explore new kinds of experience with confidence. (p. 3)

Although this "impulse to defend the predictability of life" offers many benefits (not the least of which is a sense of stability, certainty, and sanity), it also contains risk. To conserve meaning in the face of change, one may sacrifice an accurate perception of change itself. Behavior is selectively perceived and fitted into already constructed meanings. This feature of constructed meaning helps to explain the frustration family members often feel at not being seen as or accepted for who they really are. Parents develop images of their children that may persist despite dramatic growth and change. Likewise, children hold on to images of their parents long after the images seem appropriate. (See Chapter 2.)

When older families face a crisis, they do so in the context of that which they already know about the crisis, about the family member under threat, and about the outcome. Obviously, this knowledge can be affirmed and can be self-fulfilling. The case study in Exhibit 1–2 gives an example. What was the father's reality? Perhaps he saw Ann as distant, angry, or impatient, which confirmed his view of Ann as being insensitive to the awesome experience he was about to face.

A third feature of constructed meaning (also reflected in this case study) is the fact that two people never share the same subjective experience. Two observers of the same event inevitably interpret it differently without realizing this inevitability. Consensus may be reached, but often only as an accommodation to the friction engendered by the inevitable differences. As already noted, age and developmental differences may prompt vastly different interpretations of a given event. Such differences in interpretation may prompt dramatic and persistent conflict. For example, solicitous interest may be perceived as meddlesomeness; an expression of protection may be perceived as overcontrol. When such conflict occurs, confusion and feelings of invalidation are likely to emerge.

The potential for misperception of meaning in families (prompted by the confusion of subjective and objective, and compounded by the need to conserve one's personal view) prompts a unique adaptation by the family as a whole. Partly to avoid a continuous struggle over diverse perspectives, the family develops a shared illusion of agreement. In effect, the family pretends, without knowing it is doing so, that certain actions have certain meanings, that members' intentions are

---

Exhibit 1–2 Case Study 2

Ann's father, now in his 70s, was facing an impending heart bypass operation. He faced the possibility of dying on the operating table or, if he survived, the possibility of some unknown physical handicap. As an observer, Ann knew her father to be an independent, sometimes stubborn, man who would not welcome advice and counsel willingly. Hence, before the fact, Ann knew her father would not accept her efforts to assist him emotionally through his (and her) ordeal. As a result, Ann recreated her "reality" by acting in ways that confirmed it: by withholding advice or by being indirect or by withholding counsel until the tension was too great. Then she mixed her caring with frustration and made its acceptance even harder.

known to each other, and that family roles are real. Apparently, these subjective meanings of the family system are even more persistent than are the meanings of individual members. They endure longer, they may misrepresent behavior more extremely, and they are less easily revealed to the family than to the individual person.

This persistence of family "illusions of agreement" may help to explain why parent-child role relationships are so difficult to alter; why children and their parents seemingly never finish with issues of autonomy and independence; and why families may get stuck in the repetition of unfulfilling authority-dependency relationships.

Family Myth

When the construction of meaning occurs within families, certain views of the family itself and of persons' roles within the family also stabilize. These are called family myths. Many of the crises encountered in older families directly challenge long-held myths. One such myth is that the parents in a family are the primary caregivers: they nurture more, and they yield personal concerns to those of their children. A second myth is that the intensity of family life will decrease as the family ages and as the children lead their own independent lives. A third myth, perhaps less overt in many families, is that the parents, by virtue of being adults, are complete in their development: stable, mature, capable, and less needful of care and nurturance. Insofar as the disruption in older families may involve changes for the elderly parents, there may be urgent need for nurturance and caring. The new demands and expectations placed on the entire family may be fundamentally incongruent with how they perceived their roles, responsibilities, and capacities in the past.

Structural Perspective

Three important perspectives have been suggested: (1) that family life requires an understanding of the ways interaction provides the groundwork for defining roles and identities; (2) that different developmental needs of family members guarantee conflict; and (3) that meaning is constructed and conserved, often leading to misunderstanding and inappropriately stabilized definitions of persons and events. Embedded in these perspectives are two overarching statements about family life: First, a constant state of tension exists in families and is created by the pressure between forces that promote or demand change and the need to stabilize and conserve the meanings made of past experience. Second, families accommodate to this tension as a unit. Family myths and stabilized illusions of agreement are formed and exist as a feature of the family as a whole. This final perspective, of the family as a stabilized structure, warrants fuller attention.

Three quite different uses of the term *structure* are described below. In each, structure and function are intertwined. Hence, each usage of the term makes comment, implicitly or explicitly, about the way members interact, about expectations, duty, and much more.

Membership Identification

The first usage concerns the identification of family membership. Who is the family and on what basis is this defined? In some contexts, the family is *nuclear*; in others it is *intergenerational*. The family is also *extended* to include more distant relations or it may be a *network*, including friends and neighbors. By marriage, the family establishes affinity; by divorce or other disruptions, it becomes *single-parented, fractured*, or *blended*. A person is usually a member of all of these families—a child in one, a parent in another, an in-law in another. Different roles, expectations, loyalties, and lines of authority are called into play, depending on which family is in the foreground. Frequently, conflict is generated as different families claim their power over members.

In the case of the older family (i.e., when children are adults with adult parents), the structural definitions are complex and subsume confusing or often vague expectations. Because society provides poorly articulated guidelines for grand-parenting or for being an adult child to an older parent, the extended family must evolve its own roles, often with little formal guidance from society. If the progression from generation to generation is broken through separation or divorce or other means, the connections between members may also be broken, even though blood ties still exist.

A major theme in this study is that as older families face crises—especially when the crises involve the elderly family member—conflict and confusion is generated over the struggle about which person in the family is to deal with the demands. Who will be the "burden bearer," and on what basis is this choice justified? Adult daughters and daughters-in-law are often assigned the weight of caretaking responsibility. Notwithstanding the question of justice or fairness, this choice is often made at considerable emotional cost to the family.

Pattern of Interaction

A second usage of the concept *family structure* deals with the pattern of stabilized interactions and alliances families form. According to Minuchin (1974), family structure is "the invisible set of functional demands that organize the ways in which family members interact" (p. 51). The demands are formed by universal rules governing family organization (power, authority, and complimentarity of function) and by expectations of particular family members. "The origin of these [rules] expectations is buried in years of explicit and implicit negotiations, often around small daily events. Frequently the nature of the original contracts has been forgotten, and they may never have ever been explicit. *But the patterns remain* [italics added]—on automatic pilot, as it were—as a matter of mutual accommodation and functional effectiveness" (Minuchin, 1974, p. 52).

As patterns stabilize, families begin to look quite different. Minuchin distinguishes between the *enmeshed* and the *disengaged* family structure. The enmeshed family has poorly defined rules around loyalty and responsibility. Interactions are close, intense, and unclear. The disengaged family has overly rigid rules, which result in tight and strained communication. These two family types are extremes. Most families fall somewhere in the middle. Kantor and Lehr (1975) describe three family structures: the open, the closed, and the random.

Although the focus in Minuchin's and Kantor and Lehr's works is on younger families, the concept of family structure as these authors use it is useful for the study of the older family. Many questions need to be explored as to how these different families cope with their aging. Do they follow a different family cycle? How is generational continuity affected by structure? Do children of enmeshed nuclear families repeat this pattern? In times of crisis, especially if various families are affected, which are more able to cope successfully? Although we must await further examination of such questions, the claim that the concept of family structure is central in the study of older families can be made. Stabilized patterns of "invisible functional demands" (Minuchin, 1974) and "invisible loyalties" (Boszormenyi-Nagy & Spark, 1973) mediate between forces that promote stability and those that promote change. Predictions of an older family's ability to cope with threat rest in part on the nature and quality of these stabilized features of the family as a system.

Elements of Interaction

A third way of viewing family structure deals with the various elements of family interaction that comprise the family as a system. These may be considered the elements Minuchin or Kantor and Lehr (and others) combine in their larger structural patterns.

The McMaster's model of family functioning (Epstein & Bishop, 1981) identifies six elements: (1) problem solving process, (2) communication, (3) roles, (4) affective responsiveness, (5) affective involvement, and (6) behavioral control. In Minuchin's work, consideration is given to the clarity and the flexibility of boundaries between persons and roles, and to alignments and coalitions and how they occur by virtue of age or sex. The circumplex model (Olson, Sprenkle, & Russell, 1979) defines cohesion and adaptability within families as central elements. Finally, systems theory as it is applied to the family places special emphasis on (1) subsystems within the family, (2) boundaries between subsystems, (3) feedback mechanisms that serve to stabilize the system, (4) purpose or mission; (5) causality, and (6) family rules (Bross, 1982).

These different elements are mentioned not so much to explore their special application or to debate differences between authors as to reveal their range. Another important perspective is understanding how older families negotiate the issues and threats of aging associated with stabilized patterns of interaction. These form a system. They influence how members see themselves and their roles in the family. They predict different responses to crises. Ultimately, they provide the context in which persons who wish to assist the older family in trouble must initiate their work and assess their effectiveness.

COMPETENCE—AN ORGANIZING PRINCIPLE

Clearly, families differ widely in their ability to cope with challenge and threat. Some become stronger as they confront crises; others break down and only partially recover. In many cases the issues families face call forth new knowledge about their strength. Some authors express surprise at the capacities families show in the light of their weakness as an organization. According to Hill (1970), the family is a vulnerable organization.

> Compared with other associations in society, the average family is badly handicapped organizationally. Its age composition is heavily weighted with dependents, and it cannot freely reject its weak members and re-cruit more competent teammates. Its members receive an unearned acceptance: there is no price for belonging. Because of its unusual age composition and its uncertain sex composition, it is intrinsically a puny work group and an awkward decision-making group. This group is not ideally manned to withstand stress, yet society has assigned to it the heaviest of responsibilities: the socialization and orientation of the young, and the meeting of the major emotional needs of all citizens, young and old. (p. 14)

When one tries to understand how families differ as they confront conflict and crisis, the concept of competence is a useful organizing principle. There are three ways of conceptualizing competence: (1) as effective social role performance, (2) as ability to cope, and (3) as experienced mastery. Combined, they reveal how competence is multifaceted.

Competence As Effective Social Role Performance

As social role performance, competence is defined by how well or how completely a person enacts the duties and the expectations of certain roles. One sociologist has defined role types variously as "those which one's society will normally assign one, those in the repertoire of one's social system that one may reasonably aspire to, and those one might reasonably invent or elaborate " (Inkeles, 1966, p. 266).

Society often withdraws and leaves unreplaced a firm and valued set of roles for an aged person (Kuypers & Bengtson, 1973). Because social information and guidance and validation for behaving in socially central roles may be lacking, a special vulnerability may be created for the elderly person. A kind of social invisibility is often prompted.

This invisibility may exist within the family as well as in the wider society. Existing roles for older members may be vaguely defined or may involve a decrease in centrality or responsibility. Yet, in the relative absence of socially defined roles in the wider society, the members may look to the family as a means to replace and to substitute lost roles. Such competence is reflected by how clearly and how adequately family roles are created and enacted. As it has been suggested in prior analysis, many of these family roles may be formed on images of younger family life and may not serve well the unique demands of older family life. Hence, certain established family roles may not be functional for issues of the aging family. Because many of the challenges to older families are unprecedented and involve loss of capacity or loss of members, competence in older families may be measured by how well they can transform roles in its members, substitute for roles that are lost, or compensate for role performance that is made problematic because of the loss of physical or mental capacity.

Competence As Ability To Cope

A second perspective views competence as an adaptation to the unique and present demands of the environment. A key element here is the meaning given to environmental change and the kinds of action taken to cope with the perceived demands. Gladwin (1967) defines it thus:

> Competence . . . develops along three major axes, all closely inter-related. First is the ability to learn or to use a variety of alternative pathways. Second, the competent individual comprehends and is able to use a variety of social systems within the society, moving within these systems and utilizing the resources they offer. . . . Third, competence depends upon effective reality testing. Reality testing involves a positive, broad, and sophisticated understanding of the world. (p. 32)

This more psychological perspective on competence focuses on how a person perceives, interprets, and then interacts with environment. Competence is not solely a matter of acting out a preset role; rather, it involves how accurately a person perceives an event, how flexibly he can respond, and how well that response engages with the available resources.

This view of competence amplifies in considerable detail the first view of competence as role performance. Older family competence involves (1) how flexible the family, as a system, can be to seek out alternative and new responses to challenge; (2) how integrated these responses are with supports and resources outside the family; and (3) how clearly and accurately the family can assess the meaning of change and challenge.

Many older families are vulnerable to failure when they define a catastrophe where there is none. The social context in which they perceive events often distorts the meaning of change; it appears to be more threatening than necessary. This perception, in turn, limits flexibility and reduces the ability to establish a responsive and connected use of social resources.

This second view of competence emphasizes the nature of person and system interaction. Flexibility, rigidity, accuracy of perception (among others) are hallmarks of this perspective (Haan, 1969).

Competence As Experienced Mastery

The third perspective of competence is defined, not in terms of role performance per se or processes of coping (e.g., accurate perception and flexible response), but on the basis of the feelings the person (or family) has about the ability to influence outcome. In a discussion of competence, Smith (1968) suggests that "coordinate with the feeling of efficacy is an attitude of hope. . . . The world is the sort of place in which given appropriate efforts, I can expect good outcomes" (p. 282).

Feelings of personal power, of the ability to influence one's environment, and of self-determination are characteristics of the competent person. Even without a clearly defined and supported role a person can still experience competence by feeling and acting powerfully. Faith and optimism are important. A crucial assumption of this perspective is that the feeling level is a prerequisite for action. Without the sense of successful outcome before the fact, little corrective action can be forthcoming. A pessimistic, hopeless, or helpless perception yields to inaction and to dependency.

Applied to the older family, this perspective of competence has several manifestations. The first concerns the shared family view of its capacity to be effective. Clearly, this sense of family strength is rooted in the family's history and may serve either to block or to release family action in times of challenge. A second meaning concerns the objective realities likely to prevail in many of the situations older families face. In the face of death, accident, or mental deterioration, many families may find it hard to hold a feeling of hope. Accuracy of perception may be compromised by a more fundamental and emotionally immobilizing feeling of despair and helplessness.

Competence—A Combined View

In the process of providing an understanding of how families cope with threat, these three perspectives of competence identify various levels of competence: the changing nature of roles and role performance, accuracy of perception, use of resources, and the power of optimism. Each view determines how corrective action is blocked or unleashed. They interact with and influence each other.

The three views of competence also question whether some of the challenges to older families present unique threats to competence. Are role losses more massive and more difficult for older members to replace? Does family history and the transfer of loyalty guarantee a unique vulnerability in older families? Do cultural views of aging (as loss or decay) precondition the older family to an unrealistic and perhaps overly fearful approach to problem definition? Are resources too sparse or too focused on the young family to be easily accepted and used? Finally, can confidence and optimism be held in the face of impending death or mental deterioration or stroke? Do all these conditions promote incompetence in the family as it ages?

Combined, the three views also show that competence in the older family is influenced by many factors. It is a process that is never complete. In understanding this process, some of the organizing perspectives are called into play. By examining how family members interact with each other, insight is gained into how bounded families are by inflexible roles; how families recreate images of members and expectations of loyalty that affect their capacity to shift roles, when required; how accurately members perceive the unique context of a clear and present threat; and how families recreate a sense of optimism or despair.

The developmental perspective shows how the issues of family members invariably differ in times of threat, how family competence resides, and how these differences are accommodated. The phenomenological view shows that members give meaning to events and that this meaning (as a family myth and as an individual response) affects the ways families mobilize in times of threat. The structural view highlights the understanding that issues of stability and flexibility of the family as a unit are of crucial importance. In times of threat, when the tempo of change increases, families experience an upset in the balance between the need to conserve a stable sense of family order and the need to adjust to the realities of change, which sometimes become radical and irreparable. Furthermore, competence must be defined on many levels: a personal sense of competence, the roles and myths shared by the family, the connections of family to social systems, and the cultural context in which family and aging are embedded.

SOCIAL BREAKDOWN SYNDROME

Competent adaptation to stress or threat is a process that unfolds over a period of time. In previous work, the authors have examined a process called the social breakdown syndrome (SBS) as it may apply to elderly persons (Kuypers & Bengtson, 1973). In the SBS, a series of steps or episodes connect in a circular process that eventually folds in upon itself and creates a repeating pattern of stress reaction. Adaptation is not a single reaction to a single event; rather, it is influenced by one's history, which, in turn, influences future adaptations. Furthermore, the SBS suggests that a repeating negative cycle may become established that, without special corrective action, may be resistant to change. In another work the authors applied this model to the older family and considered practical steps for reversing the negative cycle (Kuypers & Bengtson, 1983). In this section, the negative cycle of breakdown is explained as it applies to individuals.

As originally introduced by Gruenberg and Zusman (1964), the SBS offers a seven-stage formulation of the development of negative psychological functioning. The authors have reduced these stages to six (see Figure 1–1):

1. precondition of susceptibility to vulnerability
2. dependence on external labelling
3. social labelling as incompetent
4. induced dependency
5. atrophy of previous skills
6. internalization and self-labelling as incompetent

This formulation contains many analytically useful concepts. First, the SBS shows that individual competence is directly connected to the way in which a person interacts with social and environmental conditions. Second (and like the combined view of competence), it focuses on many levels of action: a person's sense of self and the degree to which this inner and personal construction is related to information provided by the outside world; the skills a person carries into a new situation and how these are continuously being either strengthened or weakened; and the power of environmental feedback to undermine or to strengthen existing perspectives and adaptive capacities.

Vulnerability

As a single cycle of person-environment interaction, the six-stage process should have special emphasis placed on certain elements. Perhaps most important is step one, the *pre-condition of susceptibility*. To begin the negative cycle, the person may be in a temporary state of vulnerability. Many factors may prompt this situation. A person may approach an event feeling powerless to have a positive effect, and so he may feel defeated—incompetent—before he starts. (Initial re-

Figure 1–1 Social Breakdown in Old Age: A Vicious Cycle of Induced Incompetence

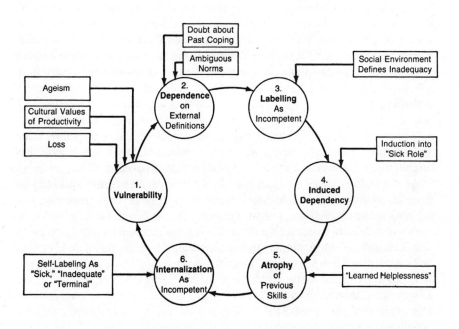

sponses to the event are marked by inactivity and confusion.) A person's past experiences may give little evidence of coping in the face of threat and may lead to the likelihood that a new event will confirm and recreate poor resolutions. The image of the future may be essentially negative. Furthermore, a person's relative social isolation may directly affect his sense of vulnerability. Ample evidence exists in the crisis intervention literature to show that positive crisis resolution is often related to the presence of *usable* social supports (Parad, 1966). The absence of a support network for a person increases personal vulnerability and increases the chances of establishing a negative cycle of breakdown. Moreover, the timing of a threatening event is crucial, whether it is expected or not; whether it can be prepared for or not; whether it is combined with other threats and becomes magnified by virtue of being embedded in other challenges. Finally, the issue of vulnerability rests on the degree to which the threat is fundamental to the values or the hopes a person holds. Family therapists would add that vulnerability is also measured by how directly the perceived threat disrupts formal (structural) connections to the family.

Many changes in later life may increase vulnerability. The list is well known (if incomplete) and includes widowhood, retirement and loss of income, child launching, the onset of disease, and impending death. The authors see such events as stimulants to breakdown, but not as sufficient cause. Obviously, not all persons experience breakdown in these circumstances. As in the case of competence, the power of the event is seen in its interaction with the way people sense it (its subjective meaning) and in how, consequently, the event sets in motion a series of interactions. Breakdown is a statement of process, not an outcome of an event.

Labelling

Whatever the source of vulnerability and susceptibility, the SBS suggests that a generalized reaction is prompted that fosters breakdown. Step two is described as an overreliance on external labels or external definitions of capacity and potential. If the externalization and guidance is basically positive, the negative cycle may be reversed; however, if the labelling is negative (step three) and, especially, if it supports the initial conviction of hopelessness, the cycle is accelerated. Much research in the past two decades has focused on externalization of control over one's fate (Lefcourt, 1976). According to this literature, if a person perceives his fate to be external to and independent of his actions, he develops a fatalistic, passive, and nonaffirming position in the world. Such an external locus of control cycles back to step one and increases vulnerability. It also renders the person susceptible to steps four and five of the SBS. In these steps, the person loses any existing adaptive capacities and eventually learns to act in ways that confirm his developing sense of helplessness and dependency.

Internalization

This condition leads to the final and crucial step of the SBS—internalization— in which the person reconstructs the meaning of the event and of his capacity to successfully adapt to its demands. The person has internalized and now believes in his weakness and incompetence. This affirmation of a negative reality then closes the negative cycle and increases vulnerability (step one) in the face of new threat.

In prior work the authors argued that the SBS could be fruitfully applied to problems of aging in two ways. The first way is to understand the basically negative position elderly persons have in their wider society and the way in which lack of social support and negative labels combine to generate loss of competence.

Even though the elderly may not have specific sick roles into which they are ceremonially induced (except for the few who may find themselves in specialized institutions for the elderly), the atrophy of work and social skills is likely to occur. The critical question then becomes whether basic psychological skills previously used to cope with and adapt to environment might also atrophy. Indeed, if this is the case, then the social labelling as incompetent is eventuated in the loss of mechanisms—coping processes—which provide the foundation for competent behavior. The cycle of interaction is created in which a person, rendered susceptible, is ascribed a negative value, is encouraged to develop skills and behavior in concert with this value, and finally incorporates the negative value as true for the self. This, in turn, leads to further susceptibility, dependence, low self-assessment, and the atrophy of coping skills. (Kuypers and Bengtson, 1973, p. 190)

A second value of the SBS is in the way it shows the various levels of intervention possible to reverse the cycle—attitudinal, systems, and cultural (see Kuypers & Bengtson, 1983). Here, however, the SBS is presented not as a statement of the *inevitable*, but rather as one of *potential* risk. As a model, it embeds the authors' conceptions of competence in a time line and highlights the chaining of experience into a possible negative cycle that folds back upon itself.

The family as it ages is placed in a vulnerable position as it attempts to cope with challenges to its integrity. The authors have attempted to show that an understanding of this vulnerability calls forth different perspectives on family life. The older family was discussed as an interacting system whose members create unique meanings of family life—meanings formed in part by the different developmental agendas of members. Family structure was discussed as an important perspective that reveals stabilized patterns in families as they age.

Tension exists in family life between forces that maintain stability and forces that promote change. The challenge to older families is often concerned with the way to cope with such tensions when they reach crisis proportions. Considerable attention was given in this chapter to the concepts of competence and breakdown. Reseachers and theoreticians must focus on these concepts in the hope of better charting the struggles of older families in the course of their aging.

REFERENCES

Bengtson, V.L., & Kuypers, J.A. (1971). Generational difference and the developmental stake. *Aging & Human Development, 2,* 249–260.

Biddle, B.J., & Thomas, E.J. (Eds.). (1966). *Role therapy: Concepts and research.* New York: John Wiley & Sons.

Boszormenyi-Nagy, I., & Spark, G. (1973). *Invisible loyalties: Reciprocity in intergenerational therapy.* New York: Harper & Row.

Bronson, W. (1968). Stable patterns of behavior: The significance of enduring orientations for personality development. In J.P. Hill (Ed.), *Minnesota Symposium on Child Psychology* (Vol. 2). Minneapolis: University of Minnesota Press.

Bross, A. (1982). *Family therapy: A recursive model of strategic practice.* Toronto: Methuen.

Bugenthal, J. (1967). *Challenges of humanistic psychology*. Toronto: McGraw-Hill.

Epstein, N., & Bishop, D. (1981). Problem center system therapy of the family. In A. Gurman & D. Kniskern (Eds.), *Handbook of family therapy*. New York: Brunner & Mazel.

Frank, J. (1961). *Persuasion and healing: A comparative study of psychotherapy*. Baltimore: Johns Hopkins Press.

Freud, A. (1964). *The ego and the mechanisms of defense*. New York: International Universities Press.

Gladwin, T. (1967). Social competence and clinical practice. *Psychiatry, 30*, 30–43.

Goffman, I. (1967). *Interaction ritual: Essays on face to face behavior*. New York: Anchor Press.

Gruenberg, E., & Zusman, J. (1964). The natural history of schizophrenia. *International Psychiatric Clinic, 1*, 699.

Haan, N. (1969). A tripartite model of ego functioning values and clinical and research applications. *Journal of Nervous and Mental Disease, 148(1)*, 14–30.

Haan, N. (1977). *Coping and defending: Processes of self-environment organization*. New York: Academic Press.

Haley, J. (1971). Changing families: A family therapy reader. New York: Grune & Stratton.

Hartman, H. (1958). *Ego psychology and the problem of adaptation*. London: Image Publication.

Havighurst, R. (1973). *Developmental tasks and education*. New York: D. McKay.

Hill, R. (1970). *Family development in three generations: A longitudinal study*. Cambridge, MA: Schenkman.

Inkeles, A. (1966). Social structure and the socialization of competence. *Harvard Educational Review, 36*, 265–283.

Kantor, D., & Lehr, W. (1975). *Inside the family: Toward a theory of family process*. New York: Harper & Row.

Kuypers, J.A., & Bengtson, V.L. (1973). Social breakdown and competence. *Human Dev. 16*, 181–201.

Kuypers, J., & Bengtson, V. (1983). Recurrent threats to the older family. In T. Brubaker (Ed.), *Family Relations in Later Life*. Beverly Hills, CA: Sage Publications.

Laing, R.D. (1971). *The politics of the family*. New York: Pantheon Books.

Lefcourt, H. (1976). *Locus of Control: Current trends in theory and research*. Hillsdale, NJ: L. Eoribaum.

Marris, P. (1975). *Loss and change*. Garden City: Anchor Press.

Minuchin, S. (1974). *Families and family therapy*. Cambridge, MA: Harvard University Press.

Olson, D.H., Sprenkle, D.H., & Russell, C. (1979). Circumplex model of marital and family systems: I. Cohesion and adaptability dimensions, family types, and clinical applications. *Family Process, 18*, 3–28.

Oppenheimer, J.R. (1954). *Science and common understanding*. New York: Simon & Schuster.

Parad, H. (1966). The use of time limited crisis intervention in community mental health programming. *Social Service Review, 40*, 275–288.

Patterson, G.R. (1971). *Families: Applications of social learning to family life*. Champaign, IL: Research Press.

Pelletier, K. (1977). *Mind as healer, mind as slayer*. New York: Delta Books.

Piaget, J. (1929). *The child's conception of the world*. New York: Harcourt, Brace.

Satir, V. (1972). *People making*. Palo Alto, CA: Science and Behavior Books.

Smith, M.B. (1968). Competence and clinical practice. *Psychiatry, 30*, 30–43.

Watzlawick, P., Beavin, J.H., & Jackson, D.D. (1967). *The pragmatics of human communication: A study of interactional patterns, pathologies, and paradoxes*. New York: W.W. Norton.

Chapter 2

Autonomy, Interdependence, and Developmental Delay in Older Generations of the Family

William H. Quinn

The notion of family intergenerational bonds and involvement of older persons is an acceptable one, confirmed over the years by empirical and clinical studies. Parents and children remain important to one another through the lives of each cohort group (Mancini, 1979; Troll & Bengtson, 1979). For some older persons, family members become the final interpersonal connection and support, characterized by disengagement *into* rather than *out of* the family system (Rosow, 1967).

INTERGENERATIONAL INTERACTION: INTERDEPENDENCE

Although intergenerational studies on contact patterns, mutual exchange, and geographical proximity have been accumulated in a consistent manner, very little is known that can be used with any assurance to describe the elements of interaction that become conducive or disturbing to the intergenerational relations of adult family members. Kaplan (1975) has stated this reality succinctly:

> Qualitative interactional research is now a requisite. How do we measure the ebb and flow of interaction between the old parent and the adult child, perhaps also old? Who benefits according to what value and under what conditions? And who has more taken away from this value than that person is able to give? It is apparent greater qualitative knowledge is needed on the forms of interdependence by the generations. (p. 385)

Clinically and empirically, the family field has suffered from a less than workable understanding of older generational relationships. Filial attitudes (such as loyalty and expectation) and individual developmental issues become the "field of play" (and often "work") in which the two family generations attempt to discover or to maintain a comfortable emotional closeness while they attempt to reconcile longstanding or contemporary social-emotional conflicts. As each generation struggles with tasks pertaining to its own needs and demands, the overlay on interactional style can become a powerful inhibitor to closeness and satisfaction. In a persuasive documentation of this reality, Cohler and Grunebaum (1981) report the burdens older women carry as their grown daughters call and visit so frequently that older mothers become resentful and bitter. The young women expect advice, affection, companionship, and baby-sitting. At the same time, older mothers expect some freedom from those family responsibilities. They define their lives in ways that promote personal satisfaction, and so they sometimes obstruct obligatory responses. Older women seek friends and activities of personal value. According to the authors, the younger female generation had little understanding of their parents' need and interpreted responses from mothers as showing disloyalty or little concern for legacy and family continuity. Peterson (1982) suggests that maybe these older women do not go south to retire but to "leave the nest," much as adolescents do when they go to college to make a statement of independence. From the perspective of the younger generation, adult daughters wish the older generation to be more supportive, concerned, and involved. This idea is counter to the one that suggests that our society has assumed that the older generation carries family loyalty to a limit beyond which younger generations can reach or maintain.

Brody (1981) describes a related phenomenon in which middle-aged women are in the middle (from a generational position) and are required to meet demands of older and younger generations. These women are also caught in the middle between two values—one traditional and one contemporary—in which care of the elderly as a family responsibility competes with a desire to be free to work outside the home and to establish autonomy. This prototype that Brody constructs is, in part, a result of demographic and social changes; however, the consequential stress and pull of being in the middle is of interest here as it relates to family interaction and satisfaction.

CONFLICTUAL INTERACTION

Conflictual interaction processes can evolve in a variety of ways. For example, conflict can occur when an older parent appeals to someone who will understand and will help alleviate circumstances brought on by aging phenomena. A causal influence between the plea and the conflict is not suggested; other factors that influence the relationship certainly affect the call and response of such a plea. The request for help itself does not necessarily create a strain between the generations. The life situation of parent or child, or the history and development of the relationship, such as the movement toward the challenging of the parent's authority by the child, may be present at the time of such a plea. Thus, the consequence of the parent's request for help is influenced by timing—forces presently acting upon the individual within the relationship.

Frequently, adult children are sought as confidants and supports during stressful periods experienced by aged parents. These adult children sometimes find it difficult or are uncertain about the way to respond and to provide support while meeting responsibilities in their own immediate families. Simos (1973) reported that in a study of both adult children and aging parents, only one-fourth of the sample reported cordial or warm relationships. The majority of the others complained of no privacy, demandingness of the other person, chronic complaints, and longstanding interpersonal problems. Many children felt guilty but did not know how to help parents who had financial and housing problems. Watson (1982) contends that taking on filial care can be to the detriment of meeting other personal and family responsibilities. Although this dilemma does occur, Cicirelli (1981) warns us that the situation for these children often results in fatigue and frustration, not necessarily because of other stresses or responsibilities not fulfilled, but simply because of the disappointments or agonizing moments arising from a sense of failure in meeting the requests or needs of one's parent. Somehow, expectations or sense of loyalty play a significant part in role satisfaction and can threaten the relationships, regardless of external demands in the life of the child.

Help for these adult children is important. Hausman (1979) found that in counseling groups of adult children, confusion existed in determining the extent of, and the limits to, duties and obligations to parents and the behaviors expected of them as children. Opportunities to discuss these anxieties and difficulties can allow these adult children to derive, in groups, creative and useful solutions. These successes seem to provide a sense of competence out of despair, thereby assuring children of some confidence and hope.

A psychological burden exists within this precarious situation and dilemma for the child. An adult child, relinquishing autonomy and freedom, may receive pity for sacrificing for an aged parent. Yet, the child in our culture can be criticized and can be guilt-ridden if parents are neglected. As Reid (1966) stated, married people in middle age may well be faced with responsibility for taking care of as many as four parents and one to eight grandparents, as well as their own children. Cicirelli (1981) claims that we may be developing a "countermyth" that stipulates that adult children can and always will provide help. This notion is unrealistic. In the future, we may observe more "filial anxiety" in which children experience the anticipation of necessarily giving help to parents. Children may carry through middle age the expectation of family care-giving, which may manufacture anxiety and may interfere with accomplishing their other life tasks. This anxiety carried by children may work to the detriment of fostering healthy relationships because it threatens confidence in the future and all that goes with it—loyalty and legacy, continuity and family satisfaction.

Although adult children may have to confront this developmental phenomenon of greater filial responsibility, they may also contribute to the relationship conflict. The source of conflict is not necessarily entirely from the older generation.

Children may mistakenly maintain behavior detrimental to the fostering of healthy relationships with aged parents. As Lerner (1979) and Troll and Smith (1976) propose, socialization continues throughout the life span, and the child's influence on the parent may be as crucial to development as is the parent's influence on the child. Cicirelli (1981) suggests that children potentially contribute to learned helplessness in parents by providing whatever parents need or request. Parents may fail to comprehend their children's resistance to what they, as parents, perceive to be real and legitimate demands, while children ineffectively clarify their own reluctance to respond as their parents expect.

Brody (1970) described the infinite cultural expectations of ritual behavior and stereotyped attitudes in intergenerational relations that have become unrealistic with changing social conditions. Adult children unable to relinquish the old etiquette of filial behavior may find relationships with parents that create or sustain intimacy and enhance the well-being of both generations inaccessible. Consequently, generational continuity is disturbed as rifts and the threat of disloyalty become possible. As role theorists contend (Brim, 1968; Turner, 1970), what is appropriate is defined by cultural prescriptions surrounding the role and by each person's needs, resources, and expectations. Functional relationships are, in part, determined by the ability of children to view their parents as individuals who desire affection and caring while recognizing the necessity of individuality or independence.

QUALITY IN INTERGENERATIONAL RELATIONSHIPS

Affection

In reports of studies about the nature and the characteristics of human relationships, an overriding conclusion exists that affection or sentiment is an essential element of a meaningful relationship. Although the level of affect in a relationship is crucial, it is difficult to define. We may think of it as "loving" or "liking." Yet, this may be too global or only a composite of other relationship dynamics of more specificity. As Black and Bengtson (1973) noted, sentiment was an early social and psychological construct, but we know little about how it develops or how we measure it. Although the definition by Black and Bengtson ("a mutual positive sentiment among group members and their expressions of love, respect, appreciation and recognition of others" (1973, p. 4)) is a broad and encompassing one, more appealing is the simply put second definition given in Webster's *New Collegiate Dictionary*: "a tender attachment: fondness."

Affection is a vital element of intergenerational ties. Sussman and Burchinal (1962) report that emotional support by adult children has altered physical support and care and is the overriding relationship dimension. Johnson and Bursk (1977) contend that close intergenerational ties are based on mutual affection, trust, and respect, as well as interdependence and reciprocal giving. Quinn (1982) discusses the ancedotes that parents and children offer to describe strong affectional ties with pride and gratitude. The conviction with which they are delivered confirms the importance of affection in mapping the relationship.

In the three-generation study by Bengtson (1971), older parents and adult children were asked for their perceptions of affection toward the other and from the perspective of the other in terms of five dimensions: degree of understanding, trust, fairness, respect, and sentiment. Both dyad members showed high levels of perceived affectional solidarity. By using the same measures of affection, Quinn (1983) found similar results and demonstrated a significant causal association between affection and each generation's perception of relationship quality with the other generation.

Affectional ties and feelings of closeness can affect the quality of intergenerational relationships of institutionalized, as well as noninstitutionalized, older persons. Smith and Bengtson (1979) interviewed 100 older persons in an institutional setting and their adult children about solidarity in these relationships. They found that the majority of relationships were characterized by closeness, love, and affection, which contributed to strengthening these bonds. The reasons for such increased solidarity included relief from strains on the family, physical or mental improvement of the parent, more opportunity for social-emotional interaction as basic needs were met through the facility, and the parents' involvement with other residents. These factors relieved some of the pressure from kin. Possibly, as parental needs are met by other care-givers, more opportunity can exist within the family relationship for conversation, reminiscing, and participating together in social events. Butler and Lewis (1982) suggest that some governmental support of aged persons and the recognition of forces confronting adult children (some aged themselves) would allow family members more opportunity to meet psychosocial needs of elder family members and would contribute to more harmonious relationships. Although the development of affection in relationships is a complex and not easily explained phenomenon, it does seem clear that the presence of such characteristics as sentiment, respect, trust, understanding, and fairness enhance relationship quality. Tender attachments mean much to parents and children of these generations. Perhaps these bonds can be achieved with the more impaired parents only when care-giving support from others can be harnessed.

Communication

One primary dimension of any human adjustment problem is the nature of communication within the interactional context. Aspects of communication within intergenerational relationships can be conceptualized as comprising three dimensions: the manner in which thoughts and feelings are transmitted, the extent of arriving at congruence in negotiating expectations of one another, and the extent of mutual aid in the form of information exchanged.

The struggles of resolving conflict relate to ineffective communication patterns. Hawkinson (1965) confirmed the presence of this existing conflict in his studies of personal communication. A substantial discrepancy was found among the wishes, expectations, and practices in the relationship of parents and adult children. This finding may indicate the unrealistic wishes and expectations parents have of children, but they may also suggest communication patterns that do not transmit thoughts and feelings accurately and so restrict agreement and understanding of each other.

Role expectations in these relationships appear to be a part of relationship satisfaction, which is partly due to effective responses to impending changes in the context of relationships. Hess and Waring (1978) predicted that role expectations developed at earlier life stages required negotiation as the distribution of needs and resources shifted the balance of power—just as Williamson (1981) vividly described. The issue of dependence in the parent-child relationship requires negotiation across the life span. The idea that structurally carving out a relevant, age-appropriate intergenerational relationship as children reach middle age (the fourth decade of life is the beginning of this restructuring according to Williamson) and the process of communication (including the transmission of thoughts, feelings, and expectations) are integral parts of this relationship shift of two adult generations. Johnson (1978) found in her interviews that when mothers and daughters were asked why they thought their relationships were good or bad, 47 percent of the mothers and 38 percent of the daughters responded that the other person met family role expectations. Each generation, then, required some keen sense of what was expected (conveyed necessarily in a communicative way) to satisfy these expectations.

A more recent focus in these relationships regarding communication is around mediation (Sussman, 1977). Some instrumental functions in contemporary society are being accepted by formal institutions. This acceptance provides a new role for kin as mediators between the bureaucracy and the elderly parents. Family members, including adult children, begin accepting a position in which they indirectly help older parents meet the tasks of daily living. Advice-giving, supplying information, and serving as a consultant to aged persons making decisions about their lives may increasingly play a part in the communication process. By possessing effective communication in the mediating arena and thereby facilitating decision making by elderly parents, children can promote their parents' well-being.

Filial Expectations

Conclusive evidence exists that aged persons expect help from their families. Many aged persons, especially those without a spouse, find themselves dependent upon offspring for various forms of aid. Although this family solidarity of need fulfillment can generate contact and loyalty, it can also threaten the satisfaction in interactional experience. Elderly parents with greater filial expectations of children are more likely to place greater demands on them. This intimidation can produce resentment in children and frustration from their inability or unwillingness to satisfy requests. Hence, the resulting anger and the failing loyalty inhibit sentiment and affection, and possibly morale (Kerckhoff, 1966; Robinson & Thurnher, 1979; Seelbach & Sauer, 1977). At the same time, appropriateness of expectation and desirability and comfort in parent-child interdependency engenders expression of positive feeling (Cantor, 1975).

The idea of comfort in the management of interdependency between the generations is a crucial one because it influences relationship contentment. As communication and other intrafamilial dimensions influence these bonds, so have social changes added a great challenge to the management and the promotion of rewarding interaction. Brody (1970) sensed the inappropriateness of traditional cultural and social attitudes about filial demands. She outlined several developments that explain this contradiction: (1) the dramatic increase in the aged population and in longevity, inducing more responsibility; (2) the decrease in large families, limiting opportunity for mutual support; (3) the aging of family members (including children) on whom older people rely, which diminishes full-fledged efforts to help while struggling with individual demands (children's developmental tasks); and (4) an increase in three- and four-generational families, which confounds responsibilities and obligations in the emotional, financial, and instrumental areas.

This etiquette of filial behavior is most tested in families most vulnerable to these social changes. Family members, particularly children who are experiencing the shift in family structure and are themselves experiencing aging phenomena, are most challenged to revise this traditional etiquette. Those families who continue to accept it are burdened by having to meet service, financial, and affective needs of older parents; or, as a substitute, they struggle with their own guilt if they choose not to try to meet these demands. If a child has career, caregiving, and parenting responsibilities in the procreative family, resentment, bitterness, neglect, and jealousy may surface. For instance, a child may feel ambivalent in accepting a job promotion if it means a geographical move away from a parent who may need aid. Although there are positive outcomes in accepting a helping role with a parent, potentially negative consequences far outweigh positive ones when filial expectations are high.

Filial Responsibility

The concept of filial responsibility is significant for the intergenerational relationship, because it contributes to a determination of the type and the amount of support provided and the nature of the interaction. The concept of filial responsibility (maturity) refers to an adult child's sense of obligation in meeting the needs of parents. Blenkner (1965) defined filial maturity as a newly found recognition of and commitment (in middle age) to being depended upon. Frequently overlooked in the discussion of this concept, but as important, is the understanding that this maturity means a new identification with the older parent. A child begins experiencing a support-giving role while viewing the parent as the person was before the birth of the child. This positive identification and multidimensional perspective can provide the foundation for the resolution of dependency issues and for the creation of an interdependence that characterizes healthy emotional bonds. This interdependence is further solidified if the parents can successfully manage their own aging and accept their own late-life development as meaningful or satisfying. In order that the child may develop this filial maturity, the parent also must participate in that process—both in modeling successful development and in possessing the capacity to help modify the interaction with the child, not as a "parent" to a "child," but as a partner in an emotional experience of peers.

Managing this filial responsibility in a way that promotes a reconstructed, yet more healthy, relationship requires successful individual coping as other life stressors appear. A child with personal and family demands that are unresolvable when parents transmit unrealistic notions of loyalty and support will fail to achieve a sense of successful filial responsibility that promotes the independence of both and a mature family bond. The impact of a number of stressors is not the only threat to filial care. There is also the resulting disappointment and frustration derived from parental expectations that are not met and so become an interference in relationship development. This disappointment of the child becomes a pervasive and ongoing threat to resolving the autonomy-connectedness balance so crucial for the structure of healthy relationships.

Consensus

It is commonly assumed and stated that persons who have similar interests and values seek out each other and achieve potential closeness. Hess and Waring (1978) discuss the changing social conditions and the personal characteristics that have shifted intergenerational relationships toward a voluntaristic context. As relationships between parents and children become more focused on friendship patterns, characteristics of mutual respect, common interests, affection, and emotional support become primary. In fact, empirical analysis of consensus as it relates to affection, communication, and the quality of parent and adult child relations indicates high correlations (Quinn, 1983; Quinn & Keller, 1983).

Recent social policy suggests that social and governmental institutions will continue to accept a role in meeting instrumental needs of the aged. Family members in contemporary society are challenged, therefore, with shaping relationships with aged family members in a more nonobligatory manner. As Kreps

(1977) pointedly asked, "Except for periods of psychological stress, illness and the like, will there be sufficient mutuality of interest to hold [them] together on a continuous basis?" (pp. 23–24).

Although it is known that parents and youth do not have unity on value sets such as political views, similarity of values between older parents and children in middle age may be more closely tied. As parents and children age, socialization continues to be nonlinear, and children remain influential in their parents' development. Children mature, and both generations learn together from their position in the same social structure (Troll and Bengtson, 1979). Perhaps, when these two generations pass into a more stable period, values and attitudes may take on greater resemblance, provided cohort differences do not dominate lineage transmission. Profiles of interviewed pairs in the Johnson and Bursk (1977) study indicated that parents and adult children who shared similar values gave the quality of their relationships a higher rating.

In summary, the outcome of consensus on the quality of relationship can be viewed from the following partial paradigm that Heider (1958) constructed (*P* means person, *O* means other): If P is similar to O, P is induced to like O (consensus promotes the quality of the relationship); if P likes O, P is induced to benefit O (quality of relationship enhances well-being). As Bengtson and Kuypers (1970) have noted, the final proposition suggests in practical terms the possibility of psychosocial well-being influenced by similarity of values and interests. Hess and Waring (1978) conclude that regardless of developmental stake, in which value similarity is judged by each generation's identity needs, sufficient areas of basic agreement exist to allow family members of different ages to share perceptions and experiences while engaging a sense of responsibility for one another.

CONCEPTUAL INTEGRATION AND FAMILY TRANSITION

Each of the concepts mentioned previously that describes quality of relationship relates to the attempt at or the eventual reconciliation of personal differences between parents and adult children and the acceptance of each other's developmental changes. The impasse reached in these relationships can be the consequence of unsuccessful attempts to negotiate and to discover compatible distributions of power and agreement of changed status. A dysfunctional style of interaction can include a parent and a child who are openly conflictual or are suspiciously careful in insuring distance and avoidance. A fragility about the relationship is evident because one or the other is fearful of upsetting the established family loyalty, which has been fervently maintained over the years. The independence-dependence imbalance must give way to a new-found structure of interdependence that allows both generations to establish autonomy while remaining connected to each other. The challenge for these generations appears to be the accomplishment of a comfortable shift toward acceptance of equal status while retaining (and in some cases redefining) the meaning of family loyalty. This shift includes commitment to the transcendence of values and attitudes through the generations and a willingness to remain emotionally connected to those family members of other generations.

A broad, yet integrative, conceptual schema has been proposed; it deals with the necessity "to terminate the hierarchical boundary" (Williamson, 1981, p. 443). The relational shift is seen as developmental and necessary to establish peer identity in the relationship and to resolve the sound emotional conflict arising from inappropriate power imbalances. This attempt at restructuring the relationship begins during the fourth decade of life for the child. The thrust of Williamson's treatise "has to do with intimidation, power and hierarchy" (p. 442) and posits that dependency and intimidation are relationship dynamics that maintain— possibly strengthen—the imbalance in power and block negotiation processes. To arrive at the point of initiating renegotiation strategies, the child must have achieved certain developmental tasks, including relational intimacy with another person (spouse or otherwise), vocational progress, and emotional maturity. Otherwise, the groundwork for dealing with the issue of dependency and peer establishment is absent and blocks renegotiation attempts. To be more explicit, the adult child must have become emotionally and physically separate from the parent, must have claimed a territory of unique life goals, and must have achieved an emotional bond with another person to replace the intimate bond with a parent. Simultaneously, the older parent must have developed a sense of individualism, a life apart from the constant connection to younger generations. Cohler (1983) suggests that we must turn from focusing our ideas singularly on familial support and obligation to adding an emphasis on personal autonomy. He claims that, as a result, we develop a "dual paradox" whereby society emphasizes independence in early life, and obligation and relational responsibility in later life. Instead, psychological adjustment in later life requires personal autonomy. These developmental tasks are required to restructure a relationship with a parent into one of equality, autonomy, and interdependence. The case study in Exhibit 2–1 provides a clinical illustration of this process of conceptual integration.

Intergenerational Resolution

Parents and children who fail to accomplish this restructuring do so because they are compelled to execute expectations of family loyalty. Boszormenyi-Nagy and Spark (1973) propose that children possess such a sense of indebtedness to parents that they have a compelling desire to satisfy family mottos or themes enforced by parents. This compelling drive is conducted to the exclusion of self-identity. The consequences of this covert loyalty are a disallowance of the child's

Exhibit 2–1 Clinical Case Study

Jennifer, age 29, and her husband, Kevin, age 32, were seen in marital therapy. They came in for an initial interview because of increasingly hostile behavior toward one another. In large part, this conflict was a consequence of the recent death of an infant son. Jennifer attributed this loss to the incompetence of medical personnel in the military force, with which Kevin was associated. She felt they were negligent in treating the child, and her anger was fueled by her perception of Kevin's lack of courage in helping Jennifer care for a terminally ill son. Kevin, in turn, resented these accusations and pointed to the financial demands that separated him from fully caring for the son.

Further data gathering provided some understanding of the historical development of the relationship. Jennifer married Kevin at age 17, using the opportunity to leave home—particularly her mother. Jennifer reported that her mother had been irresponsible as a parent, intrusive and stern, and had had little understanding of her while she was growing up. The mother consistently treated Jennifer as younger and more immature than she was. After 12 years as a military family, Jennifer, Kevin, and their 10-year-old daughter, Stacy, had been reassigned by the military to a base back in their hometown. Consequently, Jennifer's parents became much more involved in their family life, to the extent of wanting to "parent" Stacy and, in a way, Jennifer also. This involvement was viewed as a response to the need to absolve guilt over failure to be responsible parents to Jennifer as a child.

Jennifer and her mother quickly grew to resent each other as the mother tried to make decisions that Jennifer saw as her own to make and consistently tried to tell Jennifer how to parent. Furthermore, the mother treated her as the same daughter who had left home at 17. That the mother owned the house in which Jennifer and her family lived gave the mother another vehicle for her domineering activity. After one argument, the mother put a "for-sale" sign in Jennifer's front yard. Furthermore, the mother interfered with Jennifer's marital troubles, attempting to manipulate the relationship in a way that would "keep" Jennifer 17 and using her immaturity and marital conflict as a means of getting custody of Stacy. In turn, Jennifer fought her mother's control tactics with childish responses—yelling and screaming, avoiding her mother, and being revengeful.

This relationship pattern became central to intervention, because the intergenerational conflict fostered disagreements and disloyalty within the marriage and prevented Jennifer from becoming more independent at a time in which the inner strength gained from caring for a terminally ill child provided impetus for a new-found maturity and autonomy. This development was seen in career success, in interior design, and in a confidence about constructing solutions to life's problems. The focus of therapy became the reconstruction of the mother-daughter relationship. The goal was the achievement of more balanced power and status and a renewed sense of interdependence as peers. Although the process was difficult and sometimes painful, it was accomplished as the roles of parents and spouse were redefined and accepted. Jennifer and her mother were prone to argument, which would lead to closeness; too much togetherness, however, would lead to argument again. A more stable and balanced relationship was derived from Jennifer's ability to be assertive and not aggressive, and the therapist's maneuvers to push the twosome to work through long-lasting resentments and regrets. A new peerlike interaction surfaced.

In the final stage of therapy, Jennifer and her mother reconstructed their relationship and developed changed perceptions about themselves and each other. The mother came to realize that Jennifer needed to have authority over Stacy and that her daughter's marriage was not her

Exhibit 2–1 continued

responsibility, but that of Kevin and his spouse. As these changes occurred, a reconstructed mother-daughter relationship and an interaction pattern characterized by the expression of personal value and by convictions with feelings of affection for one another emerged. As a consequence, Jennifer and Kevin could struggle directly with their own relational problems with a renewed strength and sense of energy.

uniqueness and sense of psychological independence, which prohibits proclamation of personal convictions and beliefs in experiences with parents. Williamson (1981, p. 442) argues that this sense of loyalty and the need to enforce family legacies by the child must be shaken; a declaration of "personal authority" must emerge. This change is accomplished by the "task of renegotiating the politics of the relationship structures and the interactional pattern between the generations" (Williamson, 1982, p. 24).

The term "former parents" is put forth by Williamson (1978, p. 93) to describe biological parents in this relationship stage because elements of parental nurturing, protecting, and guiding must be forfeited to establish this restructuring of power and a new sense of peer interaction. Thus, the shifting of this power hierarchy between these generations allows new, more creative and developmentally appropriate dialogue of a friendship to come forth. With this positive restructuring, the children no longer feel obliged to say what parents want to hear (or to say nothing to avoid conflict). Children are released from the urge to hide aspects of their lifestyle that are not in accord with the parent's views, or they no longer need to accede to the wishes of a parent in order to remain loyal and to absolve guilt. Wilen (1979) discovered that improvement in the relationship was often attributed to the result of a long and careful negotiation between the two generations. When the relationship was not improved, the child frequently pointed to the lack of negotiation growing out of the child's desire for independence. Conversely, parents viewed conflict as the critical issue of the child's lack of maturity (accomplishing life tasks of vocation and leaving home). The satisfaction in this intergenerational relationship, then, is not arrived at when family loyalty is forsaken, but when this loyalty is exhibited in a peer context and when the two family members become free to exercise their individuality to meet challenges of longevity of life and personal fulfillment. Simultaneously, the parent and the child connect with each other (on different terms than when the hierarchical incongruity existed) in an interactional context of new meaning, creativity, and informality. The parent-child relationship is a dynamic one that undergoes change. One must accept the idea that differing vantage points are used by each generation to assess and to experience the relationship and that restructuring over the life span is a developmental and reciprocal process.

REFERENCES

Bengtson, V.L. (1971). Inter-age differences in perceptions of the generation gap. *The Gerontologist*, *11*, 85–89.

Bengtson, V.L., & Kuypers, J.A. (1970). Generational differences and the "developmental state." *Aging and Human Development*, *2*, 249–260.

Black, K.O., & Bengtson, V.L. (1973). The measurement of family solidarity: An intergenerational analysis. Paper presented at the meeting of the American Psychological Association, Montreal, Canada.

Blenkner, M. (1965). Social work and family relations in later life with some thoughts in filial maturity. In E. Shanas & G. Streib (Eds.), *Social structure and the family*. New York: Prentice-Hall.

Boszormenyi-Nagy, I., & Spark, G. (1973). *Invisible loyalties*. New York: Harper & Row.

Brim, O.G. (1968). Adult socialization. In J. Clausen (Ed.), *Socialization and Society*. Boston: Little Brown & Co.

Brody, E. (1970). The etiquette of filial behavior. *Aging and Human Development*, *1*, 87–94.

Brody, E. (1981). "Women in the middle" and family help to older people. *The Gerontologist*, *21*, 471–480.

Butler, R., & Lewis, M. (1982). *Aging and mental health* (3rd ed.). St. Louis: C.V. Mosby.

Cantor, M. (1975). Life space and the social support system of the inner city elderly of New York. *The Gerontologist*, *15*, 23–27.

Cicirelli, V. (1981). *Helping elderly parents: The role of adult children*. Boston: Auburn House.

Cohler, B. (1983). Autonomy and interdependence in the family of adulthood: A psychological perspective. *The Gerontologist*, *23*, 33–39.

Cohler, B., & Grunebaum, H.U. (1981). *Mothers, grandmothers and daughters*. New York: John Wiley & Sons.

Hausman, C.P. (1979). Short-term counseling groups for people with elderly parents. *The Gerontologist*, *19*, 102–107.

Hawkinson, W.P. (1965). Wish, expectancy and practice in the interaction of generations. In A.M. Rose & W.A. Petersen (Eds.), *Older people and their social world*. Philadelphia: F.A. Davis.

Heider, F. (1958). *The psychology of interpersonal relations*. New York: John Wiley & Sons.

Hess, B.B., & Waring, J.M. (1978). Parent and child in later life: Rethinking the relationship. In R.M. Lerner & G.B. Spanier (Eds.), *Child influences on marital and family interactions*. New York: Academic Press.

Johnson, E., & Bursk, B.J. (1977). Relationship between the elderly and their adult children. *The Gerontologist*, *17*, 90–96.

Johnson, E.S. (1978). "Good" relationships between older mothers and their daughters: A causal model. *The Gerontologist*, *18*, 301–306.

Kaplan, J. (1975). The family in aging. *The Gerontologist*, *15*, 385.

Kerckhoff, A.C. (1966). Family patterns and morale in retirement. In I.A. Simpson & J.C. McKenney (Eds.), *Social aspects of aging*. Durham, NC: Duke University Press.

Kreps, J.M. (1977). Intergenerational transfers and the bureaucracy. In E. Shanas & M.B. Sussman (Eds.), *Family bureaucracy and the elderly*. Durham, NC: Duke University Press.

Lerner, R.M. (1979). A dialectical concept of individual and social relationship development. In R. Burgess and T. Huston (Eds.), *Social exchange in developing relationships*. New York: Academic Press.

Mancini, J.A. (1979). Family relationships and morale among people 65 years of age and older. *American Journal of Orthopsychiatry, 49*, 292–300.

Petersen, L.S. (1982). Young and old are leaving the nest. *Family Therapy News, 13*, 4.

Quinn, W.H. (1982). Older parent and adult child interaction: Qualitative dimensions in building family strengths. In N. Stinnett, J. DeFrain, K. King, H. Lingren, G. Rowe, S. VanZandt, & R. Williams (Eds.). *Family Strengths 4: Positive Support Systems* (pp. 235–250). Lincoln, NE: University of Nebraska Press.

Quinn, W.H. (1983). Personal and family adjustment in later life. *Journal of Marriage and the Family, 45*, 57–73.

Quinn, W.H., & Keller, J.F. (1981). A family therapy model for preserving independence in older persons. *American Journal of Family Therapy, 9*, 79–84.

Quinn, W.H., & Keller, J.F. (1983). Older generations of the family: Relational dimensions and quality. *American Journal of Family Therapy, 11*, 23–34.

Reid, O.M. (1966). Aging Americans: A review of cooperative research projects. *Welfare in Review*, U.S. Department of HEW, *4*, 1–2.

Robinson, B., & Thurnher, M. (1979). Taking care of aged parents: A family cycle transition. *The Gerontologist, 19*, 586–593.

Rosow, I. (1967). Social integration of the aged. New York: The Free Press.

Seelbach, W.C., & Sauer, W.J. (1977). Filial responsibility expectations and morale among aged parents. *The Gerontologist, 17*, 492–499.

Simos, B.G. (1973). Adult children and their aging parents. *Social Work, 18*, 78–85.

Smith, K.F., & Bengtson, V.L. (1979). Positive consequences of institutionalization: Solidarity between elderly parents and their middle-aged children. *The Gerontologist, 19*, 438–447.

Sussman, M.B. (1977). Family, bureaucracy and the elderly individual: An organizational linkage perspective. In E. Shanas & M.B. Sussman (Eds.), *Family, bureaucracy and the elderly*. Durham, NC: Duke University Press.

Sussman, M.B., & Burchinal, L. (1962). Kin family network: Unheralded structure in current conceptualizations of family functioning. *Marriage and Family Living, 24*, 320–332.

Troll, L.E., & Bengtson, V.L. (1979). Generations in the family. In W.R. Burr, R. Hill, F.I. Nye, & I.L. Reiss (Eds.), *Contemporary theories about the family* (Vol. 1, pp. 127–161). New York: The Free Press.

Troll, L., & Smith, J. (1976). Attachment through the life-span: Some questions about dyadic bonds among adults. *Human Development, 19*, 156–170.

Turner, R. (1970). *Family interaction*. New York: John Wiley & Sons.

Watson, W. (1982). *Aging and social behavior*. Monterey, CA: Wadsworth Health Services Division.

Wilen, J.B. (1979). Changing relationships among grandparents, parents, and their young adult children. Paper presented at the annual meeting of the Gerontological Society, Washington, DC.

Williamson, D.S. (1978). New life at the graveyard: A method of therapy for individuation from a dead former parent. *Journal of Marital and Family Counseling, 4*, 93–101.

Williamson, D.S. (1981). Personal authority via termination of the intergenerational hierarchical boundary: A "new" stage in the family life cycle. *Journal of Marital and Family Therapy, 7*, 441–452.

Williamson, D.S. (1982). Personal authority via termination of the intergenerational hierarchical boundary: Part II—the consultation process and the therapeutic method. *Journal of Marital and Family Therapy, 8*, 23–37.

Chapter 3

Grandparents and Family Relations

Helen Q. Kivnick

A general consensus has emerged that family involvement is important to aging individuals, despite controversies among scholars about the most prevalent family structure in contemporary America; the specific functions the family performs for aging members; the predominant modes of intergenerational interaction; and the relative importance to the aging of various dyadic relationships (e.g., friendship, sibling, parent-child, grandparent, or other kin). In reviewing kinship research and theory done in the 1970s, Lee (1980) observes that emphasis has shifted from *whether* kin are important to the aging to *how and when* they are important. There is little doubt that elderly parents and their adult children play important roles in each other's lives. The remaining questions are concerned with the nature of those important roles (Lee & Ellithorpe, 1982). Bulter and Lewis (1982) and Hess and Waring (1978) note that feelings of community, intimacy, and solidarity based on kinship are central to a person's orientation as a significant human being in space and time. Schulman (1975) reports an age-correlated tendency for the elderly to name kin as the persons with whom their relationships are closest. Society undermines the functionality of the aging, but the family represents an island of safety and support from which the elderly are integrated into society at large (Shanas, 1980; Sussman, 1976). Families transcend societal age segregation (Hagestad, 1981a) and have managed, historically, to contain conflicts between the needs of individual members and those of the family group within the larger, ever-changing social context (Hareven, 1977). Nurturance, filial maturity and responsibility, guilt, and moral obligation are all viewed by recent research as central to the relationships between aging persons and their families. (See Chapters 6, 7, and 14 for elaboration of these concepts.)

Note: Some of the ideas in this chapter were developed by Dr. Kivnick in 1982.

Dr. Kivnick would also like to thank Gary Gardner and Michael Smyer for their comments on the early drafts of this chapter.

FAMILY CONTACT

Throughout 20 years of descriptive research on the aged population in the community, Ethel Shanas (1979, 1980) has consistently spoken out against the widespread belief that older people are alienated from their families. There are undoubtedly elements of truth in the observations that the American population is geographically mobile, that the nuclear family predominates in the United States, and that human service agencies are available to the elderly. Nonetheless, Shanas's findings disconfirm the derivative hypotheses that most older people live at great distances from their adult children; that most older people rarely see their children, parents, siblings, or other relatives; and that families are no longer an important source of care for older people. In surveys conducted in 1952, 1967, and 1975 the proportion of older people living within ten minutes' distance of at least one child has remained relatively constant—at somewhat higher than 50 percent. In 1975, 75 percent of older parents lived within 30 minutes' distance of at least one child. In this same year, 53 percent of older parents had seen at least one of their children within the past 36 hours, and 77 percent had seen a child within the past week. From 1952 through 1975, only 10 percent of older parents had not seen at least one child within the previous month. Thus, although actual living arrangements reflect generationally reciprocal desires for independence and privacy, the modified extended family emerges as the dominant family form for old people in the United States (Shanas, 1979).

Contact Patterns

Within the broad contours of the intergenerational proximity and interaction described above, investigators have sought to identify and to explain specific patterns and associations. As an indication of changing demands within the family an hourglass shape has been used to describe the frequency pattern of intergenerational interaction across the life cycle (Schneider, in Shanas, 1979; Schulman, 1975). According to this description, involvement with kin is high during childhood and youth, lower in the face of the immediate responsibilities of adulthood and middle age, and high, once again, in later life. Recent contradictory findings (Gibson, 1972; Leigh, 1982), however, report that the amount of interaction with kin is not at all related to the life-span variable. Instead, the critical variables appear to be kinship propinquity (closeness in the family tree), geographical proximity, affectional closeness and enjoyment, feelings of obligation, exchange of aid, and parental need for help.

Lee (1980) cites several studies that demonstrate the primary influence on contact frequency of geographical distance and resulting kin availability. Both he and Gibson caution that kin availability is such an important factor that if it is not analytically controlled, it may interact with other variables (e.g., age, contact functionality) and thereby may obscure meaningful relationships between these variables and contact frequency or obscure the relationships. Despite relative geographic closeness within cities, researchers disagree over the relationship between urbanization and kin contact. Hendrix (1976) asserts that urbanization reduces motivation for kin contact. By contrast, Cohler and Grunebaum (1981) explain that urban society creates so many professional and social opportunities that geographic closeness to kin and its accompanying high contact frequency are widely available.

Serious doubt exists as to whether frequency of face-to-face contact, per se, conveys anything meaningful about the subjective qualities of the relationships involved (Rosow, 1967). Troll and Smith (1976) point out that family bonds override separation, distance, and their attendant paucity of contact. Although distance does limit face-to-face interaction, it seems to have no effect on such contact as phoning, writing, or giving and receiving financial aid (Wilkening, Gurrero, & Ginsberg, 1972). More than contact frequency, this exchange of aid is regarded as a general expression of family solidarity, intergenerational ties, and mutual concern (Lee and Ellithorpe, 1982). Research has failed to confirm the hypotheses, however, that providing aid to children is associated with higher morale in the elderly and that receiving aid from children is associated with lower morale. Investigators have been able to conclude only that family generations seem to be interdependent and seem to exchange various forms of mutual aid in both directions (Lee & Ellithorpe, 1982).

Despite the acknowledged importance of family involvement to the elderly, most research has found no association between frequency of kin contact and emotional well-being among the elderly (Arling, 1976; Lee, 1980; Wood & Robertson, 1978). Two studies stand in notable exception to this widespread, perplexing finding. In the first, Bock and Webber (1972) suggest that strong kin ties may be inversely related to suicide among elderly widows. In the second, Watson and Kivett (1976) found that frequency of visits from children was related to life satisfaction among fathers over 60 years old. In contrast to contact with kin, there is a definite, positive association between morale and contact with friends, according to Lee and Ellithorpe (1982). This difference between contact with family and contact with friends is explained by differences underlying the two kinds of relationships. While family relationships are likely to be based on a lifelong sense of duty, of obligation, and of shared values, friendships rest on mutual choice, shared interests, and shared recreational activities (Lee and Ellithorpe, 1982). Although these underlying differences make sense, it is not conceptually apparent why contact with friends should be more closely associated with high morale than is contact with family.

What does seem to be apparent are the observations that research has provided little information about the quality of the relationships between the aging and their families (Shanas, 1980), and that studies of kinship interaction and well-being have failed to tap the critical dimensions of interaction or subjective well-being, or both (Kivnick, 1982a; 1982b; Lee & Ellithorpe, 1982). Clearly, if we are interested in the impact of family relationships on the lives of the aging, we must look beyond convenient, available measures toward more qualitative factors.

Parent-Child Relationship

Persons over 65 years old represent an increasing proportion of the population, creating families in which both Generations No. 1 and No. 2 are in old age (Gelfand, Olsen, & Block, 1978). Thus, the members of Generation No. 2 find themselves in filial crisis. Not only are they squeezed between pressures from their parents and pressures from their own adult children, but also they are likely to be involved in confronting the social and psychological issues of their own aging. In addition, they are likely to be experiencing ever-diminishing personal resources (e.g., energy, mobility, wealth), and, therefore, they are likely to be increasingly unable to respond to demands from either parents or children or to satisfy their own emerging needs. Underlying the straightforward pressures and tensions inherent in such a squeeze, unresolved loyalty conflicts and unsettled personal accounts (Spark, 1974) among the members of Generations No. 1, No. 2, and No. 3 exacerbate tensions and disrupt the inter- and intrapersonal equilibria essential to satisfactory resolutions.

As a function of longer postchildrearing adulthood, elderly parents and their children share bonds that endure for unprecedented lengths of time (Hagestad, 1981a)—bonds that evolve on the basis of ever-increasing amounts of shared experience in different life stages. No consistent obligations or expectations underlie these bonds, however—either in a behavioral or an emotional sense. Indeed, few consistent behavioral or emotional expectations exist for any facet of a life stage that lasts decades longer than experience can illuminate. Today's elderly parents cannot look back to their own parents' experience as a realistic guide to family life in old age; their parents' experience is likely to have been quite different. Shanas (1980) describes old people in their families as pioneers, because, in the absence of historical precedent, today's families must develop new systems of interaction, responsibility, and exchange. Rather than simply transmit family culture and expectations, today's families must create them anew (Hagestad, 1981a). In order to understand these families, researchers must, themselves, create conceptual frameworks that are appropriate to the roles and relationships that are evolving.

The rise of various social and economic service agencies for the aging is widely viewed as having effected a shift in the primary nature of filial responsibility, away from obligations of finances toward those based on emotions (Hagestad, 1981a; Hareven, 1977; Shorter, 1975; Streib and Beck, 1980; Treas, 1977). Although adult children routinely provide their parents with companionship, services, financial aid, gifts, advice, and counsel (Treas, 1977), they are not expected in contemporary American society to constitute the primary source of all of these forms of assistance. In fact, adult children quite understandably find themselves unable to provide all of these forms of assistance in adequate measure. If major economic and instrumental support comes from outside agencies, family members are freer to provide the affective support that can come from nowhere else. This division of responsibility is problematic, however, because it is not uniformly experienced across generations. Although older parents tend to expect more affective than instrumental support from their grown children, the children themselves tend to focus on instrumental responsibilities. This imbalance is important because research suggests that older people suffer depressed morale levels when their expectations differ from those of their children (Seelbach and Sauer, 1977).

Family Structure

It is striking that the vast majority of research and reports discussing older people and their families does so almost entirely in terms of the parent-child relationship. Not only do discussions of care and responsibility in dyadic relationships focus on interchange between elderly parents and their grown children, but even studies concerning the family life cycle limit themselves to consideration of two generations. The term "family life cycle" is described as referring to "the succession of critical stages through which the typical family passes during its life span" (Glick, 1977, p. 5). However, although a typical family may include members of three or four generations, the family life span as discussed in theoretical and empirical studies (e.g., Glick, 1977; Nock, 1979; Spanier, Sauer, & Larzelere, 1979) appears to end with the empty nest, that is, with the marriage of the last child or the death of a spouse. In their empirical evaluation of the family life cycle, Spanier et al. (1979) considered "the formation, maintenance, change, and dissolution of marriage and family relations" (p. 27), and they studied families through the empty nest stage as defined above. This conceptualization implies that the dissolution of marriage relationships (through the death of one spouse) is congruent to the dissolution of family relations and also that the family life cycle concerns children only as long as they are pre-adult. It also fails to consider the pre-parental and post-empty nest or postwidowhood years, although individuals are clearly members of families during these ignored years.

It is understandable that studies of the later-life family focus largely on parents and their children. Because the parental relationship is the family relationship that has historically received most attention, it has accumulated bodies of research and theory that make it the most feasible to continue to examine. It also represents a reasonably well understood basis from which to extrapolate. Parenthood is the adult family role that persons have historically participated in for the greatest number of years. In addition to explanations of research tradition and convention, on the one hand, and empirical individual description on the other, parenthood may be the object of primary focus because of an inherent primary importance. Gutmann's concept of the parental imperative (1975) certainly supports this explanation by asserting that parenthood is the pivotal stage of the human life cycle. According to Gutmann's concept, parenthood imparts organization, form, and content to all of the stages that lead up to it and to those that follow. However, even this concept suggests consideration of the postparenthood period as different from, although clearly derivative of, parenthood itself. With the lengthening expectable life span, the postchildrearing years are increasing in number for the average person, and require most clarification. Therefore, the empirical notion of family life cycle should be expanded to incorporate those family events (e.g., grandparenthood, great-grandparenthood, temporary or permanent reentry of a parent into the home) that take place in later life after a couple's children are grown.

Spark and Brody (1970) bring a family dynamics approach to their consideration of the emotional quality and meaning of intergenerational relationships. Discussing intergenerational needs and exchange in terms of interdependence, they explain that relationships between generations are likely to be best when each family member is experienced and available as a mutual resource. Because the needs of each family member continue to change throughout that person's lifetime, a healthy intergenerational family is characterized by flexibility and the ability to meet these ever-changing needs. Spark and Brody note also that grandparents have been seen as stimulators of conflict, as competing objects of attention and sources of authority, as sources of support, and as indulgent figures. These varying emotional roles suggest that grandparents must be included if intergenerational families are to move toward higher levels of maturity and flexibility.

GRANDPARENTHOOD

Shanas (1980) reminds us that a person with children is not only a parent; he or she is also part of a lineage. For each parent, becoming a grandparent represents a new expression of that lineage. In discussing the impact of social trends on grandparenthood, Clavan (1978) observes that this role is not clearly defined for grandparents or for other relatives, that it is no longer limited to old age, and that it characterizes individuals who are integrated on a very limited basis into the life of the nuclear family. On these bases, she describes grandparenthood as an "ideological" role (i.e., a kinship position without normative rights or obligations), and she calls for the development of a "real" grandparent role to bring grandparents back into the family. This call suggests that other family members have real, clearly defined roles that include them in the family. However, because members of today's multigenerational families confront serious role ambiguities, they are called upon to develop appropriate systems of exchange and interaction. This ambiguity applies to family members in all generations, not just to grandparents. In addition, it applies to all family roles in which an individual participates (e.g., grandparent, parent, adult child, sibling). The remainder of this chapter focuses, insofar as possible, on those family relationships that explicity have to do with grandparenthood.

Conceptual Complexities

The study of grandparenthood is beset by conceptual complexities that must somehow be addressed in order to develop a meaningful understanding of this experience. One such complexity has to do with the fact that grandparents represent many different cohorts and both the first and second generations in four-generation families. Persons widely disparate in age (chronological age, historical age, and family age) are likely to face grandparenthood with different sets of hopes and capabilities, alongside different configurations of personal and professional relationships, activities, and responsibilities. As the "old-old," grandparents are fragile individuals in need of an array of services. As the "young-old," they are enjoying retirement and facing the imminence of "old-old" age. As the middle-aged, they are at the peak of their power and responsibility for both older and younger generations. However, a discussion of grandparents includes all of these persons and the relationships they have with their grandchildren.

A second conceptual complexity has to do with what Hagestad (1981a) refers to as the interweaving of lives. Within a family, individual lives are interwoven with one another in such a way that changes in the life of one family member are likely to affect the lives of all the others. This effect holds true for normative, involuntary developmental changes; for voluntary changes; and also for unexpected, unpredictable changes.

Another related complexity has to do with the fact that grandparenthood is developmental in nature, that is, that a given grandparenthood relationship grows and changes over its years of existence. As discussed at greater length elsewhere (Kivnick, 1981a; 1982a; 1982b), this developmental notion refers also to the person's current grandparenthood as it is related to relevant aspects of his or her lifelong experience and also as it is influenced by ongoing, individual developmental changes in the grandparent and in the grandchildren. As is true in most longstanding family relationships, then, grandparenthood reflects the grandparent as he or she is, has been, and will become.

Today's middle-aged grandparents are the young-old and the old-old grandparents of the coming decades; today's infant grandchildren are the schoolchildren, adolescents and young adults of years to come. A 68-year-old woman is likely to be a different type of grandmother to her newborn grandson from the kind she will be when they are both ten years older, and also from the type she will be to that grandson's younger female cousin, born on Grandmother's 80th birthday. In seeking to describe and to understand grandparenthood we must identify the presence of interwoven lives and developmental changes and also clarify the specific natures of these influences. Otherwise, we risk misinterpreting what is, in essence, a single frame of a full-length motion picture film as if that frame were the entire film. Consider the description in Exhibit 3–1 of 20 to 25 years in the life of a grandmother.

The interwoven nature of the lives of the members of this family illustrates the widespread ramifications of events occurring to any one member. The grandmother's and the grandchildren's reciprocal role behaviors have undergone many changes in response to a variety of developmental and circumstantial changes in the lives of family members in all generations. Some of these changes—e.g., divorce (Hagestad, Smyer, & Stierman, 1982; Smyer & Hofland, 1982)—have been studied in terms of their family-wide effects. Others remain relatively unexplored. As the above example shows, however, none can be ignored. Although grandparenthood is a relationship in its own right—different from the grandmother's ongoing bond with her daughter and different from the mother's raising of her children—it is nonetheless inseparable from these other family relationships, and it must be understood in the context they provide.

Methodological Complexities

Various methodological difficulties beset grandparenthood research and potentially limit the usefulness of findings. The first difficulty has to do with the meaningful nature of material tapped by objective, readily quantifiable questions. Scholars are beginning to suggest that research has not yet tapped the critical dimensions of kinship interaction, partly because qualitative dimensions of relationships are difficult to measure. They are difficult even to identify. A related issue is that those relationship dimensions that are easy to measure may not convey much meaningful information about the overall relationship. For example, although frequency of contact with grandchildren may be easy to measure, such frequency has been viewed as unrelated to grandparent morale (Wood and Robertson, 1978) and also as not indicative of the actual nature of the relationships involved (Blau, 1973). How can we articulate and quantify, though, what it is that lights up an old grandfather's eyes when he talks about his grandson?

A second difficulty in grandparenthood research has to do with who or what the unit of statistical analysis is in any given study. This difficulty suggests that even easily quantifiable dimensions of grandparenthood may not be easy to measure meaningfully. To date, research on grandparenthood as it is experienced by grandparents has been conducted by gathering data from grandparents. Such data include, among other things, information about activities with and attitudes

Exhibit 3–1 A Case Study of a Grandmother

A widow in her early 60s lived in New England within easy walking distance of her married daughter. She thoroughly enjoyed caring for her infant (and then toddler) grandson while the child's mother was employed. This grandmother's surrogate parent role provided her with much personal satisfaction. In addition, it permitted her daughter to derive the experiential and the financial satisfactions of full-time employment. In this mutually beneficial situation, feelings of reciprocal gratitude and affection provided further enhancement of the relationships among this grandmother, her daughter, and her daughter's husband and young child. As the grandmother aged, however, and as her grandchild matured, she found that she did not have the energy to be the primary daytime caretaker for an energetic 4-year-old. She had begun to develop arthritis, and so when she bent down she was not sure that she would be able to stand up again. Particularly when her daughter had a second child, this grandmother began to resent the self-encouraged expectation that she would provide child care for her grandchildren. She also felt guilty for being unable to fulfill what she regarded as her part of a bargain. Although these shifts resulted from expectable developmental changes in the grandmother and her grand-children, renegotiating the scope of her grandparental responsibilities understandably affected the balance of intergenerational gratitude and cooperation and the nature of interdependence existing between her and her daughter's family. These altered balances, in turn, affected the behavior, meaning, and satisfaction that comprised her experience of grandmotherhood.

When this grandmother was in her mid-to-late 60s, her daughter was divorced. This semi-voluntary change created for the daughter and her children a new constellation of emotional and financial needs and pressures, which, in turn, created new changes in the feelings of interdependence and in the behavior between herself and her mother. In this case, the middle-aged mother remained single for 8 to 10 years, and the grandmother came to represent a critical second adult in the lives of her grandchildren, even though she remained unable and unwilling to assume full-time, day-to-day parenting responsibilities for them.

When the grandmother was in her mid-70s she married a man she had known since childhood, whose wife had recently died of cancer. Together, they moved to the Sun Belt to accommodate her new husband's lifelong retirement plans. Quite expectably, this voluntary change necessitated yet another reorganization in this three-generation family's system of emotional, financial, and service-related interdependence. Remarriage introduces a new person into the intergenerational family and rearranges the interpersonal priorities and responsibilities of various other family members. Although this woman's grandmotherhood experience had been changing all along in response to the grandchildren's constantly maturing interests and to her own gradually deteriorating physical strength, now, suddenly, she was subject to a different kind of change. Now she found herself geographically removed from the grandchildren she had been used to seeing almost every day, if only for a quick hello or to watch them compete in athletic events. Correspondingly, the grandchildren found themselves no longer able to take her for granted, to be enjoyed, indulged, or ignored as their moods and other activities dictated. Grandparent-grandchild contact now had to be thoughtfully planned. Phone calls had to be timed so that both parties were home, awake, and free to talk. Letter-writing consumed time and provided satisfactions quite different from those resulting from regular informal contact. Visits over long distances represented major interruptions in normal life, and for grandmother, mother, and grandchildren, such visits carried different expectations and demanded very different kinds of attention from those to which these family members had grown accustomed.

Over the years, the grandmother's arthritis had become increasingly incapacitating. When she was in her mid-80s, her second husband died. In addition to her arthritis, she suddenly developed incurable shingles, and she found herself unable to live alone. At the time at which

Exhibit 3–1 continued

> decisions needed to be made, her daughter was recuperating from coronary bypass surgery, living on her company's disability insurance and relying on her own daughter to maintain the household until she could resume her normal responsibilities. The oldest grandson was now married and living 3,000 miles away from his mother. He and his wife were expecting their first child; Mother was about to become a first-time grandmother, and Grandmother was about to become a great-grandmother. This young man had just lost his managerial position, because a local fruit packing plant had closed. Because he worked for a major national food processing company, he did not face indefinite unemployment; nevertheless, the geography and the finances of his short-term future were highly uncertain.

toward "your grandchildren." Because such studies are concerned with grandparenthood to and for grandparents, they have analyzed their data by regarding each grandparent as one case. Respondents may be expected, however, to have difficulty giving meaningful answers to general questions about such aspects of grandparenthood as frequency of contact, satisfaction with contact, and concern or worry about or feelings of closeness or identification with "your grandchildren." In the author's research (Kivnick, 1982b), respondents had an average of 2.6 children and from 1 through more than 15 grandchildren (mean = 4.5). Quite understandably, different families of grandchildren lived at widely different distances from the grandparents, and respondents felt that general statements obscured meaningful differences. As a middle-aged, very wealthy grandmother explained, "Those who live in Canada I don't see nearly enough, and, quite frankly, those who live here in the city I see more often than I'd like. With the ones from Canada every visit is a treat, and I only see them at their best. But for those who are right here, I see them at their best and at their worst—and I know their worst much better than I'd like to." In response to a precoded multiple choice question, this woman's best description of her level of satisfaction with the frequency of grandchild contact was "about as much as you'd like to have " (Kivnick, 1982b), but she reminded me that this answer conveyed neither her frustration with the local children nor her powerful longing for those at great distance.

In order to understand the grandparenthood experience across individual persons, we must analyze such variables as the geographical proximity, the age of the grandchildren, and the number of grandchildren. Such analysis is complicated, however, in cases like that of the grandmother, in which the grandchildren live at distances varying from one to several thousand miles. Such analysis is even more complicated for those grandparents whose grandchildren range in age from infancy through young adulthood. Failing to provide control for these variables or adequately explore them in data analysis may lead to findings that are confounded and misleading. However, failing to address these complexities while designing an experimental instrument leads all too easily to the collection and the analysis of data that are straightforward to gather but must be recognized at the outset to be of limited validity. (See Chapter 17 for an elaboration of this caution.)

A promising solution to many of these problems seems to be to regard each grandparent-grandchild relationship as a separate unit of statistical analysis. This analytic procedure would be conducted in addition to the traditional procedures noted above and would provide a complementary focus. In order to implement this procedure, each grandparent would be asked to provide the desired information about each grandchild, which would then appear in a data set once for each grandchild. Although grandparents having many grandchildren would be over-represented in such a set of grandparenthood dyads, this method would enable us to construct a more realistic picture of the overall grandparenting experience of each respondent than we are now able to do. Despite its potential methodological difficulties and high financial cost for data gathering and analysis and despite the potential burden it places on research respondents, this method would permit consideration of the characteristics of the individual relationships that comprise any person's grandparenthood experience. Its use with traditional methods could begin to encourage both researchers and practitioners to consider the meaningful components of an experience that has been described only in terms of gross contours.

Role Components

In considering grandparenthood, researchers and practitioners must recognize that the notion of role behavior is different from that of role meaning, which is, in turn, different from that of role satisfaction. Possibly, because all three aspects are difficult to measure in a meaningful fashion, research has referred simply to the grandparent role without systematically differentiating among these role components or without investigating relationships among them. Clearly, however, these facets are related; just as clearly, too, a difference exists between a grandmother's behavior in a role, in the meaning and importance the role holds for her, and in her satisfaction in that role. For example, taking grandchildren to their favorite restaurants has been discussed in the following very different ways by different grandparents: "It's a chance to show her off to my friends." "That's one way I can introduce him to my world, so he'll have some idea of what my life is like." "Going out to eat at her local deli was a real ritual for my grandmother and me. I still remember the smell of that place, and the way she looked so carefully at each kind of meat. It's only natural that I'd want to do the same kind of thing with my own grandchildren." "His parents don't have much money right now, so I think it's important for me to introduce him to the finer things in life." "I'm a very busy woman, with little time to spend thinking about what might suit his fancy. When he comes to stay with me, I take him along on whatever I had planned to do—to the Club or out to lunch, or whatever." "I get a bang out of arranging what I know will be a real treat for her." "One of my jobs as a grandmother is to teach him to be a little grownup." "I never was good with children. Taking her to a nice place lets me spend some time with her, where I don't have to think up something to do or love her up and down. And she knows she'll have to behave well and not give me any trouble. And even if it doesn't work out all that well, it doesn't last all that long."

Conversely, very different behavior can have similar meanings to different grandparents. For example, several different grandparents have spoken about feeling a sense of timelessness and identification as they watch a grandchild "just be himself," and each has cited one of the following activities as an occasion for such feelings: watching him in a swimming meet once in a while; taking her to dancing lessons each week and watching how well she does; babysitting for them in the evenings when they do their homework; being there to watch each new grandchild be born and cry his first cry; keeping a collection of up-to-date photographs of the grandchildren on the dressing table.

The same grandparent may find himself sharing quite different kinds of activities with the grandchildren, but as circumstances change, role meaning remains relatively constant. For example, a grandmother in her early 50s spoke of romping and roughhousing with her two young granddaughters. She tremendously enjoyed joining them as they played with their hamsters and their puppies, and she became enmeshed so frequently with them in laughing, tickling matches that they called her "La La" for "Laughing Lady." This woman developed spinal cancer, however, when her granddaughters were eight and six years old, and she could no longer move freely. When she was not in incapacitating pain, she watched them play with their pets and with each other, and she laughed from the sidelines. When she could no longer leave her home, she had snapshots taken of the two girls and their pets, and she wrote them letters asking about the animals.

Attributing a particular quality or intensity of meaning to grandparenthood does not necessarily imply satisfaction. Consider the following grandfather, who thinks about grandparenthood primarily in terms of passing on knowledge and wisdom to his grandchildren, and being respected for such teaching. This man has three families of grandchildren (ten grandchildren in all), but most of them live more than a day's drive away. Unfortunately he has had little opportunity to establish with his grandchildren the kinds of relationships in which it would be natural to teach skills like fishing or to tell stories of family or personal history. It is particularly unfortunate for this grandfather that the two grandchildren who live nearby are the children of his now-divorced son. The son's ex-wife has remarried, and she actively impedes the children's contact with all members of her ex-husband's family. When he spoke, this grandfather was, understandably, extremely bitter and dissatisfied with his grandparenthood.

If a man with the same geographic and family circumstances thought about grandparenthood in a more distant or formal way, wishing only to send cards and gifts on holidays and to keep track of school graduations, he would be more likely to be satisfied with his current grandparenthood situation. If this man were to have grandchildren who were both geographically and emotionally available, he might be more likely to experience the kind of grandfatherhood for which he longs.

Simply regarding grandparenthood, overall, as an extremely important part of life carries no implication of satisfaction. Although a woman who spends the majority of her waking minutes thinking about her grandchildren may be quite gratified if they are available and desirably attentive, she may be correspondingly disappointed and bitter if they are unavailable, antagonistic, or simply not interested in her. Whereas such a woman may be expected to experience high morale if this crucial area of her life proves satisfying, she may also be expected to experience seriously lowered morale if it proves disappointing. By contrast, the well-being of a woman to whom grandparenthood represents one small part of a life full of people and activities would be expected to be far less susceptible to either positive or negative influences of grandparenthood.

Behavior

Various researchers have noted the difference between objective grandparenthood behavior and subjective aspects of grandparenthood, such as meaning or significance (Clavan, 1978). Nevertheless, the field as a whole has not clearly articulated the distinction between role behavior, meaning, and satisfaction; nor has it systematically investigated the relationships among them. Nonetheless, the accumulated body of grandparenthood research may be categorized according to these three role components. Early work considered the grandparent's effect on the family and, in so doing, focused almost entirely on the behavioral component of grandparenthood. This work was based primarily on clinical case materials and gathered its data from families and persons with levels of pathology severe enough that they sought psychiatric treatment (Campbell & Bubolz, 1982). It should not be surprising, then, that many early professional reports describe the grandparent's role within the family in negative terms, such as usurping and dominating the mother's role (Bordon, in Campbell & Bubolz; Vollmer, 1937); monopolizing parental time and interfering with parent-child relationships (Fox, 1937); precipitating antisocial behavior in adolescents by transmitting excess hostility to children (Strauss, 1943); overindulging the grandchildren (Fried & Stern, 1948); encouraging unhealthy rejection of the parent (Abraham, 1955); and infantilizing the parent and stimulating the development of undesirable character traits (Rappaport, 1958).

By contrast, there are positive functions of the grandparent's role in the family: providing an opportunity for the child to sublimate negative feelings toward the parents; functioning as a helpmate to the parents (Deutsch, 1945); stepping in, in time of crisis to fill the position of a missing nuclear family member (Von Hentig, 1946; Young & Wilmot, 1957); housesitting and supplementing family income through gifts (Sussman, 1953); serving as surrogate parents; serving as babysitters (Lajewski, 1959); exemplifying for children the positive characteristics of old age; serving as an antidote to parental physical or psychiatric disabilities (Kahana & Kahana, 1971); providing a corrective influence in families in which parents are abusively disturbed (LaBarre, Jessner, & Ussery, 1960); and contributing to the complementarity of goals and self-evaluation within the family (Ackerman, 1961). In reviewing grandparenting over four decades, Campbell and Bubolz (1982) conclude that parenting in most families is the responsibility of parents and that grandparents are neither expected nor permitted to share in this responsibility.

Other research concerned with grandparent role behavior shifts its focus from evaluating the effects of grandparental behavior on the family to describing grandparent-grandchild interaction. Several researchers discuss such interaction in terms of differential levels of grandparent-grandchild formality and friendliness (Boyd, 1969; Burgess & Locke, 1950; Neugarten & Weinstein, 1964; Radcliffe-Brown & Forde, 1950). These researchers concur in describing an inverse relationship between the amount of functional authority the grandparent wields in society and the extent to which friendly equality and warmth characterize their relationships with granchildren. Neugarten and Weinstein differentiated five behavioral styles of grandparenting: formal; fun seeker; surrogate parent; reservoir of family wisdom; and distant figure. For present purposes, Wood and Robertson's finding (1976) that grandparenthood activity is unrelated to life satisfaction is categorized as another study of grandparent role behavior.

Satisfaction

Comparatively little work has been conducted on grandparental satisfaction with the grandparenthood experience, per se. Some researchers report that many grandparents enjoy their created role (Robertson, 1977); others report that grandparents find only limited satisfaction in this role (Lopata, 1973). Neugarten and Weinstein (1964) found that although the majority of their subjects enjoyed grandparenthood, a sizeable minority of their sample expressed some kind of disappointment with this role. These conflicting findings clearly indicate that grandparenthood satisfaction cannot be taken for granted, and they suggest that persons may be satisfied with some aspects of grandparenthood at the same time as they are unhappy with others. Boyd (1969) and Troll (1971) cite a distinction between simply becoming a grandparent (an ascribed status), and becoming a valued grandparent (an earned and acquired status). Although Clavan (1978) observes that both grandmothers and grandfathers are valued in their families when they ease parental child care burdens, she fails to differentiate between being valued in a role by people outside the self, on the one hand, and valuing a role and being satisfied in it according to one's own internal feelings on the other. This distinction is important because being valued by grandchildren and grown children may be necessary for grandparenthood satisfaction. However, being valued in this way has not been demonstrated to be sufficient for such satisfaction or for a grandparent's valuing this experience within himself.

Meaning

Research on the meaning of grandparenthood focused originally on single dimensions of meaning. For example, Benedek (1970), Blau (1973), and Boyd (1969) all discussed grandparents and their grandchildren in terms of providing mutual affection, acceptance, and support. Albrecht (1954) and Apple (1956) explored the issue of socialization responsibility and found that grandparents were glad to be free of responsibility for all aspects of their grandchildren's failures, shortcomings, and mistakes. In their consideration of interactional responsibility, Kahana and Kahana (1971) placed responsibility in the hands of the grandparent. Cohler and Grunebaum (1981) assert that because working-class people place more value on comfort and pleasure in interpersonal relationships, they attribute more importance to family stability and solidarity than do their middle-class counterparts. This assertion suggests that as a potential embodiment of family solidarity, grandparenthood may be more meaningful among working-class grandparents than among middle-class grandparents. Gorlitz and Gutmann (1981) discuss the psychodynamic meaning of grandparenthood in terms of its representing a new phase of parenthood for the grandparent; in terms of its reviving earlier internal struggles with issues of dependence, separation, and individuation; and in terms of its exacerbating or ameliorating the narcissistic vulnerability of the postparental years.

Differentiating role significance from behavioral style, Neugarten and Weinstein (1964) deductively identified five categories of grandparenthood meaning: the source of biological renewal; an opportunity to succeed in a new emotional role; a teacher-resource person role; a vicarious achievement; and a remote role. Wood and Robertson (1976) posited that role meaning is a product of anticipatory socialization and that a person's attitudes upon assuming the grandparent role are determined by social forces (directed toward meeting society's needs) and by personal forces (directed toward meeting the person's own needs). In Wood and Robertson's empirical work, respondents were scored on these two attitudinal dimensions. Four grandparent role types were identified, based on high-low distributions of subjects: apportioned (high on both personal and social determinants); individualized (high on personal and low on social determinants); symbolic (low on personal and high on social determinants); and remote (low on both personal and social determinants).

Until 1980, these were the only two-dimensional frameworks cited as describing grandparenthood meaning. Each framework has an inherent problem, however, that has limited its immediate usefulness in subsequent grandparenthood research. Although the Neugarten and Weinstein (1964) framework is valuable in its breadth, the fact that it does not exist in quantitatively measurable form means that it has been difficult to incorporate into quantitative exploration. The Wood and Robertson framework is desirably quantifiable; however, it rests on only two dimensions of grandparenthood meaning—i.e., grandparenthood attitudes determined by social forces and grandparenthood attitudes determined by personal forces. On the basis of pilot interviews from the author's work, these two dimensions seemed inadequate to describe the full range of grandparenthood meanings noted by respondents.

In designing the study (Kivnick, 1980; 1982a; 1982b; 1983), the author tentatively attributed earlier findings of no relationship between grandparenthood meaning and grandparent mental health to the use of inadequate measures of grandparenthood meaning. The first task of the project was, therefore, the development of a quantifiable, comprehensive conceptualization of grandparenthood meaning. Questionnaire items were developed from qualitative interviews with eleven grandparents. Five dimensions of grandparenthood meaning were then derived by analyzing quantitative questionnaire data obtained from 286 grandparents: centrality; valued elder; immortality through clan; reinvolvement with personal past; and indulgence. The significance subsumed in each dimension is discussed elsewhere in summary form (Kivnick, 1982a) and also in detail (Kivnick, 1982b; 1983). Because this study had been designed explicitly to clarify and to quantify grandparenthood role meaning, the derived dimensions of meaning could be used in a quantitative exploration of the relationship of grandparenthood meaning to psychological well-being and to personal life history. Despite the exploratory nature of this study, findings suggest that dimensions of role meaning are differentially associated with psychological well-being according to a deprivation-compensation model. Grandparents seem to be able to use grandparenthood meaning to maximize psychosocial and circumstantial strengths, to rework psychosocial deficits, and to compensate for circumstantial weaknesses.

This study differs from earlier work in terms of the conceptual breadth of the empirical data used to derive dimensions of grandparenthood meaning and also by the extensive analysis of the grandparenthood well-being connection. The promising nature of these findings suggests that these methods are well-suited to the study of subtleties and complexities of the grandparenthood experience and may profitably be applied to a consideration of role behavior and satisfaction, as well. These findings also suggest that the distinction among grandparent role behavior, meaning, and satisfaction may be critical to the development of a comprehensive understanding of grandparenthood—both in and of itself and in the context of other aspects of grandparents' lives.

Autonomy and Control

At all developmental stages, family dynamics involve struggle for control. All family members simultaneously attempt to control themselves and their own behavior within the family and also to influence the behavior of other members. They further struggle for control and autonomy through family-based interactions and also through the family's mediation between its members and society at large. Though these issues have long been focal with respect to the child-rearing stages of family life, their relevance to the family life of grandparents remains to be fully explored.

Hagestad (1981b) asserts that the parent-child influence is a lifelong process, and she notes that, when questioned, respondents in three generations acknowledge their parents as the persons who are most influential in their current lives. In contrast to this unidirectional view, Walters and Walters (1980) emphasize a move toward reciprocal models of influence and causality. Although they speak directly only about parent-child relationships, this reciprocal causality is also applicable to grandparent-parent, and grandparent-grandchild relationships. Reciprocity suggests that a unilateral influence is not exerted by an authoritative person on a powerless dyadic partner; rather, influence in a relationship is exerted by both partners, regardless of vested authority, as they respond to expressions of each other's demands, needs, wishes, and satisfactions. Thus, grandparents should not be considered to be omnipotent and manipulative or helpless and wholly reactive in their relationships to their families; instead, they may profitably be viewed as participating in a network of reciprocal influences that may be modified, when adequately understood, in order to maximize the satisfactions of all participants. Grandparenthood research directly relevant to this issue is concerned with the relationship between grandparent functional authority and friendly cordiality in intergenerational relations. Likewise, it is concerned with the extent to which grandparents have real control and responsibility vis-à-vis their grandchildren. Both of these areas, which have been discussed earlier, are relevant to the present context because the notion of reciprocal influence may be used effectively to defuse conflicts around intergenerational control and to mitigate their negative consequences.

The concept of control has to do with one person's influence on another; the concept of autonomy has to do with a person's capacity to control one's own life. Issues of intergenerational autonomy and control involve grandparents as they do or do not overinfluence the younger generations and as they are or are not subject to control by these same persons (Kivnick, 1981b). For example, Boyd (1969) asserts that the best relationship between two adult generations exists when grandparents are willing to provide help and assistance while recognizing the need of the young adult generation for autonomy and independence. Cohler and Grunebaum (1981) cite numerous findings that indicate that issues of the younger generation's autonomy are the major source of intergenerational conflict. Bengtson and Kuypers's description of parent-child differences in generational stake (1971) is consistent with these findings.

Although their terminology is different, Cohler and Grunebaum (1981) present findings that illustrate precisely the reverse situation. They identify as a major source of intergenerational conflict the feeling among grandparents that their young adult offspring expect advice and assistance they are unwilling to provide. In the traditional negative view, grandparents are seen as intruding on the autonomy of other family members. This view attributes to grandparents sufficient power and control for them to effect their detrimental influence. Cohler and Grunebaum make the further important observation that grandparents frequently experience their own autonomy as intruded on by their children and, perhaps, by their grandchildren as well. In describing grandparents' desire to maintain their own autonomy, Cohler and Grunebaum return to the research that indicates that older family members enjoy the empty nest. They relish their new, hard-won freedom from the responsibilities of guiding and disciplining their children and also of functioning as exemplary role models. They look forward to being able to live for themselves. This reluctance to be constrained by other people's demands is consistent with Neugarten's (1964) assertion that the aging are increasingly concerned with their own internal life and with the tasks of coming to terms with aging and death. These internal concerns take time and energy, and they may well make external demands seem particularly burdensome.

Reseach on the locus of control (Gatz & Siegler, 1981) differentiates between locus of control for a particular event (does a person cause or anticipate an event?) and locus of control for handling the event (does a person accept responsibility for coping with an event?). Both facets of control are relevant to older people in their families. It is clear that such parameters of older family life as widowhood, divorce or death in the middle generation, residential proximity of members of other generations, and affinity for in-laws in all generations are likely to remain outside the control of the grandparent. To the extent that relationships with grandchildren are mediated by parents (Lowenthal and Robinson, 1976), both the grandparents and the grandchildren are subject to control by the parent generation. Grandparents do have control, however, over the way they deal with these various situations. They may choose to exert the effort to maintain contact across geographic distance. They may continue to participate in family rituals, despite the pain caused by the death of a spouse. In cases of acrimonious middle-generation divorce, they may try to overcome personal feelings of bitterness or disappointment, to express support for both divorcing parents, and to maintain direct contact with the grandchildren. Because family bonds are permanent, grandparents need not fear that a single instance of conflict can terminate relationships and leave them helplessly abandoned.

Locus-of-control research also differentiates between actual locus of control (can the person control events in his or her life?) and perceived locus of control (does the person feel that he or she has control of life's events?). Reid, Haas, and Hawkings (1977) have demonstrated the centrality of a perceived sense of control and effectance to adjustment and well-being among the elderly, particularly in those areas the elderly evaluated as most important. In addition, Abramson, Seligman, and Teasdale (1978) have found that as the perception of a lack of personal control (i.e., the perception of external control) becomes increasingly global and stable, such psychological deficits as depression and helplessness are likely to become unfortunately general and chronic. These negative consequences of perceived external control suggest that the reciprocal control grandparents experience within their families may provide a critical defense against chronic depression. The longstanding nature of family relationships provides an ongoing context in which grandparents can use the control they do wield to maximize essential life satisfactions. In so doing, they reinforce their perception of effectiveness and self-determination and thus limit the extent to which helplessness and its consequent emotional deficits become generalized and chronic.

The recognition of grandparents' need for autonomy and to have a measure of interpersonal control makes the notion of reciprocal influence among the generations seem more realistic than it may frequently appear to be. Of course, the simple existence of this reciprocity does not guarantee its positive effects. Its mutual recognition is central to the differentiated, uniformly responsible functioning of the intergenerational family as a whole and also to the grandparents' maintaining maximum levels of personal independence. Spark and Brody (1970) emphasize the fact that pathological dependence at any age must be differentiated from healthy interdependence, in which each family member is experienced as an autonomous individual and also as an available resource. Like all family members, grandparents have personal conflicts, weaknesses, and strengths. Like all family members, they are both controlled and controlling. Like all family members, they must balance the need for autonomy with that for assistance. Like all family members, they must engage in a complex network of compromises to minimize weaknesses and to enhance strengths for the benefit of all members.

As a family relationship, grandparenthood represents a series of ongoing, longstanding bonds. As a role, it comprises a unique range of behaviors, meanings, and satisfactions. Within the context of the intergenerational family, grandparenthood behavior, meaning, and satisfaction must be negotiated to achieve optimal levels of overall need satisfaction for all family members. Although this chapter has focused on grandparenthood from the grandparent's point of view, it must be remembered that, like all family relationships, grandparenthood is mutual in nature. In the face of increasing lack of internal control over their physical, social, and internal worlds, aging family members must ideally be able to take advantage of the unique qualities inherent in grandparenthood in order to maximize actual and perceived internal control. These controls, in turn, may be crucial to the grandparents' own immediate well-being and to the long-term well-being of the entire intergenerational family.

REFERENCES

Abraham, K. (1955). Some remarks on the role of grandparents in the psychology of neuroses. In *Clinical papers and essays on psychoanalysis, II*. New York: Basic Books.

Abramson, L.Y., Seligman, M.E.P., & Teasdale, J.D. (1978). Learned helplessness in humans: Critique and reformulation. *Journal of Abnormal Psychology, 87*(1), 49–74.

Ackerman, N.W. (1961). A dynamic frame for the clinical approach to family conflict. In N.W.Ackerman et al. (Eds.), *Exploring the base for family therapy*. New York: Family Service Association of America.

Albrecht, R. (1954).The parental responsibilities of grandparents. *Marriage and Family Living, 16*(3), 201–204.

Apple, D. (1956). The social structure of grandparenthood. *American Anthropologist, 58*(4), 656–663.

Arling, G. (1976). The elderly widow and her family, neighbors, and friends. *Journal of Marriage and the Family, 38*, 757–768.

Benedek, T. (1970). Parenthood during the life cycle. In E.J.Anthony & T. Benedek (Eds.), *Parenthood during the life cycle*. Boston: Little, Brown, & Co.

Bengtson, V.L., & Kuypers, J.A. (1971). Generational difference and the developmental stake. *Aging and Human Development, 2*, 249–260.

Blau, Z.S. (1973). *Old age in a changing society*. New York: Franklin Watts.

Bock, E.W., & Webber, I.L. (1972). Suicide among the elderly: Isolating widowhood and mitigating alternatives. *Journal of Marriage and the Family, 34*, 24–31.

Boyd, R.R. (1969). The valued grandparent: A changing social role. In W.T.Donahue, J.L. Kornbluh, & L. Power (Eds.), *Living in the multigenerational family*. Ann Arbor: Institute of Gerontology, University of Michigan.

Burgess, E., & Locke, H.J. (1950). *The family: From institution to companionship*. New York: American Book Company.

Butler, R.N., & Lewis, M. (1982). *Aging and mental health*. St. Louis: The C.V. Mosby Company.

Campbell, V., & Bubolz, M. (1982). Parenting by related adults. In M. Kostelnik & H. Fitzgerald (Eds.), *Patterns of supplementary parenting*. New York: Plenum Publishing.

Clavan, S. (1978). The impact of social class and social trends on the role of grandparent. *The Family Coordinator, 27*, 351–357.

Cohler, B.J., & Grunebaum, H. (1981). *Mothers, grandmothers, and daughters: Personality and child care in three generations*. New York: John Wiley & Sons.

Deutsch, H. (1945). *The psychology of women, II, Motherhood*, New York: Grune and Stratton.

Fox, F. (1937). Family life and relationships as affected by the presence of the aged. In Committee on Mental Hygiene, Family Welfare Association of America (Eds.), *Mental hygiene and old age*. New York: State Charities Aid Association.

Fried, E.G., & Stern, K. (1948). The situation of the aged within the family. *American Journal of Orthopsychiatry, 18*, 31–54.

Gatz, M., & Siegler, I.C. (1981, August). *Locus of control: A retrospective*. Paper presented at the annual convention of the American Psychological Association, Los Angeles, CA.

Gelfand, D.E., Olsen, J.K., & Block, M.R. (1978). Two generations of elderly in the changing American family: Implications for family services. *The Family Coordinator, 27*, 395–403.

Gibson, G. (1972). Kin family network: Overheralded structure in past conceptualizations of family functioning. *Journal of Marriage and the Family, 34*, 13–23.

Glick, P. (1977). Updating the life cycle of the family. *Journal of Marriage and the Family, 39*, 5–13.

Gorlitz, P., & Gutmann, D.L. (1981). The psychological transition into grandparenthood. In J.G. Howells (Ed.), *Modern perspectives in the psychiatry of middle age*. New York: Brunner/Mazel.

Gutmann, D.L. (1975). Parenthood: A key to the comparative study of the life cycle. In N. Datan & L. Ginsberg (Eds.), *Life-span developmental psychology: Normative life crises*. New York: Academic Press.

Hagestad, G.O. (1981a). Problems and promises in the social psychology of intergenerational relations. In R. Fogel, E. Hatfield, S. Kilser, & J. March (Eds.), *Aging: Stability and change in the family*. New York: Academic Press.

Hagestad, G.O. (1981b). Parent and child: Generations in the family. In T. Field (Ed.), *Human development*. New York: John Wiley & Sons.

Hagestad, G.O., Smyer, M.A., & Stierman, K. (1982). Parent-child relations in adulthood: The impact of divorce in middle age. In R. Cohen, S. Weissman, & B. Cohler (Eds.), *Parenthood as an adult experience*. New York: Guilford Press.

Hareven, T.K. (1977). Family time and historical time. *Daedalus, 106*(1), 57–70.

Hendrix, L. (1976). Kinship, social networks, and integration among Ozark residents and out-migrants. *Journal of Marriage and the Family, 38*, 97–104.

Hess, B.B., & Waring, J.M. (1978). Parent and child in later life: Rethinking the relationship. In R.M. Lerner & G.B. Spanier (Eds.), *Child influences on marital and family interaction*. New York: Academic Press.

Kahana, E., & Kahana, B. (1971). Theoretical and research perspectives on grandparenthood. *Aging and Human Development, 2*, 261–268.

Kivnick, H.Q. (1980). *Grandparenthood: Meaning and mental health*. (Doctoral dissertation, University of Michigan). University Microfilms No. 81-6165.

Kivnick, H.Q. (1981a). Grandparenthood and the mental health of grandparents. *Ageing and Society, 1*, 365–391.

Kivnick, H.Q. (1981b, August). *Perceived control in the family*. Paper at the annual convention of the American Psychological Association. Los Angeles, CA.

Kivnick, H.Q. (1982a). Grandparenthood: An overview of meaning and mental health. *The Gerontologist, 22*(1), 59–66.

Kivnick, H.Q. (1982b). *The meaning of grandparenthood*. Ann Arbor, MI: UMI Research Press.

Kivnick, H.Q. (1983). Dimensions of grandparenthood meaning: Deductive conceptualization and empirical derivation. *Journal of Personality and Social Psychology, 44*(5), 1056–1068.

LaBarre, M.B., Jessner, L., & Ussery, L. (1960). The significance of grandmothers in the psychopathology of children. *American Journal of Orthopsychiatry, 30*, 175–185.

Lajewski, H.C. (1959). Working mothers and their arrangements for the care of their children. *Social Security Bulletin, 22*, 8–13.

Lee, G.R. (1980). Kinship in the seventies: A decade review of research and theory. *Journal of Marriage and the Family, 42*, 923–934.

Lee, G.R., & Ellithorpe, E. (1982). Intergenerational exchange and subjective well-being among the elderly. *Journal of Marriage and the Family, 44*(1), 217–224.

Leigh, G.K. (1982). Kinship interaction over the family life span. *Journal of Marriage and the Family, 44,* 197–208.

Lopata, H. (1973). Widowhood in an American city. Cambridge: Schenkman.

Lowenthal, M.F., & Robinson, B. (1976). Social networks and isolation. In R.H. Binstock & E. Shanas (Eds.), *Handbook of aging and the social sciences.* New York: Van Nostrand Reinhold.

Neugarten, B.L. (Ed.). (1964). *Personality in middle and later life: Empirical studies.* New York: Atherton Press.

Neugarten, B.L., & Weinstein, K.K. (1964). The changing American grandparent. *Journal of Marriage and the Family, 26,* 199–204.

Nock, S.L. (1979). The family life cycle: Empirical or conceptual tool? *Journal of Marriage and the Family, 41,* 15–26.

Radcliffe-Brown, A.R., & Forde, D. (Eds.). (1950). *African systems of kinship and marriage.* London: Oxford University Press.

Rappaport, E.A. (1958). The grandparent syndrome. *Psychoanalytic Quarterly, 27,* 518–538.

Reid, D.W., Haas, G., & Hawkings, D. (1977). Locus of desired control and positive self-concept of the elderly. *Journal of Gerontology, 32*(4), 441–450.

Robertson, J. (1977). Grandmotherhood: A study of role conceptions. *Journal of Marriage and the Family, 33,* 165–174.

Rosow, I. (1967). *Social integration of the aged.* New York: The Free Press.

Schulman, N. (1975). Life cycle variations in patterns of close relationships. *Journal of Marriage and the Family, 37,* 813–821.

Seelbach, W.C., & Sauer, W.J. (1977). Filial responsibility expectations and morale among aged parents. *The Gerontologist, 17,* 492–499.

Shanas, E. (1979). Social myth as hypothesis: The case of the family relations of old people. *The Gerontologist, 19*(1), 3–9.

Shanas, E. (1980). Older people and their families: The new pioneers. *Journal of Marriage and the Family, 42,* 9–15.

Shorter, E. (1975). *The making of the modern family.* New York: Basic Books.

Smyer, M.A., & Hofland, B.F. (1982). Divorce and family support in later life: Emerging concerns. *Journal of Family Issues, 3,* 61–77.

Spanier, G.B., Sauer, W., & Larzelere, R. (1979). An empirical evaluation of the family life cycle. *Journal of Marriage and the Family, 41,* 27–38.

Spark, G.M. (1974). Grandparents and intergenerational family therapy. *Family Process, 13,* 225–237.

Spark, G.M., & Brody, E.M. (1970). The aged are family members. *Family Process, 9,* 195–210.

Strauss, C.A. (1943). Grandma made Johnny delinquent. *American Journal of Orthopsychiatry, 13,* 343–346.

Streib, G.F., & Beck, R.W. (1980). Older families: A decade review. *Journal of Marriage and the Family, 42*(4), 937–956.

Sussman, M.B. (1953). The help pattern in the middle class family. *American Sociological Review, 18,* 22–28.

Sussman, M.B. (1976). The family life of old people. In R.H. Binstock & E. Shanas (Eds.), *Handbook of aging and the social sciences.* New York: Van Nostrand Reinhold.

Treas, J. (1977). Family support systems for the aged: Some social and demographic considerations. *The Gerontologist, 17*(6), 486–491.

Troll, L.E. (1971). The family of later life: A decade review. *Journal of Marriage and the Family, 33,* 263–290.

Troll, L.E., & Smith, J. (1976). Attachment through the life span: Some questions about dyadic bonds among adults. *Human Development, 19,* 156–170.

Vollmer, H. (1937). The grandmother: A problem in childrearing. *American Journal of Orthopsychiatry, 7,* 378–382.

Von Hentig, H.V. (1946). The sociological function of the grandmother. *Social Forces, 24,* 389–392.

Walters, J., & Walters, L.H. (1980). Parent-child relationships: A review, 1970–1979. *Journal of Marriage and the Family, 42,* 807–822.

Watson, J.A., & Kivett, R. (1976). Influences on the life satisfaction of older fathers. *The Family Coordinator, 25,* 482–488.

Wilkening, E.A., Gurrero, S., & Ginsberg, S. (1972). Distance and intergenerational ties of farm families. *Sociological Quarterly, 13,* 383–396.

Wood, V., & Robertson, J.F. (1976). The significance of grandparenthood. In J. Gubrium (Ed.), *Time, roles, and self in old age.* New York: Behavioral Publications.

Wood, V., & Robertson, J.F. (1978). Friendship and kinship interaction: Differential effect on the morale of the elderly. *Journal of Marriage and the Family, 40,* 367–375.

Young, M., & Wilmot, P. (1957). *Family and kinship in East London.* London: Routledge & Kegan Paul.

Chapter 4

Leisure Lifestyles and Family Dynamics in Old Age

Jay A. Mancini

Benefits attributed to family interaction and to leisure participation for older adults are remarkably similar. These two life domains are typically identified by laymen and professionals in the course of discussing that which promotes well-being as one ages and experiences change in work and family responsibilities (Atchley, 1971; Thompson & Streib, 1961). In both cases, the outcomes for older adults are said to include increased self-esteem, better mental health, and a feeling that life is more meaningful. The assumptions regarding leisure and family in later life, however, may not accurately reflect the aging experience. It is not yet fully known how discretionary time and family life are meaningful for older people. These domains require continued research and theoretical activity if social science is to achieve closure on the question of how leisure participation and family interaction are associated with and contribute to well-being in old age.

Several assumptions about leisure, the family, and old age undergird the present review. First, the interplay between the leisure and the family domains is potentially substantial. Second, leisure participation and family interaction can influence well-being in old age. Third, the relational dimensions of leisure participation must be understood to understand adequately the impact of leisure on well-being. Fourth, the leisure context should be considered to understand adequately the impact of family interaction on well-being.

The primary goal is to identify and to elaborate the interface between leisure lifestyles and family dynamics and to demonstrate the importance of this interface for well-being in later adulthood. The chapter discusses the role of leisure in the lives of the elderly, the family life of old people, the functions of interpersonal relationships, and a leisure lifestyle typology. The chapter concludes with an integrative approach to understanding the interface of leisure and the family in old age and to the delineation of implications for independent aging.

Note: Dr. Mancini wishes to thank Professor Vira Kivett for her comments during the writing of this chapter.

LEISURE AND THE ELDERLY

Rapoport and Rapoport (1975, p. 312) have noted that the "meaning of leisure in later life is complex and variable." Their suggestion is well taken because even though older people have relatively more time that could be defined and used as leisure, there is considerable variation in how that time is actually used. Leisure is not the absence of work; rather, it involves the definition that whatever one is doing is owing to discretion and choice, not to obligation. Older people orchestrate their leisure time in varying ways, with differing degrees of physical activity and levels of companionship with others. Nevertheless, however the time is actually spent, people who are satisfied with the leisure and recreational aspects of their lives report higher levels of well-being.

Family systems therapists have suggested that "one's satisfaction with existence is closely dependent on whether he feels he is getting what he wants out of life, a goal irrevocably connected with the utilization of time" (Kantor & Lehr, 1975, p. 89). The research results on leisure satisfaction appear to support their viewpoint. Studies of older adults in urban settings have found that general well-being is substantially and positively associated with two dimensions of leisure satisfaction: the extent to which it is felt that recreational patterns are meeting individual needs; and contentment with the way that available free time is being spent (Mancini, 1978; Mancini & Orthner, 1980). More importantly, these associations held even when the influence of such situational constraints as health and socioeconomic status are taken into account. A related aspect of leisure satisfaction is the congruence between actual time use and the way the older person prefers to use leisure time. In studies by Peppers (1976) and Seleen (1982), well-being was positively associated with a closer correspondence between time use or activity preferences and actual behavior. These findings reflect the importance of personal discretion in the way time is organized and utilized by the elderly.

Activity theories of successful aging suggest that leisure participation also promotes well-being. Peppers's (1976) research examined the relationship between leisure activity type and well-being, and found that higher adjustment scores were reported by those in the "active-social" category. This category was comprised of "activities which require considerable physical effort and normally take place in a group" (p. 442). The relationship between leisure participation and well-being has also been investigated by Mancini and Orthner (1980), who focused on activity in community events, volunteer activity, and activity in meeting one's own needs in the area of leisure and recreation. They found that these forms of activity were positively related to well-being. Investigations on leisure participation indirectly reflect the significance of interpersonal association and reasonable health levels for successful aging and well-being.

A question posed some years ago by Atchley (1971) involved whether leisure provides the kind of identity that one would receive from active employment. This question is at the core of much of the interest in the study of leisure in old age. Atchley's view was that although leisure could fill the time previously committed to work, there was less certainty that leisure pursuits would facilitate maintaining a positive sense of self. There is some danger in assuming that one domain of life must compensate for change in another domain, partially because, to begin with, various domains are not of equal interest and value. Secondly, personal rewards across life domains are sometimes distinctly different. For example, the tangible monetary benefits of employment are not found in leisure pursuits. Nevertheless, the leisure domain may be effective in its ability to provide for needs for association and personal contact with others.

Miller (1965) has discussed the "social dilemma" pertaining to the older adult and leisure. An aspect of this dilemma as it is conceptualized by Miller is that leisure activities may not fulfill the older person's associational needs to the degree that they were once met by co-workers. His assumption is that association provides a great deal of the meaning found in activities, whether they be work or nonwork oriented. Though Miller's assumption about the function of activities in meeting association needs is accurate, the leisure and work worlds probably do not significantly differ in meeting such needs. Much leisure activity occurs in a group context, and much of this association is, in fact, with members of one's family. Much of what has been noted concerning the general role of leisure in the lives of older adults suggests that well-being varies positively with leisure participation, leisure satisfaction, and congruence between leisure behavior and leisure preferences. This insight points to the importance of association in the lives of older adults and to a personal need that can be potentially addressed by family relationships.

FAMILY RELATIONS AND OLDER ADULTS

Although it may be argued that family relationships are among the more significant social relationships for older adults (Thompson & Streib, 1961), the cumulative knowledge base about this domain is, for the most part, limited (Kaplan, 1975). A major obstacle thus far to an adequate understanding of how family life can facilitate successful aging has been a disproportionate focus on the amount of contact between family members (see Chapters, 2, 14, and 17). Studies have generally not examined the more qualitative dimensions of family life, such as communication styles between the generations, power relationships, and affective intergenerational exchange (Mancini, 1980).

One of the more pressing research needs is a study about the way older people involve their families in their use of discretionary time. Because detailed reviews of the research on family life have been published elsewhere (e.g., Troll, Miller, & Atchley, 1979), the current treatment is abbreviated. Studies that are discussed have particular relevance for understanding the interface of leisure and family dynamics. They fall into two categories: contact with family and family support. In both cases, the implications for well-being are discussed because a major outcome of family interaction is presumed to be increases in how positively one experiences the older adulthood years. The focus on family contact is germane to the current review because it is a use of time in a family context, even though the studies tell little about that which really occurs during contact with family. Similarly, family support and exchange are relevant to our discussion because various kinds of exchange occur during the time spent with one's family.

Family Contact

In contrast to popular belief, older adults have considerable contact with members of their family (Shanas, 1979). About three-fourths have face-to-face contact with a middle-age child on a weekly or semi-weekly basis, and when face-to-face contact is not possible, some other means of staying in touch is relied upon (Troll, Miller, & Atchley, 1979). Often the contact is brief and—at least for the middle-age child with a very old parent—may function as a way to monitor the parent's welfare. Though the data are quite conclusive in demonstrating that the average older American is not isolated from the family (Shanas, 1979; Troll, Miller, and Atchley, 1979), the meaning that contact has for well-being is undetermined.

An "enrichment myth" now exists concerning family relations; it suggests that the lives of older adults are necessarily bettered by interaction with family members (Mancini, 1980). A direct link is made between spending time with family and well-being, without consideration of the vast array of potential intervening variables. The research that correlates the amount of family contact with well-being usually concludes that there is no direct relationship (Edwards & Klemmack, 1973; Lee, 1979; Mancini, 1979; Mancini, Quinn, Gavigan, & Franklin, 1980). Some studies even suggest a negative impact on well-being (Kerckhoff, 1966; Bell, 1976), but no research investigation has demonstrated that family contact per se promotes successful aging. Unfortunately, researchers persist in directing rudimentary studies of contact and well-being without attempting to specify the conditions under which these two dimensions may be related, either positively or negatively. That it is unlikely the contact promotes well-being (and vice versa) when the nature of contact is conflictual, when the contact is purely obligatory, or when the spirit of the contact unnecessarily exposes the dependencies of older adults is an example of the form that specification could take. Likewise, well-being would not be enhanced if any party felt exploited or if their presence meant that they were prevented from participating in preferred uses of time. In short, future empirical work must take a creative and systematic approach to examining the nature of time spent by the older person with the family. One dimension of a varied approach involves family support behaviors.

Exchange and Expectations of Support

One indicator of family life quality may be found in the breadth and the extent of mutual support reflected in both instrumental and affective exchange. An examination of the nature of actual exchange, as well as expectations of support, is relevant for understanding the relationship of family and leisure because these activities occur in a temporal context; also, much of affective exchange can occur specifically within a leisure time context. The kind of exchange between the elderly and their kin assumes various forms. In research conducted in Chicago, help from older people to kin included advice on life's problems, advice on jobs and business, housekeeping assistance, household maintenance, financial support, gift-giving, assisting with shopping and running errands, child care, and care in time of illness (Bild & Havighurst, 1976). Forms of help from family members to the aged focused on much the same areas but also included providing transportation. The kinds of support most often received by older people who owned their own homes were care during illness, assistance in shopping, gifts, help with household maintenance, and transportation. In general, assistance was more commonly received from the family than given to the family on the part of older people. In the case of the financially able elderly, however, help was more likely to flow to kin.

A point worth noting here is that intergenerational relationships are not only characterized by continued contact but also by the mutual exchange of a variety of services. It is not apparent, however, that exchange of support influences the well-being of older adults. Recently, Lee and Ellithorpe (1982) conducted a multivariate study of the way exchange of aid between older persons and their children covaried with successful aging. Domains of exchange included advice on decisions, help during illness, financial assistance, gifts other than money, household task help, and help with transportation. Neither support provided by elderly parents nor support received by elders was related to well-being. An avenue of further research could entail identifying the circumstances under which exchange occurs. In addition, it may be fruitful to explore what the exchange may represent. For example, if an older person feels that the overall exchange level is inequitable (far less is received than is given), then well-being may be adversely influenced. Likewise, if the older adult perceives that far more is received than is given, then well-being may be lowered on account of feeling ineffective and dependent.

A related area of support pertains to the expectations older people have of their families and the importance these expectations have for well-being. This attitudinal approach has focused on many of the same areas of exchange or support that are found in the studies of reported behavior. Seelbach and Sauer (1977) tapped what lower-income older adults expected of their children in terms of generally being responsible for an aged parent—visiting and contact patterns, financial aid, care during illness, and residential proximity. Although there was no relationship for the sample as a whole, greater expectations among certain subgroups were related to lower well-being—those who were black, younger, male, and married. The author's research employed a wider range of the types of support that could be expected from kin: risking personal safety; sharing gossip heard about the older adult; efforts to maintain contact; inclusion in the adult child's friend network; sharing intimate feelings; acceptance in spite of flaws; visiting in time of illness; providing shelter; giving advice; financial assistance; and, support in disputes with others (Mancini & Simon, 1982). The only areas in which less than three-fourths of the interviewees expected family support were in disputes with others and sharing gossip. Even though a great deal was expected from family members, these expectations were not related to well-being.

It can be concluded from the studies on kin contact and on exchange and support that although older adults have considerable contact with family, exchange a wide variety of instrumental and affective services with them, and expect a wide array of support from kin, none of these dimensions of family appear relevant for morale. All of the studies reviewed are linked by the dimension of time; contact and exchange require the use of time. A general limitation of this research is the lack of specification of what occurs during these times that has meaning for relationship quality. Relationships are known to meet particular human needs and time affords the opportunity for relationship development. A general focus on relationship functions suggests that understanding such functions helps direct the identification of variables that connect well-being with family relationships.

FUNCTIONS OF INTERPERSONAL RELATIONSHIPS

Family relationships can potentially influence the quality of life an older adult experiences, though researchers have not yet isolated the significant conditional variables. The particular benefits provided by an active relationship ought to be an important determinant of whether spending time with family members is conducive to well-being. A typology of relationship functions developed by Weiss (1969, 1976) appears to have some utility for understanding the leisure participation and family interaction interface. Weiss's research with a Parents-Without-Partners group, in which his goal was to identify how relationships mitigated stress, led him to challenge the "fund of sociability," a perspective on human relationships proposing that "relationships are relatively undifferentiated in their provisions" (Weiss, 1976, p. 21). Quite to the contrary, he concluded that various relationships functioned in varying ways for persons and proposed the notion of the "functional specificity of relationships" (Weiss, 1969, p. 38). This perspective suggests that certain human needs can be met only in an interpersonal context (another family systems idea), that relationships become specialized in terms of the needs they address, and, consequently, that persons require a variety of interpersonal relationships in order to be satisfied with life. Though the situation of older adults is probably unlike that of the average participant in Parents Without Partners, the typology is applicable to them in a general sense.

Six relationship categories are given in Table 4–1, in which their respective functions are considered as opportunities. (Weiss's ideas are slightly modified by

Table 4–1 Functional Specificity of Relationships

Relationship Category	Function	Potential Sources
Intimacy/ Attachment	Opportunity to express freely one's feelings and emotions; a gain in feeling secure and connected with another	Spouse, dating relationship, close friend, some relatives
Social Integration	Opportunity to share experience, ideas, and information; source of companionship; a basis of social engagement and social activity; sharing owing to commonality of experience and to having similar goals	Friends, colleagues, family
Nurturance	Opportunity to take responsibility for a child and therefore development of a sense of being needed; provides meaning to life	Children
Worth	Opportunity to demonstrate competence in a social role, to prove value, and to receive recognition	Family, colleagues
Assistance/Alliance	Opportunity to take advantage of consistent assistance, provision of services, and resources	Family, kin
Guidance	Opportunity during time of stress to assess support from one who is trusted and authoritative and to receive emotional support and guidance in developing a plan of action	Helping professionals, others defined as having skills in problem-solving, perhaps some family members

Notes: The table is an elaboration of Weiss's discussion (1969, pp. 38–40; 1976, pp. 23–24) of relationship categories. Weiss feels that a fully functioning individual has a set of relationships that provides for these opportunities as specific needs arise.

using the term *opportunities.*) It is felt that adults act on their own behalf to develop interpersonal relationships; for example, these relationships serve to provide the opportunity for social integration or worth. All of the functions require the allocation of time—preferably that which is discretionary—and many functions could potentially be met by one or more family relationships. Whether we are speaking of expressing feelings, sharing experience, demonstrating competence, providing and receiving assistance, feeling needed, or assessing problem-solving expertise, it is conceivable that a family member can be a source of opportunity. It is unlikely, however, that a single relationship would provide all of these opportunities.

Most of the relationship functions can be thought of as intervening determinants of whether spending time with family promotes well-being. If the time spent provides a sense of connectedness or belonging, an opportunity for the sharing of independent and mutual experience, and a sense of being needed and feeling valued, then it is reasonable to assume that the life quality of an older person will be enhanced. It also appears that leisure participation with family that is freely chosen ought to optimize the probability that these relationship functions become reality. If we can determine the degree to which family relationships provide these opportunities, then perhaps the studies of contact, exchange, and expectations of support can demonstrate the implications for well-being.

Thus far, the roles that leisure and family play in the lives of older adults have been discussed, and an overview of how relationships can be categorized has been presented. Throughout, the interplay between discretionary time use and family relations has been noted. In moving more explicitly to an explanation of how the structure of leisure time influences relationships to others, it is suggested that the organization of time represents a lifestyle.

LEISURE LIFESTYLES

Social scientists use the word *lifestyle* to describe differences in the manner in which people organize their lives. As a rule, only one or two variables are employed as the critical benchmarks of lifestyle differences. Those who study the contemporary American family, for example, speak of alternative marriage lifestyles; it is described as an alternative lifestyle because a couple cohabits, yet the everyday life of the couple may be like that of a legal marriage. Lifestyle typologies become artificial when they are applied on a broad, general level, but they are efficient for conceptualizing everyday life when they are directed at particular life domains. The following leisure lifestyle schema is such a directed focus; it targets four dimensions: time, activities, preferences, and competence (Mancini and Orthner, 1982).

Time Dimensions

Perceptions of time determine how leisure is organized because these perceptions assign legitimacy to particular uses of time. A person is socialized to work but does not readily learn to participate in leisure. Full participation in leisure and recreation partially depends upon whether the older adult feels that nonwork activities are worthwhile and appropriate uses of time, and whether time is seen as having a future orientation. Those who do not see themselves as having much of a future have a different perspective on how they should use their time. The elder who has little sense of future may be reluctant to pursue unfamiliar leisure pursuits, particularly if they require an extended period of learning and refinement.

Activity Patterns

Within time parameters, a variety of predominant leisure activity patterns exist, and each represents a different level of interaction with others. Also, costs and rewards are associated with each pattern, and they partially explain why family contact and well-being are not positively associated. Independent activities are those done by oneself and do not require any participation with others. Activities in this category include reading, watching television, relaxation and reflection, and a number of crafts and hobbies (such as sewing, collecting, and woodworking). Of course, any of these could be done with others, but it is not necessary in order to complete successfully the activity. Parallel activities essentially are independent pursuits in a group context. If done in the presence of others, watching television qualifies as a parallel activity; other examples are spectator sports and cultural events. Though the potential for interaction is present, successful completion of a parallel activity is not dependent on the cooperation and participation of others. Collaborative activities require interaction with others. They include visiting with friends and relatives, team sports, and playing cards and board games. Without cooperation, an individual cannot participate in the activity. The various personal and interpersonal outcomes of these patterns are elaborated in the following integrative section.

Preferences Dimension

Leisure preference is the third component of a leisure lifestyle that directs how time is used. It involves general categories of activities and particular activities. Leisure preferences and leisure behavior may be quite different—especially if the older person is constrained by frail health, inadequate income, limited personal mobility, or by continual negotiation with others and their leisure preferences. In the latter case, interpersonal conflict may result if one feels that his preferences are rarely considered or acted upon by other family members. Another aspect of leisure preference is the degree to which elders spend time with the family by choice as opposed to obligation. This factor may be critical in determining whether the older person benefits from family interaction.

Competence Dimension

The final lifestyle dimension is leisure competence—i.e., whether older people feel effective as leisure participants. A personal sense of competence directs how one actually behaves, especially in the presence of others. Across the adult life cycle, unfamiliar activities are avoided because one might be unsure as to whether they can be mastered; this reluctance is pronounced when a person fears or anticipates changes in abilities because of aging.

How older people organize their discretionary time is directed by perceptions of time, the activity patterns they seem to practice, preferences for leisure pursuits, and feelings of competence. A leisure lifestyle also influences the nature and the content of family interaction because of the diverse costs and rewards associated with it. The balance of these benefits and constraints has a profound influence on the interface of leisure participation and family interaction.

FAMILY DYNAMICS AND LEISURE: AN INTEGRATION

The relationship between the leisure and family domains is potentially significant because the family is a primary vehicle for leisure behavior and because leisure participation can support quality family life (Orthner & Mancini, 1980). Over twenty years ago, Thompson and Streib (1961) discussed this relationship as it pertained to older adults, and they suggested that the understanding of how discretionary time is used should include a consideration of social relationships. They assumed that "the use of free time is determined, facilitated, or limited by the social setting" (p. 177). The earlier discussion of variation in leisure lifestyles reflected by the level of interaction with others parallels Thompson and Streib's line of reasoning. Participation in particular leisure pursuits reflects both the necessity for and the actual level of interaction with the family. The relationship between leisure and family in the lives of older people is evident from the events described below:

- Older adults are expected to spend time with their children and grandchildren.
- The regular contact older people have with members of their family can be through leisure and recreational activities.
- Particular leisure experiences, such as family gatherings on special occasions, are important to a family's sense of history. These experiences often

focus around older family members and traditionally occur at their place of residence.

- Spending time together provides the opportunity for the exchange of affectional or emotional support between generations in the family.

Common to each of the above points is interaction and its outcomes. A great deal of the interface between the leisure and the family domains revolves around family interaction.

Many years ago, the family was defined as a "unity of interacting personalities" (Burgess, 1926). From this perspective, it is clear that meaning and value in family life originate from the interaction and the interchange among its members. This process of family interaction involves *communication* (the ongoing transmission and reception of ideas and feelings), *mutual feedback* (reflecting and responding reciprocally to the communication of others), *defining situations* (perceiving the environment and the behavior of others and acting accordingly), *role patterning* (behaving in a particular way because it is expected by tradition, position, and status) and relating to *significant others* (assigning value to the thoughts, feelings, and behavior of those who are defined as having a special place in one's life). When these concepts are brought to bear on the family leisure experiences of older adults they can have the following consequences:

- Spending time together provides family members with opportunities to process the behavior of one another by attaching meaning to what they do and say.
- Shared leisure experience provides access to significant others, many of whom are family members.
- Spending time together in shared leisure encourages communication and interpersonal stimulus and response.
- Shared leisure experience provides the opportunity to depart from typical roles and authority configurations.

The "enrichment myth" of aging and the family has been identified as a constraint on the accurate understanding of successful aging. Though it is often assumed that shared leisure experience is important for family life quality and for well-being, it should be recognized that such experience contains both benefits and liabilities. Table 4–2 suggests the effects of these shared experiences.

In general, when generations in the family spend time together, the potential exists for being drawn closer together in a cohesive network; however, the potential exists also for promoting greater interpersonal distance. Even though interpersonal learning and community can develop through shared family leisure experiences, the positive expectations of what the experience will do for the

Table 4–2 Consequences of Family Leisure Experiences between Generations

Benefits	Liabilities
1. Provides opportunity for mutual sharing and interpersonal learning during time defined as nontask oriented	1. Potential for exacerbating ongoing tensions and unresolved interpersonal conflicts
2. Provides opportunity to participate in the grandparent role	2. Draining of personal energy
3. Provides opportunity to build sense of togetherness, belonging, and community	3. Incongruency with discretionary time use preference
4. Provides a forum for participation in the individual development of others	4. Regret when experiences are generally negative and personally destructive
5. Provides opportunity for enjoyment that comes from planning and anticipating future experiences and from recollection of past experiences	5. Difficulty in coping with conflict when expectation of positive experiences from family leisure experiences are not met

generations may be in distinct contrast to what is actually gained. Determinants of whether spending time together is beneficial include whether the older adult is invited to be a full participant in family life, as opposed to being defined as a bystander; the past history of family relationships (i.e., what conflict patterns have existed over the years); whether the generations feel obligated to spend time together and do so with reluctance; whether cooperative decisions are made about the nature of leisure experiences not mandated by a particular individual; and the quality of current interaction that may leave family members feeling motivated to spend either more or less time in shared leisure.

IMPLICATIONS FOR INDEPENDENT AGING

This study was undertaken to demonstrate the interplay between family interaction and leisure participation and to suggest their role in successful aging. Among the conclusions of this review are the following observations:

- Well-being varies positively with leisure participation and satisfaction and with the congruence between leisure preferences and leisure behavior.
- Contact and intergenerational exchange are not directly related to well-being.
- Current research on the family life of older people has not specified what occurs during contact with family that may have an impact on relationship quality.
- Time spent with family members can have an impact on well-being when the various family relationships function to provide a sense of belonging, a sharing of mutual experiences, and a feeling of being valued.

- The organization of discretionary time is directed by perceptions of time, activity patterns, leisure preferences, and feelings of competence. The resulting leisure lifestyle influences the nature and the content of family interaction.
- A great deal of the interface between the leisure and the family domains revolves around family interaction; a symbolic orientation to family relationships suggests that the meaning in family life originates from the interaction and the interchange among its members.
- Shared leisure experience contains both benefits and liabilities for older people and their families.

These are several of the ways in which the leisure and family domains contribute to independent aging.

In conceptualizing independent aging one must account for the constraints imposed by frail health and limited resources. An older adult who has limited mobility, debilitating chronic disease or acute illness, and a sub-standard of living will not, in all likelihood, be aging independently; in fact, to attempt to do so would not be in the best interests of that person. To age in an independent fashion implies some amount of control over one's life, but not detachment and isolation from informal and formal support sources. The core of well-being includes independent aging—general self-care, facility in making decisions that influence one's own welfare, accessing support systems as required, and maintaining reasonable continuity with one's lifestyle in earlier years. Leisure participation and family interaction can promote independent aging. Because selected leisure lifestyles encourage association (which in turn supports community and a sense of belonging) the likelihood of social lifestyle continuity is increased. When association pertains to the family in particular, it supports relationships that can provide a reservoir of support. Furthermore, independent aging covaries with the leisure and the family domains because it enables an older adult to fully participate in family relationships and activities.

REFERENCES

Atchley, R.C. (1971). Retirement and leisure participation: Continuity or crisis? *The Gerontologist, 11*, 13–17.

Bell, B.D. (1976). Role set orientation and life satisfaction: A new look at an old theory. In J.F. Gubrium (Ed.), *Time, roles, and self in old age* (pp. 148–164). New York: Behavioral Publications.

Bild, B., & Havighurst, R.J. (1976). Senior citizens in great cities: The case of Chicago. *The Gerontologist, 16*, 3–88.

Burgess, E.W. (1926). The family as a unity of interacting personalities. *The Family, 7*, 3–9.

Edwards, J., & Klemmack, D. (1973). Correlates of life satisfaction: A re-examination. *Journal of Gerontology, 28*, 497–502.

Kantor, D., & Lehr, W. (1975). *Inside the family: Toward a theory of family process.* New York: Harper Colophon.

Kaplan, J. (1975). The family in aging. *The Gerontologist, 15,* 385.

Kerckhoff, A.C. (1966). Family patterns and morale in retirement. In I.H. Simpson & J. McKinney (Eds.), *Social aspects of aging* (pp. 173–192). Durham, NC: Duke University Press.

Lee, G. (1979). Children and the elderly: Interaction and morale. *Research on Aging, 1,* 335–360.

Lee, G.R., & Ellithorpe, E. (1982). Intergenerational exchange and subjective well-being among the elderly. *Journal of Marriage and the Family, 44,* 217–224.

Mancini, J.A. (1978). Leisure satisfaction and psychologic well-being in old age: Effects of health and income. *Journal of the American Geriatrics Society, 26,* 550–552.

Mancini, J.A. (1979). Family relationships and morale among people 65 years of age and older. *American Journal of Orthopsychiatry, 49,* 292–300.

Mancini, J.A. (1980). Stengthening the family life of older adults: Myth-conceptions and investigative needs. In N. Stinnett (Ed.), *Family strengths: Positive models for family life* (pp. 333–343). Lincoln, NE: University of Nebraska Press.

Mancini, J.A., & Orthner, D.K. (1980). Situational influences on leisure satisfaction and morale in old age. *Journal of the American Geriatrics Society, 28,* 466–471.

Mancini, J.A., & Orthner, D.K. (1982). Leisure time, activities, preferences, and competence: Implications for the morale of older adults. *Journal of Applied Gerontology, 1,* 95–103.

Mancini, J.A., Quinn, W., Gavigan, M.A., & Franklin, H. (1980). Social network interaction among older adults: Implications for life satisfaction. *Human Relations, 33,* 543–554.

Mancini, J.A., & Simon, J. (1982, June). When push comes to shove: Older adults' expectations of support from family and friends. Paper presented at the annual meeting of the Southern Gerontological Society, Orlando, FL.

Miller, S.J. (1965). The social dilemma of the aging leisure participant. In A.M. Rose & W.A. Peterson (Eds.), *Older people and their social world: The subculture of aging* (pp. 77–92). Philadelphia: F.A. Davis.

Orthner, D.K., & Mancini, J.A. (1980). Leisure behavior and group dynamics: The case of the family. In S. Iso-Ahola (Ed.), *Social psychological perspectives on leisure and recreation* (pp. 307–328). Springfield, IL: Charles C Thomas.

Peppers, L.G. (1976). Patterns of leisure and adjustment to retirement. *The Gerontologist, 16,* 441–446.

Rapoport, R., & Rapoport, R.N. (1975). *Leisure and the family life cycle.* London: Routledge & Kegan Paul.

Seelbach, W.C., & Sauer, W.J. (1977). Filial responsibility expectations and morale among aged parents. *The Gerontologist, 17,* 492–499.

Seleen, D.R. (1982). The congruence between actual and desired use of time by older adults: A predictor of life satisfaction. *The Gerontologist, 22,* 95–99.

Shanas, E. (1979). Social myth as hypothesis: The case of the family relations of old people. *The Gerontologist, 19,* 3–9.

Thompson, W.E., & Streib, G.F. (1961). Meaningful activity in a family context. In R.W. Kleemeier (Ed.), *Aging and leisure: A research perspective into the meaningful use of time* (pp. 177–211). New York: Oxford University Press.

Troll, L.E., Miller, S.J., & Atchley, R.C. (1979). *Families in later life.* Belmont, CA: Wadsworth.

Weiss, R.S. (1969). The fund of sociability. *Trans-Action, 6,* 36–43.

Weiss, R.S. (1976). The provisions of social relationships. In Z. Rubin (Ed.), *Doing unto others* (pp. 17–26). Englewood Cliffs, NJ: Prentice-Hall.

Chapter 5

Marital Quality in Later Life

Charles Lee Cole

Independence in later life is a cherished value in American society. Research on mental health (Gove, 1978; Gove, Style, & Hughes, 1981) and on physical health (Renne, 1971; Verbrugge, 1979) has consistently demonstrated the importance of marriage in maintaining the resources for independence in later life. *Independence* in this context means maintaining control over life decisions that affect the quality of the aging person's living situation. Married couples, for example, are able to maintain their own homes or to select a retirement community of their choice with less interference from adult children than are widowed and divorced elderly persons (Lee, 1980; Robinson & Thurnher, 1979; Seelbach, 1977; Sussman, 1976). Chapters 6 and 7 present a fuller discussion of this point.

Furthermore, married persons have longer life expectancies than do never-married persons, divorced persons, or widowed persons (Binstock & Shanas, 1976). These data can be explained in terms of the social integration function of marriage. Durkheim's (1951) theory of anomie suggests that marriage provides a normative basis for societal integration (Bachrach, 1980; Ryan, 1981). Social relationships, including spousal bonds, establish meaningful anchors for each person to evaluate life experiences and to provide an opportunity for social interaction with significant others that gives a sense of importance to that person. Berger and Kellner (1970) suggest that marriage tends to reduce anomic states by establishing nomos-building instrumentality.

The central thesis developed in this chapter is that marriage provides elderly couples with a variety of life-sustaining resources that contribute to the quality of life during the retirement phase of the family life cycle. The general objective of this chapter is to sensitize health care providers, practitioners, policymakers, and

Note: The author wishes to acknowledge the support of the Iowa State University Home Economics Research Institute.

family gerontologists to the importance of understanding the marital dynamics of couples in the later years of life. The specific objectives are:

- to review research about the nature of marriage for husbands and wives over the family life cycle as it contributes to our understanding of marriage for couples in the retirement phases of the family life cycle;
- to examine the nature of the contributions marriage and marital satisfaction make to a variety of social and psychological aspects of human development in later life;
- to discuss how retirement offers unique opportunities for married couples to enhance their relationship and to develop support systems for the continued growth of their full marital potential.

MARRIAGE AS A PROCESS

Marriage is a dynamic relationship in the process of continual change with each new phase of the family life cycle. Unfortunately, few studies in gerontology have bothered to examine the dynamic aspects of marriage (Quinn, 1983; Streib & Beck, 1980; Troll, Miller & Atchley, 1979). For the most part, these studies have treated marriage primarily as a social status that influences life changes. Writings about the family, marital and family therapy, and marriage enrichment, on the other hand, place emphasis on research on the dynamics of marital interaction processes. See, for example, Lewis and Spanier's (1979) theory of marital quality, which is based upon extensive research reviewed in the marital quality studies (Lerner & Spanier, 1978; Lewis and Spanier, 1979) and the writings on marital interaction processes (Cromwell & Olson, 1975; Gottman, 1979; Scanzoni, 1979; Scanzoni & Szinovancz, 1980).

Examination in this chapter of the marital quality and interaction process writings is restricted to the following areas:

- marital satisfaction throughout the family life cycle
- roles and the division of labor for couples at the retirement stage of the family life cycle
- marital interaction patterns of retired couples
- marital problems and the stressors commonly experienced in the retirement stage of the family life cycle

Before moving on to a discussion of these four focal points, however, it is necessary to lay out the conceptualization of marital quality that will be used throughout this discussion.

Marital Quality

Lewis and Spanier (1979) note that the concept of marital quality is a generic construct that encompasses a wide range of terms—marital satisfaction, marital adjustment, marital happiness, marital-role strain, marital conflict, marital communication, marital cohesion and integration, marital adaptability, marital potential, and marital commitment—which have frequently been treated as the dependent variable in marriage research. Each of these terms attempts to assess qualitative aspects of the marriage relationship. In a detailed definition of the concept, the authors declare that

> marital quality thus is defined as a subjective evaluation of a married couple's relationship. The range of evaluations constitutes a continuum reflecting numerous characteristics of marital interaction and marital functioning. High marital quality, therefore, is associated with good judgment, adequate communication, a high level of marital happiness, integration, and a high degree of satisfaction with the relationship. The definition does not convey a fixed picture of discrete categories, i.e., a high- versus low-quality marriage, but rather suggests the existence of a continuum ranging from high to low. Thus a couple's placement on the continuum would represent a composite picture which used many criteria. These criteria, when operationalized, would be dimensions of marital interaction and functioning which have traditionally been studied as well as some criteria which may not have yet been either proposed or studied. (p. 269)

Because marital quality is a subjective evaluation of the marital relationship, it is continually reassessed and reevaluated in terms of each partner's subjective definition of the marital situation that exists at any given moment. In part, this is a consequence of how well each perceives that needs are being met. Each person carries into the marriage a set of expectations of how these needs should be attended to. Some persons expect their spouses to provide all of their needs, even though, in reality, this is an impossible expectation. (For a more extensive discussion of this point, see Cole & Hulbert, 1981; Framo, 1982; Lewis, 1979; Mace, 1982; Napier & Whitaker, 1978; Sager, 1976; Singer & Stern, 1980.) Others, however, do not expect their spouses to meet very many of their needs because they expect to have their needs satisfied primarily outside of the relationship. (For a further discussion of this point, see Libby & Whitehurst, 1977.) Over the course of the marriage, the expectations of each partner about the way needs are to be satisfied and what the needs are at any given point in time are continually being reshaped and modified (Carter & McGoldrick, 1980; Framo, 1982; Mace, 1982; Sager, 1976; Singer & Stern, 1980). This reshaping and modification of the marital relationship is a function of a variety of changes in the life experiences of each spouse.

Furthermore, the way spouses adapt to the reshaping and the restructuring of the marital relationship is a cumulative experience contingent upon prior changes they have experienced as a couple. This adaptation is also influenced by the quality of the marital relationship in the context of the previous stage (or life situation) and the current transition point, which serves as a hinge to move into future stages of the relationship's developmental sequence.

Marital Adjustment

Bernard (1964) notes that the concept of adjustment refers to the dynamic process of making functional changes in the relationship. She furthermore notes that the adjustments occur at different levels.

Individual Adjustments

At the personal level, each partner adjusts to a set of situational changes (uniquely experienced separately by each person) that occur in (and make an impact on) the marriage over the life course of the relationship. Bernard (1964) points out that the processes by which the individual partners adjust to these situational changes are shaped partly by the unique biographies each brings to the situation (i.e., what they have learned from prior life experiences before they met each other) and partly by the concomitant dyadic interaction processes that have reciprocal influences on each partner's individual life situation and, therefore, individual adjustments.

Marital Pair-Bond Adjustments

At the dyadic level, the couple adjusts to living together and to the day-to-day interaction patterns that emerge and forge the roles each play in the relationship. One of the critical marital pair-bond adjustments includes the way each couple develops and changes their communication processes and patterns. Another key adjustment the spouses make to each other and with each other is the way they establish, maintain, and change their decision-making pattern and their division of responsibility and labor, which dictates who is responsible for what, to whom they are responsible, and so on.

Social Adjustments

Social adjustments are the collective responses of the couple to external systems. For example, the married couple's adjustments to the community constraints—neighbors, school systems, job demands from the occupational work place—are not so much marital adjustments between the spouses as they are the spouses' collective adjustments and social front as a couple in response to the demands and the constraints of community life every married couple is subjected to throughout married life. Another type of social adjustment is concerned with the way the couple collectively interacts with their in-laws, their children, and the friends whom they choose to relate to as a couple rather than as individuals (friends of one spouse or the other).

Later, in this chapter, an attempt is made to illustrate how a typical couple would make adjustments at these three levels as the couple moves from the middle-aged phase of life to the later stages of life.

MARITAL QUALITY THROUGH THE FAMILY LIFE CYCLE

An examination of the quality of the marital relationship throughout the family life cycle makes it clear that the marriage relationship is heavily influenced by life stressors that vary in the impact they have on the marriage. This point is explicated in detail, however, in a subsequent section of this chapter, after a review of the relevant studies that provide information about the marital relationship over the family life cycle. Basically, two primary sources of data exist: (1) the longitudinal studies on marriage, and (2) the cross-sectional studies that have treated marital quality variables as the dependent variables throughout the family life cycle. Unfortunately, few longitudinal studies have been made of the marriage career (Clark & Wallin, 1965; Feldman, 1965; Luckey & Bain, 1970; Paris & Luckey, 1966; Pineo, 1969; Ryder, 1973). What is more, the bulk of the longitudinal work done has been restricted to the initial phases of the marriage career (Luckey & Bain, 1970; Rausch, Barry, Hertel, & Swain, 1974; Ryder, 1973) and to the transition into parenthood (LaRossa, 1977; Luckey & Bain; Ryder). Very few studies have focused in depth on the transitions that occur in the later stages of the family life cycle (Ade-Ridder & Brubaker, 1983; Swenson, Eskew, & Kohlhepp, 1981).

A number of studies have treated the stages of the family life cycle as a key independent or intervening variable that has an effect on the quality of the marital relationship (Anderson, Russell, & Schumm, 1983; Hudson & Murphy, 1980; Medling & McCarrey, 1981; Swensen, Eskew, & Kohlhepp, 1981; Tamir & Antonucci, 1981). A few quasi-longitudinal studies have examined marital adjustment in the same community over an extended time (Cole, Cole, & Dean, 1980), and a few have studied the quality of the marital relationship for more than one generation of the same family (Gildford & Bengtson, 1979; Hill, 1970). Each of these studies contributes something to our knowledge base, and each has some limitations inherent in the research design used.

Spanier, Lewis, and Cole (1975) caution against making inferences from cross-sectional design data because cross-sectional designs are insensitive to changes that occur in the marriage relationship over the marriage career. Furthermore, these designs cannot be sensitive to life-course differences between generations, to cohort effects, to age-correlated effects, to social desirability (or other response-set tendencies), and to survivor effects. (The design is insensitive to survivor effects because a number of low-quality marriages drop out along the way and so attenuate the results in subsequent stages of the family life cycle.) Troll, Miller, and Atchley (1979) note that developmental psychologists and other life-span developmental theorists have warned against the exclusive use of either cross-sectional designs or longitudinal designs to study developmental changes. Schaie (1967) and Baltes (1968) point out that cross-sectional designs may result in a generation fallacy by ignoring life-course developmental differences. Furthermore, Baltes points out that the use of longitudinal designs without cross-sectional panels has a tendency to produce a life-course fallacy because the longitudinal design ignores age-cohort differences. The preferred methodology is the use of sequential-longitudinal research designs (Nesselroade, Schaie, & Baltes, 1972). The sequential-longitudinal design permits the researcher to start with two or more panels of couples married for varying lengths of time and to continue the study of each group with periodic assessments over a number of years of the couples at each stage along the way. Unfortunately, no studies known to this author have included the later stages of the marriage career by use of a sequential-longitudinal design. Therefore, we must rely upon the limited available data bases and note that they may not be indicative of the nature of the changes that actually occur in a marriage over the family life cycle.

In Medley's (1977) review of the marital quality research concerning the family life cycle, he notes that three patterns are reported:

1. A continual decline takes place in the level of marital satisfaction and happiness over the life course of the marriage.
2. An initial period of marital happiness and relationship satisfaction declines rapidly with the onset of children, continues to remain low throughout the childrearing phases of the family life cycle, and then increases to near prechildbearing levels during the postparental phases of the family life cycle. When plotted out, this pattern is a U-shaped curve.
3. No systematic pattern develops over the life course of the marriage. Neither an inverse relationship (which would show a gradual decline over time) nor a direct relationship (which would show a gradual increase in marital quality over time) is supported; nor is there any evidence of a curvilinear relationship, which would suggest a recovery to prechildbearing levels of marital satisfaction.

Pattern of Decline in Marital Quality

All studies done before the 1960s showed a decline in marital happiness and satisfaction over an extended time. For a discussion of them, see Hicks and Platt (1970) and Ade-Ridder and Brubaker (1983). Most of the research showed that the majority of the marriages had disintegrated a great deal by midlife (Blood & Wolfe, 1960; Clark & Wallin, 1965; Luckey, 1966; Paris & Luckey, 1966; Pineo, 1961, 1969). For example, in Blood and Wolfe's study of 909 Detroit wives, they report a steady decline in marital satisfaction, love, and companionship over the life course of the marriage. They also note that couples participate in fewer joint activities in the retirement phase of the family life cycle and have less resources for participation in leisure activities that cost money because they have reduced financial resources owing to the constraints of living on a retirement pension. Pineo, in a re-analysis of the longitudinal study by Burgess and Wallin (1953) of over 1,000 couples who were interviewed during the first year of the marriage and at subsequent intervals (the 5th, the 15th, and the 25th years of marriage), reports that the marital satisfaction and adjustment had declined by middle age. Pineo attributes this decline in marital adjustment and marital satisfaction to feelings of disenchantment expected to arise from the changes each spouse makes that are incongruous with the mate's expectations of what he or she should be like at that phase of life. That is, the couple's initial criteria for selecting each other may have changed and now seem inappropriate to meeting their current needs. Pineo further suggests that it is inevitable for the couple to experience disenchantment during the middle and later years of life, because the more each of them changes, the more likely the couple fit (which may have been very good when they selected each other over a quarter of a century ago) and it is unlikely to ever be as good as it was in the initial phases of their relationship.

Curvilinear Pattern of Marital Quality

The results of most of the marriage research lends some support to the contention that the quality of the marriage varies over the life course of the relationship (Gilford & Bengtson, 1979; Hudson & Murphy, 1980; Medling & McCarrey, 1981; Swenson, Eskew, & Kohlhepp, 1981; Tamir & Antonucci, 1981). In general, these studies have found that marital satisfaction declines with the onset of parenthood, and that the number of marital problems decrease after the children are launched and the couple has moved from the empty-nest stage to the retirement years and later phases of life together. These data have consistently demonstrated that the presence of children produces role strain, which has a negative effect upon the couple's marital relationship (Bernard, 1972; Figley, 1973; Rollins & Cannon, 1974). In Feldman's (1965) sequential-longitudinal design study of 852 middle and upper-middle class couples, he notes that the role strain is exacerbated by life-cycle squeeze, which creates time conflicts for the marriage couple. For example, a couple with school-aged children have to juggle the schedules of the children's activities with their own activities; the husband and the wife each move in separate and parallel directions, with less time for joint and shared activities as a couple.

According to theories of marital quality based on the curvilinear pattern of relationship change, the marriage will recover the quality lost in the childrearing stages of the family life cycle when the children leave home and the couple has less competing demands in their lives. There are two competing theories of marital quality that attempt to interpret the curvilinear pattern as a support of their theories. The two theories are Abelson et al.'s (1968) cognitive consistency theory and Rosow's (1967) life continuity theory of interpersonal relations and aging.

Cognitive Consistency Theory

Cognitive consistency theory (Schumm, 1979; Spanier, Lewis, & Cole, 1975; Streib & Beck, 1980) suggests that the longer a couple is married, the greater is the investment they make in each other and their relationship, and the greater is their tendency to report the marriage as being a happy one and as satisfying their needs. This line of reasoning contends that, as the couple continues to invest more and more in the relationship, it will increase in value because not to do so would imply that one has not had a rewarding life. This tendency to report high levels of marital happiness in the later stages of the family life cycle has been criticized by some researchers because it reflects perceptual distortions that give a more favorable image of the marriage than it could actually produce (Hawkins, 1966; Edmonds, Withers, & Dibatista, 1972).

This contention that older couples tend to report distorted images of their marital quality can be challenged from symbolic interactionism theory. Thomas (1923) reminds us that situations defined as real are real in their consequences. This line of reasoning suggests that, if the couple defines their marriage as satisfying their needs, they will act accordingly and thereby increase the mutually rewarding behaviors of both spouses. Therefore, if the couple defines the relationship as fulfilling their needs, it can satisfy their subjectively defined standards and meet their relationship expectations.

Marriage is as much a subjective state of mind and being, which molds the individual's perception of the world, as it is an objectively observable reality (Berger & Luckman, 1966; Berger & Kellner, 1970). To discount the subjective constructions of reality reported by the individual marriage partners or to ignore the importance of the external sources of validation that come from the perceptual images of outsiders would be equally invalid (Olson, 1976). These perceptual judgments of outsiders are used as a basis for evaluating observations of the couple's interaction patterns and levels of functioning.

Life Continuity Theory

Longitudinal data on marital adjustment (Clark & Wallin, 1965; Dentler & Pineo, 1960; Pineo, 1961, 1969) suggest that couples' adjustment patterns in earlier stages of development within the marriage are the best predictors for adjustment patterns in subsequent stages. Couples having high levels of adjustment in and satisfaction with their relationships in the early stages of marriage were found to return to high levels of adjustment in and satisfaction with the relationships as they completed the launching phase and moved through the empty-nest stage into the retirement stage of the family life cycle.

Couples with low levels of adjustment in and satisfaction with their relationship in the initial phases of the marriage were found to have low levels of adjustment in and satisfaction with the relationships throughout the life cycle. They did not make the same type of recovery from parenthood as that made by the couples with initially high levels of marital adjustment and relationship satisfaction. For these couples with low satisfaction, the marriage becomes utilitarian, and the primary focus is on the performance of instrumental tasks. Children become a primary source of satisfaction and the marriage relationships are never established as meaningful sources of personal identity and life satisfaction. Their identity needs center around their parenting and occupational roles. External ties to friends, extended family, and the community provide their bases for emotional support and satisfaction.

Luckey and Bain (1970) report a similar finding about the sources of satisfaction for spouses as they move from a childfree marriage through childbearing and childrearing phases of the family life cycle. For couples with high levels of satisfaction with the relationship before the arrival of children, the marital relationships retained a primary role in providing a basis for life satisfaction and self-other validation and identity.

Couples with low levels of initial satisfaction with the relationship were more likely to develop child-centered marriages. In a child-centered marriage, the spousal roles and commitments are considered to be of secondary importance as the parenting roles emerge in importance to become the central focus of the couple's lives. For these couples, the marriage is evaluated on a utilitarian basis whereby the performance of key roles related to being a good parent, a good provider, or a good housekeeper is of more importance than the quality of companionship the couple share.

For the high satisfaction group, the marriage is based more on intrinsic qualities central to the husband-wife relationship, such as the quality of companionship and self-other disclosure that they share together. These intrinsic marriages characteristically have very high levels of commitment to the relationship and to each other as marriage mates who value each other as best friends with whom they enjoy sharing life (Cuber & Harroff, 1965).

These data lead to the hypothesis that couples with child-centered marriages may find the retirement years of their marriage to be the least rewarding and the most stressful because the couples will be forced into close proximity with no means of interacting with each other, except through the children who have already left home. Beavers (1977) points out that these couples have not established a solid foundation for the marriage to develop into a meaningful relationship, and so they are typically functioning at moderately low levels. Because these couples are incapable of handling differences and resolving conflict they are likely to have their marriage relationship become an empty shell, without emotional depth and sharing.

Furthermore, one can hypothesize that these couples with child-centered marriages in the earlier phases of the family life cycle can remain heavily invested in the parenting role after the children leave home; they can attempt to be centrally involved in the lives of their children and grandchildren, even to the point of being intrusive and interfering in the normal adult development of their grown children (Stierlin, 1974). They can resist their children's attempts to individuate and to separate from the family of origin. Hence, one can further hypothesize (Medley, 1977) that, as the children separate from their parents in these child-centered marriages, the parents can reorganize the marital relationship, which probably results in a reshaped skewed form in which one spouse parents the other spouse. This parentification style of marital interaction during the retirement phase of the family life cycle can produce asymmetrical patterns of interaction; the parenting spouse can assume an overly responsible role, and the spouse being parented can assume an underresponsible role. The overresponsible spouse becomes the dominant spouse, treating the other spouse as incompetent and relegating the spouse to play a submissive role. Lewis (1979) describes this dominant-submissive pattern of marital interaction as one that has low levels of self-other respect and a lack of mutual trust, which produces a marriage in which self-other disclosures are infrequent and feared by both partners. These couples can remain together out of habit and as long as the utilitarian needs are satisfied. These couples also can be expected to remain in an empty-shell type of relationship with few intimacy needs being met by either partner.

Conversely, one can hypothesize that couples with a history of having a high level of marital quality based upon an intrinsically valued relationship can be more likely to experience the launching, empty-nest, and retirement stages of the family life cycle as being a rewarding time in their lives. These couples can view the empty-nest and retirement years as an opportunity for them to reestablish the high levels of satisfaction with the relationship they had experienced before they became parents (Clark & Wallin, 1965). Data from the marital quality studies (Stinnett et al., 1970, 1972; Medley, 1977; Sporakowski & Hughston, 1978; Swenson, Eskew, & Kohlhepp, 1981) support the hypothesis that retirement can be a time of rediscovery for couples with intrinsically based marriages. These couples can welcome having more uninterrupted time together so that they may rediscover the joys of having their emotional needs more fully met and may focus their attention on discovering and claiming the hitherto untapped resources they have for achieving an even higher level of marital functioning (Mace, 1982). For these couples, retirement can be experienced as a time in which the marital partners are freed of the time constraints and the role demands of raising children and occupational involvements.

MARITAL INTERACTION PATTERNS AMONG RETIRED COUPLES

As the couple moves into the empty-nest stage, they are forced to reexamine their interaction patterns to determine what types of adjustments need to be made in order for them to function as a marital dyad without the children. Orthner (1975) suggests that couples in the empty-nest and retirement stages of their marital career need to realign their patterns of separateness and connectedness. With increased time to interact, they have to establish a balance of the time spent away from each other and the time spent together. Orthner found that leisure activities were approached and experienced differently by husbands and wives. To some degree, wives in the retirement stage have mixed feelings about having their husbands around all the time. These wives probably experience their husbands' continual presence as a stifling of their own personal freedom by too much togetherness and too many demands on their time (Jackson, 1972; Keating & Cole, 1980). Furthermore, Orthner (1975) suggests that a predominance of individual activities by wives is probably indicative of marital dissatisfaction. In general, though, wives' adjustments to having their husbands around all the time were characterized by the wives perceiving they had less time for themselves and less privacy, also by a shift from internal to external structuring and monitoring of their time (Keating & Cole, 1980).

Husbands in the retirement stage frequently experience the new-found freedom to spend more time in leisure as a mixed blessing. They may enjoy the more relaxed pace and the less structured schedule, but they also miss the routine of having a job to go to each day. Husbands who have established diverse interests and hobbies before retirement seem to make an easier adjustment to retirement than do husbands with narrow interests clustered around their job. To this latter group of husbands, individual leisure activities may seem less meaningful than joint and parallel leisure pursuits. This experience of solitude as a meaningless, lonely experience may lead them to want to spend more time with the spouse. The more lonely the husbands feel, the more pressure they are likely to put on their wives to include them in their own activities (Keating & Cole, 1980; Napier & Whitaker, 1978).

Communication Patterns

Keating and Cole (1980) noted that the amount of communication between mates did not show an appreciable increase at the retirement stage, and the spouses' satisfaction with levels of communication did not change significantly in retirement. Stinnett et al. (1972) found that retired couples tended to enjoy having the opportunity to share their feelings and to develop depth in their relationship by more frequent sharing of mutual interests, which they discovered through meaningful self-other disclosure dialogues. The results of research on older couples (Sporakowski & Hughston, 1978; Stinnett et al., 1970; Stinnett et al., 1972) suggests that mutual trust and respect are essential for the couple to feel comfortable disclosing their inner feelings to each other. Trust and respect help to build esteem and encourage an in-depth sharing that fuels the development of greater understanding and appreciation (Mace, 1982).

The couple's communication pattern reflects how they handle differences and deal with conflict (Hof & Miller, 1981; Mace, 1982). Couples who are uncomfortable acknowledging differences tend to use an avoidance or denial strategy; couples who deny differences tend to restrict that which they talk about to topics they consider "safe." Furthermore, this denial of differences and the avoidance of discussing the topic keeps the couple from clearing up misunderstandings and learning new things about each other. Couples who fear differences frequently restrict their discussions to instrumental, task-oriented topics that have little emotional content. These couples seal themselves off from each other emotionally and they are prevented from discussing their own style of interaction to identify misunderstandings that occur or to solve the problem that keeps them distant from each other.

Another key aspect of the communication pattern is the level of exchange or the style of communication. Studies in the field of marital and family communication continually expand our knowledge base of how communication styles influence the couple's interaction pattern (Gottman, 1979). The communication style determines how open or how closed the couple is in dialogue with each other; it further determines the degree of congruence between the verbal and the nonverbal aspects of the message. Couples with a closed style of communicating are less likely to achieve a very high level of self-other understanding because the communication process is guarded and stilted by defensive postures.

Conversely, couples with an open style of communication are more likely to express their feelings, thoughts, intentions, and actions in a congruent fashion that leads to mutual understanding, empathy, trust, and respect, and thus builds a depth of relationship capable of accepting and appreciating spousal differences.

Roles: Responsibility and Divisions of Labor

The results of research on spousal activities among retired couples indicate that at this stage in their lives husbands and wives develop a more flexible pattern of carrying out the household tasks (Jackson, 1972; Keith & Brubaker, 1979; Keith, Powers, & Goudy, 1981; Schafer & Keith, 1981). The wife perceives her husband's increased interest in performing domestic tasks as short-lived and that the bulk of the responsibility for doing the household chores remains within her domain (Keating & Cole, 1980). According to Keating and Cole, wives contend that the completion and organization of role responsibilities (such as the household tasks of shopping, cooking, and cleaning) require more energy and take more time after the husband retires. These retired wives, however, did find the increased time for interaction as a couple rewarding enough to make accommodations to their husbands' retirement needs, even though these accommodations frequently produced added stress for the wives.

Ballweg (1967) points out that these role adjustments in the retirement years can usually be made relatively smoothly if the level of couple communication is high enough to facilitate conflict resolution. He goes on to suggest that role sharing in the retirement stage is partly a function of the wife's self-concept. If the wife has a sufficiently high level of self-esteem, she is less likely to perceive the husband's increased participation in household tasks as threatening to her sense of well-being. Keith et al. (1981) found that role sharing of domestic tasks has functional significance for enhancing the self-esteem and the sense of well-being of husbands who increased their participation in household activities after they retired. Schafer and Keith (1981) examined the issue of equity and marital roles across the family life cycle and found that retired couples perceived the division of labor and role responsibilities as being generally equitable. In the incidences in which retired couples perceived the role responsibilities to be inequitable, both husbands and wives perceived the inequity in their favor for the most part. This response suggests that each partner is making a significant contribution to the maintenance of the relationship. It furthermore suggests that the contributions of one's spouse are recognized and appreciated. Whether the spouses who perceived the inequity in their favor vocalized this concern to their mate is unclear.

Value Orientation

Couples in the retirement stage of the family life cycle tend to be more consciously aware of values than do couples at the earlier stages. Medling and McCarrey (1981) examined the relationship between value similarity among mates and the couple's level of marital adjustment over the family life cycle. They found that couples with a high degree of value similarity during the retirement years had substantially higher levels (40 points higher) of marital adjustment.

Value similarity was not significantly related to marital adjustment for couples in the earlier stages of the family life cycle. They interpreted these data as indicating that retired couples had less competing role demands (such as raising children and occupational involvements) which gave them the luxury of time to be conscious of their values and consequently more likely to make day-to-day life decisions from a value conscious sense of reality.

Tamir and Antonucci (1981) found that, in the later stages of the family life cycle, men became more affiliative and women became more achievement-oriented. Through the early years of the marriage, husbands typically focused a great deal of energy on achieving financial security, community prestige, and so forth, which took their attention from direct involvement in the development and maintenance of the marriage and family relationships. As the husbands reached middle age, they typically reassessed their priorities and began to make shifts away from the values of achieving career advancements and prestige. As they did this, the husbands began to rediscover the importance of getting to know their wives and children better and began to want to redirect their energies to work on the development and maintenance of these interpersonal relationships within the family.

At the same time, the wives began to reassess their own values and priorities. Middle-aged wives typically shifted their attention away from children and spouse and became more aware of their own needs as middle-aged women. This shift away from the development and maintenance of family affiliative bonds was frequently resisted by the husbands and the children. Keating and Cole (1980) noted that during this stage of the marriage, wives became accustomed to not having their husbands around to share things with, and because their children were leaving or had already left home and thus did not need full-time active mothering, they were just beginning to have time for their own interests and activities. As these middle-aged wives became more self-reliant and independent, they began to focus their attention and energies on meeting their own needs and frequently increased their involvement in the world outside the home by seeking paid employment and by becoming more achievement-oriented. These differing motivational shifts can produce value conflicts for couples in retirement.

Swenson et al. (1981) suggest that value awareness is related to ego development. They found that couples with ego development at or below the conformist stage of ego development were less aware of their own values and less likely to use their values as a source of direction for guiding their own behavior. Couples with greater self-awareness were more conscious of their own values and used these values to guide their behavior. Furthermore, they found that couples with higher levels of ego development were more likely to have increased levels of commitment to the marriage relationship and to their partner, which was evidenced by expressions of love, affection, self-disclosure, acceptance, and affirmation of their partner. They also found that the incidence of marital problems decreased, probably because the retired couple's value awareness mediated their interaction exchanges together as a couple.

CONCLUSIONS AND RECOMMENDATIONS

It is evident from this review of research into the marital quality in later life that retired couples have in their marriage a valuable resource that can facilitate their continued personal development in the retirement years. Couples with partner-centered (as opposed to child-centered) marriages tend to make mutually satisfying adjustments in the retirement years and usually perceive the postparental stages of life as being a time of increased marital quality. These partner-centered marriages have a high level of marital functioning, which is evidenced by their ability to communicate effectively, to solve problems, and to resolve conflicts in a manner that builds self-other esteem (Mace, 1982). Having a meaningful marital relationship can offer life-sustaining supports that help to buffer the aging person against an assortment of life stresses that have an impact upon the quality of life during the later years. Physical health and emotional well-being are higher for married persons than for singles—especially for men.

That older couples do change and make adaptations to changes in life situations has been demonstrated in this chapter. Furthermore, the studies on marital quality in later life suggest that marital interaction patterns that were established in the preretirement stages of the family life cycle tend to be the best predictor of the couple's marital quality in the retirement years. This pattern of continuity and change in the relationship is consistent with life continuity explanations of adjustment to retirement (Rosow, 1967). To fully understand the complexities of the dynamics of the marital relationship in its continuities and changes over the life course, researchers must move beyond the current cross-sectional research designs, which treat marriage as a static relationship. Studying marriage as a process, we must focus on the dynamic aspects of marital interaction over the marital career by the use of a longitudinal-sequential perspective and research design (Feldman & Feldman, 1975).

REFERENCES

Abelson, R.P., Aronston, E., McGuire, W., Newcomb, T., Rosenberg, M., & Tannenbaum, P. (1968). *Theories of cognitive consistency: A sourcebook.* Chicago: Rand McNally.

Ade-Ridder, L., & Brubaker, T. (1983). Marital quality and retirement among older couples. In T. Brubaker (Ed.), *Family relationships in later life* (pp. 21–30). Beverly Hills, CA: Sage Publications.

Anderson, D., Russell, C., & Schumm, W. (1983). Perceived marital quality and family life cycle categories: A further analysis. *Journal of Marriage and the Family, 45,* 127–139.

Bachrach, C. (1980). Childlessness and social isolation among the elderly. *Journal of Marriage and the Family, 42,* 627–637.

Ballweg, J. (1967). Resolution of conjugal role adjustments after retirement. *Journal of Marriage and the Family, 29,* 277–281.

Baltes, P. (1968). Longitudinal and cross-sectional sequences in the study of age and generation effects. *Human Development, 11,* 145–171.

Beavers, W. (1977). *Psychotherapy and growth: A family systems perspective.* New York: Brunner/ Mazel.

Berger, P., & Kellner, H. (1970). Marriage and the construction of reality. In H. Dreitzel (Ed.), *Recent sociology 2.* New York: Macmillan.

Berger, P., & Luckman, T. (1966). *The social construction of reality* (pp. 50–73). New York: Doubleday.

Bernard, J. (1964). The adjustment of married mates. In H. Christensen (Ed.), *Handbook of marriage and the family.* Chicago: Rand McNally.

Bernard, J. (1972). *The future of marriage.* New York: World Publishing.

Binstock, R., & Shanas, E. (1976). *Handbook of aging and the social sciences.* New York: Van Nostrand Reinhold.

Blood, R., & Wolfe, D. (1960). Husbands and wives: The dynamics of married living. New York: The Free Press.

Burgess, E., & Wallin, P. (1953). *Engagement and marriage.* Philadelphia: J.B. Lippincott.

Carter, E., & McGoldrick, M. (1980). *The family life cycle: A framework for family therapy.* New York: Gardner Press.

Clark, A., & Wallin, P. (1965). Women's sexual responsiveness and the duration and quality of their marriages. *American Journal of Sociology, 71,* 187–196.

Cole, C.L., Cole, A.L., & Dean, D.G. (1980). Emotional maturity and marital adjustment: A decade replication. *Journal of Marriage and the Family, 42,* 533–539.

Cole, C.L., & Hulbert, J.R. (1981, October). Need fulfillment patterns in health families. Paper presented at the annual meeting of the National Council on Family Relations, Milwaukee, WI.

Cromwell, R., & Olson, D. (1975). *Power in families.* New York: John Wiley & Sons.

Cuber, J., & Harroff, P. (1965). *Sex and the significant Americans.* New York: Appleton-Century-Crofts.

Dentler, R., & Pineo, P. (1960). Marital adjustment and personal growth of husbands: A panel analysis. *Marriage and Family Living, 22,* 45–48.

Durkheim, E. (1951). *Suicide.* New York: The Free Press.

Edmonds, V., Withers, G., & Dibatista, B. (1972). Adjustment, conservatism and marital conventionalization. *Journal of Marriage and the Family, 34,* 96–103.

Feldman, H. (1965). *Development of the husband-wife relationship* (Report of research, pp. 1–152). Washington, DC: National Institute of Mental Health.

Feldman, H., & Feldman, M. (1975). The family life cycle: Some suggestions for recycling. *Journal of Marriage and the Family, 37,* 277–284.

Figley, C. (1973). Child density and the marital relationship. *Journal of Marriage and the Family, 35,* 272–282.

Framo, J. (1982). *Explorations in marital and family therapy.* New York: Springer-Verlag.

Gilford, R., & Bengtson, V.L. (1979). Measuring marital satisfaction in 3 generations: Positive and negative dimensions. *Journal of Marriage and the Family, 41,* 387–398.

Gottman, J. (1979). *Marital interaction*. New York: Academic Press.

Gove, W. (1978). Sex differences in mental illness among adult men and women: An evaluation of 4 questions raised regarding the higher rates of women. *Social Science and Medicine, 12*, 187–198.

Gove, W., Style, C., & Hughes, M. (1981, August). *The function of marriage for the individual: A theoretical formulation and empirical evaluation*. Paper presented at the annual meeting of the American Sociological Association, Montreal, Canada.

Hawkins, J. (1966). The Locke marital adjustment test and social desirability. *Journal of Marriage and the Family, 28*, 193–195.

Hicks, M., & Platt, M. (1970). Marital happiness and stability: A review of research in the sixties. *Journal of Marriage and the Family, 32*, 553–574.

Hill, R. (1970). *Family development in three generations*. Cambridge, MA: Schenkman.

Hof, L., & Miller, W. (1981). *Marriage enrichment: Philosophy, process, and program*. Bowie, MD: Brady.

Hudson, W., & Murphy, G. (1980). The non-linear relationship between marital satisfaction and stage of the family life cycle: An artifact of type I error. *Journal of Marriage and the Family, 42*, 263–267.

Jackson, J. (1972). Marital life among aging blacks. *Family Coordinator, 21*, 21–27.

Keating, N., & Cole, P. (1980). What do I do with him 24 hours a day? Changes in the housewife role after retirement. *Gerontologist, 20*, 84–89.

Keith, P., & Brubaker, T. (1979). Household roles in later life: A look at masculinity and marital adjustment. *Family Coordinator, 28*, 497–502.

Keith, P., Powers, E., & Goudy, W. (1981). Older men in employment and retired families: Well-being and involvement in household activities. *Alternative Lifestyles, 4*, 228–241.

LaRossa, R. (1977). *Power and conflict in marriage: Expecting the first child*. Beverly Hills, CA: Sage.

Lee, G. (1980). Kinship in the seventies: A decade of research and theory. *Journal of Marriage and the Family, 42*, 193–204.

Lerner, R., & Spanier, G. (1978). *Child influences on marital and family interaction*. New York: Academic Press.

Lewis, J. (1979). *How's your family?* New York: Brunner-Mazel.

Lewis, R., & Spanier, G. (1979). Theorizing about the quality and stability of marriage. In W. Burr, R. Hill, F.I. Nye, & I. Reiss (Eds.), *Contemporary theories about the family* (Vol. I) (pp. 268–294). New York: The Free Press.

Libby, R., & Whitehurst, R. (1977). *Marriage and alternatives: Exploring intimate relationships*. Glenview, IL: Scott, Foresman, and Company.

Luckey, E. (1966). Number of years married as related to personality perception and marital satisfaction. *Journal of Marriage and the Family, 28*, 44–48.

Luckey, E., & Bain, J. (1970). Children: A factor in marital satisfaction. *Journal of Marriage and the Family, 32*, 43–44.

Mace, D. (1982). *Love and anger in marriage*. Grand Rapids, MI: Zendervan.

Medley, M. (1977). Marital adjustment in the post-retirement years. *Family Coordinator, 26*, 5–11.

Medling, J.M., & McCarrey, M. (1981). Marital adjustment over segments of the family life cycle: The issue of spousal value similarity. *Journal of Marriage and the Family, 43*, 195–203.

Napier, A., & Whitaker, C. (1978). *The family crucible*. New York: Harper & Row.

Nesselroade, J., Schaie, K., & Baltes, P. (1972). Ontogenetic and generational components of structural and quantitative change in adult cognitive behavior. *Journal of Gerontology, 27*, 222–228.

Olson, D. (1976). *Treating relationships*. Lake Mills, IA: Graphic Publishing.

Orthner, D. (1975). Leisure activity patterns and marital satisfaction over the marital career. *Journal of Marriage and the Family, 37*, 91–102.

Paris, B., & Luckey, E. (1966). A longitudinal study of marital satisfaction. *Sociology and Social Research, 50*, 212–222.

Pineo, P. (1961). Disenchantment in the later years of marriage. *Marriage and Family Living, 23*, 3–11.

Pineo, P. (1969). Development patterns in marriage. *Family Coordinator, 18*, 135–140.

Quinn, W. (1983). Personal and family adjustment in later life. *Journal of Marriage and the Family, 45*, 57–73.

Rausch, H., Barry, W., Hertel, R., & Swain, M. (1974). *Communication, conflict and marriage*. San Francisco: Jossey-Bass.

Renne, K. (1971). Health and marital experience in an urban population. *Journal of Marriage and the Family, 33*, 338–348.

Robinson, B., & Thurnher, M. (1979). Taking care of aged parents: A family cycle transition. *The Gerontologist, 19*, 586–593.

Rollins, B., & Cannon, K. (1974). Marital adjustment over the family life cycle: A reevaluation. *Journal of Marriage and the Family, 36*, 271–283.

Rosow, I. (1967). *Social integration of the aged*. New York: The Free Press.

Ryan, J. (1981). Marital status, happiness and anomie. *Journal of Marriage and the Family, 43*, 643–649.

Ryder, R. (1973). Longitudinal data relating marriage satisfaction to having children. *Journal of Marriage and the Family, 35*, 604–606.

Sager, C. (1976). *Marriage contracts and couple therapy*. New York: Brunner-Mazel.

Scanzoni, J. (1979). Social processes and family power. In W. Burr, R. Hill, F.I. Nye, & I. Reiss (Eds.), *Contemporary theories about the family* (pp. 295–316). New York: The Free Press.

Scanzoni, J., & Szinovancz, M. (1980). *Family decision-making*. Beverly Hills, CA: Sage.

Schafer, R., & Keith, P. (1981). Equity in marital roles across the family life cycle. *Journal of Marriage and the Family, 43*, 359–367.

Schaie, K. (1967). Age changes and age differences. *The Gerontologist, 1*, 128–132.

Schumm, W. (1979). Marital satisfaction over the family life cycle: A critique and proposal. *Journal of Marriage and the Family, 41*, 7–12.

Seelbach, W. (1977). Gender differences in expectations for filial responsibility. *The Gerontologist, 17*, 421–425.

Singer, L., & Stern, B. (1980). *Stages: The crises that shape your marriage*. New York: Grosset & Dunlap.

Spanier, G.B., & Lewis, R.A. (1980). Marital quality: A review of the seventies. *Journal of Marriage and the Family, 43*, 825–839.

Spanier, G.B., Lewis, R.A., & Cole, C.L. (1975). Marital adjustment over the family life cycle: The issue of curvilinearity. *Journal of Marriage and the Family, 37*, 263–268.

Sporakowski, M., & Hughston, G. (1978). Prescriptions for happy marriage: Adjustments and satisfactions of couples married for 50 or more years. *Family Coordinator, 27*, 321–327.

Stierlin, H. (1974). *Separating parents and adolescents*. New York: Quadrangle.

Stinnett, N., Carter, L., & Montgomery, J. (1972). Older persons' perceptions of their marriages. *Journal of Marriage and the Family, 34*, 665–670.

Stinnett, N., Collins, J., & Montgomery, J. (1970). Marital need satisfaction of husbands and wives. *Journal of Marriage and the Family, 32*, 428–434.

Streib, G., & Beck, R. (1980). Older families: A decade review. *Journal of Marriage and the Family, 42*, 937–956.

Sussman, M. (1976). The family of old people. In R. Binstock & E. Shanas (Eds.), *Handbook of aging and the social sciences* (pp. 218–243). New York: Van Nostrand Reinhold.

Swenson, C., Eskew, R., & Kohlhepp, K. (1981). Stage of family life cycle, ego development, and the marriage relationship. *Journal of Marriage and the Family, 43*, 841–853.

Tamir, L., & Antonucci, T. (1981). Self-perception, motivation, and social support through the family life cycle. *Journal of Marriage and the Family, 43*, 151–160.

Thomas, W.I. (1923). *The unadjusted girl*. Boston: Little and Brown.

Troll, L., Miller, S., & Atchley, R. (1979). *Families in later life*. Belmont, CA: Wadsworth.

Verbrugge, L. (1979). Marital status and health. *Journal of Marriage and the Family, 41*, 267–285.

Part II

Treatment and Care Issues

Chapter 6

Filial Responsibility and the Care of Aging Family Members

Wayne C. Seelbach

The rapidly expanding professional concern with intergenerational relations and the rapidly increasing numbers of three-, four-, and even five-generation families have heightened interest in the various aspects of filial responsibility. Recent extensions in life expectancy have produced such considerable generational overlap that today the obligations (or privileges) associated with filial responsibility have become a significant reality for greater numbers of families (Simos, 1970). The steady increases in the number and the proportion of older persons coupled with an era of "New Federalism," the reductions in many social services, and serious concerns about the viability of the Social Security system collectively underscore the importance of directing even greater attention to the role of families as a primary support system for the aged. Such informal support networks particularly are vital to maintaining older persons' well-being and to prolonging their independence (Black, 1973).

There are, of course, increases in physical, economical, social, and psychological dependencies among the elderly population (Kalish, 1969; Bloom & Monroe, 1972). These increasing dependencies along with the more frequent crises that are associated with the later years of life require major adaptive efforts by individual persons and their families. The central or immediate task for family members and for professionals is the avoidance of a tendency toward premature or unnecessary dependencies in later years. This chapter should help in this regard by (1) reviewing the concept of filial responsibility in relation to the maintenance of independence for the elderly; (2) describing the nature of filial responsibility in industrial societies; (3) identifying empirically validated patterns of filial responsibility; and (4) discussing some trends and issues concerning filial responsibility.

THE CONCEPT OF FILIAL RESPONSIBILITY

Providing care for an elderly parent, which many persons believe is one of the positive universal features of family systems, has not actually been present at all times and in all places (Hess & Markson, 1980). The Eskimos and some other societies, for example, expect very little from their offspring and make relatively few demands for care. The needs of the aged in most societies, nevertheless, are frequently fulfilled through expressions of filial responsibility. Typically emphasizing duty, protection, and care, the concept of filial responsibility is an attitude of personal obligation toward the maintenance of parental well-being. Schorr (1960) stated simply that filial responsibility referred to the obligations of adults to meet their parents' needs. Specific varieties of filial responsibility usually include personal contact with elderly parents, shared living arrangements, shopping, escorting, helping with household tasks, and assistance in meeting their daily needs.

Preventive Aspects

Although filial responsibility is generally viewed as a response to an immediate and acute need or crisis, it also involves an important preventive dimension that is seldom considered in the studies made in this field. This preventive aspect must be emphasized so that adult children and their parents discover and develop ways of learning and growing to meet their personal and family needs before and during periods of decline and dependence. Adult children frequently place too much emphasis upon strategies of helping in which they attempt to provide whatever the elderly parent needs (Cicirelli, 1981). Such a tendency may contribute to learned helplessness and premature dependence.

Cultural Expectations

Butler and Lewis's (1982) review of the concept of filial responsibility indicates that adult children were held accountable for their parents under medieval church law and that the concept of community assistance was not introduced until the Elizabethan Poor Laws. Nevertheless, the expectation continued and still continues that families should do as much as possible for their older parents before receiving formal help from outside sources. The issue of filial responsibility versus government aid was tested to a greater degree early in the twentieth century as a result of the increasing numbers of old people and the dramatic social and technological changes that characterized the transition from a traditional, agricultural society.

In contemporary society parents have a legal responsibility to provide for their children, but the reverse is not true; adult children are generally not legally bound to do anything for their parents (Eckhardt, 1970; Fox, 1972; and Hueber, 1971). Any discussion of filial responsibility must also note the implicit cultural assumption that family responsibility is serial, not reciprocal in nature. That is to say, that each generation is viewed as being primarily responsible for the support of the succeeding one. Parents care for their children, and those children are generally expected to give first priority to their own children, not to the same parents who cared for them. This cultural practice and expectation create potential difficulties with respect to filial responsibility and the relationship between formal and informal support systems. Adults' obligation to aged parents are rooted in social, emotional, and moral values such as the fourth commandment in the Judeo-Christian tradition, which admonishes "Honor thy father and thy mother." Thus, it is not totally clear just exactly what parents expect, although there is evidence that they do not expect complete repayment of all that they do for their children (Williamson, Evans, & Munley, 1980).

Parent-adult child relationships are frequently guilt-ridden. One reason for this guilt is the assumption that in one sense children can never fully repay their parents—even if there were a strong cultural mandate to do so. Children are indebted to their parents for nurturance, for socialization, and for life itself. Because there is no way the voluntary aspects of these original gifts can be matched with return gifts, children will perpetually remain in their parents' debt (Blau, 1973). Some older parents exploit this debt; others become its victims. Wentkowski (1981) examined the cultural rules directing exchange of support within networks along with variations in the ways in which older persons interpret these rules. Her study emphasized the great personal significance of reciprocity in the exchange of support for preserving the self-esteem of the elderly. This significance of reciprocity has obvious implications for the maintenance of independence in later life.

Effect of Generational Differences

Differences in backgrounds, experiences, and lifestyles make it difficult for each generation to fully appreciate and to understand the needs of the other. Although older parents have, for example, experienced the stage of midlife, their experiences occurred at a different historical time. Another potential source of poor understanding is people's tendency to become somewhat more egocentric with age and consequently to assume that everyone should live the way they do and provide for them as they so desire. Some older parents also possess difficult personality characteristics. They can be demanding tyrants who pretend helplessness or dependency, others can be unduly rigid, while still others simply delight in being impossible to deal with (Cicirelli, 1981). Such parental characteristics certainly affect the nature of filial responsibility and the extent to which it is demonstrated.

Some observers maintain that as parents age, the parent-child relationship reverses itself, and the parent assumes the former dependency role of the child while the child takes on the supportive role of the parent. Blenkner (1965), however, argues that role reversal is a pathological condition. She believes that instead of adult children's assuming the parents' role, they should take on a more mature filial role. The mature role involves being depended upon and, therefore, being dependable insofar as parents are concerned. This is the stage of "filial maturity."

Effect of Governmental Agencies

Although some pessimists believe that the American family is disintegrating partly because family members no longer seem obligated to provide care, Hess and Markson (1980) contend that removing care from the "emotion-laden uncertainties of family politics" could actually strengthen family bonds. Social services and programs, by assuming some of the financial burden and helping with instrumental tasks, may enhance the likelihood that adults will be able to satisfy their aged parents' important psychological and affective needs (Seelbach & Sauer, 1977). This point is reiterated by Butler and Lewis (1982) who note that although government agencies do provide some financial support and services for older persons, many politics continue to reflect the earlier traditions of total filial or family responsibility. A notable example is the "responsible relative" clause still found in many welfare programs. Middle-aged couples who may have as many as four parents and eight grandparents alive simply cannot afford to be financially or emotionally "responsible" relatives to all. Compounding the difficulty is the fact that since approximately 10 percent of the elderly population has a child over age 65, many aged parents have aged children who themselves require some care. Government and welfare agencies must, in sum, help alleviate some of the financial and instrumental burdens from contemporary families, in order that family members can attend to the many important emotional and personal needs of their elderly.

FILIAL RESPONSIBILITY IN INDUSTRIAL SOCIETY

There has been much debate and discussion, if not controversy, concerning the nature and extent of filial responsibility in contemporary industrial societies. Some observers have noted a decline in the family's traditional protective functions because of the combined influences of urbanization and industrialization (Albrecht, 1953; Beard, 1949). With the change from a traditional family system based on consanguine values to one based upon bonds of conjugality and sentiment, many of the general obligations of kinship have been reduced (Hess & Waring, 1978). For example, Winch and Blumberg (1974) analyzed the relationship between societal complexity and familial organization. They concluded that familism is high in stable, agricultural societies and low in hunting and gathering societies because older parents consequently may come to be placed outside their children's "circle of privatized domesticity" (Hareven, 1976).

Recent developments in the political economy of modern, industrialized nations have tended to further erode filial obligations and duties. These trends, as they were described earlier, have extended public responsibility to matters previously left to the family. The current generation of middle-aged adults represents the first cohort of offspring to be more or less released from the need to provide income maintenance or health care for aged parents. Such developments do not necessarily imply that filial responsibility has disappeared; rather, its manifestations and nature have changed. Although some researchers have speculated that filial responsibility is rapidly diminishing in the United States and that adults no longer feel responsible or obligated to meet the needs of their aging parents (Treas, 1977), Sussman (1976) has challenged this view by noting that the nature of filial responsibility has changed. Contemporary filial responsibility involves helping parents understand or utilize local, state, and federal resources in order to remain independent.

Although the traditional family has certainly lost some of its traditional functions as industrialization proceeds, it has strengthened others and gained new ones. Most importantly, the family has become a major source of affectional and emotional support. Shorter (1975) observes that the historical emergence of the modern family has been marked by unprecedented demands on kin for intimacy and affection. In an urban, industrialized society, these functions are just as—if not more—essential as the economic and instrumental functions were in former times. Relatedly, a new set of tasks confronts the middle-aged offspring in industrialized society. They now are called upon to act as protectors, guides, and coordinators in dealing with the bureaucracy that presently surrounds family life and aging. Filial responsibility will increasingly involve intervention on behalf of aged parents to ensure their various entitlements and to deal with bureaucratic red tape (Shanas & Sussman, 1977). It is certain that adult children's advisory roles and psychological supports are becoming increasingly important in contemporary society (Sussman & Burchinal, 1962).

A strong need exists for effective coordination of services from various formal and informal helping networks in contemporary society. Adult children generally are the persons most able to individualize or tailor the care needed to fit the idiosyncratic situation and the preferences of their elderly parents. They also may provide the best assessments of the type and the degree of supplemental services required to prolong and to preserve their parents' independence. Moreover, adult children can control, coordinate, and monitor the quality of care given, not only from formal sources but from within the kin network itself (Cicirelli, 1981).

Although only the nature and the character of filial responsibility have changed, the myth of family alienation from old people remains. Because this myth is so persistent and so pervasive, Shanas and Sussman (1977) refer to it as a "hydra-headed monster." Moreover, it has spawned some related myths. According to one of these, the formal support system provides the bulk of the care received by the dependent elderly; according to another, the provision of formal services undermines filial responsibility; and according to a final myth, elderly parents are abandoned by their families. Ample empirical evidence exists to dispel these myths and to slay the hydra-headed monster. This evidence is summarized in the following section.

FILIAL RESPONSIBILITY: EMPIRICAL FINDINGS

Independence, highly valued at all stages in the family life cycle, has contributed to the "intimacy-at-a-distance" characterization of intergenerational relations. Most older persons strongly desire to remain independent of their children for as long as possible; but, when they absolutely become unable to manage for themselves, they do expect help from their offspring (Sanders & Seelbach, 1981; Neugarten, 1975; Streib, 1972). In a three-generation study of filial care-giving made by Brody, Johnsen, and Fulcomer (1981), a majority of each generation ranked child first as the person to serve as confidant, to manage finances, and to do grocery shopping. Johnson and Bursk (1977) found reciprocal patterns of exchange in 93 percent of the aged who had children. Indeed, as mentioned in an earlier section, an overwhelming amount of empirical research documents the fact that most elderly are not abandoned, isolated, neglected, or rejected by their adult children or by other kin (e.g., Bild & Havighurst, 1976; Litwak, 1960; Rosow, 1967; Shanas, 1961, 1974).

As elderly persons grow even older, lose friends, and become increasingly dependent, they tend to be more involved with their families than with nonkin (Sussman, 1965). Troll (1971) indicates that because ties with family may, in fact, be their only remaining attachments, the importance of adult children as sources of assistance increases (Adams, 1970; Cantor, 1975). Cicirelli (1981) found that adult children frequently provided help in illness or crises as well as in other areas such as home repairs, housework, gifts, and negotiations with various bureaucracies. Protection and negotiations with bureaucracies are highly important services in contemporary, complex industrial societies.

Other research has demonstrated that adults and their elderly parents can have differing views about the importance of various types of aid and services. For example, adult children seemed not to appreciate their elderly parents' concerns with crime and safety or with the difficulties of dealing with bureaucratic business or government agencies. Children, conversely, were greatly concerned about home health care and personal care, to which the elderly attached relatively low priority (Cicirelli, 1981).

Older persons may want and expect aid from offspring when the need arises, but it appears that the desire stops short of expecting financial aid (Wake & Sporakowski, 1972; Seelbach, 1977). Tibbits (1977) sees a trend toward a decrease in older persons' financial reliance on their children, noting that less than five percent of the elderly's income comes from a direct transfer of money from children to parents. Financial aid generally is of less importance to the elderly than are love, respect, and emotional support from their children.

A large amount of additional research has examined variables such as gender, social class, ethnicity, and residence in relation to filial responsibility expectations and realizations. Seelbach (1977) found that older women expected more filial support than did their male counterparts. Williamson, Evans, and Munley (1980) discovered that adult males receive more monetary or instrumental aid from their parents, but females receive more services or expressive aid. Similarly in later life, sons are more likely viewed as sources of financial support; daughters are frequently asked to help older parents meet daily responsibilities and to be available for companionship. Brody (1981) calls attention to the special needs of daughters who are "women in the middle."

Lowenthal and Robinson (1976) observed that middle-class parents tend to offer money and goods to their offspring, but working-class parents more typically exchange services. Middle-class elders were also less likely to have recently seen their children, but working class parents were more likely to have lived with their offspring. Mindel (1979) and Watson (1982) suggest that older people who have children but who do not share a household with them tend to live near at least one of them.

Variations in racial and ethnic attitudes toward filial responsibility have also been documented (Hayes & Mindel, 1973; Mutran, 1981; Seelbach, 1977, 1978, 1981; Weeks & Cuellar, 1981). The general, albeit not unanimous, conclusion is that the minority elderly are more likely to have somewhat closer family bonds inasmuch as economic necessity, religious values, and mutual protection from the effects of discrimination tend to sustain kinship ties at each stage of the family life cycle. Schorr (1960) particularly observed that blacks were more likely than whites to endorse filial responsibility norms.

Other studies, which have produced contradictory findings, have centered on rural-urban differences in the familial interactions of the elderly. Dinkel (1944), for example, found rural respondents most supportive of filial responsibility, but Bultena (1969) found family interaction greatest among urbanites. In a study by Sauer, Seelbach, and Hanson (1981), urbanites were more likely to endorse filial norms than were rural residents; however, Wake and Sporakowski (1972) found no differences in the filial attitudes of rural and urban respondents.

In sum, although empirical research has clearly dispelled the myth of abandonment, Cicirelli (1981) cautions that in rejecting one myth there may be a temptation to embrace an opposite notion. This "countermyth," as he terms it, is that adult children automatically can and will provide adequate and effective help to their dependent elderly parents. Cicirelli's study found that most adults presently provide rather little service and that they feel a commitment to provide only limited amounts in the future. The study suggested the presence of a phenomenon Cicirelli termed "filial anxiety," which resulted from children's anticipating the potential necessity of providing help to elderly parents. Finally, older parents who were socialized into a traditional set of expectations about filial responsibility may not have been able to understand their children's resistance to these "legitimate" demands for dependence and care. Indeed, an inverse association has been found between aged parents' filial responsibility expectations and their levels of life satisfaction (Seelbach & Sauer, 1977).

FILIAL RESPONSIBILITY: TRENDS AND ISSUES

Relationships between aged parents and adult children as well as relationships between "ancient" parents and aged children are somewhat anomic in their lack of clear normative prescriptions while the range of choices of action is expanding (Hess & Waring, 1978). Adult children traditionally have been the elderly's primary support system, and they continue to provide such help today—partly, because the elderly may believe that "no one does it better." Some demographic, economic, and social trends suggest, however, that adults may have to limit the amount and kinds of help they can provide to their elderly parents, despite the New Federalism and the reductions in social services (Cicirelli, 1981; Treas, 1977). If such is the case, the filial support system must be continually and thoroughly evaluated for its limitations in meeting the needs of the elderly. Adult children often are physically, emotionally, or economically unable to provide long-term care. Relatedly, the amount of help required may be so great that it is disruptive to normal family functioning and morale. In fact, some evidence exists that adult children often take on filial responsibilities to the detriment of other individual and family responsibilities (Watson, 1982). Hence, a vitally important implication of filial responsibility involves the individual and the familial consequences of providing long-term care to older relatives.

Cicirelli's notion of "filial anxiety" includes a recognition that degrees of personal strain and negative feelings are prevalent among the elderly's offspring. The strains that are most prevalent and most strongly related to parental dependency tend to arise directly from helping the relationship itself. They often are not due to secondary problems with spouse, children, finances, or job. The most typical strains involve instead a sense of physical and emotional fatigue along with persistent feelings of being unable to satisfy the parent no matter what one does (Cicirelli, 1981; Silverstone & Hyman, 1976). This response has clear implications for family therapists and interventionists as they strive to strengthen the informal support system.

Provisions for Help

Certainly, the availability of formal help can assist the informal network in meeting the needs of the elderly by dissipating the burden of care. In addition to the more comprehensive types of care, a particular need exists for part-time care or respite services. Counseling and self-help groups can provide outlets in which strains and feelings can be shared. Adult children can be helped to resolve the conflicts and issues of earlier years that may influence their reactions to parents, to gain a more mature perspective, and to learn more effective ways of maintaining and enhancing the independence of their aging parents (Troll, Miller, & Atchley, 1979). Silverstone and Hyman (1976) suggest that adults begin preparation for filial duty by asking themselves five questions:

1. Can you accept your parents' old age?
2. Do you like your aging parents?
3. Can you accept a different role?
4. Can you accept your own aging?
5. Are you overburdened?*

Many conflicts probably stem from conflicting generational views on the importance of various types of help. Counseling and group work could aid in clarifying and resolving such differences so that the viewpoints and needs of each generation are more accurately understood and appreciated. In a rapidly changing modern society, filial responsibility may be encompassed in various continuing education offerings wherein the generations compare their expectations and discover the extent to which they are in agreement. Heretofore, filial responsibility has not been explicitly taught or discussed; rather, it has been passed on from one generation to the next in a set of implicit assumptions that foster misperceptions and dysfunctional communication.

Demographic Trends

Beyond the sheer increases in the number and the proportion of older persons, other demographic trends, such as smaller families and increases in the "old-old" age category, seriously stretch the resources of the informal, filial support network (Treas, 1977). Additionally, today's elderly produced relatively few children; thus, the number of adult children available to provide services is somewhat smaller than in previous times. The trend toward zero population growth will exacerbate this situation (Shanas & Hauser, 1974).

---

*Adapted from material in B. Silverstone and H. Hyman (1976), *You and your aging parent*. New York: Pantheon Books, pp. 24–28.

Concurrent with these developments, the children of advanced aged parents, who are themselves aging, are becoming more prevalent. This growth creates situations in which two generations of elderly may require aid from other family members, which thereby increases the burdens on the informal support system (Gelfand, Olsen, & Block, 1978). Three- and four-generation families are not uncommon and the number of five-generation families is on the increase. Determining which generation should have priority in the allocation of finite family resources and energies is the critical issue.

Social Trends

Another issue flows from social trends such as changes in women's roles, the emergence of variant family forms, and alternative lifestyles; together, they may reduce feelings of filial responsibility. Also important are the increasing numbers of divorced, separated, widowed, and remarried middle-aged children, which create situations in which family relationships may become blurred or may be maintained with less sense of obligation. Hess and Waring (1978) observe that helping behaviors are indeed becoming more voluntary than obligatory. Inflation is steadily and dramatically eroding the economic resources of the elderly and their adult children, which simultaneously makes the elderly more likely to require financial help and their children less able to provide it. Cicirelli (1981) concludes that if adult children cannot meet all the needs of their elderly parents, it then becomes all the more important to coordinate the family network with other support systems for the elderly—a recurring theme throughout this chapter. Lastly, there are other issues that pertain to the ways of distributing filial responsibilities among family members, which includes sex-role flexibility. At times, it seems that the least "logical" offspring is the one who has the most filial duties. How does one acquire this role? Silverstone and Hyman (1976) note that caretakers (1) may volunteer; (2) may be chosen by their parents; (3) may function as pseudo-caretakers who claim credit but actually render little aid; (4) may use their role to achieve martyrdom; and (5) may be perceived as a friend or an enemy.*

Social Policy

The concept of filial responsibility has important implications for social policy—particularly in respect to the question of reinforcing adults' obligation to care for and to support their dependent parents versus the further development or curtailment of governmental and community services. If adult offspring are capable, dependable, and desirable sources of affective and instrumental support

---

*Adapted from material in B. Silverstone and H. Hyman (1976), *You and your aging parent*. New York: Pantheon Books, pp. 46–51.

for their aged parents, the burden upon extra-familial sources may then be lessened. If, however, offspring are not reliable, capable, or desirable, programmatic efforts are then needed as a substitute.

Social policy must, of course, be cognizant of the preferences and the needs of elderly parents. For example, some evidence exists that elderly parents differentiate between instrumental and affective types of filial responsibility (Sussman, 1965). The tendency is for parents to expect more from their offspring in the way of social and affective support than in the area of instrumental and economic types of assistance. By assuming many of the more instrumental tasks, social services and programs may enhance the likelihood that adults will be able to meet their aged parents' affective and social needs. Being released from the responsibility for instrumental and economic support, adults could then devote more of their energies to providing the kinds of affective supports their elderly parents tend to deem as most important.

Weeks and Cuellar (1981) call attention to another policy issue, which concerns the minority elderly. Policymakers must be aware that helping networks are not evenly distributed throughout the older population, and that they are most pronounced in segments of the population that are most sensitive about receiving a fair share of public benefits. Policymakers and service providers, therefore, simply need to be aware that major group differences exist in older persons' helping networks.

Research Issues

Important empirical research issues concerning filial responsibility remain. Most research on the topic has focused on frequency of contact and assistance; relatively little attention has been given to the perhaps more important qualitative dimensions. Because there surely are varying degrees of help given between the extremes of abandonment and total commitment, data are needed that document the specific conditions under which adult children can and will provide effective help to their elderly parents. More particularly, the importance and the effects of parents' and children's contingent circumstances have been generally overlooked. Future studies should explore the complex interrelationships among filial responsibility expectations, realization of filial responsible behaviors, and the contingent circumstances of older parents and their offspring. Another area for future investigation involves the complex social and psychological processes by which filial responsibility expectations are formulated.

In conclusion, interventionists should anticipate increasing problems stemming from the multiplicity of emotions and feelings associated with filial responsibility. Feelings of guilt, resentment, duty, anxiety, love, jealousy, insecurity, and compassion all become intricately activated when the time comes for filial responsibility to be discharged. Perhaps this chapter can help to extend the thinking and the research about filial responsibility and its implications for maintaining and prolonging independence in later life.

REFERENCES

Adams, B.N. (1970). Isolation, function, and beyond: American kinship in the 1980's. *Journal of Marriage and the Family, 34,* 575–597.

Albrecht, R. (1953). Relationships of older people with their own parents. *Marriage and Family Living, 15,* 296–298.

Beard, B. (1949). Are the aged ex-family? *Social Forces, 27,* 274–279.

Bild, B.R., & Havighurst, R. (1976). Family and social support. *The Gerontologist, 16,* 63–69.

Black, D. (1973). The older person and the family. In R. Davis (Ed.), *Aging: prospects and issues.* Los Angeles, CA: Andrus Gerontology Center.

Blau, Z. (1973). *Old age in a changing society.* New York: New Viewpoints.

Blenkner, M. (1965). Social work and family relationships in later life. In E. Shanas & G. Streib (Eds.), *Social structure and the family: generational relations.* Englewood Cliffs, NJ: Prentice-Hall.

Bloom, M., & Monroe, A. (1972). Social work and the aging. *The Family Coordinator, 21,* 103–115.

Brody, E., Johnsen, P., & Fulcomer, M. (1981, November). What should adult children do for elderly parents: Expectations of three generations of women. Paper presented at annual meeting of the Gerontological Society of America, Toronto, Canada.

Bultena, G. (1969). Rural-urban differences in the familial interaction of the aged. *Rural Sociology, 34,* 5–15.

Butler, R., & Lewis, M. (1982). *Aging and mental health* (3rd ed.). St. Louis: C.V. Mosby.

Cantor, M. (1975). Life space and the social support system of the inner city elderly of New York. *The Gerontologist, 15,* 23–27.

Cicirelli, V. (1981). *Helping elderly parents: the role of adult children.* Boston: Auburn House.

Dinkel, R. (1944). Attitudes of children toward supporting aged parents. *American Sociological Review, 9,* 370–379.

Eckhardt, K. (1970). Family responsibility and legal norms. *Journal of Marriage and the Family, 32,* 105–109.

Fox, S. (1972). The past, present, and future of a child's legal responsibility for support of his parents. *Journal of Geriatric Psychiatry, 5,* 137–147.

Gelfand, D., Olsen, J., & Block, M. (1978). Two generations of elderly in the changing American family: Implications for family services. *The Family Coordinator, 27,* 395–404.

Hareven, T. (1976). The last stage: historical adulthood and old age. *Daedalus,* Fall, 13–28.

Hayes, W., & Mindel, C. (1973). Extended kin relations in black and white families. *Journal of Marriage and the Family, 35,* 51–57.

Hess, B., & Markson, E. (1980). *Aging and old age.* New York: Macmillan.

Hess, B., & Waring, J. (1978). Parent and child in later life: Rethinking the relationship. In R. Lerner & G. Spanier (Eds.), *Child influences on marital and family interaction.* New York: Academic Press.

Hess, B., & Waring, J. (1978). Changing patterns of aging and family bonds in later life. *The Family Coordinator, 27,* 303–314.

Hueber, D. (1971). The effects of relatives' responsibility laws on the family. Unpublished doctoral dissertation, Case Western Reserve University, Cleveland, Ohio.

Johnson, E., & Bursk, B. (1977). Relationships between the elderly and their adult children. *The Gerontologist, 17*, 90–96.

Kalish, R. (Ed.). (1969). *The dependencies of older people.* Ann Arbor: University of Michigan Institute of Gerontology.

Litwak, E. (1960). Geographical mobility and extended family cohesion. *American Sociological Review, 25*, 9–21.

Lowenthal, M., & Robinson, B. (1976). Social networks and isolation. In R. Binstock and E. Shanas (Eds.), *Handbook of aging and social sciences.* New York: Van Nostrand Reinhold.

Mindel, C. (1979). Multigenerational family households: recent trends and implications for the future. *The Gerontologist, 19*, 456–463.

Mutran, E. (1981, November). Family support and the well-being of the widowed: Black-white comparisons. Paper presented at annual meeting of the Gerontological Society of America, Toronto, Canada.

Neugarten, B. (1975). The future and the young-old. *The Gerontologist, 15*, 4–9.

Rosow, I. (1967). *Social integration of the aged.* New York: Free Press.

Sanders, L., & Seelbach, W. (1981). Variations in preferred care alternatives for the elderly: family versus nonfamily sources. *Family Relations, 30*, 447–451.

Sauer, W., Seelbach, W., & Hanson, S. (1981). Rural-urban and cohort differences in filial responsibility norms. *Journal of Minority Aging, 5*, 299–305.

Schorr, A. (1960). *Filial responsibility in the modern American family* (U.S. Dept. of Health, Education, and Welfare). Washington, D C : U.S. Government Printing Office.

Seelbach, W. (1977). Gender differences in expectations for filial responsibility. *The Gerontologist, 17*, 421–425.

Seelbach, W. (1978). Correlates of aged parents' filial responsibility expectations and realizations. *The Family Coordinator, 27*, 341–350.

Seelbach, W. (1981). Filial responsibility among aged parents: a racial comparison. *Journal of Minority Aging, 5*, 286–292.

Seelbach, W., & Sauer, W. (1977). Filial responsibility expectations and morale among aged parents. *The Gerontologist, 17*, 492–499.

Shanas, E. (1973). Family kin network and aging: A cross cultural perspective. *Journal of Marriage and the Family, 35*, 505–511.

Shanas, E. (1961). *Family relationships of old people.* Chicago: Health Information Foundation.

Shanas, E., & Hauser, P. (1974). Zero population growth and the family life of old people. *Journal of Social Issues, 30*, 79–92.

Shanas, E., & Sussman, M. (Eds.). (1977). *Family, bureaucracy, and the elderly.* Durham, NC: Duke University Press.

Shorter, E. (1975). *The making of the modern family.* New York: Basic Books.

Silverstone, B., & Hyman, H. (1976). *You and your aging parent.* New York: Pantheon Books.

Simos, B. (1970). Relations of adults with aging parents. *The Gerontologist, 10*, 135–139.

Streib, G. (1972). Older families and their troubles: familial and social responses. *The Family Coordinator, 21*, 5–19.

Sussman, M. (1965). Relations of adult children with their parents in the United States. In E. Shanas & G. Streib (Eds.), *Social structure and the family: Generational relations.* Englewood Cliffs, NJ: Prentice-Hall.

Sussman, M. (1976). The family life of old people. In R. Binstock and E. Shanas (Eds.), *Handbook of aging and the social sciences*. New York: Van Nostrand Reinhold.

Sussman, M., & Burchinal, L. (1962). Parental aid to married children: implications for family functioning. *Marriage and Family Living, 24,* 320–332.

Tibbits, C. (1977). Older Americans in the family context. *Aging,* April-May.

Treas, J. (1977). Family support systems for the aged: some social and demographic considerations. *The Gerontologist, 17,* 486–491.

Troll, L. (1971). The family of later life: A decade review. *Journal of Marriage and the Family, 33,* 263–290.

Troll, L., Miller, S., & Atchley, R. (1979). *Families in later life.* Belmont, CA: Wadsworth Health Services Divisions.

Wake, S., & Sporakowski, M. (1972). An intergenerational comparison of attitudes towards supporting aged parents. *Journal of Marriage and the Family, 34,* 42–48.

Watson, W. (1982). *Aging and social behavior.* Belmont, CA: Wadsworth Health Services Divisions.

Weeks, J., & Cuellar, J. (1981). The role of family members in the helping networks of older people. *The Gerontologist, 21,* 388–394.

Wenktowski, G. (1981). Reciprocity and the coping strategies of older people: Cultural dimensions of network building. *The Gerontologist, 21,* 600–609.

Williamson, J., Evans, L., & Munley, A. (1980). *Aging and Society.* New York: Holt, Rinehart, & Winston.

Winch, R., & Blumberg, R. (1974). Societal complexity and familial organization. In R. Winch & G. Spanier (Eds.), *Selected studies in marriage and the family* (4th ed.). New York: Holt, Rinehart & Winston.

Chapter 7

Family Support of Older Persons in the Long-Term Care Setting: Recommendations for Practice

Timothy H. Brubaker and Ellie Brubaker

Long-term care for the elderly has become an important issue within recent years as human service professionals have directed their attention to the care of older people with chronic health problems. For example, social gerontologists, social workers, and other social service professionals have begun to explore the effects of long-term care on older people and their families. The interest of these professionals is important because long-term care involves services in the home, in the community, and in the institutions that provide for older persons over an extended time. Koff (1982) defines long-term care as "those services designed to provide diagnostic, preventive, therapeutic, rehabilitative, supportive and mainte- nance services for individuals . . . who have chronic physical and/or mental impairments, in a variety of institutional and noninstitutional health care settings, including the home" (p. 3).

In the case of approximately 5 percent of persons aged 65 years and older, long- term care is viewed from an institutional perspective. These persons experience long-term care primarily in nursing homes or by periodic stays in hospitals. In the case of another 20 to 25 percent of the elderly, long-term care involves a large array of community services. These older persons and their families seek services to assist them in living outside the institutional setting. Community services can help an older person live independently at home, or they can provide services that encourage adult children to invite older parents into their own homes. Many times, the services provided within the community are the crucial factors that keep the older person out of an institutional setting. In either case, family involvement in the long-term care of older persons is an important issue for gerontological re- searchers and practitioners.

FAMILY INVOLVEMENT

Just as families are actively involved with their older relatives who live independently, they also maintain helping relationships with older members who are involved in long-term care (Shanas, 1979a, b; O'Brien & Wagner, 1980). Shanas (1979a) suggests that families can continue to provide services even though nonfamilial long-term care is utilized. Rathbone-McCuan (1976) describes the ways adult day-care programs help families who have an elderly family member living with them. When community long-term care services are used, family members can act as a liaison between their older relative and the community service (Shanas, 1979b).

The data also clearly indicate that families continue their involvement in the support of older people who live within an institutional long-term care setting. The support provided may take the form of visitation. Two studies indicate that children, grandchildren, and other relatives visit their elderly members after admission to an institutional long-term care setting (Hook, Sobal, & Oak, 1982) and continue their visits after the older person has become settled (Spasoff et al., 1978). It has been suggested that visits from family and friends contribute positively to the well-being of older persons (Noelker & Harel, 1978; Greene & Monahan, 1982).

Because family relationships with older persons involved in long-term care are valuable, providers of services need to be aware of ways to enhance those relationships. Service providers of long-term care are aware that family relationships with older persons exist and that those relationships are advantageous to their clients. Nevertheless, practitioners are best able to put their knowledge into use when they develop skills that successfully promote family involvement and that deal with the difficulties older families may experience.

The general objective of this chapter is to present ways in which service providers can reinforce the ties older persons in the long-term care setting have with their families. The specific areas to be discussed include (1) assessment, (2) utilization of appropriate resource systems, (3) coordination of service delivery, and (4) dealing with barriers that deter the delivery of services.

LONG-TERM CARE PRACTICE

The primary goal of the practitioner involved in providing long-term care services to older clients (institutional or community based) is the matching of resources to client need. The following case example (Exhibit 7–1) demonstrates the manner in which service providers can employ their skills to relieve family concerns, while they engage family members in tasks that can strengthen their relationship with older persons receiving long-term care.

The several recommendations to providers of long-term care are now presented in more detail. Followed, they can assist the practitioner in achieving the primary goal of long-term care services—the matching of resources to client need.

Exhibit 7–1 Case Study

Mrs. Lane lived in the same midwestern community throughout her lifetime. She had married her childhood sweetheart and had had three children. Some years ago, when her son moved to the East Coast with his family, she regretted that she was able to see him only several times a year. Her two daughters lived within walking distance, and her grandchildren often stopped by for cookies on their way home from school. Two years ago, after a stroke, her husband died. Mrs. Lane began to complain to her family that she felt lonely. In the past several months, Mrs. Lane called her daughters frequently at night, saying that she was frightened. All three of her children invited her to move into their homes, but Mrs. Lane refused, saying that she felt it would harm the good relationship she had always had with them and their families.

When Mrs. Lane was 80 years old, she moved from her own home into a long-term care facility. There were several nursing homes in her community, and Mrs. Lane asked her daughters to choose one for her. After talking with the social worker employed by each facility, her daughters took her to visit the one with which they felt most comfortable. Mrs. Lane and her daughters met with Mrs. Sanders, the social worker at the facility her daughters had chosen. Mrs. Sanders described the nursing facility to Mrs. Lane, as she had done for her daughters. She had been provided with some information about Mrs. Lane by the daughters, but she talked with Mrs. Lane herself at length in order to answer any questions Mrs. Lane might have and to determine her feelings about entering the facility. In addition, she questioned Mrs. Lane concerning her reasons for wanting to enter a long-term care facility. She found that Mrs. Lane had always been fearful of staying alone and had been uncomfortable in her home since her husband had died. Mrs. Sanders encouraged Mrs. Lane to discuss these feelings and stated that Mrs. Lane's concerns were not unusual ones.

During their meeting, Mrs. Lane related that her relationship with her children and the friendships she had in the community were important to her. She also indicated that she did not want to become dependent on one person or resource. She was particularly interested in continuing attendance at her church. Mrs. Sanders suggested that the daughters contact Mrs. Lane's friends from church to determine how they could remain involved. Mrs. Lane agreed to this and, as a result, received regular invitations to Sunday dinner from church acquaintances.

Both daughters offered to take their mother shopping with them when she needed clothing or other incidentals. Mrs. Saunders supported this offer by agreeing to help Mrs. Lane let them know when she needed to purchase items. In addition, the daughters clearly let their mother know that they would continue to visit her on a regular basis and would also be available if she wished to telephone them.

Assessment of Client and Relationships

In order to match resources to need, the service provider determines the "goals" that need to be set and the "action" that should be taken (Lowy, 1979). This process involves several steps. First, the practitioner gathers information about the client's situation to determine the unmet needs that exist. Then, the practitioner investigates the impact of the older person's relationships with others upon the needs experienced. To accomplish these steps, contact is made with the older client and with those persons involved in the client's support network.

Knowledge about older persons and their families provides information about factors contributing to the client's problems and about potential resources to deal with those problems. The format used in assessing those needs depends upon the stage of the professional's relationship with the client. If the client is entering long-term care, the professional requires different information from the client and the support systems than that required had the person been in long-term care for an extended time.

The first step, gaining information about the elderly person's situation, involves obtaining factual information about the older person. If the provider has not previously been involved with the client, information is required concerning age; the client's marital status; the number and the names of children and other relatives; the client's housing situation; the client's health status and the services received from medical professionals—including medical history and medications taken; the client's reactions to the need for long-term care services; the client's emotional status; and details about the formal and the informal support the client is receiving. As the professional-client relationship progresses, assessment continues; relevant information about the older person requires an updating of data gathered earlier in the helping process.

The second step involves investigating the impact of support systems on the needs experienced by the client. The service provider can benefit from developing an assessment format that investigates whether the older person's needs are exacerbated or relieved through relationships with others. Such a format includes information about (1) the client's perception of needs, (2) significant others' perceptions of the client's needs, (3) current resources, (4) past use of available resources, (5) current relationships, (6) the historical content of current relationships, and (7) changes in the client's relationships to others.

When the professional enters into a relationship with a client, information about current resources and relationships and the historical content of those relationships is necessary. This information can help the service provider avoid repeating "past interventive mistakes and to better assess the client's capabilities and motivation to work on the problem" (Fischer, 1978, p. 250). In addition, the service provider may be called upon to act as a mediator between the family and the older person when a difference in opinion occurs about the best way to deal with the older person's needs. These data can be gathered by questioning the older persons and their family members concerning the current and the historical status of their relationships.

Specific historical information helpful to the practitioner includes the impact of previous helping relationships (Hartman, 1981). For example, did the relationships themselves bring about the problem, and were problems present in earlier helping transactions? All information about elderly persons and their family situations are important at this point. In the case example (Exhibit 7–1), Mrs. Sanders questioned Mrs. Lane, her family, and others involved in her support network to gather information necessary for service provision. In addition, Mrs. Sanders gained information about Mrs. Lane's situation at the time her need for services began, and she investigated the changes that contributed to the development of her current need. The manner in which this was done facilitated Mrs. Sanders' ability to meet her client's needs.

Utilization of Resource Systems

For those attempting to match resources to the needs of older persons in long-term care, several sources of help are available. These sources of help include resources provided by institutions or agencies (formal resources), services provided by the older person's social network (generally, this involves help given by the extended family), and resources the older person is able to provide.

Social Support

Research on practice with the elderly indicates that involving the older person's informal social systems in the treatment process increases the person's ability to function appropriately (Ruevini, 1975; Tolsdorf, 1976). Because family members often comprise the largest portion of the older person's support network, the worker can best help clients by involving them in long-term care service provision.

Much has been written about blending family help with formal resource systems (Sussman, 1977). How can this blending be accomplished best in order to benefit the older client? First, the family can be used to "link" the elderly client and other resources (Silverman & Brahce, 1979). The family may be used as a liaison between the older client and the service provider, if the client so desires. In the case of Mrs. Lane, the social worker (at Mrs. Lane's request) first met with the daughters to give information about the nursing facility. The daughters then prepared their mother by giving her information about the facility.

Formal Support

For the practitioner providing long-term care services within the community, numerous resources exist (Kamerman & Kahn, 1976). These resources include meals on wheels, homemaker-home health aid services, telephone reassurance, friendly visiting (volunteers), senior centers, information referral centers, and congregate meals. Often, information concerning these services is available from an adult service worker employed by the county welfare department or from the area council on aging.

For elderly persons living within an institutional long-term care setting, formal and informal resources can include services within as well as outside the institution. For example, meeting clients' needs may require the service provider to develop resources that can be available to present and future clients. How can this be accomplished? The activities director in the long-term care facility can make contact with a local high school home economics class and request that students, when they are studying the family life cycle, volunteer to visit persons at the facility. Visits from young students to elderly persons who do not have grand-children nearby can add a positive dimension to their emotional functioning. Social workers in long-term care facilities may also need to work in consultation with community mental health professionals for difficulties their clients are experiencing. Church groups can be asked to take elderly residents to church and then home for dinner before returning them to the nursing facility.

Merging Social Network and Formal Support

In the case described in Exhibit 7–1, Mrs. Lane had an active relationship with her family. The social worker at the nursing facility recognized, however, that Mrs. Lane did not want to be totally dependent on the family for her emotional support. The worker also recognized the wisdom of helping Mrs. Lane make a successful transition from the community to the nursing facility. The use of Mrs. Lane's acquaintances from church helped her through a time that might have been difficult. This experience also exemplified for Mrs. Lane the idea that residency in a long-term care facility does not have to mean the end to existing friendships; rather, it can strengthen them. In the case of Mrs. Lane, the social network that the social worker used was already in existence. Of course, service providers can develop and contribute to the social networks of their long-term care clients.

After Mrs. Lane moved to the facility, her family continued to shop with her for necessities and to launder the items she did not entrust to the nursing home laundry. Conclusions drawn from consultation with long-term care facility profes-sionals have revealed that families are most likely to continue active involvement with their older, institutionalized members when they feel they have a function to perform. That function can involve material, social, emotional or other support. For Mrs. Lane, the active involvement of her family provided her with some autonomy from the nursing facility. In the same way, her relationship with her friends allowed more functional dependence on both her family and the facility.

Another resource frequently available to the service provider is the older client. To meet their needs, elderly clients can often become active team members with their families and the formal resources that serve them. An example is a situation in a small midwestern community in which several elderly clients complained about the lack of an available person to contact them on a regular basis. These clients were concerned that when they encountered a physical problem, they might not receive help for several days. Some of these persons were receiving long-term care services, which facilitated their ability to remain in their own homes. The practitioner asked the clients and their families whether they would be willing to become involved in the development of a telephone reassurance system for the community. They accepted the invitation and supplied names of other older persons and family members who might be willing to become involved. The practitioner contacted these persons, who developed a board of directors and attended the first meeting. Subsequently, the older persons and their families developed the telephone reassurance line.

Institutionalized older persons maintain a greater sense of competency and are more likely to retain the ability to meet their needs in the future when they are given responsibility for meeting some of their own needs. There are numerous ways in which this can be accomplished. For example, professionals within institutions can involve older residents and their families by inviting them to serve on policy and planning committees. Given financial and nutritional guidelines, older residents and their families can be asked to develop menus for the facility. Obviously, the more resources older people have, the less dependent they are on any one relationship and the more power they have in their interactions with others. Appropriately matching resources to needs is successful when the family and the older clients are involved as resources.

Coordination of Service Delivery

Various persons may be involved in determining and carrying out services to be provided to older persons. If practitioners, families, and older clients are to work together successfully in providing services to the elderly, their work must be coordinated. Services to the elderly are often disorganized and uncoordinated (Friedman & Kaye, 1979; Bradshaw, Brandenburg, Basham, & Ferguson, 1980). Attention to the strengths and the weaknesses of each helping party enhances maximization of the benefits of sharing service tasks. For example, a family may have few financial resources with which to support an elderly member, but it may have time to help that member with shopping and cleaning. In this case, the service provider could investigate resources that meet the financial needs of the client. Fischer (1978) suggests that various roles for the social worker include "clinical/behavior change role," "consultant/educator role," and "broker/advocate role." In addition to the service provider enacting several roles, the family and the older person could carry out roles often filled by the practitioner. Consequently, the service provider could tap the instrumental or "broker/advocate" role to ensure that the client receives necessary resources, while the client's family could carry out the more affective "clinical/behavior change" role.

The case example (Exhibit 7–1) illustrates the manner in which a practitioner can work with the client's support system to coordinate services and to ensure that needed services are provided. Mrs. Sanders requested the family to take over some of the instrumental tasks for Mrs. Lane, while she saw that the nursing home carried out others. In the same way, Mrs. Sanders and family members both provided some affective services to Mrs. Lane. Duplication of tasks and gaps in service can be avoided by regular conferences with other employees of the facility, with family members, and with the older person. In these conferences, discussion of the elderly person's needs and the way those needs are being met is productive. Also, it is helpful to persons providing services for meeting needs to talk about the stresses they experience and their satisfaction with the tasks they have completed. Through dealing with the specific services provided and by establishing a forum in which the providers and the recipients can discuss the helping process, the professional coordinating services can see that the older person's needs are successfully met.

Whatever the division of tasks between service provider and the family member may be, it is vital for the provider to be a responsible advocate for the older client. In so doing, the provider becomes a case manager, ensuring that needs are met by various resources.

Dealing with Barriers to Service Delivery

A problem the service provider often encounters when working with the elderly is the difficulties between the clients and their social systems. The long-term care professional is likely to be called upon to deal with stressful relationships between older clients and their families. The service provider has several tasks to complete when a stressful situation becomes apparent. First, the provider must see that the needs of the elderly person are met and that problematic family relationships do not interfere with service delivery. Second, the provider can help the family deal with the difficulty it is experiencing.

The first task, ensuring service provision, can be completed through case coordination, as discussed above. The service provider can support family help-giving in the face of conflict, and so enable the older client to receive the resources the family has committed itself to provide.

The second task, helping the family to overcome stressful relationships, can again be dealt with by utilizing the recommendations suggested above. A family in conflict requires resources to deal with that conflict. Both the family and the aged persons can be active participants in securing those resources, even though the resource involves counseling services, self-help groups, or clarification of difficulties and tasks under the direction of the service provider.

CONCLUSION

This chapter has focused on recommendations for long-term care providers working with older persons and their families. Recommendations for practice include (1) assessment of the client's social environment so that service provision is correctly targeted and relationship difficulties are successfully handled; (2) utilization of appropriate resources so that practitioner, family, and client successfully share in the service delivery process; (3) case management to allow for appropriate delegation and delivery of shared services; and (4) working with barriers to service delivery to ensure that extended family problems do not hinder services and to facilitate the resolution of family problems.

REFERENCES

Bradshaw, B.R., Brandenburg, C., Basham, J., & Ferguson, E.A. (1980). Barriers to community-based long-term care. *Journal of Gerontological Social Work, 2*, 185–198.

Fischer, J. (1978). *Effective casework practice: An eclectic approach.* New York: McGraw Hill.

Friedman, S.R., & Kaye, L.W. (1979). Homecare for the frail elderly: Implications for an interactional relationship. *Journal of Gerontological Social Work, 2*, 109–123.

Greene, V.L., & Monahan, D.J. (1982). The impact of visitation on patient well-being in nursing homes. *The Gerontologist, 22*, 418–423.

Hartman, A. (1981). The family: A central focus for practice. *Social Work, 26*, 7–13.

Hook, W.F., Sobal, J., & Oak, J.C. (1982). Frequency of visitation in nursing homes: Patterns of contact across the boundaries of total institutions. *The Gerontologist, 22*, 424–428.

Kamerman, S.B., & Kahn, A.J. (1976). *Social services in the United States: Policies and programs.* Philadelphia: Temple University Press.

Koff, T.H. (1982). *Long-term care: An approach to serving the frail elderly.* Boston: Little, Brown & Co.

Lowy, L. (1979). *Social work with the aging: The challenge and promise of the later years.* New York: Harper & Row.

Noelker, L., & Harel, Z. (1978). Predictors of well-being and survival among institutionalized aged. *The Gerontologist, 18*, 562–567.

O'Brien, J.E., & Wagner, D.L. (1980). Help seeking by the frail elderly: Problems in network analysis. *The Gerontologist, 20*, 78–83.

Rathbone-McCuan, E. (1976). Geriatric day care: A family perspective. *The Gerontologist, 16*, 517–521.

Ruevini, U. (1975). Network intervention with a family in crisis. *Family Process, 14*, 193–203.

Shanas, E. (1979a). Social myth as hypothesis: The case of the family relations of old people. *The Gerontologist, 19*, 3–9.

Shanas, E. (1979b). The family as a social support system in old age. *The Gerontologist, 19*, 169–174.

Silverman, A.G., & Brahce, C.I. (1979). As parents grow older: An intervention model. *Journal of Gerontological Social Work, 2*, 77–85.

Spasoff, R.A., Kraus, A.S., Beattie, E.J., Holden, D., Lawton, J.S., Rodenburg, M., & Woodcock, G.W. (1978). A longitudinal study of elderly residents of long-stay institutions. *The Gerontologist, 18*, 281–292.

Sussman, M.B. (1977). Family bureaucracy and the elderly individual: An organizational/linkage perspective. In E. Shanas & M.B. Sussman (Eds.), *Family, bureaucracy and the elderly.* Durham, NC: Duke University Press.

Tolsdorf, C.C. (1976). Social networks, support, and coping: An exploratory study. *Family Process, 15*, 407–417.

Chapter 8

Support for the Impaired Elderly: A Challenge for Family Care-Givers

Carla Masciocchi, Adria Thomas, and Tamerra Moeller

The proportion of the elderly in the population is increasing. With advanced age, comes an increased vulnerability to chronically disabling diseases and the attendant need for long-term support. Irrespective of the availability of formal services, which ebb and flow, the provision of care falls primarily on the informal support system. More specifically, it is the family who provides the bulk of home care services to the impaired aged. Despite the devolution of care-giving to kin, families are not socialized to assume the role of care-giver and are ill-equipped to manage the emotional and physical requirements of such a role. Families experience periods of disequilibrium and growth as they respond to changed circumstances among their members. New sets of demands may shift a relatively balanced system of relationships into disequilibrium, which requires transformation of the members' functions. During these periods of transition, families often face crises as they adapt to new roles and expectations.

The period in the family life cycle in which an elder is unable to maintain an independent existence presents such a crisis to a family—i.e., for the impaired person and for other family members. Adult children may take a dependent parent into their home and become the care-giver to that parent. Whether care is provided in the household or from a separate residence, a redefinition of roles for the elder, for the focal care-giver, and for other family members is necessary. Adult children, who may be in the process of accommodating to their lessened parenting role, must relinquish their more independent position to reenter a care-giving situation. Spouses again need to share the care-giver with a dependent family member. Dependent children still in the home may have to adjust to the decreased availability of their parents or may themselves assume care-giving functions. Siblings of the caretaker and extended family members may be called upon to support the care-giving family, initiating new interactions. These changes disrupt the homeostasis of the family and challenge the system to modify itself.

In this chapter, the potential consequences to families as they adapt to their roles as providers of care is explored. The provision of support by families to their impaired elderly relatives is illustrated through studies conducted at the University of Pennsylvania. In addition, extant services to meet the needs of the caring family are discussed.

PROJECTED POPULATION AND NEEDS OF THE ELDERLY

Major shifts in population age patterns during the twentieth century have significantly affected the configuration of families, especially the generational constellation and concomitant role expectations. Of signal importance is the fact that the American population is growing notably older. The number of the elderly (defined as 65 years of age and older) has grown dramatically since 1900, and represents a larger share of the total population for each succeeding decade. Not only has the older population grown from 3.1 million in 1900 to 25.5 million in 1980; but proportionally, older Americans represented 11.3 percent of the total population—nearly 300 percent greater than their proportional representation at the turn of the century. Moreover, the older population is expected to increase by 30 percent, to at least 32 million, over the next 20 years. The oldest members of this aging population, those 85 years and older, are growing even faster than the total aged population; more than doubling over the last 20 years, this group is projected to increase at least twofold by the year 2000 (Special Committee on Aging, U.S. Senate, 1982).

With survival to old age comes greater vulnerability, however, to such degenerative diseases as heart disease, stroke, and cancer. Moreover, the incidence and prevalence of chronic mental disorders among the aged is high. Significantly, aging is often associated with progressive mental deficiency (Butler & Lewis, 1977). Organic brain disorders affect over 3 million elderly Americans, one-third of whom are afflicted with severe forms (Special Committee on Aging, U.S. Senate, 1982). In addition, the President's Commission on Mental Health reported in 1979 that 18 to 25 percent of the elderly population manifest other significant mental health symptoms.

The prevalence of chronic disease also increases markedly with age. Of persons 65 years old and over living in noninstitutional arrangements, 85 percent report at least one chronic disease, and 46 percent (nearly twice as many as in the age category 45 to 64 years) report some limitation of normal activity related to chronic health conditions. The proportion of the elderly who are severely limited rises as the population grows older; almost one-third (31%) of the "old-old" are totally unable to carry on one or more major activities (Federal Council on Aging, 1981). The national average of 108 restricted-activity days and 47 bed-disability days for the noninstitutionalized elderly who are most severely functionally limited illustrates the extent of the support required by this group (National Center for Health Statistics, 1981).

In terms of living arrangements, the elderly generally maintain independent households, either alone or with a spouse. Brody, Poulshock, and Masciocchi (1979) indicate that community elderly who are not disabled or only mildly disabled maintain living arrangements normative for the general population. On the other hand, research findings demonstrate that residence with children or other family members is often characteristic of those with serious disabilities requiring long-term support (Brody et al., 1978, 1979; Hess & Waring, 1978; Mindel, 1979). Most of this support emanates from the immediate family who provides substantial physical, emotional, social, and economic assistance to their chronically ill, impaired elderly relatives.

FAMILIES AS CARE-GIVERS

A significant body of research demonstrates that the bonds of kinship provide the major resources for the maintenance and support of the vulnerable elderly. The family is the primary and largest unit of service for the impaired aged; families serve as effective resources for the elderly and, in fact, are often exceedingly responsive to the critical needs of elderly persons (e.g., S.J. Brody, 1979; Shanas, 1979). Family aid to the elderly may range from periodic financial assistance to living arrangements that include an older person too ill or otherwise incapable of residing alone. The extent of dependence, primarily determined by functional disability, dictates the type of aid. The burden borne by the care-giving family generally becomes much greater as the impaired aged family member grows older and the dependency becomes multidimensional (Sainsbury & Grad de Alarcon, 1970; Berezin, 1972). Other variables, such as the nature of the disease conditions and disability and the identity of the care-giver, have been proposed as significantly associated with the determination of family care-giving roles. Isaacs (1971), for example, noted that the conditions found most difficult for family care-givers to bear are long-term mental disorders. Yet, significantly, statistics illustrate that approximately 80 percent of long-term health and social services to the elderly and the chronically ill are provided by family members (S.J. Brody, 1982; Special Committee on Aging, U.S. Senate, 1982).

It has been suggested that the most exacting care-giving roles and tasks primarily devolve on the female family members in a generationally linked family network—i.e., upon the middle-generation woman who may then be in a "squeezed" position of providing support to both younger and older kin (Blenkner, 1965; E. Brody, 1981). Moreover, a number of studies have found that the daughter, the daughter-in-law, or other female relative of the impaired aged family member provides the bulk of support (Blenkner, 1965; Isaacs, 1971;

Kahana and Levin, 1971; Sanford, 1975; Danis, 1978; Shanas, 1979). These observations are increasingly salient when linked with the realization that it is among this middle cohort of women that current societal demands for role change and adaptation may be having their greatest impact. If the trend toward increased numbers of women entering the labor force and heading single-parent homes continues, the future availability of these care-givers becomes more questionable. Current policy discussions on extension of the mandatory retirement age give rise to further questions about the family's capability to carry on substantial care-giving tasks.

Total family impact is expected; the "functional and personal losses experienced by the older members of the family and their changing roles initiate shifts in the qualitative emotional balance of relationships, as well as in the instrumental activities of the entire family" (E.M. Brody, 1974, p. 24). Minuchin (1974) has pointed out that responding to the demands from within and without, which chronic episodes and long-term care imply, requires a constant transformation and repositioning of family members in relation to one another; so both change and continuity are achieved.

FAMILY INVOLVEMENT IN PROVIDING CARE

Studies conducted in the late 1970s by researchers at the University of Pennsylvania demonstrated that the presence of the spouse and the living children was a critical factor that allowed elderly persons, despite serious physical impairment, to remain in the community (see Chapter 9 for further evidence). A pilot study was undertaken to identify variables that controlled the placement of chronically disabled elderly in the long-term care system. The study population consisted of institutional residents and community respondents who were recipients of a variety of community-based services. Results of the study indicated that placement of the elderly was not solely conditioned by age, functional level, or economic status; the critical controlling variable was the living arrangement available to the disabled older person. In fact, the entire subsample of seriously disabled community respondents resided with spouse or children. In turn, the major determinant of the living arrangement was an evironmental support network in which the major service givers were family (Brody et al., 1977, 1978).

This pilot study was then replicated in a survey of the chronically ill elderly population in an eight-county health system area (HSA) in Pennsylvania. In the expansion concluded in 1979, the findings of the previous study were confirmed when a considerably larger sample of respondents was drawn from the active caseloads of area agencies on aging (AAA) and home health agencies (HHA). This study illustrated the significant role that near kin play in providing assistance to their ill, elderly relatives, in terms of self-maintenace and instrumental activities (Brody et al., 1979).

More specifically, when attention was focused on community respondents who were functionally impaired in one or more activities, the data indicated that almost everyone who required assistance on any Activities of Daily Living (ADL) or Instrumental Activities of Daily Living (IADL) received it. The exceptions were miniscule, one here and one there. On the ADL items, the critical providers of assistance to AAA clients were spouse, children, and agency workers. Spouse and children emerged as the major source of support for HHA clients when ADL items were viewed as a composite. Home health aides did not figure in heavily as a central source of assistance in personal care—with the possible exception of bathing, in which equivalent numbers of agency workers and immediate family provided the requisite assistance.

Siblings were an inconsequential factor in providing support. One might speculate that siblings were in a similar age cohort and so might have themselves been afflicted with chronic illnesses or disabilities. Based on the data obtained in this study, grandchildren and other relatives participated in care-giving to some extent, but, clearly, they were not significant sources of help. These data suggest that relatives beyond the nuclear family assume minor responsibilities in the provision of care to their elderly relatives.

In terms of the IADL items (in which significantly more community residents required assistance than was the case for ADL items), the categories of critical providers were again spouse, children, and agency workers for AAA clients, and spouse and children for the HHA subsample. Siblings, grandchildren, and other relatives did not enter into the calculations of major sources of support. One distinct difference between care-givers in ADL and IADL activities was the greater reliance by the AAA subsample on friends for assistance in shopping.

In addition to identifying their network of support, respondents were asked to indicate the hours of assistance received per week from the various categories of helpers. Spouses and children devoted a significant bulk of time to care-giving. Spouses of AAA clients spent a median of 9 hours providing assistance in ADL; spouses of HHA respondents contributed a median 12 hours per week of care-giving time. Children of AAA clients reportedly participated in care-giving tasks associated with personal care for 7 hours per week, on the average; the offspring of home health respondents provided assistance for 4 hours per week. All other categories of family care-givers (including siblings, grandchildren, and other relatives) contributed, as a median, approximately 2 hours of support per week to their disabled elderly relatives.

Similarly, spouse and children spent considerable time assisting the elderly disabled respondents in instrumental activities. AAA clients received a median of ten hours of help per week from spouse and seven hours of assistance from children. On the average, HHA clients were recipients of four hours and two hours of care from their offspring and spouse, respectively. The remaining categories of family care-givers assisted the elderly in instrumental activities for two hours per week.

Although respondents who lived alone were significantly less impaired than the group that lived with family or in other congregate arrangements, those who required help on ADL and IADL items were—without exception—recipients of aid. In terms of the configuration of family support, children provided critical elements of assistance to those living alone, while the elderly who were married were found to have both spouses and children as important care-givers. In addition, friends were more significant as care-givers for the elderly living independently. Children and friends expended the greatest amounts of care-giving time; although, consistently, less time was spent providing assistance to respondents who lived alone than to those who lived with others. This difference could be attributed to the higher functional status of those living alone and to the inconvenience of providing help from the base of another household.

In sum, 21 percent of the total sample were severely or totally impaired. Nearly 80 percent of this group lived with family; the remainder lived alone. All community residents who were seriously disabled reported that near kin provided the bulk of care-giving; agency workers were a secondary source of assistance. In addition, analysis of the data on care-giving revealed that distant kin, in the main, did not function as primary care-givers and, for the most part, were an inconsequential factor in the care-giving network. Even those severely disabled elderly who lived alone had a strong network of family support as shown from the data on time spent in care-giving—from 7 to 40 hours per week. Moreover, it appears from these data that when impairment is confined to instrumental activities, friends are a key source of aid; however, as the elderly become dependent on personal care, friends drop off as important care-givers.

CARE-GIVING AND FAMILY DYNAMICS

Data refute the myth that families abandon their aged relatives. Numerous studies attest to the fact that most families provide substantial support to their elderly members (E.M. Brody, 1967, 1977, 1981; Cantor, 1981; Kerckhoff, 1965; Shanas, 1979; Sussman, 1965; Treas, 1975; Weber & Blenkner, 1975). Recently, gerontologists have turned their attention to investigating the family dynamics of coping with the care-giving role; yet, little is known about the experience of families who care for the impaired elderly over time.

Stress

Although it is generally assumed that emotional decrements are related to the stress associated with both the impaired person's dependency role and the family's care-giving role, it is also conceivable that stress may have positive effects. The caring environment may function as the medium through which affective bonds among family members are enhanced and strengthened. When effective coping mechanisms are employed to meliorate the stress engendered by care-giving, families may view the success in managing the situation as a significant factor in contributing to cohesion and solidarity within the family unit. The care-giving experience can be a source of emotional gratification for family members.

In contrast, given the value that society places on independence, the old person's loss of self-mastery and the resulting dependence on others for care can have negative psychic consequences. For family members assuming the care of the older person, the loss of freedom, mobility, energy, and time can produce stress and may result in psychological problems for the care-givers individually and the family collectively. The burden of caring for an impaired aged relative can add significantly to other types of problems that families more normatively experience; inability to manage the elevated level of stress may result in pathological symptomatology and behavior among family care-givers. Similarly, chronic illness or disability and its concomitant dependency can produce depression or other types of psychological decrements in the impaired aged person.

Once self-mastery is lost in the context of chronic illness (unlike acute illness), the need for care may be long-term and indefinite. Likewise, the response of care-givers to the expressed need may be equally long-term and indefinite. Particularly for the family, this situation can produce a sense of entrapment. Perception of problems, the scope and the intensity of stress, and the family's responses may vary over time, reflecting in part previously established behavioral patterns.

Most of the vanguard studies on families and the consequences of care-giving emanated from Great Britain. In their longitudinal study of familial burden in caring for a mentally impaired relative, Hoenig and Hamilton (1966) bifurcated burden into two distinct but interacting types—subjective and objective. Subjective burden was viewed as the mental outlook and feelings of the family concerning the extent to which the patient's illness was burdensome. Objective burden was defined as aberrant behavior of the impaired person and adverse effects on identifiable family resources (e.g., income loss and deteriorated health status). The authors found that 80 percent of the families experienced some type of burden, a finding replicated by Sainsbury and Grad de Alarcon (1970). Examination of the objective burden specifically revealed that the patient's illness adversely affected two-thirds of the family households, most frequently in terms of consequent disruption in family routine and physical strain on family members. The most burdensome behaviors manifested by the impaired person were physical or nursing care needs, followed by excessive demands for companionship.

Sanford (1975) retrospectively studied families with an aged relative residing in a hospital geriatric unit in London. Family members principally responsible for home support of the impaired person were interviewed to determine which problems required resolution before the elderly person could be restored to the family living arrangement. Problems encountered by the care-giver fell into three groups: the behavior patterns of the dependent person, the care-giver's own limitations in the care-giving role, and environmental and social conditions. The results indicated that the most stressful problems were those associated with the behavior of the dependent person. Nocturnal disturbance, a frequently cited problem, generated the most stress and was poorly tolerated by care-givers. Interestingly, although similar percentages of the elderly were incontinent of urine or feces, a significant difference existed in the proportion of families able to tolerate these two conditions: almost twice as many family supporters reported stress related to fecal incontinence. Mobility limitations of the impaired aged also caused significant stress for care-givers. Finally, over half of the care-givers reported anxiety or depression as their major limitation, and these were usually attributed to caring for the dependent person. Restriction of social participation was also cited as a critical problem area for care-givers; findings were similar to those reported by Bergmann, Foster, Justice, and Matthews (1978).

Case studies have illustrated that families, when exposed to the continuing burden of caring for a severely ill parent, pursued a pattern of behavior that reestablished family splits and alignments that predated the illness of the parent (Miller & Harris, 1967). Savitsky and Sharkey (1972) and Simos (1973) noted the same phenomenon. When a crisis brings parents and children together, the latter's capacity to be depended on by the parents is tested; likewise, the aged person's capacity to handle feelings of dependency is also tested. Savitsky and Sharkey report significant levels of stress for the impaired aged and their care-giving children as a result of the reversed dependency relationships. The authors use the term *role reversal*, a misnomer, because the symbolic role of parent is not abrogated and the affective bonds, although they may be different, are nonetheless present; however, the *de facto* role of parent in relation to the care-giving child does change at important levels. Shellhase and Shellhase (1972) make the additional point that the impaired person and the family are ill-prepared to assume their new roles. Just as the old person is not socialized to dependency in later life, appropriate role models are not available to families functioning as care-givers to their impaired older relatives. The significant ambiguity surrounding these changes in terms of role expectations and the absence of a clear socialization process can induce considerable stress for the dependent person and the supportive family members.

Recent studies have generally confirmed earlier findings and have been consistent in terms of the types of stress that accompany care-giving. The presence and the degree of emotional, physical, and financial strains appear to be associated with the personal and the situational characteristics of the care-giver. Most pervasive is emotional stress (Cantor, 1981; Horowitz, 1981; Johnson, 1979) whereas financial burden is least often reported to be a major source of strain (Cicirelli, 1980; Horowitz, 1981; Horowitz & Shindelman, 1981). Much of the emotional stress emanates from the care-giver's isolation, which results in decreased opportunities for friendships, interrupted participation in community activities, and infrequent contact with persons who are acting in similar roles (Archbold, 1979; Crossman, London, & Barry, 1981; Fengler & Goodrich, 1979; Gibson, 1980b). The lack of these social supports and contacts decreases the care-giver's emotional resilience and lowers morale (Archbold, 1980). The emotional consequences of isolation are accentuated as the care-giver's interactions are increasingly confined to an impaired relative who has a reduced capacity for intimacy and companionship because of cognitive confusion or other communicative disorders. Moreover, the care-giver is unable to grieve for such an impaired relative who, though significantly changed, remains alive (Fengler & Goodrich, 1979; Crossman et al., 1981).

Although almost two-thirds of the care-givers in Cantor's study (1981) cited substantial emotional stress and nearly half (47%) experienced considerable physical strain in caring for their frail elderly relative, the burden was found to fall differentially on various care-giving groups. For example, child care-givers were less likely to report great financial burden and reported feeling less socially isolated than did spouses providing care. Although both groups experienced great emotional strain, spouses were more likely to report physical and financial strain, largely because of their own age, health, and income limitations. Corroborative evidence of the physical strain of care-giving is offered by Crossman and his associates (1981), who found not only that extant health problems were exacerbated but that an increased predisposition to a number of physically disabling conditions was evidenced by spouse care-givers.

Adjustment

In terms of adjustment, care-givers have consistently reported a circumscribed lifestyle: restrictions on their own leisure activities, personal wants, and freedom of choice about time expenditure (Cantor, 1981; Zarit, Reever, & Bach-Peterson, 1980). Role overload is almost inevitable as the care-giver attempts to balance the responsibilities of care-giving with demands from other family members and the care-giver's own personal needs, which may include an occupational role (Archbold, 1979). Although the full impact of care-giving on the care-giver's occupational role has not been extensively investigated, Cantor (1981) found the negative effects to be minimal. Whether the job functions as a counterforce to the social isolation frequently referenced by care-givers or as respite from care-giving responsibilities is not clear from the studies. The effects of care-giving on the relationships with the immediate family are also debatable. Cantor (1981) found familial relationships to be relatively uninfluenced, but Horowitz (1981) noted stress in this area, although the strains were more often with siblings than with the provider's spouse and children. Conversely, interactions with the family have been shown in some cases to meliorate the feelings of burden experienced by the primary care-giver (Zarit et al., 1980).

In summary, then, the studies reveal disparate conclusions about the positive and negative effects of care-giving on the family. Clinical observations and research findings document that stress can occur and pathology may manifest itself in family members faced with the responsibility of caring for an impaired elderly member (Hoenig & Hamilton, 1966; Baer et al., 1970; Sainsbury & Grad de Alarcon, 1970; Isaacs, 1971; Cath, 1972; Savitsky & Sharkey, 1972; Sanford, 1975; Zarit et al., 1980). Evidence from research and clinical practice suggests, however, that care-giving can also be a positive experience that enhances and cements family ties (Blenkner, 1965; Cath, 1972; Horowitz & Shindelman, 1981). These conflicting reports of positive and negative effects on family care-givers are not surprising, given the paucity and the limitations of actual research on the care-giving process (Robinson & Thurnher, 1979).

The importance of these statistics for service support lies in their indication of probable vulnerability in family functioning; for although families do, in fact, take on major care-giving responsibilities for their disabled aged members, the crisis nature of nursing home intake and the extent of the stress families often evidence before and during the placement decision point up the extremes to which they are willing to go to support their older members. Thus, the family is coming to be recognized as the appropriate focal point for social or clinical intervention (Dobrof & Litwak, 1977; Blazer, 1978; Lebowitz, 1978). Organized community services are extended almost exclusively to the elderly alone; few, if any, service configurations focus on family need under circumstances of care-giving for an aged member. There are no legislative or reimbursement policies that enable such family services to be offered, although the need for and the efficacy of family and group-oriented counseling, for example, has been clearly demonstrated (Michaels, 1977).

A stated goal of public policy is to retain the impaired elderly person in the community as long as possible. Inasmuch as continuing and unmeliorated stress can be a significant factor in the decision to institutionalize, it is necessary to determine not only the types of problems experienced by family care-givers but also the points at which the stress becomes intolerable and the coping mechanisms become ineffective so that institutionalization becomes a major consideration. Elaine Brody (1977) underlines this point:

> Studies of the paths leading to institutional care have shown that placing an elderly relative is the last, rather than the first, resort of families. In general, they have exhausted all other alternatives, endured severe personal, social, and economic stress in the process, and made the final decision with the utmost reluctance. (pp. 113–114)

SOME INTERVENTIONS FOR FAMILY CARE-GIVERS

These personal, social and economic stresses can be mitigated through programs such as support groups, respite care, home health services, housing, and
transportation. Although most community-based programs developed to complement the informal support of the family have largely been designed to assist with
personal care and homemaking tasks (Callahan, Diamond, Gield, & Morris, 1980), support and educational groups centered on the broader issues of aging
and care-giving are now offered by a variety of community organizations.

Support Groups

Support groups have been shown to counteract the isolation cited by many care-
givers. In most such groups, participants experience psychological relief by
sharing common difficulties, engaging in mutual problem-solving, and receiving
recognition and support from other group members (Crossman et al., 1981;
Gibson, 1980b; Hausman, 1979; Lazarus, Stafford, Cooper, Cohler, & Dysken, 1981). Members are able to express fears about their own aging as they
encounter the indignities of mental and physical deterioration in aging parents.
Support groups offer an acceptable outlet for the anger, the frustration, and the
guilt felt by care-givers who are confronted with their impaired relative's increasing dependence and the necessity of altered plans, such as the caretaker's own
retirement options (Lazarus et al., 1981; Robinson & Thurnher, 1979). In addition, these groups provide a supportive environment for exploring the difficult
decision to institutionalize one's relative (Hartford & Parsons, 1982).

Support groups are also a source of instrumental aid to the care-giver. Members
can learn to evaluate their own capacity to care for a disabled relative as well as to
recognize and to accept realistic goals for themselves and the dependent family
member (Lazarus et al., 1981). It is important for the family to acknowledge that
gains achieved by the disabled older person are often incremental and modest.
Many families report feelings of frustration in their attempts to converse with a
relative who suffers from a severe organic impairment. Similarly, ambivalence
toward health professionals may become marked during particularly stressful
periods of care, and families often express difficulty in communicating assertively
and effectively with physicians and other professionals (Fengler & Goodrich, 1979; Hausman, 1979). Support groups serve as a means of learning new
modes of communication.

Respite Care

The daily care required by many impaired elderly persons and the care-giver's
subsequent need for relief from the ensuing physical demands and emotional

isolation can be mitigated through respite care (Archbold, 1980; Blazer, 1978; Crossman et al., 1981; Fengler & Goodrich, 1979). Respite care, which can assume multiple forms, is frequently mentioned by families as a primary incentive to their continued involvement in care-giving (Howells, 1980). This type of relief can be provided through various sources: day-care centers, geriatric day hospitals, nursing homes, or other facilities specially designed for the frail elderly (Gibson, 1980b). Families can utilize this service for periods ranging from overnight to weekends or to more extended stays. A particularly advantageous arrangement is one in which the day-care center staff also serves as the respite-care staff. In this case, a family may become familiar with staff members on a daily basis before a longer respite period (Crossman et al., 1981). Families participating on an intermittent basis in such temporary institutional care report a greater determination and encouragement to continue caring for their relatives at home (Howells, 1980).

Such day-care arrangements are not suitable, however, for those elderly who are bedridden or too disabled to participate. Persons who require considerable preparation to go outside of their living quarters also present the need for other alternatives. Home care is such an alternative. Families may receive a few hours each week, overnight sitting, or a certain number of hours each month which they may utilize as best fits their needs. The care-givers' concern for the quality of care received by impaired relatives has been an impetus to use registered nurses in respite care. Crossman and associates (1981) found that provision of respite care in the home by a registered nurse, regardless of the older person's impairment level, had several advantages. A nurse could detect health problems among the care-givers, could provide them with the confidence to leave their impaired relatives, and (through repeated interaction) could act as a liaison with the formal health care system. Care-givers have frequently expressed frustration in maintaining contact with formal health services when the impaired relative is largely bedridden (Archbold, 1980).

Education

Education constitutes another mode of assistance to family care-givers. Programs are needed to acquaint families with the special problems associated with care-giving. Although not numerous, various types of educational activities are currently offered, primarily under the aegis of community mental health centers, educational institutions, and long-term-care facilities. The content of these programs varies according to the focus of the sponsoring agency and ranges from information dissemination to skill development. Informational sessions may be built around disease progression, access to the formal support systems, or eligibility requirements for entitlement programs. The central thrust of skill-building courses may be the exploration and the development of coping mechanisms or applied care-giving skills. The target audiences of educational programs should be broadened to include all categories of health professionals and informal care-givers. As the family's initial contact with the health care system, primary care physicians are an appropriate focal group for continuing education on support of families under conditions of care-giving.

Home Health Services

Historically, in-home service programs were designed to support mothers and their young children, particularly under the auspice of The Maternal and Child Health Care Act. It was only with the advent of Medicare, Medicaid, and the Older Americans Act that home health care programs began to focus on the older person. Consistent with all other programs, the needs of family members providing support were virtually ignored, and, consequently, home care services lacked the comprehensiveness, the flexibility, and the overall adequacy to deal with the complex and varied problems faced by these care-givers (Gibson, 1980a). Transportation services have been subject to similar limitations. Although the older person may need transportation for health care, such services could be expanded to benefit family care-givers. For instance, a sibling may be better able to provide respite care if transport funds are made available (Gross-Andrew & Zimmer, 1978). To the extent that transportation and home care services help the impaired person they *de facto* assist the family. Inasmuch as these services are extant, large capital outlays are not necessary for program development; legislative changes in eligibility requirements are needed to include families.

Residential Options

Another family-oriented service involves the current development of residential options. Housing allowances or low interest loans would permit families to remodel or build extra rooms if additional space is needed to care for an impaired relative. Public housing with annexes that allow families to provide services yet maintain some privacy has been suggested, as well as prefabricated mini-houses that can be removed when they are no longer needed (Gibson, 1980b). Similarly, zoning ordinances must take into account the increased need for the care of impaired older persons by their families and must allow for the construction of an additional unit onto an existing family dwelling. For housing and other service options, consideration must be given to the constellation of the family it is meant to serve—e.g., the elderly couple alone, the family in which the adult child care-givers may be disabled, or the family whose members are geographically dispersed.

DIRECTIONS FOR THE FUTURE

The belief that families relegate the care of their impaired elderly to others has been dispelled through gerontological research; yet the myth of family abandonment persists among the general populace and the policymakers. The tenacity of this fiction is evident in current legislative concern that the provision of formal services will reduce family participation in care-giving. The evidence does not support such concern. Preliminary studies have indicated no weakening of family involvement with the introduction of formal services, although this has yet to be tested definitively. Families provide the bulk of care to their impaired relatives, often at great emotional, physical, and financial expense to themselves.

A major thrust of this chapter has been to create an awareness of the need for instrumental and emotional support of families in their care-giving role. The existence of a responsive back-up array of formal services can enable families to gain a sense of security in, and minimize the stress of, care-giving. The creation of such supports requires a restructuring of government programs to make them more relevant to the needs of the caring family. In many western societies, there are elaborate provisions for family support. In the United States, only two federal programs directly furnish support to caring families: small subsidies provided through the Internal Revenue Service, and the provision of "aid and assistance" by the Veterans Administration. Additional federal supports could be achieved through the augmentation of SSI (Title XVI, SSA) to include family caretaker needs. Another option is the revision of Titles XVIII, XIX, Title III (AOA) and the block SSA grants to make families, as well as individual persons, eligible for services such as home health care, homemaker, day care, day hospital, respite, companion and escort. Housing, mental health, and rehabilitation services can also be made more responsive to the caring family's needs. The role of the acute-care hospital should be reevaluated so that the discharge process reflects the needs of both the impaired person and the family. Reducing barriers to existing services is another focus for action.

The dual approach of augmentation of resources and improved utilization of existing services would foster a supportive community climate for the family. Should a crisis arise in the family, instrumental and emotional support would be available and accessible. Most importantly, by helping families in the caring effort, the quality of their lives and that of the impaired elderly relative would be enhanced. To achieve these objectives, research is needed on the optimal combination of public and family responsibility. The long-term effects of interventions on the mental and physical well-being of the care-giver must also be examined. New policies, based on empirical evidence, are critical to meet the challenges faced by today's families.

REFERENCES

Archbold, P.G. (1979). Caregivers. *American Health Association, 5*(4), 61–62.

Archbold, P.G. (1980). Impact of parent caring on middle-aged offspring. *Journal of Gerontological Nursing, 6*(2), 78–85.

Baer, P.E., Morin, K., & Gaitz, C.M. (1970). Familial resources of elderly psychiatric patients. *Archives of General Psychiatry, 22*(4), 343–350.

Berezin, M.A. (1972). Psychodynamic considerations of aging and the aged: An overview. *American Journal of Psychiatry, 128*(12), 1483–1491.

Bergmann, K., Foster, E.M., Justice, A.W., & Matthews, V. (1978). Management of the demented elderly in the community. *International Journal of Psychiatry, 132,* 441–449.

Blazer, D. (1978). Working with the elderly patient's family. *Geriatrics, 33,* 117–118, 123.

Blenkner, M. (1965). Social work and family relationships in later life with some thoughts on filial maturity. In E. Shanas & G. Streib (Eds.), *Social structure and the family: Gerontological relations* (pp. 46–61). Englewood Cliffs, NJ: Prentice-Hall.

Brody, E.M. (1974). Aging and the family personality: A developmental view. *Family Process, 13*(1), 23–27.

Brody, E.M. (1967). Aging is a family affair. *Public Welfare, 25*(2), 129–31.

Brody, E.M. (1977). *Long term care of older people—A practical guide.* New York: Human Sciences Press.

Brody, E.M. (1981). "Women in the Middle" and family help to older people. *The Gerontologist, 21*(5), 471–480.

Brody, S.J. (1979, June). *Planning for the long-term support/care system: The array of services to be considered.* Philadelphia: Health Services Council.

Brody, S.J. (1982). The hospital role in providing health care to the elderly: Coordination with other community services. In *The hospital role in caring for the elderly: Leadership issues* (pp. 20–35). Chicago: Hospital Research and Educational Trust.

Brody, S.J., Poulshock, S.W., & Masciocchi, C. (1977, July). *Studies in chronic illness, disability and long term care: A pretest of a methodology* (Final Report). Harrisburg: Commonwealth of Pennsylvania, Department of Health, Department of Public Welfare.

Brody, S.J., Poulshock, S.W., & Masciocchi, C. (1979). *Studies in chronic illness, disability and long-term care: Pennsylvania health systems area IV* (Project Report). Harrisburg: Commonwealth of Pennsylvania, Department of Health, Department of Public Welfare.

Brody, S.J., Poulshock, S.W. & Masciocchi, C. (1978). The family caring unit: A major consideration in the long-term support system. *The Gerontologist, 18*(6), 556–561.

Butler, R.N. & Lewis, M.I. (1977). *Aging and mental health* (2nd ed). St. Louis: C.V. Mosby.

Callahan, J.J., Diamond, L.D., Gield, J.Z. & Morris, R. (1980, Winter). Responsibilities of families for their severely disabled elderly. *Health Care Financing Review, 1*(3), pp. 29–48.

Cantor, M.H. (1981, November). *Factors associated with strain among family, friends and neighbors caring for the frail elderly*. Paper presented at the Annual Scientific Meeting of the Gerontological Society of America, Toronto, Canada.

Cath, S. (1972). The institutionalization of a parent: A nadir of life. *Journal of Geriatric Psychiatry, 5*, 25–46.

Cicirelli, V.G. (1980, November). *Personal strains and negative feelings in adult children's relationships with elderly parents*. Paper presented at the Annual Scientific Meeting of the Gerontological Society of America, San Diego, CA.

Crossman, L., London, C., & Barry, C. (1981). Older women caring for disabled spouses: A model for supportive services. *The Gerontologist, 21*(5), 464–470.

Danis, B.G. (1978, November). *Stress in individuals caring for ill elderly relatives*. Paper presented at the 31st Annual Scientific Meeting of the Gerontological Society, Dallas, TX.

Dobrof, R., & Litwak, E. (1977). *Maintenance of family ties of long-term care patients: Theory and guide to practice*. (National Institute of Mental Health) Washington, DC: U.S. Government Printing Office.

Federal Council on the Aging. (1981). *The need for long term care: Information and issues* (DHHS Publication No. OHDS 81-20704). Washington, DC: U.S. Government Printing Office.

Fengler, A., & Goodrich, N. (1979). Wives of elderly disabled men: The hidden patients. *The Gerontologist, 19*(2), 175–183.

Gibson, M.J. (1980a). Family support for the elderly in international perspective: Part I. *Ageing International, 7*(3), 12–17.

Gibson, M.J. (1980b). Family support for the elderly in international perspective: Part II, policies and programs. *Ageing International, 7*(4), 13–19.

Gross-Andrew, S., & Zimmer, A.H. (1978). Incentives to families caring for disabled elderly: Research and demonstration project to strengthen the natural supports system. *Journal of Gerontological Social Work, 1*(2), 119–130.

Hartford, M.E., & Parsons, R. (1982). Groups with relatives of dependent older adults. *The Gerontologist, 22*(3), 394–398.

Hausman, C.P. (1979). Short-term counseling groups with elderly parents. *The Gerontologist, 19*(1), 102–107.

Hess, B.B., & Waring J.M. (1978). Changing patterns of aging and family bonds in later life. *The Family Coordinator, 27*, 303–314.

Hoenig, J., & Hamilton, M. (1966). Elderly psychiatric patients and the burden on the household. *Psychiatria et Neurologia, 152*(5), 281–93.

Horowitz, A. (1981, November). *Sons and daughters as caregivers to older parents: Differences in role performance and consequences*. Paper presented at the 34th Annual Scientific Meeting of the Gerontological Society of America, Toronto, Canada.

Horowitz, A., & Shindelman, L.W. (1981, November). Reciprocity and affection: Past influences on current caregiving. Paper presented at the 34th Annual Scientific Meeting of the Gerontological Society of America, Toronto, Canada.

Howells, D. (1980, November). Reallocating institutional resources: Respite care as a supplement to family care of the elderly. Paper presented at the 33rd Annual Scientific Meeting of the Gerontological Society of America, San Diego, CA.

Isaacs, B. (1971). Geriatric patients: Do their families care? *British Medical Journal, 4*, 282–286.

Johnson, C.L. (1979, November). Impediments to family supports to dependent elderly: An analysis of the primary caregivers. Paper presented at the Annual Scientific Meeting of the Gerontological Society of America, Washington, DC.

Kahana, R.J., & Levin, S. (1971). Aging and the conflict of generations. *Journal of Geriatric Psychiatry, 4*(2), 115–162.

Kerckhoff, A. (1965). Nuclear and extended family relationships: A normative and behavioral analysis. In E. Shanus & G. Streib (Eds.), *Social structure and the family: Generational relations.* Englewood Cliffs, NJ: Prentice-Hall.

Lazarus, L.W., Stafford, B., Cooper, K., Cohler, B., & Dysken, M. (1981). A pilot study of an Alzheimer patients' relatives discussion group. *The Gerontologist, 21*(4), 353–358.

Lebowitz, B.D. (1978). Old age and family functioning. *Journal of Gerontological Social Work, 1*(2), 111–118.

Michaels, F. (1977). *The effects of discussing grief, loss, death, and dying on depression levels in a geriatric outpatient therapy group.* Unpublished doctoral dissertation, Auburn University.

Miller, M., & Harris A. (1967). The chronically ill aged: Paradoxical patient-family behavior. *Journal of the American Geriatrics Society, 15*(5), 480–495.

Mindel, C.H. (1979). Multigenerational family households: Recent trends and implications for the future. *The Gerontologist, 19*(5), 456–463.

Minuchin, S. (1974). *Families and family therapy.* Cambridge: Harvard University Press.

National Center for Health Statistics. (1981). *Health characteristics of persons with chronic activity limitation: U.S. 1979* (DHHS Publication No. 82-1565). Washington: DC: U.S. Government Printing Office.

Robinson, B., & Thurnher, M. (1979). Taking care of aged parents: A family cycle transition. *The Gerontologist, 19*(6), 586–593.

Sainsbury, P., & Grad de Alarcon, J. (1970). The effects of community care on the family of the geriatric patient. *Journal of Geriatric Psychiatry, 4*(1), 23–41.

Sanford, J.R.A. (1975). Tolerance of debility in elderly dependents by supporters at home: Its significance for hospital practice. *British Medical Journal, 3,* 471–473.

Savitsky, E., & Sharkey, H. (1972). The geriatric patient and his family: Study of family interaction in the aged. *Journal of Geriatric Psychiatry, 5*(1), 3–19.

Shanas, E. (1979). The family as a social support system in old age. *The Gerontologist, 19*(2), 169–174.

Shellhase, L.J., & Shellhase, F.E. (1972). Role of the family in rehabilitation. *Social Casework, 53*(9), 544–550.

Simos, B. (1973). Adult children and their aging parents. *Social Work 18*(3), 78–85.

Special Committee on Aging, U.S. Senate. (1982). *Developments in aging: 1981.* Washington, DC: U.S. Government Printing Office.

Sussman, M.B. (1965). Relationships of adult children with their parents in the United States. In E. Shanas & G.F. Streib (Eds.), *Social structure and the family: Generational relations* (pp. 62–92). Englewood Cliffs, NJ: Prentice-Hall.

Treas, J. (1975). Aging and the family. In D.S. Woodruff and J.E. Birren (Eds.), *Aging: Scientific perspectives and social issues* (pp. 92–108). New York: Van Nostrand Reinhold.

Weber, R.E., & Blenkner, M. (1975). The social service perspective. In S. Sherwood (Ed.), *Long term care: Handbook for researchers, planners, and providers* (pp. 253–314). New York: Spectrum Publishers.

Zarit, S.H., Reever, K.E., & Bach-Peterson, J. (1980). Relatives of the impaired elderly: Correlates of feeling of burden. *The Gerontologist, 20*(6), 649–655.

Chapter 9

The Family, Public Policy, and Long-Term Care

Greg Arling and William J. McAuley

Complete independence is seldom a realistic or even desirable goal in old age, especially for the minority of older people who experience a loss in health or mental status. The chronically impaired elderly must learn to depend upon others for help in meeting some of the most basic needs of daily living. Having someone to depend upon, while avoiding excessive dependency, is the basis for well-being and personal autonomy in any stage of the life cycle, but particularly in old age. In most cases, the family is the major source of support for the older impaired person residing in the community.

In the past, those responsible for long-term-care policy have rarely given adequate attention to the importance of family members in the overall system of services (Lebowitz, 1979; Maddox, 1975; Shanas & Maddox, 1976). Long-term care policymakers only recently have suggested that formal services may be displacing, duplicating, or discouraging family care. The increasing interest in the role of the family in long-term care has been brought about by concerns about the cost and the appropriateness of institutionalization and about apparent shifts in the demography of the family and in the roles of family members (see Chapter 7 and Chapter 8).

The purpose of this chapter is to describe the role of the family in community long-term care for the impaired elderly. The authors add to the growing body of research in social gerontology that debunks the myths that families no longer provide care for their elders, that community agencies or other formal sources of care in the home replace or crowd out family care-givers, and that families dump their elders into nursing homes or other institutional settings. The chapter also describes the types of community care provided by family members and other sources, and examines the circumstances associated with the use of family care versus non-family assistance among the impaired elderly.

BACKGROUND

Extent of Family Care

A number of studies have shown that the elderly expect family members to step in and to provide help if they should become ill or disabled. The General Accounting Office study of older people in Cleveland, Ohio (Comptroller General of the United States, 1977) reported that 87 percent of the elderly had someone who would provide care to them as long as needed. Children were most frequently mentioned as the potential care-givers (42%); the next most frequent source was a spouse (27%). An additional 19 percent mentioned siblings and other relatives as the sources of care. Shanas and her associates (Shanas, Townsend, Wedderburn, Friis, Milhoj, & Stehouwer, 1968) found that between one-third and two-fifths of older persons living in communities reported they relied on their spouses in times of illness; an additional one-fifth to one-third relied on children and other relatives. An earlier investigation by Shanas (1961) indicated that approximately 95 percent of older persons had someone who felt responsible for them, and approximately 60 percent said they had a son or a daughter from whom they could receive help. Rosow (1967) reported strong expectations of reliance on family among older apartment residents in Cleveland, Ohio. His findings suggest, however, that the working class and those without nearby relatives are more likely to expect formal organizations or agencies to provide help in time of need.

Older people not only expect but receive assistance from the family when the need arises. Data from the General Accounting Office study in Cleveland suggest that over 90 percent of older people who receive personal care or have someone to check in regularly get this help from relatives or friends (Comptroller General of the United States, 1977). More than half of those receiving homemaker assistance, administrative and legal services, meal preparation, and continuous supervision rely upon family and friends for these forms of help. York and Calsyn (1977), in a study of nursing home applicants, found that families had been providing household and personal care for the majority of applicants before their nursing home applications. Morris (1975) cited evidence from a recent study that 75 percent of the elderly discharged from hospitals received follow-up care from relatives. Shanas (1979) reported from a nationwide study that spouses, children, and other relatives were the primary sources of help to the bedfast elderly residing in the community. The elderly who were not bedfast but had been ill in bed at some point during the year before the interview were also very likely to have received help from relatives.

Situations Affecting Family Care

Elders who become ill or impaired frequently move into the household with relatives (Murray, 1976). Studies of nursing home admissions suggest that it is not unusual for families to take in older persons before institutionalization and that the care provided by relatives may in many cases act to avoid or at least delay institutionalization (Miller & Harris, 1965; Townsend, 1965; York & Calsyn, 1977). In a comparison of chronically ill elderly in institutions and community settings, Brody and his associates (Brody, Poulshock, & Maschiocchi, 1978) reported that those elderly living with a spouse, child or other relative were able to remain outside institutions despite serious functional impairments. Wan and Weissert (1981) found that living alone and lack of availability of children or grandchildren was associated with higher rates of institutionalization among participants in an experimental study of geriatric day-care and homemaker services. They suggest that social-support networks may serve as buffers between physical decline and institutionalization.

What determines the use of family resources versus other sources of care? The prior research dealing with this question is sketchy and unclear. Cantor (1980) has suggested that the degree of dependence, which is associated with age, may influence the relative helping roles played by family and nonfamily sources. She notes that as age and dependency increase, the balance in care should shift toward greater involvement of the formal system.

Living arrangements, marital status, and the proximity of children can also be important factors in the relative distribution of help from family and nonfamily sources. As Streib and Beck (1980) have noted, the involvement of children and other family members in care-giving is usually less important among married elderly than among those who live alone. Stoller (1982), in an investigation of 753 older community residents, found that those living alone and those without living children were most likely to rely on help from nonfamily sources such as friends or neighbors. Elders who were married and living with their spouses in independent households reported heavy reliance upon their spouses for care during illnesses and emergencies. Rosow (1967) found that household living arrangements and having children nearby can influence the sources of help received. Those living with others tend to rely heavily upon household members in time of need. Additionally, having children nearby is associated with higher levels of help from offspring.

Weeks and Cuellar (1981), studying the helping networks of 1,139 older people in San Diego County, found that those living alone relied least on family members in times of need. Their results further indicate that ethnic factors may play a role in family care-giving. Older people born into cultures with traditionally strong family relationships are more likely to seek help from the family.

Stoller's (1982) investigation, described earlier, examined how metropolitan versus nonmetropolitan residence related to sources of help. Nonmetropolitan elderly were somewhat less likely than metropolitan elderly to be able to name someone who could help them during periods of illness or functional incapacity. Stoller noted relatively little difference, however, among metropolitan and nonmetropolitan residents in their reliance on family versus other sources of help.

METHOD

Sample Design

Data for this chapter came from the Statewide Survey of Older Virginians, a household survey of 2,146 older people (over 60 years old) conducted in 1979 (McAuley, Arling, Nutty, & Bowling, 1980). The survey was based on a multistage statewide area probability sample of noninstitutionalized older people. The response rate was 87 percent of all persons who lived in sampled housing units and who were identified as age eligible. Informants were used in 8 percent of the cases. Information was obtained from informants when the target respondent was unable to carry out the interview. A weighting scheme, compensating for unequal selection probabilities and response, was used to enhance the representativeness of the sample. All results in this chapter are based upon weighted class.

The characteristics of the weighted sample closely reflect census data for Virginia's older population. Approximately three-quarters are in the "young-old" category (60–74 years old), about one-fifth are nonwhite, and slightly more than two-fifths are men. Three-fifths of the sample have less than a high school education. Approximately 56 percent reside in small towns with a population of less than 25,000 or in rural areas.

Measures

The questionnaire was based on the OARS multidimensional functional assessment instrument (Duke University Center for the Study of Aging and Human Development, 1978). A number of tests of reliability and validity (Fillenbaum, 1978; Fillenbaum & Smyer, 1981) have been carried out on sections of the OARS instrument. These studies have reported levels of reliability and validity that are comparable to other general assessment instruments.

Only a small proportion of the variables in the OARS instrument are being used in this chapter. The demographic variables are age (60–64 years old, 65–74 years old, 75 years old, and older); gender (male, female); marital status (married, widowed, single, divorced or separated); race (white, nonwhite); living arrangement (alone, spouse only, spouse and adult child or other relative, adult child, other relative, and unrelated person); and community size (farm, small towns with a population of less than 25,000, and cities with a population of 25,000 or more).

Activities of daily living (ADL) is summarized in the OARS instrument by interviewer ratings of excellent, good, mildly impaired, moderately impaired, severely impaired, and totally impaired. The moderately to totally impaired require assistance in four or more activities of daily living (e.g., bathing, shopping, housekeeping or meal preparation). The moderately impaired are able to get through a single day without help, but the severely impaired require help each day, and the totally impaired require this help continuously during the day or night.

Information about types of care and sources is based upon self-reports by respondents. The types of care were described in generic terms so that respondents were not biased to report on only formal service delivery. Information about sources of care was obtained in a similar manner. The respondent was asked to identify the source of care, and the interviewers recorded the answers into response categories.

RESULTS

Characteristics of Impaired Elderly

The term impaired elderly is used to refer to persons who have moderate to total impairment in activities of daily living. They are contrasted in Table 9–1 with respondents who have excellent to good ADL status or only mild impairment. The impaired elderly are significantly older, more likely to live with an adult child, and less likely to live alone or with a spouse. They are also more likely to be widowed. The impaired do not differ significantly from the unimpaired in terms of gender.

Over half of the impaired elderly (56%) are 75 years of age or older. Sixty percent are female, and 40 percent are male. Half of the impaired elderly are widowed; only 35 percent are married; and an additional 15 percent are single, separated, or divorced. Despite the high percentages of widowed and never married persons among the impaired, only 10 percent live alone. Nineteen percent live with only a husband or wife, and 16 percent live with a spouse and another relative. In comparison to the unimpaired, a considerably higher percentage of impaired (35%) live with an adult child, 14 percent live with other relatives, and 7 percent live with an unrelated person, such as a friend or a live-in care-giver.

Major Helpers

The majority of the impaired elderly require and receive care in the home. Because 90 percent live with someone else, they generally draw their support from within the household.

The respondents were asked to identify one or two individuals who were their major helpers—i.e., assisted with daily living activities such as bathing, dressing, shopping, housekeeping, or other needs. The major helpers are presented in Table 9–2. (Because respondents could name two major helpers, the percentages total more than 100%.)

Marital status definitely influences the choice of the major helper. The spouse is the major helper for 70 percent of the married respondents. Twenty-five percent

Table 9–1 Social Characteristics by ADL Status for Total Sample

Social Characteristics	ADL Status*	
	Excellent, Good or Mildly Impaired† (%)	Moderate to Total Impairment‡ (%)
Age§		
60–64	31	16
65–74	49	29
75 and older	20	56
Gender		
Female	59	60
Male	42	40
Marital Status§		
Married	58	35
Widowed	32	50
Single (never married)	5	10
Divorced	4	2
Separated	1	3
Living Arrangement§		
Alone	25	10
Spouse only	43	19
Spouse and other relative	15	16
Adult child	9	35
Other relative	6	14
Unrelated person	3	7

Notes:

* Percentages may not total 100% because of rounding error

†n = 1,927

‡n = 219

§$p<.001$, Chi-square

Source: Constructed from *Final report of the statewide survey of older Virginians*. Richmond, VA: Virginia Center on Aging, © 1980.

rely on an adult child, 5 percent on a sibling, 7 percent on another relative, 1 percent on a neighbor or friend, and 12 percent on an agency or paid source. Eleven percent report no major helper, despite their impairment.

The data in Table 9–2 suggest that adult children and other relatives (not including siblings) tend to become more centrally involved when an impaired elderly cannot rely upon a spouse as the major helper. The majority (56%) of the unmarried respondents rely upon an adult child, 9 percent on a sibling, 38 percent

Table 9–2 Major Helpers for Moderately to Totally Impaired in ADL

Major Helper*	Percentage†
Married respondents‡	
Spouse	70
Adult child	25
Sibling	5
Other relative	7
Neighbor or friend	1
Agency or paid source	12
No major helper	11
Unmarried respondents§	
Adult child	56
Sibling	9
Other relative	38
Neighbor or friend	10
Agency or paid source	19
No major helper	3

Notes:

* Major helpers include in-laws for each category—e.g., adult child includes son-in-law and daughter-in-law.

†Percentages do not total 100% because respondents have up to two major helpers.

‡$n = 73$

§$n = 146$

Source: Constructed from *Final report of the statewide survey of older Virginians.* Richmond, VA: Virginia Center on Aging, © 1980.

on another relative, and 10 percent on a neighbor or friend. Although relatively more of the unmarried impaired elders rely on an agency or paid source as major helper, the percentage (19%) is still quite low—3 percent of the unmarried have no major helper.

Types and Sources of Care

The types of care being received by the impaired elderly are presented in Table 9–3. To obtain this information, respondents were asked whether they were currently receiving help with each activity because they could not perform the task without help. The types of care examined here were selected from a larger set of possibilities because they comprise the core services the impaired elderly might need in order to remain in the home.

The data in Table 9–3 suggest that the impaired elderly are heavy users of all five types of assistance. The most commonly received types of care are homemaking

Table 9–3 Types and Sources of Care for Moderately to Totally Impaired in ADL

Type of Care	Receiving Assistance* (%)	(n)	Source†		
			Family (%)	Neighbors/ Friends (%)	Agency or Paid Source (%)
Homemaker/Housekeeping	82	(181)	81	7	12
Meal preparation	80	(176)	72	7	21
Personal care	50	(109)	79	13	20
Continuous supervision	48	(114)	88	6	6
Nursing care	31	(68)	69	9	25

Notes:

* Total n = 219. Percentages for sources are based upon the total number of persons (n) receiving each type of care. Percentages may not total 100% because of rounding error.

†Only one source was recorded for homemaker/housekeeping, meal preparation, and continuous supervision. Respondents could name up to three sources for personal care and nursing care; therefore, these percentage totals exceed 100%.

Source: Constructed from *Final report on the statewide survey of older Virginians.* Richmond, VA: Virginia Center on Aging, © 1980.

(82%) and meal preparation (80%). Exactly half the respondents receive personal care, 48 percent receive continuous supervision, and 31 percent receive nursing care.

The family (e.g., spouse, adult child, or other relative) is the most frequent source of all five types of care. Eighty-eight percent of the respondents who are continuously supervised receive this assistance from a family member. Eighty-one percent receiving homemaking assistance, 79 percent receiving personal care, 72 percent receiving meal preparation, and 69 percent receiving nursing care get these services from a family member. Much smaller percentages (6% to 13%) receive assistance from neighbors and friends. Agencies or paid sources provide assistance to 25 percent of those receiving nursing care, to 21 percent receiving meal preparation, to 20 percent receiving personal care, to 12 percent receiving homemaker assistance, and to 6 percent receiving continuous supervision.

Comparison of Family and Nonfamily Sources

Distribution

The vast majority of the impaired elderly receive care either exclusively from the family or from the family in combination with other care-givers. Table 9–4

Table 9–4 Distribution of Care by Family and Nonfamily Sources for Moderately to Totally Impaired in ADL

Sources of Care	Percentage*
Family sources of care†	
Family member only	65
Family and neighbors/Friends	2
Family and agency/Paid sources	15
Family, agency/Paid sources, and neighbors/Friends	2
TOTAL	(84)
No Family sources of care	
Neighbors/Friends only	5
Agency/Paid sources only	9
Neighbors/friends and agency/Paid sources	2
TOTAL	(15)

Notes:

* $n = 207$. A total of 219 persons are moderately to totally impaired in ADL. Only 207 receive homemaker/housekeeping, meal preparation, personal care, continuous supervision, or nursing care in the home. Percentages do not total 100% because of rounding error.

†Family sources include spouse, children, sibling, other relatives and in-laws.

Source: Constructed from *Final report on the statewide survey of older Virginians.* Richmond, VA: Virginia Center on Aging, © 1980.

presents the sources of care for the five types of in-home care according to whether a family member is involved in care-giving.

Among the elderly who are receiving one or more of the five forms of help, 84 percent receive care from family members and 65 percent rely exclusively upon the family. Fifteen percent have care from the family and an agency or paid source, 2 percent get help from both family and a neighbor or friend, and 2 percent have all three types of care-givers.

Only fifteen percent of the impaired who receive care have no family care-givers. Five percent rely exclusively on such nonfamily informal care-givers as friends or neighbors, an additional 9 percent rely solely on agency or paid sources, and 2 percent have help from both paid sources and neighbors or friends.

Sources

The patterns in family and nonfamily care-giving are presented in Table 9–5. Sources of care are divided into three categories: care exclusively from the family, the family in combination with a nonfamily source, and nonfamily sources only.

Table 9–5 Family and Nonfamily Sources of Care by Other Variables for Moderately to Totally Impaired in ADL

Variables	(n)†	Sources of Care* Family Only (%)	Family and Nonfamily (%)	Nonfamily Only (%)
Number of types of care§				
One	(27)	66	3	31
Two	(51)	74	5	30
Three	(45)	59	30	11
Four	(35)	62	28	10
Five	(46)	64	24	11
Level of impairment‡				
Moderate	(91)	71	12	17
Severe	(64)	62	17	21
Total	(52)	58	31	11
Living arrangement§				
Unrelated persons	(13)	4	0	96
Alone	(20)	38	9	53
Spouse only	(38)	76	19	5
Spouse and other relative	(34)	74	10	15
Adult child	(72)	68	27	5
Other relative	(28)	75	22	2
Marital status‡				
Married	(74)	76	15	10
Unmarried	(132)	59	21	20
Community size‡				
Farm	(77)	76	12	11
Small town (less than 25,000 population)	(38)	68	17	15
Urban (25,000+ population)	(92)	54	24	22
Race				
White	(147)	66	18	15
Nonwhite	(59)	60	20	20

* Family sources are spouses, adult children, other relatives and in-laws; nonfamily sources are neighbors, friends, and agency or paid sources.

†Total n = 207 or the number receiving one or more of the five types of care (e.g., meal preparation, personal care, continuous supervision, or nursing care). Percentages may not total 100% because of rounding error.

‡$p<.05$, Chi-square

§$p<.001$, Chi-square

Source: Constructed from *Final report on the statewide survey of older Virginians.* Richmond, VA: Virginia Center on Aging, © 1980.

Certain characteristics of the impaired person influence the distribution of family and nonfamily sources.

One important consideration is the extent of need for care. This is measured in two ways—the number of types of care received and the level of ADL impairment. Table 9–5 shows a statistically significant relationship between the number of types of care and the sources of care. Those people receiving only one or two forms of care tend to rely exclusively on either family or nonfamily sources. As the number of types of care increases to three or more, the proportion of persons receiving care from both family and nonfamily sources also increases. The proportion relying exclusively on the family does not decline as types of care increase. It remains relatively constant at about two-thirds. The proportion relying exclusively on nonfamily sources declines, from 31 percent to 11 percent, as the number of types of care increases.

Level of ADL impairment also influences the distribution of care. The proportion of elderly receiving help from both family and nonfamily sources increases directly with the level of ADL impairment. In addition, the proportion of people who rely exclusively on family or nonfamily sources declines as ADL impairment increases.

Living arrangement also has a statistically significant relationship to sources of care. Nonfamily providers are the exclusive source of care for 96 percent of those living with unrelated persons and 53 percent of those living alone. In contrast, family members are the exclusive source of care for 68 percent to 76 percent of those who share their households with family members. Between 10 percent and 27 percent of those living with family members rely upon combined family and nonfamily sources. Relatively few (between 2% and 15%) rely exclusively, however, upon nonfamily sources. It should be noted that although people who live alone or with unrelated persons constitute only 17 percent of the impaired elderly, they represent 68 percent of those who rely exclusively on nonfamily sources for care.

Married persons are significantly more likely than others to rely upon family members, including the spouse. Seventy-six percent of married persons receive care from family members only, 15 percent have combined family and nonfamily sources, and only 10 percent rely exclusively on nonfamily sources. Unmarried persons are more likely to rely upon combined family and nonfamily sources (21 percent) and nonfamily sources only (20 percent). A majority (59 percent) of unmarried persons rely exclusively, however, upon the family for their care.

The involvement of nonfamily sources tends to increase with community size. Seventy-six percent of the impaired who live in rural areas rely exclusively on the family. Fifty-four percent of those who live in urban areas (population 25,000 or more) have family sources only, 24 percent have combined family and nonfamily sources, and 22 percent have nonfamily sources only. Race, the final variable, is not significantly related to sources of care.

DISCUSSION

There is no doubt that families have the primary role in community long-term care. For the majority of impaired elderly in the community, the family is the exclusive source of in-home care. Ninety percent of the impaired elderly live with someone else. The spouse is the primary care-giver for the majority of the impaired elderly who are married. The widowed or otherwise unmarried rely heavily upon adult children and other relatives. Neighbors and friends assist in care-giving for about 10 percent of the unmarried and a much smaller percentage of those who are married. Only 9 percent of the impaired elderly rely totally upon agencies or paid sources of care. This category includes private housekeepers or nurses who may be paid directly by the older person or the family.

The results suggest that nonfamily sources of care supplement rather than displace family care-giving. Neighbors, friends, and agencies and other paid sources are most commonly used in conjunction with family care-givers when the impaired person receives several types of care (especially three or more) or when severe or total impairment creates an extensive need for assistance. Furthermore, findings not reported in the tables show that approximately two-thirds of those who rely exclusively upon nonfamily sources live alone or with an unrelated person; therefore, they have more limited access to family help.

The Family and the Nursing Home

The sources of care in the community contrast sharply with care in the nursing home. Families may visit and give emotional support to nursing home residents, but they are seldom directly involved in care-giving. The number of nursing home residents is less than one-third the number of impaired elderly who live in the community. In Virginia, the number of impaired elderly in the community is estimated to be more than 70,000; the residents of nursing homes, age 60 years and older, number fewer than 20,000 (Arling, 1981). Approximately two-thirds of nursing home residents receive public funds—particularly Medicaid—at an annual expenditure of over $15,000 per resident. What leads to this dichotomy between heavy use of family care in the community and the total reliance on formal care-giving (largely at public expense) in the institution?

One hypothesis is that institutional residents have no close family members or at least no potential for support from family in the community. They end up in institutions because they have no other possibilities. This hypothesis rests on the assumption that the impaired elderly can be divided into dichotomous categories: those whose families are willing and able to care for them, and those who have no families, weak family ties, or families that are unwilling to take on care-giving.

Public Policy and the Family

The problems presented by rising costs, inappropriate use of nursing homes and acute care facilities, and a rapidly increasing population of the very old have led many to conclude that the long-term care system must undergo major changes (Federal Council on Aging, 1979; Kane & Kane, 1980; Ruchlin, Morris, & Eggert, 1982; Somers, 1982; U.S. Congress, 1977; White House Conference on Aging, 1981). Critics of the long-term care system invariably place emphasis upon community versus institutional care, and the family as a major provider of in-home services.

Institutional Bias

Public policies have generally discouraged family care-giving in favor of the total care of the institutional setting. Technical documents dealing with long-term care presented at the White House Conference on Aging (1981) point out the bias toward institutional care that is inherent in Medicare and Medicaid. Medicare is highly circumscribed to cover only acute or episodic illness, but Medicaid financial eligibility for long-term care cannot be obtained for most older people until they have exhausted their assets through heavy medical or nursing home expenditures. Public policies, in essence, present the impaired elderly and their families with little choice. They must remain in the community and rely heavily on family or private sources for care, or they must enter a nursing home or other institution, often relegating their care-giving to the institutional staff and severing their ties with the community.

The choice is rarely to dump older family members prematurely into institutions. Shanas and Maddox (1976) have suggested that families often delay the institutionalization of older members until family resources are exhausted. Such delays may be detrimental to the older person and exacerbate family problems. Because present policies do little to support families that care for the impaired elderly, many people whose needs might be adequately met in the community are institutionalized instead.

Contractual System for Family Care-Giving

Sussman (1976) has proposed that long-term care policies should promote contractual agreements in which economic as well as service incentives are offered to families for the care of older members. Such a contract may encourage some families who are otherwise unwilling to provide care, to do so. Sussman suggests, however, that the main effect of a contract is to give the family clear expectations about care and to free their energies so that they can focus on the emotional commitments that are crucial to family relationships. The authors have suggested elsewhere that financial payments to families may pose problems for the formal service system and for family care-giving (Arling & McAuley, 1981); and yet, contractual payment systems deserve careful consideration.

Care-Giving As Shared Responsibility

Policies that make care-giving a joint public and family responsibility must take into account certain factors. First of all, such policies must be based on a recognition of the advantages and the disadvantages of family involvement. Families should be encouraged and assisted in care-giving, but any effort to force family involvement is likely to undermine emotional bonds and to create family disharmony. Monitoring or case management should be available to ensure that the care provided by relatives is adequate and that the family is not overburdened.

Secondly, since families require a number of different types of assistance, no single service can be successful in fostering and sustaining a joint effort in care-giving. Some families may need personal care or nursing care in the home during certain periods of the day; others may need adult day-care or respite care. Families may benefit from counseling to deal with emotional strain, and they may need education to enhance their care-giving skills.

Thirdly, public policies should make explicit the shared responsibility for care between public agencies and the family. Shared responsibility could be formally maintained through copayment for public services, possibly through contracts with a sliding scale based upon economic means. A direct payment to families for costs associated with care-giving is another method; although, direct payments may be difficult to administer, and families may still need the involvement of professionals to provide adequate care.

Finally, policies designed to encourage family care-giving should take into account that formal services, including nursing homes, are necessary for many impaired elderly. Some persons have no family members. For others, the family has financial, emotional, or physical limitations that should be recognized. When formal services in the home become exceedingly expensive, or when the family faces inordinate strain, nursing home care may be the only feasible alternative.

Major policy reform affecting the family should not take place without careful study and evaluation. The family is one piece in the complex puzzle of long-term care. Impaired older people and their families should have the freedom to choose among feasible alternatives. Shifting total responsibility to the family in order to reduce public expenditures may be destructive of family bonds and ultimately increase the costs to society. Public policy should strike a careful balance between the roles of government and the family in order to maximize the well-being of impaired older people.

REFERENCES

Arling, G. (1981). *Aging and long-term care through the 1980's*. Richmond, VA: Virginia Center on Aging.

Arling, G., & McAuley, W.J. (1981). Financial incentives for family caregiving: Policy and impact. *The Gerontologist, 21* (Part II), 193. (Abstract)

Brody, S.J., Poulshock, W., & Masciocchi, C.F. (1978). The family caring unit: A major consideration in the long-term support system. *The Gerontologist, 18,* 556–561.

Cantor, M.H. (1980). Caring for the frail elderly: Impact on family, friends and neighbors: 2. *The Gerontologist, 20* (Part II), 265. (Abstract)

Comptroller General of the United States. (1977). *The well-being of the elderly in Cleveland, Ohio.* Washington, DC: U.S. General Accounting Office.

Duke University Center for the Study of Aging and Human Development. (1978). *Multidimensional functional assessment of the elderly: The OARS methodology.* Durham, NC: Duke University.

Federal Council on Aging. (1979). *Annual report to the President—1979* (Appendix A). Washington, DC: U.S. Government Printing Office.

Fillenbaum, G. (1978). Validity and reliability of the multidimensional functional assessment questionnaire. In Duke University Center for the Study of Aging and Human Development, *Multidimensional functional assessment of the elderly: The OARS methodology.* Durham, NC: Duke University.

Fillenbaum, G., & Smyer, M. (1981). The development, validity and reliability of the OARS multidimensional functional assessment questionnaire. *Journal of Gerontology, 36,* 428–434.

Kane, R.J., & Kane, R.A. (1980). Alternatives to institutional care of the elderly: Beyond the dichotomy. *The Gerontologist, 20,* 249–259.

Lebowitz, B.D. (1979). Old age and family functioning. *Journal of Gerontological Social Work, 1,* 111–118.

Maddox, G.F. (1975). Families as context and resource in chronic illness. In S. Sherwood (Ed.), *Long-term care: A handbook for researchers, planners and providers.* New York: Wiley.

McAuley, W.J., Arling, G., Nutty, C., & Bowling, C. (1980). *The final report of the statewide survey of older Virginians.* Richmond, VA: Virginia Center on Aging.

Miller, M.B., & Harris, A. (1965). Social factors and family contacts in a nursing home population. *Journal of the American Geriatrics Society, 13,* 845–851.

Morris, R. (1975). *Hearing before subcommittee on long-term care of the select committee on aging, House of Representatives, 94th Congress, 1st Session.* Washington, DC: U.S. Government Printing Office.

Murray, J. (1976). Family structure in the preretirement years. In *Almost 65: Baseline data from the retirement history study.* Washington, DC: U.S. Department of Health, Education and Welfare.

Rosow, I. (1967). *Social integration of the aged.* New York: The Free Press.

Ruchlin, H.S., Morris, J.N., & Eggert, G.M. (1982). Management and financing of long term care services. *Journal of the American Medical Association, 306,* 101–106.

Shanas, E. (1961). *Family relationships of older people.* New York: Health Information Foundation.

Shanas, E. (1979). The family as a social support system in old age. *The Gerontologist, 19,* 169–174.

Shanas, E., & Maddox, G.L. (1976). Aging, health, and the organization of health resources. In R.H. Binstock & E. Shanas (Eds.), *Handbook of aging and the social sciences.* New York: Van Nostrand Reinhold.

Shanas, E., Townsend, P., Wedderburn, D., Friis, H., Milhoj, P., & Stehouwer, J. (1968). *Old people in three societies*. New York: Atherton.

Somers, A.R. (1982). Long-term care for the elderly and disabled: A new health priority. *Journal of the American Medical Association, 307*, 221–226.

Stoller, E.P. (1982). Sources of support for the elderly during illness. *Health and Social Work, 7*, 111–122.

Streib, G.F., & Beck, R.W. (1980). Older families: A decade review. *Journal of Marriage and the Family, 42*, 937–955.

Sussman, M.B. (1976). The family life of older people. In R.H. Binstock & E. Shanas (Eds.), *Handbook of aging and the social sciences*. New York: Van Nostrand Reinhold.

Townsend, P. (1965). The effects of family structure on the likelihood of admission to an institution in old age: The application of a general theory. In E. Shanas and G.F. Streib (Eds.), *Social structure and the family*. Englewood Cliffs, NJ: Prentice-Hall.

United States Congress, Congressional Budget Office. (1977). *Long-term care for the elderly and disabled*. Washington, DC: U.S. Government Printing Office.

Wan, T.T.H., & Weissert, W.G. (1981). Social support networks, patient status and institutionalization. *Research on Aging, 3*, 240–256.

Weeks, J.R., & Cuellar, J.B. (1981). The role of family members in the helping networks of older people. *The Gerontologist, 21*, 388–394.

White House Conference on Aging. (1981). *Final Report of the 1981 White House Conference on Aging* (Volume I). Washington, DC: U.S. Government Printing Office.

York, J.L., & Calsyn, R.J. (1977). Family involvement in nursing homes. *The Gerontologist, 17*, 500–505.

Chapter 10

The Dependent Elderly: Targets for Abuse

June Henton, Rodney Cate, and Beth Emery

Regardless of their age or stage of life, people who develop patterns of excessive dependence in relationships often find themselves at a serious disadvantage. When such dependence causes them to feel they cannot function without the presence or the attention of a limited few, they suddenly become at risk of tolerating unacceptable behavior directed toward them by those selected persons. Such tolerance has been demonstrated over and over again in power struggles among family members. More recently, they have been called to our attention by cases of violence in families and other close relationships.

THE TARGETS FOR ABUSE

Only in the past decade have social scientists discovered the nature and the extent of abuse occurring in "loving" relationships within this society. Violent patterns of interaction have been documented between premarital partners (Cate, Henton, Koval, Christopher, & Lloyd, 1982), married couples (Straus, Gelles, & Steinmetz, 1980), parents and children (Gil, 1970), and siblings (Steinmetz, 1977), as well as between elderly persons victimized by various family members (Rathbone-McCuan, 1980). Elder abuse has often been described as occurring in situations in which the aged victims are in the care of only one or two persons, and in which they are incapable of fending for themselves. Persons who have a mental or physical handicap or are otherwise unable to attend to their own needs (such as in the case of financial negotiations) are particularly vulnerable to becoming excessively dependent and, therefore, a target for abuse (Douglass, Hickey, & Noel, 1980).

To illustrate the situation, consider the case of Emily T (Exhibit 10–1), reported by Rathbone-McCuan (1980).

Exhibit 10–1 The Case Study of Emily T

Mrs. T. a seventy-two-year-old white widow, lived with her daughter and her son-in-law. Her daughter had told her mother she could live with them. The daughter and son-in-law were part owners of Mrs. T's house, and all three of their names were on the deed. Emily's daughter maliciously hit her mother on the right hand with a telephone, causing the hand to become swollen and bruised.

Another daughter took Mrs. T to the emergency room of an acute care hospital for treatment. This daughter stated that there was confusion and hostility in her mother's house, exacerbated by alcoholism. Mrs. T was discharged from the hospital to the non-abusing daughter's house. The hospital social worker set up an appointment for the mother to consult a lawyer. It was learned that there had been several other instances of physical abuse by the daughter, as well as instances when the son-in-law had used abusive language and threatened his mother-in-law. (Rathbone-McCuan, 1980, p. 298)

This case study portrays a situation with positive chances for rehabilitation and a potentially happy outcome for the abused victim. The sequence of events can be summarized thus: The mother was abused by a daughter; a second daughter found out, took her out of the abusive environment, and provided her with medical and legal help and a place to stay. In this case, the mother's support group extended beyond one or two people, which gave her other options for assistance. But what if there had not been a second daughter or anyone else attending to the mother's welfare?

Too often persons who become the victims of violence have no good alternatives to their current situation, or they at least perceive that to be the case. This pattern of extreme dependence is particularly apparent in instances of child abuse and abuse of the frail elderly. Researchers have found, however, that even among young adults (e.g., in cases of premarital and spouse abuse), many persons perceive their alternatives to their current relationships to be limited and, therefore, choose to remain with their violent partners (Henton, Cate, Koval, Lloyd, & Christopher, in press; Gelles, 1976).

The vulnerability felt by people who perceive that they have nowhere to turn in times of need acts as a powerful inhibitor to their acquiring help. In cases of abuse, many elderly victims refuse to report the violence to authorities because they fear retaliation by the abuser, they are ashamed to admit the punitive treatment, or they have no other place to live (Block & Sinnott, 1979). Reports of elder abuse to social service agencies come from hospital staffs, nursing agencies, community service agencies, relatives, friends, and sometimes from the abused victims themselves (Lau & Kosberg, 1979). Even with this large variety of reporting sources, however, it is assumed that these referrals represent only a small proportion of the actual number of abuse cases. The reporting of elder abuse may be even less frequent than the reporting of spouse and child abuse because few states have mandatory reporting laws. In addition, the lower reporting rate may exist because people have only recently become aware of elder abuse as a problem (Pedrick-Cornell & Gelles, 1982). The underreporting of elder abuse will continue until the public becomes sensitive to the fact, the extent, and the severity of its existence.

Without adequate reporting, it is impossible to determine accurately the number of elderly persons who are being abused by their care-givers. Estimates of the incidence of elder abuse range from 500,000 to 2.5 million cases per year ("Aging committees consider programs," 1980). Several researchers (e.g., Block & Sinnott, 1979; Lau & Kosberg, 1979) have attempted to extrapolate abuse rates to the larger population from their data based on limited samples. These attempts have not been very successful, however, on account of a number of methodological problems. Pedrick-Cornell and Gelles (1982) have noted the following limitations to one or more of these studies: (a) the small, nonrepresentative samples; (b) the extremely low questionnaire return rates by respondents, which further limits generalizability; and (c) the possible reporting of the same incident of abuse by different professionals, thus distorting the reported rate. Consequently, an immediate need exists for researchers to generate data that would yield an accurate national incidence statistic in order to determine how widespread the problem is.

DEFINING ELDER ABUSE

Although the need for information about the frequency and the nature of elder abuse is clear, the study of violence against the elderly is complicated by the lack of adequate definition. Research within this area has addressed many types of abusive behaviors toward the elderly; yet, the question of what actually constitutes abuse still causes confusion among researchers, professionals, and practitioners. This problem is by no means a new or unique one for family violence researchers; the early literature on child abuse dealt with many of the same issues in a similar attempt to define abusive acts toward children (Pedrick-Cornell & Gelles, 1982).

The Range of Abusive Acts

The central problem of defining elder abuse lies, it seems, in determining the range of the acts considered to be abusive. In general, any act on the part of a caregiver that may result in physical injury to an elderly person is considered to constitute abuse. Many researchers, however, have suggested a broader definition that encompasses the results of other behavior: (1) verbal, emotional, or psychological injury; (2) neglect of the physical and emotional well-being of the person; and (3) misuse of funds or property or the rights of the elderly (Hickey & Douglass, 1981; Katz, 1979-80; Kimsey, Tarbox, & Bragg, 1981; Lau & Kosberg, 1979; Rathbone-McCuan, 1980; Steinmetz, 1981).

Factors other than those determining the range of behavior to be included have also caused confusion. In order to establish whether or not an act should be defined as abusive, the severity of its form (physical or nonphysical) must be discussed. Overt physical violence to the elderly may well be the most serious form of abuse because of the fragile condition of elderly persons. Pushes and shoves or even a slap may cause broken bones or severe bruises. However, the more subtle, nonphysical types of maltreatment (such as psychological abuse or neglect) should not be dismissed as any less severe (New York Subcommittee on Human Services, 1980). The effects of these types of abuse and neglect may be just as damaging and, perhaps, more pervasive than the effects of physical violence.

The Issue of Intent

Another question that must also be addressed in determining abuse is the issue of intent vs. the outcome of particular "violent" acts. How are accidental injuries interpreted within the context of abuse? How is punitive behavior viewed when there are no apparent effects? Elderly people bruise very easily. Although no ill will may be intended, merely gripping an arm or a wrist too tightly when assisting an aged person from one place to another can cause bruising. Loose slippers or inadequate lighting can result in a fall (Renvoize, 1978), having results that, on the surface, might suggest abusive treatment. It is difficult, then, for a doctor or a social worker to determine whether the injuries they observe are accidental or intentional, which adds to their apprehension about reporting them.

Clearly, all acts that infringe in any way upon the basic human rights of the elderly could potentially be classified as abusive (New York Subcommittee on Human Services, 1980). The major task, then, is the development of a common definition of elder abuse that would allow appropriate comparisons to be made with research findings derived from various projects. Some previous research has been based on very narrow and limiting definitions (Rathbone-McCuan, 1980); others employed broader perspectives (Hickey & Douglass, 1981; Lau & Kosberg, 1979). This lack of clarity and consistency in defining elder abuse serves to make accurate reporting of abuse, as well as any comparisons of the research, virtually impossible (Pedrick-Cornell & Gelles, 1982). As long as this confusion exists, it will be extremely difficult for family violence researchers to develop an accurate understanding of the problem.

TYPES OF ABUSE

Abuse of the elderly can be classified according to two basic types: neglect and abuse. More specifically, these acts include physical, verbal, and psychological assaults; financial abuse or misuse of property and belongings; and violation of the rights of the elderly. These types of abuse can and do occur within the context of the family and are not limited to formal care-givers (e.g., attendants and nurses in hospitals and nursing homes) or to strangers (Lau & Kosberg, 1979).

Neglect

A common type of violation imposed by families against the elderly is neglect (Hickey & Douglass, 1981; Kimsey, Tarbox, & Bragg, 1981; Katz, 1979-80; Lau & Kosberg, 1979; Steinmetz, 1981). Two types of neglect occur within the family environment: *passive neglect,* characterized by situations in which the elderly person is left alone, isolated, or forgotten; and *active neglect,* described as the withholding of items that are necessary for daily living, such as companionship, medicine, food, and bathroom assistance (Hickey & Douglass, 1981). Those professionals, such as adult service workers and police officers, who are likely to come in contact with cases of passive neglect do not appear to view it as a particularly critical problem (Hickey & Douglass, 1981). Explanations of passive neglect suggest that family members are too busy or too concerned with their own lives to bother with the dependent adult, or that they lack the necessary education and adequate knowledge for understanding and caring for the needs of an elderly person (Hickey & Douglass, 1981; Steinmetz, 1978).

Active forms of neglect are less common, but they do occur—primarily for the same reasons as passive neglect. Inadequate knowledge about caring for the elderly often results in physical harm. Tying an elderly person, who needs constant care and attention, to a chair or into bed so that the care-giver can complete the shopping or the housekeeping is a common example of active neglect. The excessive use of sleeping medication or alcohol to ease discomfort or to make the person more manageable, as well as withholding medication as a means of control, are also documented examples of neglect (Steinmetz, 1978).

There is some contradiction among researchers about types of behavior considered to be either neglectful or abusive. Some researchers classify physical neglect as a form of physical abuse (Kimsey et al., 1981; Lau & Kosberg, 1979). In addition to physical restraint and the improper use of medication, these studies also refer to negligence in providing appropriate diets, lack of supervision, and failure to provide a sanitary environment as being physically abusive treatment.

Assault

Other types of physical abuse are less "benign" than neglect by intent, however, and are much more obvious and detectable (Kimsey et al., 1981). The elderly are often subjected to violent acts such as slaps, burns, scratches, whippings and beatings that result in bruises, lacerations, and broken bones (Hickey & Douglass, 1981; Kimsey et al., 1981; Lau & Kosberg, 1979; Steinmetz, 1981).

Along with these physically violent acts, researchers cite psychological and material abuse and the violation of rights as the major infringements most frequently reported by professionals such as social service workers and policemen (Block & Sinnott, 1979; Hickey & Douglass, 1981; Kimsey et al., 1981; Lau & Kosberg, 1979; Rathbone-McCuan, 1980; Steinmetz, 1981).

According to Kimsey et al. (1981), psychological abuse is usually poorly defined and only lately has begun to receive much consideration. It is most commonly described as verbal and emotional assaults on the elderly person. Verbal abuse encompasses threats, yelling and screaming, insults, condemnation and intimidation (Hickey & Douglass, 1981; Katz, 1979-80; Kimsey et al., 1981; Lau & Kosberg, 1979; Steinmetz, 1981). Many older dependents are treated in a manner that lowers their self-worth and dignity. Overprotection and the denial of their need to be independent reduce many elderly individuals to a state of confusion, helplessness, and disorientation associated with infantilization (treatment of the elderly as children) and a regression to senility (Hickey & Douglass, 1981; Kimsey et al., 1981). Data suggest that verbal and emotional or psychological abuse is widespread among familial care-givers (Lau & Kosberg, 1979; Steinmetz, 1981).

Misuse of Finances and Property

Material abuse, or the theft of money and material possessions of the elderly, occurs both in and out of institutions (Kimsey et al., 1981). Elderly patients and relatives who are dependent or not clear-minded may be defrauded and are subject to the misuse of their property or funds at the hands of a relative or institutional care-giver (Katz, 1979-80; Kimsey et al., 1981). Frequently, social security checks are cashed and the money is withheld from the elderly person, or possessions may be stolen piece by piece (New York Subcommittee on Human Services, 1980).

Violation of Rights

Closely related to material abuse is the violation of the rights of the elderly. In these cases, elderly persons may be forced out of their homes—often into nursing homes by abusive relatives or care-givers (New York Subcommittee on Human Services, 1980; Lau & Kosberg, 1979).

In summary, it seems that of the various types of neglect and abuse reported, passive neglect occurs most often but is generally not seen as a serious problem (Hickey & Douglass, 1981). Psychological abuse follows in frequency, yet is viewed as having more severe and detrimental effects upon the elderly (Hickey & Douglass, 1981; Kimsey et al., 1981; Lau & Kosberg, 1979). Active neglect and physical abuse occur with less frequency as the severity of the particular acts

increases. Finally, instances of material abuse and violation of the rights of the elderly are known to occur, but they are depicted as being difficult to document or to prosecute (Kimsey et al., 1981).

FACTORS RELATED TO THE OCCURRENCE OF ELDER ABUSE

Because the study of elder abuse is in its beginning stages, direct causes of the phenomenon have not been established. As in the case of most human behavior, the causes of elder abuse are probably multiple and complex. Researchers and theorists have suggested several factors, which fall into four categories: (1) *personal* characteristics of the abusers and the abused; (2) *interpersonal* characteristics of the relationship between the abuser and the elderly person; (3) *situational* factors that increase the likelihood of abuse; and (4) *socio-cultural* factors that impinge on the use of violence.

Personal Factors

At the personal level of analysis, both the abusers and the victims of abuse may possess characteristics that increase the likelihood of elder abuse. Those characteristics that pertain to abusers will be examined first.

The Abusers

One of the most frequently mentioned attributes of spouse and child abusers is their tendency to have experienced abuse as children or to have witnessed abuse between their parents (Gayford, 1975). Although no adequate empirical evidence exists to verify such a relationship in the case of elder abuse, researchers have suggested that a "cycle-of-violence" explanation may be applicable to elder abuse (Rathbone-McCuan, 1980; Steinmetz, 1981). Abusers of the elderly within the family context may be adult children who have been abused by their parents when they were young; now, they are using similar types of violence against their parents (Kimsey et al., 1981). That a son or daughter might resort to physical or verbal abuse against an elderly parent who taught them (at least implicitly) that the use of physical force is an acceptable means of conduct between family members points out that parents can be powerful role models. Therefore, a history of family violence (i.e., child abuse and marital violence) may establish a pattern of interaction for family members throughout the life cycle.

Hickey and Douglass (1981) have suggested that one of the primary factors associated with violent behavior is the abuser-care-giver's inability to deal with the dependence of the elderly person. Much of this inadequate coping is probably due to the interpersonal and situational factors to be discussed later in this section. Straus (1973) postulates, however, that many abusers possess certain types of personality traits (such as aggressiveness) that predispose them to abusive behavior in relationships. Other researchers have found spouse abusers to be significantly less assertive than nonabusers (Rosenbaum & O'Leary, 1981). This lack of interpersonal competence may be characteristic also of other types of abusers. No doubt, a certain level of interpersonal competence is required of a care-giver to cope with the dependency of an elderly person.

In addition, abusers may suffer from personal problems, including mental or physical impairment, psychological illness, or alcoholism (Rathbone-McCuan, 1980). Most sources describe abusive care-givers as middle-aged or older, female, and, in approximately 85 percent of the cases, a relative of the victim—usually a daughter, a granddaughter, or a sibling (New York Subcommitttee on Human Services, 1980; Pedrick-Cornell & Gelles, 1982; Steinmetz, 1981). Many are by definition (60 years of age or older) elderly themselves; yet, they are still caring for dependent relatives (Steinmetz, 1981). Fatigue, which results from the hard work of providing care for the elderly person, can be overwhelming for the care-giver and can create tension that may erupt into violence.

The Abused

Any study of factors related to elder abuse must also take into account the personal characteristics of the abuser's victims; they seem also to have personal characteristics that predispose them to become the targets of aggression. One such characteristic of many victims of abuse is a feeling of helplessness at this stage in life. A major factor that contributes to this condition in many elderly persons is the state of their physical and mental health. Again, information about this factor in elder abuse is closely linked with past research on child abuse. Studies in this area report that children who have physical or mental handicaps are the children most likely to be abused (Pedrick-Cornell & Gelles, 1982). Researchers in the field of elder abuse agree that the elderly who suffer from mental and physical handicaps are at greater risk of abuse than are their relatively healthy counterparts (Block & Sinnott, 1979; Lau & Kosberg, 1979; New York Subcommittee on Human Services, 1980; Rathbone-McCuan, 1980; Steinmetz, 1978). Illness or handicaps accompanied by a loss of identity and a sense of usefulness and productivity can lead to further dependency by making the aged person particularly vulnerable to abuse. Care-givers are tempted to react to this helplessness as they would react to a child—by lashing out verbally or physically at the older person. Unfortunately, some care-givers yield to this temptation.

An analysis of the published results of research reveal that certain characteristics describe the majority of abused elderly persons. Most of the research is in agreement, stating that the victims are primarily female and 65 years of age or older—some being in their mid-70s (Pedrick-Cornell & Gelles, 1982; Rathbone-McCuan, 1980; Steinmetz, 1981). Many victims have established a pattern of dependency upon their care-givers. Often, in cases in which abuse occurs within the family, the child has assumed the care-giving role and the parent (or victim) is now in the dependent role (Rathbone-McCuan, 1980; Steinmetz, 1981). The elderly person may have become stubborn, quarrelsome, difficult to control, or senile, and may even have become aggressive or violent. In other words, some— although a minority—are capable of provoking aggression from their care-givers (Kimsey et al., 1981; Renvoize, 1978).

Interpersonal Factors

Several factors that pertain to the nature of the interpersonal relationship between the care-giver and the elderly person have been suggested as causes of elder abuse. This violence sometimes can be traced to past unresolved parent-child conflicts (Hickey & Douglass, 1981; Steinmetz, 1981). In other words, a dysfunctional relationship that was present during the care-giver's childhood and adolescent years may recur during the care-giving relationship, resulting in abusive behavior directed toward the elderly parent.

Renvoize (1978) has suggested that power conflicts between the elderly and family members can contribute to the occurrence of abuse. The aged grandparent may object to children's choices of friends, their hairstyles, their music, and so forth, which engenders struggles within the family. As in many cases, the elderly female may have conflict with the care-giving daughter or daughter-in-law over household matters or care of the children. Such power struggles can set the stage for abusive behavior to occur on the part of the care-giver.

Situational Factors

Many cases of elder abuse can be ascribed to situational factors that interact with those personal and interpersonal factors discussed previously. The most widely discussed situational factor is the increased stress experienced by the care-giver family that comes about when the older person moves into the house (Block & Sinnott, 1979; Lau & Kosberg, 1979). The inclusion of this new member into the already established family system can be traumatic, especially when the transition is sudden or when the elderly person is so physically or mentally impaired that almost constant responsibility is required of the care-giver. As previously discussed, the care-giver who has an aggressive personality or lacks interpersonal skills may be ill-equipped to deal with such constant responsibility (Lau & Kosberg, 1979). The enactment of abuse toward the elderly person would be a conceivable reaction to this situation.

Adding to this stress is the probability that the inclusion of an elderly family member into the care-giver's home may come at a difficult time in the developmental life course of the care-giver (Katz, 1979–80; Steinmetz, 1981). When parents are under strain from child-rearing and its associated economic and psychological strains is such a time. Another stressful time is when families are launching their children and women are beginning to focus their attention in the direction of personal fulfillment and careers (Steinmetz, 1978). Likewise, later in the life cycle of the care-giver, the inclusion of an elderly parent into the family may come when the care-giver is anticipating retirement and its associated benefits, such as increased freedom of activity. The added stress of taking care of an elderly person at these points in time increases the likelihood that violence might erupt.

Socio-Cultural Factors

Several factors at the socio-cultural level have been postulated to impinge on the probability of violence occurring in the relationship of the care-giver to the elderly person (Hickey & Douglass, 1981; Katz, 1979–80). First, there is the factor of "ageism," which is known to be widespread. Ageism refers to those practices, prejudices, and stereotypes that portray the elderly in a negative manner. In general, American society suffers from ageism. It is probably best typified by a recent Harris poll that showed that Americans tend to see the elderly as "senile, lonely, used-up bodies, rotting away and waiting to die" (Troll & Nowak, 1976, p. 42). If the elderly find people reacting to them according to these stereotypes, they, too, may internalize such negativism into the images they have of themselves. These negative feelings of self-worth, when added to the possibility that they are not highly valued by the care-giver, can further diminish the quality of their relationship and increase their proneness to violence.

Second, in the past few years, several structural changes in the family have occurred that may affect the relationship of the care-giver to the elderly. One structural change is the trend to smaller families. Consequently, there are relatively fewer offspring to act as care-givers, and they are likely to be geographically separated (Katz, 1979–80). Such a situation places much greater stress than normal on the care-giver. Relatedly, as the divorce rate increases, many persons (mainly women) find themselves suddenly single and oftentimes in financial difficulty. The added stress of responsibility for an elderly parent at this point may be a prime time for violence to occur.

PROMOTING INDEPENDENCE TO CURB ABUSE

Although accurate data are currently unavailable to describe fully the nature and the extent of elder abuse in America today, its occurrence is well documented. These deplorable acts of violence that characterize relationships between the elderly and their care-givers emerge out of feelings of stress and the desolation felt by those experiencing problems with no apparent solutions. Inadequate coping skills on the part of the care-givers and the inability of the elderly to assert their independence or to find alternate sources of care interact to create volatile levels of frustration.

As in the case of any problem in which the contributing factors are multiple and complex, solutions are also apt to be nonsimplistic in the case of elder abuse. It is necessary to examine the issues from perspectives of both the elderly and their care-givers, and to analyze the stressors associated with their relationships. Based on the information available about violence enacted against the elderly, what implications can be drawn for families and for public officials who are responsible for protecting the rights of the American people?

Implications for Families

Any presentation of these implications must refer to our current state of knowledge about relationship development in general, which suggests the operation of an exchange principle (Thibaut & Kelley, 1959). Persons bring certain resources into a relationship to offer in return for rewards that are given to them by the other person(s). When the exchange of rewards gets out of balance, and one side of the partnership is contributing more than its share, feelings of unhappiness and dissatisfaction may result. In addition, when opportunities for acceptable alternative relationships are minimal, a pattern of unhealthy dependence may be the outcome.

General principles such as these may be extremely useful in our deliberations about how to prevent elder abuse. From the standpoint of the elderly who are potential targets for abuse, never has the need for both financial and interpersonal resources been clearer. When the economy of the country is weak and families are struggling to survive, the addition at that time of another person in need of financial, physical, or psychological support can be devastating. This pressure can be somewhat alleviated when the elder is perceived to be contributing to the family in certain important ways, such as the provision of monetary benefits.

A review of the facts about the resources of the aged population, however, suggests that significant financial contributions may be unrealistic for most elderly persons. In those cases, expanding the support network to include persons other than the present care-giver to make various contributions to the care-giving relationship on behalf of the elderly should establish a more equal balance. Whatever form these contributions take (i.e., money, time, etc.) and whatever their amount, the critical issue in achieving satisfaction lies in the recipient's perception of their adequacy. When the care-givers still perceive an imbalance, initiating discussion about their feelings to members of the support network could be beneficial.

Much of the uncertainty, the unhappiness, and the anger that are experienced by elders and their families when additional care and support are required might be avoided by a clarification of the expectations one holds for the other's behavior. The knowledge that care-giving tends to be more stressful when it is sudden and unexpected than when it is gradual (Block & Sinnott, 1979) seems to apply not only to how abruptly the need for care occurs but also to one's cognitive preparation before the event. This insight points out the importance of anticipating events in advance (to the extent possible) and considering alternative plans for care.

The decision to follow one plan of action over another should be determined on the basis of the needs, the values, the goals, and the resources of the elderly and the providers of care; otherwise the plan will not succeed. It is important to recognize, however, that handling a problem on an intellectual level before it occurs may be very different from the solution required when circumstantial and emotional components are added at the time of the event. This inability to predict the situation in any detail suggests the need for establishing contingency plans. The flexibility of having more than one option for care allows for a selection process that best suits conditions at the time.

In addition, those plans should be developmental in perspective. One arrangement may work out very well initially; however, as circumstances change over an extended time, the burden of care can become overwhelming. Negotiating with siblings or other relatives to share responsibilities for the elderly parent can be viewed as a strategy for avoiding violent behavior. Writings about spouse abuse make it clear that persons in relationships need to be assertive in expressing their desires and concerns. Without the capability to confront issues as they arise, the small irritations accumulate and become a complex problem, emotional in nature and sometimes eventuating in violent consequences.

As family members prepare for the challenge of accommodating the needs of grandparents or other relatives, they must confront their own feelings about the role transitions that may be necessary. The ambivalence experienced by the now adult child who may have to assume the role of parent to the elder can be difficult to resolve. Personal, interpersonal, and material resources have much to do with the extent to which this shift can be accomplished satisfactorily or whether other options, such as the employment of alternate care-givers (perhaps surrogate children), provide an acceptable solution. The latter may be especially attractive when families are separated geographically from the older generation.

Implications for Public Policy

Protection of the rights and welfare of the dependent elderly is a public responsibility. Where violation of human rights is at risk, as in the case of elder abuse, public officials must ultimately consider plans for alleviating the problem. Solutions to such matters are, however, far from clear-cut. One must weigh the relative benefits and the disadvantages associated with substituting various types of institutional care for home care in the same way similar issues were faced in the case of child abuse. Merely removing a person from an abusive environment may not represent the best choice, even if adequate space were available.

The interdependencies of family members, usually characterized by a unique affectional bond, complicate attempts at intervention into even highly abusive situations. Furthermore, the unwillingness of victims to report the abuse may be a continuing problem as long as they perceive that the alternative to the abusive environment is institutional care. What can be done, then, to call attention to the existence of elder abuse, and how can the violence be stopped?

Initially, tax dollars could be well spent on further investigation into the elder abuse phenomenon. Development of a solid research base, which then provides reliable statistics for general distribution, can be extremely important in the attempt to increase public awareness of the problem. In addition, identifying ways to prolong the independent lives of the elderly (e.g., the increased age of mandatory retirement) may allow senior citizens to contribute to the national economy and to be on their own for a longer period of time. Work programs for the aged represent another way to extend economic productivity.

Families who face financial and emotional pressures in their care of the aged should be offered incentive programs (e.g., tax benefits) to encourage continued family care. Such incentives could serve to even out the exchange on behalf of the elderly. The provision of adult day care (Renvoize, 1978) or other substitute care on a routine basis (particularly in cases of abuse) could offer the added support necessary to maintain the emotional health of the family.

The importance of independent living for the aged cannot be overestimated for the prevention of elder abuse. Through private and public efforts, these persons can continue to live safe, fulfilling lives throughout their later years.

REFERENCES

Aging committees consider programs to curb growing problem of elder abuse. (1980). *Federal Contracts Opportunities, 5*(15), 1.

Block, M., & Sinnott, J. (1979). (Eds.). *The battered elder syndrome: An exploratory study.* Unpublished manuscript, University of Maryland, College Park.

Cate, R., Henton, J., Koval, J., Christopher, F.S., & Lloyd, S. (1982). Premarital abuse: A social psychological perspective. *Journal of Family Issues, 3,* 79–90.

Douglass, R.L., Hickey, T., & Noel, C. (1980). *A study of maltreatment of the elderly and other vulnerable adults.* Unpublished manuscript, University of Michigan.

Gayford, J.J. (1975). Wife battering: A preliminary survey of 100 cases. *British Medical Journal, 1,* 194–197.

Gelles, R.J. (1976). Abused wives: Why do they stay? *Journal of Marriage and the Family, 38,* 659–668.

Gil, D.G. (1970). *Violence against children: Physical child abuse in the United States.* Cambridge, MA: Harvard University Press.

Henton, J., Cate, R., Koval, J., Lloyd, C., & Christopher, S. (in press). Romance and violence in dating relationships. *Journal of Family Issues.*

Hickey, T., & Douglass, R.L. (1981). Mistreatment of the elderly in the domestic setting: An exploratory study. *American Journal of Public Health, 71,* 500–507.

Katz, K.D. (1979–80). Elder abuse. *Journal of Family Law, 18,* 695–722.

Kimsey, L.R., Tarbox, A.R., & Bragg, D.F. (1981). The caretakers and the hidden agenda. I. The caretakers and the categories of abuse. *Journal of the American Geriatrics Society, 29,* 465.

Lau, E., & Kosberg, J. (1979). Abuse of the elderly by informal care providers.

New York Subcommittee on Human Services, Select Committee on Aging. (1980). *Domestic violence against the elderly* (Publication No. 96-233), Washington, DC: U.S. Government Printing Office.

Pedrick-Cornell, C., & Gelles, R.J. (1982). Elder abuse: The status of current knowledge. *Family Relations, 31,* 457–465.

Rathbone-McCuan, E. (1980). Elderly victims of family violence and neglect. *Social Casework, 61,* 296–304.

Renvoize, J. (1978). *Web of violence: A study of family violence.* Boston: Routledge & Kegan Paul.

Rosenbaum, A., & O'Leary, K.D. (1981). Marital violence: Characteristics of abusive couples. *Journal of Consulting and Clinical Psychology, 49,* 63–71.

Steinmetz, S.K. (1978). Battered parents. *Society, 15,* 54–55.

Steinmetz, S.K. (1977). *The cycle of violence: Assertive, aggressive, and abusive family interaction.* New York: Praeger.

Steinmetz, S.K. (1981). Elder abuse. *Aging,* 6–10.

Straus, M.A. (1973). A general systems theory approach to a theory of violence between family members. *Social Science Information, 12,* 105–125.

Straus, M.A., Gelles, R.J., & Steinmetz, S.K. (1980). *Behind closed doors: Violence in the American family.* Garden City, NY: Anchor Books.

Thibaut, J.W., & Kelley, H.H. (1959). *The social psychology of groups.* New York: Wiley.

Troll, L.E., & Nowak, C. (1976). How old are you? The question of age bias in counseling adults. *The Counseling Psychologist, 6*(1), 41–43.

Part III

Special Aging Populations

Chapter 11

Aging and Social Relations in the Black Community

E. Percil Stanford and Shirley A. Lockery

As the black population continues to increase in the United States, the older population becomes proportionately more significant in terms of the make-up of the black community. This makes it necessary for community planners and developers to take into consideration the differences that exist among the black age groups. Historically, the black family has been reported to take care of itself. Recent information shows, however, that the black family is often unable to support itself and needs the assistance available through public and private agencies in the community. The interaction patterns of black families in the community have been such that the older person has been supported, in most instances, through the volunteer efforts of immediate family members or of extended formal and informal kinships in the community.

The many efforts to insure that the older person has the minimal comforts necessary have not traditionally been described as a volunteer activity. However, as voluntarism is described today, the contributions made by the many different persons in the community have certainly been of a volunteer nature. This understanding has made it important to put the value of volunteer input (which brings about many primary interaction patterns) into perspective. It is conceivable that voluntarism has been the glue that has held the black family and the community together.

Given the economic and social problems currently facing this nation and given the decline in resources and programs for minority groups and the elderly, it is timely to look at the social relationships of the black elderly in their communities. To this end, the first section presents current demographic data.

Unfortunately, there is limited information on the black elderly family and community interactions. To address this issue, the second section gives an overview of black family structures and family interaction patterns of the black elderly.

The black community has been, and continues to be, supported by black families. This support often manifests itself in a variety of ways. One way is community interaction through voluntarism. The final section of this chapter reviews the critical dimensions of the black elderly in terms of voluntarism as a method of social interaction.

DEMOGRAPHIC PROFILE

The aging population is growing dramatically. The number of persons 60 years of age or older has increased from approximately 4.9 million in 1900 to almost 35.6 million in 1980 (U.S. Bureau of the Census, 1981a, p. 3). Projected estimates for the year 2000 indicate that this same population will reach nearly 42 million or 16.1 percent (Fowles, 1978, pp. 4–7). By the year 2035, it is anticipated that the same group will reach 70 million or 23.2 percent of the total population.

Age Groups

According to a provisional report by the United States Bureau of the Census (1981a, p. 3), the 1980 population count indicates that nearly 16 percent (35,629,844) of the people in this society are 60 years of age or older. Although the black elderly are one of the fastest growing segments in this society, they represent only 1.3 percent (2,956,560) of the total population 60 years of age and over. The white population in this same age group makes up 14 percent (31,918,010) of the total population.

Approximately 11 percent of the total population and nearly 17 percent of the total white population is over 60 years old. The black elderly percentages decline further with the advancement of age. Even with the "crossover effect," in which blacks reach an advanced age at which they tend to live longer than their white counterparts, their percentage of the total population 65 years and over is still less than 1 percent (.92). Although the white population showed a decline, it was at least 10 percent of the total population.

As of March 1978, more than half (60.2%) of the black elderly 65 years of age and older resided in the South (Williams, 1980, p. 5). The remainder, in order of greatest number, lived in the North Central (16.4%), the Northeast (15.3%), and the West (8.1%). With the exception of the West, which had 15.8 percent of the white elderly population, they were very nearly evenly distributed geographically.

Marital Status

In 1980, 46.2 percent (1,773,000) of all blacks 55 years of age or older were married and living with their spouses (U.S. Bureau of the Census, 1981b, pp. 8–9). Approximately 32 percent (1,221,000) of those remaining were widowed, and 22 percent (8,460,000) were single, divorced, or separated. For whites in the same age group, the percentages were considerably higher; nearly 65 percent (26,123,000) were married and were living with their spouses (U.S. Bureau of the Census, 1981b, pp. 7–8). Almost 24 percent (9,584,000) of the white population 55 years of age and over were widowed; the remaining 11.3 percent (4,557,000) were single, divorced, or separated.

By gender, more than half (53.1%) of the black men and four-fifths (80.7%) of the white men over 55 years old were married and were living with their wives (U.S. Bureau of the Census, 1981b, pp. 7–9). For the women of both racial groups, the percentage living with their husbands was somewhat lower. More than 50 percent (52.4%) of the white females and one-third (34.7%) of the black females lived with their husbands.

As for other living arrangements, more whites (76.1%) were living in families than blacks (69.4%) (U.S. Bureau of the Census, 1981b, pp. 13–14). Conversely, approximately 30 percent of blacks, in contrast to 24 percent of whites, resided in nonfamily settings. Persons within this category lived alone or with nonrelatives.

Life Expectancy

Only 50.2 percent of the 2,028,000 black family heads of households 55 years of age and over in 1980 were men, in contrast to 86.8 percent or nearly 16.4 million elderly white families. To some extent, these differences can be attributed to the lower life expectancy of black men. Although this gap between life expectancy at birth among whites and blacks has declined in recent years there is still a difference. For example, in 1978, white men were expected to live 70.2 years while their black* counterparts were expected to live 65 years (Select Committee on Aging, 1982, p. 22). Obviously, for men there is still a gap of 5.2 years. Life expectancy for each of the groups was greatest for white women at 77.8 years, followed by black women at 73.6 years of age. Once again there was a gap of 4.2 years between the two female groups. Even larger gaps occur between the life expectancy of men and women. White women exceed white men by 7.6 years and black men by 12.8 years. Black women also exceed white men by 3.4 years and their male counterparts by 8.6 years.

Economic Status

An examination of the economic status of the black elderly reveals a dramatic increase in the number of persons 65 years of age and older living in poverty. Affeldt (1981), in his analysis of the 1980 census data, found that the poverty rate

---

*Data came from "other" category, which is primarily composed of blacks.

has increased among elderly blacks from 33.9 percent in 1978 to 38.1 percent in 1980, in contrast to 13.6 percent for elderly whites. There were 31.5 percent poor aged black men compared to 9.0 percent for older white men. The poverty rate for elderly black women was 42.6 percent as compared to 16.8 percent for aged white females.

BLACK FAMILY STRUCTURES AND INTERACTION PATTERNS

Family Structures

No one suitable model of "the" black family exists in America. This group has evolved from a mixed and unique configuration of environments and social patterns that makes it a heterogeneous group. As a result, a broad range of black families and black family trends and patterns has emerged. It is, therefore, not surprising to note controversial issues in the theoretical realm of the black family. A more acceptable premise is that, throughout time, the family has remained the primary socialization unit of society.

Conceptual Framework

In this country, black families, both structurally and functionally, are unique and highly diversified social units. The results of studies are replete, however, with conceptual frameworks that, for the most part, are premised on the values of the model white middle-class family. For example, Dodson (1981) and Mathis (1978) present from a historical perspective a review of two prominent conceptual frameworks on black families: (1) the pathological and dysfunctional view and (2) the cultural relativity view.

The pathological and dysfunctional view is primarily supported by the earlier investigations and writings of Frazier (1939) and Moynihan (1965). Emphasis by these and other scholars (Rainwater, 1965; Rodman, 1968) is on the negative, unstable, and disorganized characteristics of black families. Without exception, their findings support the concept of the black family unit as inherently ingrained with deviancy and pathology. For example, "Frazier largely attributed family disorganization among Blacks to economic factors, suggesting in the process that as Black families achieved higher economic status, their rates of disorganization would drop" (Allen, 1979, p. 302). Moynihan utilized Frazier's earlier work to bolster his conclusions that "the black community is characterized by broken families, illegitimacy, matriarchy, economic dependency, failure to pass armed forces entrance tests, delinquency and crime" (Mathis, 1978, p. 670). This perspective, by focusing only upon cultural weaknesses, has perpetuated negative myths and stereotypes; at the same time, it has had a major impact on the development of social policy for black families. Inevitably, policies and research pertaining to this group have been premised on the assumption that problems reside within the individual and not within the society or the conditions in the environment. Criticism of this perspective has been extensive (Allen, 1978; Gutman, 1976; Rainwater & Yancey, 1967; Staples, 1971), and an opposing view has been presented.

The cultural relativity view, which is supported by notable scholars, such as Billingsley (1968), Blassingame (1972), Hill (1972), and Nobles (1974), builds upon the strengths of the black family. This view is based upon one or a combination of both of the following concepts. Unlike the pathological and dysfunctional view, the first premise maintains that recognizable and acceptable cultural differences exist between black and white Americans (Valentine, 1968; Young, 1974). The second, which to a great extent builds upon Herskovits's (1966) anthropological study of African culture, argues that black family differences can be directly attributed to the survival and the retention of African cultural patterns (Blassingame, 1972; Nobles, 1974; Turnbull, 1976; Young, 1974). From this system arises the foundations for extended family patterns of black Americans (Billingsley, 1968; Hays & Mindel, 1973; Hill, 1972).

Much controversy continues around the validity of theoretical perspectives pertaining to black families. However, this study subscribes to the belief that black families are

> an important subculture of American society . . . , possessing a value system, patterns of behavior, and institutions which can be described, understood, and appreciated for their own strengths and characteristics. The black family . . . serves the peculiar survival needs of a group which continues to suffer discrimination, prejudice, and subtle institutional racism. (Peters, 1978, p. 655)

Resources for Human Care

That eleven percent of the total black population is at 60 years old and over has major implications for the distribution of resources for human care. Resources are defined in human as well as material terms. It takes considerable energy and understanding to care for the over 60-year-old population, particularly if they are not in the best of health. At the same time, those over 60 years of age can be a great resource themselves.

The results of research have shown that the family, rather than serving as an alternative support system, provides supplemental aid to those in greatest need. An additional supplement to the family structure is the informal support network of friends and neighbors (Cantor, 1979a,b; Evans & Northwood, 1978; Mindel & Wright, 1980; Stanford, 1978a). Furthermore, in times of greatest need, the black family continues to be the major source of assistance, although the elderly rely on local community services (Stanford, 1978a). That 42 percent of blacks 55 years old and over are married and living with a spouse is significant. They form an important family nucleus that many say has disappeared. This group is often the hub of important service activities.

Extended Family Structure

In *Black Families in White America,* Billingsley (1968, p. 4) developed a detailed theoretical position for understanding the Negro family. Not only did his position accentuate the interrelationship of the Negro family at different levels of society, it also stressed the group's heterogeneity. Billingsley (1968, pp. 16–21) established a framework with three types of families: nuclear, extended, and augmented. Briefly, the nuclear family is composed of the husband and wife, two parents and their children, or the single parent family; the extended family is made up of the nuclear family with the addition of other relatives; and the augmented family consists of family members and nonrelated persons residing in the same household—"roomers, boarders, lodgers or other relatively long-term guests" (p. 21).

From all indications through the use of Billingsley's typology, black family structure and relationships differ from that of white families. One of the prominent areas in which this difference occurs is that of the extended family. In a comparative study of black and white family interactions in the Midwest, Hays and Mindel (1973, p. 55) concluded that black families (with the exception of the parents) interacted more with extended family members than did the white group. Black families also viewed their relatives as having more importance to them. Hays and Mindel suggest further that the black experience in a hostile environment probably serves to strengthen kinship ties. Other scholars (Dubey, 1971; Nobles, 1974; Stack, 1974) support the preceding hypothesis. In a discussion of the black extended family as a source of strength, Mathis (1978) says that the extended family system is assumed to provide support for family members. The black extended family consists not only of conjugal and blood relatives, but also nonrelatives. The prevalence of extended families is another cultural pattern that further identifies the differences between whites and blacks. Blacks are more likely than white Americans to include the elderly in their family structures (Hill, 1972; Jackson, 1971; Mindel, 1980; Wylie, 1971). Furthermore, using data collected in the 1968 National Senior Citizen Survey, Mindel and Wright (1980) found that a major biracial difference noted in black extended family patterns was that the elderly played a more prominent role than in the white group.

Family Contact Patterns

Effect of Change

Although sparse data exist to indicate what the major interaction patterns between the black elderly and their families truly are, speculations about relationships and interactions can be made from the available data. The black extended family has not remained the same since the mid-1940s. Shifts have occurred that have not been documented in a formal fashion, and it appears that the black extended family has made shifts which have had and will continue to have a significant impact on the intergenerational relationships between the old and the younger blacks in the community.

A major impetus for some of the changes in expectations and relationships has been the mobility factor. More young and middle-aged adults are beginning to leave the community very early in their work lives, or they leave once they have become established in a particular career line. The shift may not be overwhelming at this point, but it is significant enough for researchers to begin to look at what may happen to future familial relationships in providing support for the older population.

It is not a one-way relationship that is of concern in discussing intergenerational familial interactions and patterns in the community. Younger persons will not have the benefit of the experience and the involvement of the older person that they might have had in the community in previous years. Much has been said about the richness older people provide by way of knowledge for those who are beginning to take responsibility for leadership in the community. It has been assumed that blacks and other minorities maintain their historical continuity and continue to transmit valuable information that builds tradition and stability in the community. Whether or not this assumption is valid remains to be tested. If it is found to have validity, the question remains: How long can older persons maintain meaningful relationships so that tradition is maintained and built upon in the community?

Development of Intergenerational Ties

Intergenerational bonds come about in two ways. First, spontaneous opportunities for mutual support occur; then, formal systems for persons to come together for mutual involvement and support emerge. The most natural (and sometimes most beneficial) avenues are those discovered spontaneously; however, there is much to be said for the more formal development of opportunities for people to come together. Older persons are often alone in the community and do not have spontaneous opportunities for meeting and involving themselves with others. More often than not, it is important for the continued enrichment of the community to bring together wisdom (represented by the older person) and skills (often represented by younger persons), irrespective of the process. It is not intended to suggest, of course, that older people do not bring needed skills into the relationship. The assumption is that many older persons who have not continued to keep pace with technological change and new policies and regulations need the input of younger adults and others who have been specifically trained in the newer technological arenas. The marriage of these two can certainly be a powerful influence in the immediate community and in the political arena.

The service role of the black family has been acknowledged at many levels. The family has not only depended upon the nuclear group for services, but it has looked toward the community-at-large as a part of that support network. As the black community redefines itself, patterns appear to be developing. For example, there have been times when the black family could be found ''where the blacks live or in the black part of the community.'' Today, in some parts of our country it is becoming more difficult to designate one particular area as the place where all blacks live. The important point in this discussion is that the types of support the black older people who are not necessarily within the confines of the traditional black community need are basically the same as those needed by persons who remain in the traditional black environment. Therefore, as these families or persons move away from their traditional support networks, new ways of interacting must be established.

Modes of Contact

Two levels of interaction seem important. The first level has to do with those families that are separated by many miles. The types of direct services and supports that can be expected are minimal. The types of interactions move from face-to-face contacts to communication by telephone and to using the mail services on a more regular basis. In addition, more persons find themselves setting up a variety of visiting patterns that provides support to the elderly. For example, the older persons may visit the adult children, or their children will take turns visiting the older person on a periodic basis. The notion is to establish a pattern of direct contact that allows the parties to continue to have the feeling of personal support. The second level of change that comes about is in the way services are provided among persons who find themselves away from the immediate family. The exchange of services is perhaps one of the most common ways in which individuals find themselves having their needs met. Another way in which service needs are met has to do with the service barter system. The service barter system works very well when both parties have something they can trade off. They may trade off one service for another, but in many cases, other in-kind activities or material goods may be exchanged for a variety of services. As we shall see later, this too may fall under the rubric of volunteer activities.

Informal Support System

From a research perspective, in 1970, Cantor and her associates (1979a, p. 27) conducted a comprehensive cross-cultural survey of the urban poor, 60 years of age or older, living in the inner city of New York. Forty-nine percent of the total sample (1,552) was white; 37 percent was black; and 13 percent was Hispanic. The scope of the research was narrowed down to include an in-depth look at the informal support system of the minority elderly. Although the informal support network included family, friends, and neighbors, the major emphasis was on the family—especially the children (Cantor, 1979b, p. 158). Cantor found that

> black . . . and other poor and working-class families are more likely to have highly developed patterns of child-parent interaction arising out of the economic and social necessity than is the case among more well-to-do elderly. (p. 173)

As a result, the family was acknowledged as the principal source of assistance, irrespective of the chore. In concentrating on the role of friends and neighbors, researchers found that in the absence of kin, especially children, this group became a vital substitute. Findings from a study in a black community in Seattle described the informal support system of friends and neighbors as a supplement to the family structure with distinct, but overlapping, roles (Evans & Northwood, 1978, p. 203).

In a further analysis of the 376 black aged women from the same sample, Cantor and her associates (1979) reached the conclusion that strong family ties exist within the black community and that the family structure, rather than "social class, number of children, and level of need," seems to indicate the amount of help older black women may get from their children (Cantor, Rosenthal, & Wilker, 1979, p. 59). This finding means that older black women living by themselves (who, in all probability, are in the greatest need of assistance) get a minimum amount of aid from their offspring in the routine tasks of daily living. Under these circumstances, older black women living alone have less opportunity to interact with their children.

In 1974, a major cross-cultural study of eight ethnic minority elderly groups— one of which was black—was initiated in San Diego. The research on each of the groups studied shared the same overall objectives. Specifically, as formally stated in the *Black Elder* (Stanford, 1978b), the objectives of concern to this presentation were as follows:

● First, to analyze characteristic lifestyles and customs, as well as the primary interactional networks of ethnic minority groups and in this case, especially those of black elders;

• Second, to explore and delineate the perceptions and viewpoints of the black elders toward formal programmatic assistance and human service networks with the overall intent of tracing, where possible, the interaction between the formal programs and the primary networks (p. 1).

The black study population was comprised of 101 persons between 52 and 95 years of age (Stanford, 1978b, p. 13). The fundamental purpose of the research was to take stock of the "service delivery systems" and of their suitability for the minority elderly in San Diego. Stanford (1978b, p. 43) found that (1) in times of need, the family network, both immediate and extended, continued to be the major means of assistance; (2) the black respondents tended to rely primarily on local community services; and (3) the respondents usually participated in activities composed of persons from the same racial group.

Filial Responsibility

Seelbach (1980) did a comparative analysis to determine the black and white elderly's attitude toward filial responsibility. It was anticipated that the black sample would have higher expectations of their adult children than did their white counterparts. In Philadelphia, among the low income 65 years of age and above, there were no significant differences. Seelbach contends "that many racial differences in family structures and functioning may actually be socio-economic differences" (p. 9).

In a report based on the data from a Los Angeles study, Newquist (1979) revealed some interesting findings on the different attitudes of ethnic groups toward family supports. Unlike the white group, blacks did not believe that adult children were responsible for their aged parents. The majority of the respondents were in agreement that the aged should maintain their autonomy from their families. Furthermore, most of the elderly (the white in particular) did not want to reside with their offspring when they retired, although they wanted to be in the same vicinity as their children.

In summary, emphasis tends to be on the family as the informal support network and the primary source of social interaction for aged blacks. Because of such trends as the black elderly's rapid growth, increasing poverty status, and changing family roles and patterns, alternative or supplemental support systems must be identified. These needs may be filled by social interaction within the community. One such mechanism already in existence, which can possibly be expanded upon, is that of voluntarism. Thus, the remainder of this chapter will explore concepts for the black family, the relationships with the elderly, and the potential for community interaction through voluntarism.

BLACK VOLUNTARISM

Community Interaction through Voluntarism

There are innumerable definitions of community interaction and its derivatives. One such concept is voluntarism. The volunteer is defined as:

> the individual who freely contributes his services, without remuneration commensurate with the value of services rendered, to public or voluntary organizations engaged in preventing, controlling, or ameliorating the effects of social problems experienced by individuals, groups or communities. (Sieder, 1971, p. 1525)

Voluntary associations are customarily defined as any formal organization, irrespective of size, in which the membership is optional. In recent years this definition has been extended to include the church.

Myrdal, Sterner, and Rose (1944) suggested that blacks were overinvolved in volunteer associations and labeled such activity as "pathological." Babchuk and Thompson (1962) reconciled this overinvolvement by viewing blacks' participation as "compensatory" in fulfilling the unmet social interaction needs not available in the dominant society.

Ethnicity

After the more recent civil rights movement, Olsen (1970) put forth the alternative premise of "ethnic community." The basic concept is that ethnic minorities usually adhere to the norms and pressures of their group members. Thus, members of ethnic communities tend to be more cohesive than members of the larger society. Blacks who strongly identify with their community are more likely to be active in a broad range of voluntary activities. Olsen felt that the ethnic community concept complemented the compensation premise. Together, both concepts accounted for higher black than white participation in a variety of social and political endeavors.

Religious Affiliation

In a later study by Ross and Wheeler (1971), the authors found that those persons who were not members of a church were less likely to participate in voluntary associations. One could argue that church activities tend to socialize people toward social participation and to inculcate civic awareness and responsibility values.

Although there are diverse views about the black elderly's volunteer services through traditional nonreligious associations, documentation is limited. In spite of the contradictory positions of the sociological studies cited earlier, there are clear indications that in the past, many of today's elderly were actively involved in volunteer associations. Historically, blacks have volunteered in various capacities throughout "their lifetime" in this country—starting with the Revolutionary War and including the many wars that followed. There are innumerable accounts from the time of the Reconstruction Era of blacks' endeavors in organized self-help activities. A more obvious example is the entire civil rights movement; realistically, it was no more than a voluntary, citizen participation effort. The church, one of the oldest institutions in the black community, has remained the primary vehicle through which older blacks continue to interact in the community.

Social Class

In an analysis of the lifestyles of the black elderly, Lambing (1972) identified social class differences in their community activities. Persons from each social class had some involvement in church activities, which included positions such as committee members and church officers. The professional group averaged 12.8 leisure time activities, which included civic and community volunteer work and membership in lodges and veterans organizations. Blue collar workers averaged 6.3 leisure activities and, to a large extent, were active lodge members. Finally, the low-income group averaged 4.1 leisure activities and belonged to lodges and other clubs.

Gerontologists commonly assume that voluntary efforts are a crucial means for sustaining the community and social interaction of the elderly. The anticipated results of such activity are, of course, higher morale and a sense of well-being among participants. For the black elderly, the number and type of activities are often a function of social status. For many, their roles and activities focus upon things such as supplemental income, informal activities with families and friends, and community activities that require little, if any, financial expenditures.

Retirement

From a secondary analysis of data from the nationwide study by Louis Harris and Associates, "Myths and Realities of Aging in America," Jackson and Wood (1976) obtained more generalizable information from the black aged sample of 200. An unexpected discovery was that the black aged felt less useful in retirement than other age or racial groups. The church and the role of religion continued to be most important to this group. Their evaluation of activities indicated that higher participation in church activities and visitation with neighbors was a manifestation "of a cohesive Black community for some older Blacks" (p. 17). Although volunteer work was as meaningful to the black elderly as to their white counterparts, differences existed in the types of activities in which the two groups became engaged. Jackson and Wood found that "Proportionately more of the aged Blacks than aged Whites worked in family services, civic affairs, education, interracial and cultural activities'' (p. 18). One can conclude that in spite of the hardships associated with age and race, the black elderly still exhibit a great deal of strength and desire for social interactions within the community.

The Black Volunteer and Nonvolunteer

The Volunteer

The foregoing discussion makes it clear that the black elder has traditionally had a role as volunteer. Heretofore, neither the provider nor the recipient of informal good deeds or assistance considered the act to be that of volunteering; volunteer activities were thought to be highly formal and organized and reserved for persons with better than average resources.

Black elders have normally been restricted to participating in activities sanctioned by their immediate community and peer group. Seldom has there been the freedom to consider involvement across racial lines. As a result, the role of the black elder volunteer can be narrowly described as that of being available to help in situations of need or to do good deeds to ameliorate the ills of their immediate environment. The general pattern of behavior for black volunteers has gone unchanged for a variety of reasons. The primary reason has been the little outreach to make blacks feel comfortable in settings where they have often been denied the right of membership or informal involvement.

As resources continue to become scarce, more emphasis will be placed on the reliance upon informal supports as a primary means of getting needs met. This emphasis includes our depending upon the elderly in our midst.

The volunteer role for the black elder has three guiding principles. First, persons must be convinced that what is being asked of them can be done in a manner that will not embarrass them. Next, they need to see a practical relationship between what they are doing and how it will benefit them and their community. Lastly, it must enhance their status as a person in the eyes of their peers first and then of others. When the initiator of volunteer opportunities keeps these and similar principles in mind, it is possible to develop a cadre of elder blacks who can become effective volunteers. In summary, the key to developing a volunteer group of black elders that can be depended upon to provide a service is the ability to predict that they are available, and that they will respond to the need to serve or to assist a broad constituency.

The Nonvolunteer

It is not incumbent upon all older blacks to volunteer or even to feel that it is something they should want to do. The first order of business is to insure that they are well-adjusted older persons who can, if they wish, live independent lives. It is reasonable to speculate that the nonvolunteer is apt to depend on personal resources rather than to become indebted to friends or strangers. There is no need to induce guilt feelings in those who have the time and the energy to contribute toward volunteer activity, but who choose not to do so. Furthermore, the non-volunteer in the black community (whether elderly or not) is potentially someone who has tremendous influence in the immediate environment. They are often the influential persons others seek out, and so they do not need to "go out" to provide a service.

Professional service organizations and agencies can serve as vital links in promoting the independence of those elder blacks who do not volunteer. They must be sensitive to the ways blacks have fulfilled their needs for recreation, religion, and income. There should also be an equal awareness of the health history of those being pursued. Professional service organizations can help by developing formal programs designed to educate the elderly about special avenues of assistance that ensure more independence. To achieve this goal, these agencies must devise communication stratagems that reach black elders. It means going into the community and spending time with representatives of formal and informal groups to better understand how to be of maximum use to the nonvolunteer types.

Evidence has been provided to support the position that self-help, community participation and voluntary associations have been an integral part of the black elder's life. For the black elderly, community interactions provide them with the opportunity for socialization, the acquisition of prestige, problem-solving, and expressive needs at a time when physical, social, and economic factors restrict their lives.

IMPLICATIONS

Innovative and effective program development of service delivery systems on behalf of the minority elderly requires knowledge of and sensitivity to their cultural and socio-economic history (Tamez & Hyslin, 1980, p. 17). The hetero-geneity that exists within an ethnic group and between different ethnic groups is of primary importance in the planning and the implementation of policies and programs for the elderly. More and more, policymakers and administrators are being confronted with the need for more detailed subcultural information. Such information is essential as they try to ensure a fair distribution of limited and shrinking resources among the different groups.

Demographic data indicate that the black elderly continue to increase in signifi-cant numbers. The implications for that increase are important not only for the black community but for the society at large because this group represents a major national resource. The older black person has not been thought of in such terms.

The population that is going to represent the older black group in the 1990s and beyond will be a much different older black population than has been in existence before. These will be persons who will have had different exposure and experiences and will be expecting to participate in meaningful ways in the total community. They will have had an opportunity to be exposed to much more by way of community interests and volunteer efforts. It is not enough to hope that the older black person will find ways to volunteer his or her time without the input from community agencies and organizations. Those who want to volunteer will find ways of doing it; therefore, it is time to go beyond that type of mind-set. Inasmuch as a large number of older persons are going to be in relatively good health and can be involved in meaningful activities in the community, it is paramount that they be included in the planning.

One of the fallacies in thinking about social relations in the black community centers around the notion that everything is based on a survival mode. Instead of being looked at on the basis that people are involved with each other because it is to their liking to do so, generational relationships have generally been viewed as being absolutely necessary in order for either party to survive. Undoubtedly, there are many situations in which survival is the issue, but it is not necessarily survival in the truest sense. Once it is accepted that the minority older persons and those with whom they are involved are engaged in an experience that goes beyond pure survival, there is apt to be much more quality in the relationships, which permits growth and excitement for all parties involved.

Throughout the history of politics in our society, basic tenets have prevailed that presume to be in the best interest of the black community. Nevertheless, it is evident that in many instances, neither intent nor desire exists to develop policies that have in mind the black person as the primary beneficiary of the particular legislation or laws. There has not been considerable change in that perspective; however, the black community as a whole has become more aware of some of the injustices and has taken minor steps to make corrections. Progress has come about, however, in a spiral fashion. There have been many good accomplishments, but they have been set back by major legislation or acts that nullify all the good that had come before. They, in turn, dictate new initiatives.

Being politically active and outspoken is also not new for older blacks. Many have been on the front lines for many years. It is important at this stage of the development of black communities to continue to use the wisdom and the experience that older blacks have in the area of political action. Only political involvement and political activity can effect significant change that allows for interactions and relationships among all age groups in the community to proceed in a reasonable fashion.

It is most important for those in policy-making positions to be aware of the changes that are coming about in major black communities and in areas of transition. It is also the responsibility of policymakers to insure that all constituents receive services and benefits that are forthcoming.

A number of implications can be drawn from the preceding profile of aged blacks. To begin with, blacks 50 years of age and older are one of the fastest growing segments of this society. In spite of this growth, a gap of nearly 13 percent still exists between the black aged and their white counterparts.

Close attention must also be paid to who these elderly are. They may be small in number, but they are able to have a substantial impact on their community—whether predominantly black or mixed. These are the elders who serve on boards, join clubs, and—most important—become role models for the young and middle-aged blacks.

Along with the growth of the black elderly population, there is also a notable increase (5%) in the rate of poverty among blacks 65 years of age or older. Although nearly 14 percent of the white population in this same age group lives in poverty, a disproportionate number (38%) of their black counterparts live under the same conditions. The economic status of the black elderly is one indicator of their greater relative need.

The "crossover effect" has received immense notoriety. Those who live very long lives serve a most useful function in the community. First, they represent strength and survivability and stand as living examples of what can happen when health and other life circumstances are favorable. As the number of old blacks increases, facilities in the home and the community in general must be adjusted or modified to accommodate this new segment of the black community.

REFERENCES

Affeldt, D. (1981). Fact sheet on poverty among older Blacks (65 or older). *Quarterly Contact, 3*, 6.

Allen, W.R. (1979). Class, culture, and family organization: The effects of class and race on family structure in urban America. *Journal of Comparative Family Studies, 10*, 301–313.

Allen, W.R. (1978). Black family research in the United States: A review, assessment, and extension. *Journal of Comparative Family Studies, 9*, 167–189.

Babchuk, N., & Thompson, R. (1962). The voluntary associations of Negroes. *American Sociological Review, 27*, 647–655.

Billingsley, A. (1968). *Black families in white America*. Englewood Cliffs, NJ: Prentice-Hall.

Blassingame, J.W. (1972). *The slave community: Plantation life in antebellum South*. New York: Oxford Press.

Cantor, M.H. (1979a). Effect of ethnicity on life styles of the inner-city elderly. In J. Hendricks & C.D. Hendricks (Eds.), *Dimensions of aging readings*. Cambridge, MA: Winthrop Publishers.

Cantor, M.H. (1979b). The informal support system of New York's inner-city elderly: Is ethnicity a factor? In D.E. Gelfand & A.J. Kutzik (Eds.), *Ethnicity and aging: Theory, research, and policy*. New York: Springer Publishing.

Cantor, M.H., Rosenthal, K., & Wilker, L. (1979). Social and family relationships of black aged women in New York City. *Journal of Minority Aging, 4,* 50–61.

Dodson, J. (1981). Conceptualizations of black families. In H.P. McAdoo (Ed.), *Black families* (pp. 23–36). Beverly Hills, CA: Sage Publications.

Dubey, S.N. (1971). Powerlessness and orientations toward family and children: A study in deviance. *Indian Journal of Social Work, 32,* 35–43.

Evans, R.L., & Northwood, L.K. (1978). The utility of locality based social networks. *Journal of Minority Aging, 3,* 199–211.

Fowles, D.G. (1978). *Some prospects for the future elderly population* (Statistical Reports on Older Americans, No. 3). Washington, DC: U.S. Government Printing Office.

Frazier, E.F. (1939). *The Negro family in the United States.* Chicago: University of Chicago Press.

Gutman, H. (1976). *The Black family in slavery and freedom: 1750-1925.* New York: Random House.

Hays, W.C., & Mindel, C.H. (1973). Extended kinship relations in black and white families. *Journal of Marriage and the Family,* 35, 51–57.

Herskovits, M.J. (Ed.) (1966). *The new world Negro.* Bloomington, IN: Indiana Press.

Herskovits, M.J. (1941). *The myth of the Negro past.* New York: Harper and Row.

Hill, R. (1972). *The strengths of Black families.* New York: Emerson-Hall.

Jackson, J. (1971). Sex and social class variations in black aged parent-adult child relationships. *Aging and Human Development, 2,* 96–107.

Jackson, M., & Wood, J.L. (1976). *Aging in America: Implications for the Black aged.* Washington, DC: National Council on the Aging.

Lambing, M.L. Brooks. (1972). Social class living patterns of retired Negroes. *The Gerontologist, 12,* 285–289.

Mathis, A. (1978). Contrasting approaches to the study of Black families. *Journal of Marriage and the Family, 40,* 667–676.

Mindel, C.H. (1980). Extended familism among urban Mexican-Americans, Anglos, and Blacks. *Hispanic Journal of Behavioral Sciences, 2,* 21–34.

Mindel, C.H., & Wright, R. (1980, November). *Intergenerational factors in the utilization of social services by black and white elderly: A causal analysis* (pp. 21–25). Paper presented at the 33rd Annual Meeting of the Gerontological Society of America, San Diego, CA.

Moynihan, D.P. (1965). *The Negro family: The case for national action.* Washington, DC: U.S. Government Printing Office.

Myrdal, G., Sterner, R., & Rose, A. (1944). *An American dilemma.* New York: Harper and Row.

Newquist, D., et al. (1979). *Prescription for neglect: Experience of older blacks and Mexican-Americans with the American health care system.* Los Angeles: University of Southern California, Ethel Percy Andrus Gerontology Center.

Nobles, W.W. (1974). Africanity: Its role in black families. *The Black Scholar, 5,* 10–17.

Olsen, M. (1970). Social and political participation of blacks. *American Sociological Review, 35,* 682–697.

Peters, M.F. (1978). Notes from the guest editor. *Journal of Marriage and the Family, 40,* 655–658.

Rainwater, L. (1965). *Family design.* Chicago: Aldine Press.

Rainwater, L., & Yancey, W. (1967). *The Moynihan report and the politics of controversy.* Cambridge, MA: The Massachusetts Institute of Technology Press.

Rodman, H. (1968). Family and social pathology in the ghetto. *Science, 161,* 756–762.

Ross, J.C., & Wheeler, R. (1971). *Black belonging: A study of the social correlates of work relations among Negroes*. Westport, CT: Greenwood Publishing Co.

Seelbach, W.C. (1980, November). *Filial responsibility among aged parents: A racial comparison*. Paper presented at the 33rd Annual Meeting of the Gerontological Society of America, San Diego, CA.

Select Committee on Aging. (1982). *Every ninth American*. Washington, DC: U.S. Government Printing Office.

Sieder, V. (1971). Volunteers. In *Encyclopedia of social work* (Vol. 2). (pp. 1521–1534). Washington, DC: National Association of Social Workers.

Stack, C.B. (1974). *All our kin*. New York: Harper and Row.

Stanford, E.P. (1978a). *Suburban Black elderly*. Los Alamitos, CA: Hwong Publishing Co.

Stanford, E.P. (1978b). *The black elder: A cross-cultural study of minority elders in San Diego*. San Diego: Campanile Press.

Staples, R. (1971). Toward a sociology of the black family: A decade of theory and research. *Journal of Marriage and the Family, 33*, 19–38.

Tamez, H., & Hyslin, N.G. (1980). Amigos del valle. Aging (Vols. 305–306): 14–19.

Turnbull, C.M. (1976). *Man in Africa*. Garden City, NY: Anchor Press/Doubleday.

U.S. Bureau of the Census. (1981a). *Race of the population by states: 1980*. Supplementary Reports, PC80-S1-3. Washington, DC: Goverment Printing Office.

U.S. Bureau of the Census. (1981b). *Marital status and living arrangements: March 1980*. Series P-20, No. 365. Washington, DC: Government Printing Office.

Valentine, C.A. (1968). *Culture and poverty*. Chicago: University of Chicago Press.

Williams B. (1980). *Characteristics of the Black elderly—1980*. Washington, DC: U.S. Department of Health and Human Services.

Wylie, F. (1971). Attitudes toward aging and the aged among black Americans: Some historical perspectives. *Aging and Human Development, 2*, 66–70.

Young, V.H. (1974). A black American socialization pattern, *American Ethnologist, 1*, 405–413.

Chapter 12

Older Rural Parents and Their Children

Jean Pearson Scott and Karen A. Roberto

Only in recent years has the population of rural older Americans been recognized as a group distinctive enough to warrant special examination. Approximately 9 million older persons—38 percent of the older population—live in nonmetropolitan areas of the United States (U.S. Bureau of the Census, 1979). Furthermore, many rural areas have a disproportionately high number of older persons; the highest proportion of all persons 65 years old and over reside in small towns with populations ranging from 1,000 to 2,500 people. The proportion of older persons living in rural areas reaches 40 percent or more in 21 states (Atchley, 1975). Clearly, a large number of older adults strive to maintain their independence in rural areas of the country.

The great diversity that exists among the rural elderly is only beginning to be fully appreciated; yet, a few generalizations about the characteristics of the rural elderly can be made to provide a context in which to examine their family relationships. Most older rural persons report satisfaction with their quality of life measured by such indicators as morale, satisfaction with housing and community, family and social interaction, and standard of living (Coward & Kerckhoff, 1978; Hynson, 1975; Lassey, Lassey, & Lee, 1980). Despite a high level of reported subjective well-being, rural older adults are vulnerable to a number of the problems that plague rural areas. The greater incidence of poverty and malnutrition, poor health, greater distance to services, and substandard housing are characteristics of rural areas, and these characteristics exacerbate problems of the older adult (Lassey, Lassey, & Lee, 1980; Youmans, 1967; U.S. Senate, 1976; White House Conference on Aging, 1981). For example, 60 percent of all substandard housing in America is in rural areas, and approximately 25 percent of

Note: The research for this chapter was supported by a grant from the AARP Andrus Foundation, Washington, D.C.

these homes are occupied by the elderly. Moreover, rural persons have lower incomes than urban residents, which often makes home improvement unaffordable. Approximately 20 percent of the older rural population exists on an income below the poverty guidelines, and many hover just above the poverty threshold (White House Conference on Aging, 1982). Because employment opportunities for older persons are limited in rural areas, persons who would like to be more economically independent may not have the opportunity to do so. Although objective indicators suggest that the needs of older adults are high, supportive services are limited in rural areas. Unfortunately, many services available under the Older Americans Act do not adequately serve rural or geographically isolated locations (U.S. Senate, 1976; White House Conference on Aging, 1982). Transportation programs, alternative housing, medical facilities and personnel, and food and nutrition programs are frequently not available in many rural communities (Lassey et al., 1980). These conditions present threats to the independence of older rural persons—particularly if informal networks of support (i.e., family and friend networks) are weak.

Because there is a lack of service programs for rural older adults, the presence of informal sources of support is essential to their well-being. The largest single source of informal support to older adults is adult children, second only to that provided by spouses (White House Conference on Aging, 1982). Furthermore, there is ample evidence that adult children remain an important source of contact, assistance, and emotional gratification for older parents. In view of the limited formal support and the vulnerability of the aged in rural environments, this chapter gives attention to the vital supportive role of children in the maintenance of independence among rural older parents.

Little attention has been given to the family interaction of the rural elderly in either the gerontological or rural sociology literature (Powers, Keith, and Goudy, 1975). Actually, much of what we know about the family relationships of the older adult has been based on data from urban populations—a population more easily accessible to the researcher. Furthermore, when a rural component has been included in studies, rural-urban distinctions are often ignored; therefore, generalizing from urban samples to rural populations may be misleading. Additionally, many of the existing reports about family relations are descriptive in nature and are largely based on frequency of interaction measures. Further exploration of the actual supportive relationship existing between rural older adults and their children—exploration that moves beyond frequency of interaction measures—is needed. Because adult children are the primary sources of support for their older parents, this chapter focuses on this central familial relationship and draws upon findings of a recent study about the support provided by children to a sample of rural elders. First, key factors influencing the supportive relationship of the rural elderly and their children are identified. Next, findings from our research about some neglected aspects of the parent-child relationship are discussed, and factors influencing this relationship are identified. Finally, the implications of these findings for practitioners who work with rural older families are discussed.

THE RURAL ELDERLY STUDY

The findings reported in this chapter were based on a sample of 571 adults who were 65 to 94 years of age and from rural areas in two west Texas counties. They were selected by a compact cluster sampling technique. The populations of both counties were widely dispersed, averaging 4 and 36 persons per square mile. All respondents were rural residents by census definitions (U.S. Bureau of the Census, 1981).

Women constituted 58.2 percent of the sample, and men, 41.8 percent. The racial or ethnic composition was 89.1 percent white, 3.2 percent black, and 7.7 percent Hispanic. One-half of the respondents were married, 44.9 percent were widowed, 3 percent were single, 1.8 percent were divorced, and 0.2 percent were separated. The mean educational level of the participants was nine years. Respondents ranged in age from 65 to 94 years; the average age was 74 years. The average number of living children reported by the respondents was three, 13 percent of the sample reported no living children. The mean gross monthly income of the sample fell in the $600 to $699 category. The average yearly income was approximately $8,500 when the sale of crops and other yearly income was combined with monthly income.

Of the respondents who had children, 12.2 percent had at least one child living in the same household; 45 percent had at least one child living in the same town or neighborhood; 32.3 percent of the respondents had at least one child living within 49 miles; 46.9 percent had at least one child living with 50 to 250 miles; and 65.9 percent had at least one child living more than 250 miles away. Contacts with children were frequent; 47.6 percent of the respondents who had a child in the same town or neighborhood received a daily visit, When the nearest children lived within 49 miles of their parents, approximately one-half visited once a week, and one third had at least monthly contact with their children. Even when respondents lived more than 250 miles from the nearest child, over 59 percent usually saw their children two to four times a year. When the respondents were asked how often they talked on the phone with at least one of their children, 22.1 percent of the respondents said daily, 40.9 percent said weekly, and 22.1 percent said at least monthly.

The older respondents were asked to evaluate the quality of their relationship with the child with whom they had the most contact. They were also asked to indicate how much help they received from their children and how much help they gave to their children. The type of reciprocity in the relationship was examined by subtracting help received from help given. Respondents fell then into one of three groups: (1) the overbenefited, those receiving more than giving; (2) the reciprocators, those making equal exchanges of assistance; and (3) the under-benefitors, those giving more than receiving. Also, the number and the types of joint activities with children were tallied.

KEY FACTORS IN THE PARENT-CHILD RELATIONSHIP

Much of the information about rural family life has been gleaned from research reports and bulletins of agricultural experiment stations (Powers et al., 1975). Also, several published studies provide some of the early data on parent-child contact among the rural elderly (Youmans, 1967; Shanas et al., 1968). Youmans's now classic, edited volume of articles included a chapter that summarized much of the earliest literature about the family relationships of rural older adults (Britton & Britton, 1967). Shanas and associates (1968) conducted a cross-cultural examina-tion of family relationships among older adults. Their sample from the United States included a rural component among the nearly 2,500 interviews that were obtained. These studies provided clear evidence that rural older persons main-tained close contact with their families, especially their children, and were not socially isolated.

Assistance Patterns

The reports of research about the mutual aid patterns of older rural adults and their families suggest that when help is needed, adult children are the family members most relied upon for assistance and provide the major portion of support to their older parents (Powers et al., 1975). Two studies report that approximately 60 percent of the rural elderly received help from children (Rosencranz, Philblad, & McNevin, 1968; Shanas et al., 1968). However, filial assistance has been characterized as relatively short-term (Powers et al., 1975) and usually does not involve financial support (Auerbach, 1976; Kivett & Scott, 1979).

Gender, marital status, and proximity to children are crucial factors in determin-ing the extent of assistance to older rural parents. When children live at a distance, severe constraints are placed on the concrete types of assistance (e.g., help with shopping, transportation) that children can provide and on the kind of support older parents offer to children. In general, the rural older woman is more eco-nomically disadvantaged than her male counterpart (U.S. Bureau of the Census, 1979). Loneliness and inadequate transportation are common problems for rural women (Kivett, 1978, 1979; Patton, 1975).

There is much evidence that marital status has a profound effect on the vulnerability of the married older adult (Powers et al., 1975). Being female and widowed tends to compound problems. Although the most recent findings reveal no gender differences on subjective well-being of the widowed (Liang, 1982;

Scott & Kivett, in press), the reports do suggest that widows face greater hardships (e.g., lower economic status, poorer health) than widowers. Consequently, widows are more vulnerable at this life stage. The special problems of older rural widows include vulnerability to loneliness, greater dependence upon others for transportation, and difficulties reintegrating into society after the death of a spouse (Hooyman, 1980; Kivett, 1978, 1979; Patton, 1975). As it would be expected, the widowed do receive greater assistance than the married (Powers et al., 1975).

A norm of reciprocity is evident in the assistance patterns of children and other family members (Powers et al., 1975); however, changes of assistance have not been studied in depth. We do not know what other factors influence patterns of exchange (e.g., why some receive more than they give or give more than they receive). Nor do we know the impact of assistance patterns on the quality of the relationship.

Our findings indicated that the most frequent types of assistance older parents received from their children were assistance when ill (59.1 percent), help in making important decisions (37.5 percent), transportation (32.3 percent) and making household repairs (32.3 percent). Consistent with other research, the widowed received more help from children in the 13 assistance areas in which responses were obtained than did the married respondents, t (447) = -6.40, p <0.001. Also, females received significantly more help than males across the thirteen areas.

The respondents were also asked about the kinds of help they gave to their children. Assistance when ill (40.4 percent), help in making important decisions (23.3 percent), and sharing garden produce with children (27 percent) were the categories named most often. The only major differences according to the marital status of the respondent were that married persons gave more help to their children in the area of sharing garden produce (X^2 = 11.61, p <0.001).

In terms of reciprocity, the majority (62.7 percent) of older parents were receiving more types of assistance than they were giving, 15.8 percent exchanged equally, and 21.3 percent gave more than they received. A discriminant analysis utilizing 11 demographic, physical, and social variables was used to determine whether older parents could be classified according to three exchange patterns: overbenefiting, reciprocating, and underbenefiting. Two significant functions were derived; the first accounted for 80 percent of the explained variance. The sex of the parent made the largest contribution to the first function, followed by age, marital status, and self-rated health. The first function was represented by older widows who were in poor health. They were classified in the overbenefited group. The second function was represented by the total number of activities with children. Those parents engaging in the highest number of activities with children tended to fall in the underbenefited group.

These findings underscore the greater dependence and need for assistance experienced by women in rural areas, particularly the widowed at advanced ages.

The results indicate that the children of older widowed women are heavily relied upon for assistance and that the need for help is greater when resources, such as personal health, are diminished. In an opposite light, men tended to give assistance to children, perhaps as a result of having greater economic resources or from being more reluctant to accept help.

Mutual Activities with Children

Although there is much evidence of the frequent contact that is maintained among the rural elderly and their children (Shanas et al., 1968; Kivett & Scott, 1979), few studies have directly examined the types of activities older rural persons and their children enjoy together. Visiting, whether face-to-face, by letter, or by telephone, obviously takes place among older parents and their children, but we know very little about social interaction and the mutual leisure activities enjoyed by rural older families.

Results from the present study indicated that the most common activities were spending happy occasions together (82 percent), vacation visits (69.3 percent), drop-in visits (67 percent) and home recreation (56.8 percent). Widows were involved to a greater extent with their children in the areas of going to church together ($X^2 = 4.10$, $p < 0.05$), and shopping together ($X^2 = 6.42$, $p < 0.01$). Married persons were more involved in outdoor recreation with their children than were widowed persons ($X^2 = 10.81$, $p < 0.001$).

As the results of the discriminant analysis showed, participating in activities with offspring was a significant variable that distinguished older parents who gave more assistance to their children than they received. Activities also figured significantly in the analysis of perceived quality of the parent-adult child relationship.

Quality of the Parent-Child Relationship

Virtually no substantive information is available about the quality of the rural elderly's relationship with children. Neither do we know what factors influence the quality of the parent-child relationship in later life. This lack of information is due in large part to failure in the past to ask questions about the qualitative elements of relationships. The findings reported in the literature reveal that the rural elderly are generally satisfied with the amount of contact they have with family members (Britton & Britton, 1967; Kivett & Scott, 1979).

In the present study, the quality of the parent-child relationship was measured with a four-item index that included questions about the overall relationship with the child, how well the respondent enjoyed visits from the child, similarity of views to those of the child, and similarity of interests to those of the child. The responses to the items were weighted equally and summed for a composite score of the quality of the relationship. The vast majority of respondents rated the relationship with the most contacted child very highly. Out of a highest possible score of 1.0 on the quality index, the mean for the sample was 0.90 (SD = 0.10).

The relative importance of several demographic, physical, and social variables in accounting for variation in quality of relationship scores was investigated through the use of multiple regression analysis. Sex, education, age, race, and marital status were entered first into the regression analysis; these were followed by self-rated health, income, and proximity to child. The last set of variables entered into the analysis were reciprocity of parent-child assistance (coded as a dummy variable), total help received from children, total help given to children, and total activities with children.

Despite the limited variability of the scores on the quality of the relationship variable, the analysis resulted in a significant regression equation [F (14,398) = 3.76, p < 0.001], which explained approximately 12 percent of the variance in the dependent variable. The variables making the greatest contributions to the quality of the parent-adult child relationship were marital status, race, activities with children, and sex. Respondents who rated the quality of their relationships the highest tended to be married, rather than widowed; white, rather than black; engaged in a higher number of activities with children; and were female. Marital status and total activities with children were the only familial variables having an influence on the quality of the parent-adult child relationship. Neither assistance nor the direction of the assistance seemed to have a significant effect in and of itself upon the quality of the relationship.

Interestingly, variables that one might think would enhance the quality of a relationship (e.g., income, health) did not figure prominently in explaining the qualitative dimension of the relationship of parent to adult child. As the results indicated, women found their relationships with children to be more highly satisfying. This finding may stem from the close bonds mothers form with their children early in the childrearing years or from women's greater dependency upon children in later life. Although the literature (Powers et al., 1975) indicates that the widowed depend upon children and have more interaction with their children than the married, the married (as the results reveal) rated their relationships higher on qualitative dimensions. There may be several possible explanations for these results. Widowed persons may place greater expectations upon children than can be met. Another possibility is that increased interaction of an obligatory nature may bring differences in values and viewpoints more sharply into focus—differences that cannot easily be overlooked when persons are more involved in each other's lives. There is evidence also that children may be unaware of and ill-prepared to meet the social-emotional needs of the bereaved parent.

The positive association of activities and the quality of the parent-child relationship suggest that activities to some extent are voluntarily engaged in because they have positive intrinsic value. Also, a higher number of joint activities probably reflects a greater similarity of interests. The relatively strong racial influence on relationship quality deserves further study. The findings are surprising in view of past reports demonstrating strong extended family structures among blacks (Jackson, 1971; Sussman, 1976). The low proportion of older blacks in the sample may suggest differences in the filial relationship for this particular group.

Although assistance patterns did not negatively or positively affect the quality of the parent-child relationship, a post hoc analysis revealed that morale scores (measured by the *Philadelphia Geriatric Center Morale Scale*) were significantly different according to the type of parent-child exchange [F (2,527) = 10.39, $p < 0.001$]. Rural older parents who were giving more than they were receiving had significantly higher morale scores than those who reciprocated and those who received more than they gave. Also, the group that reciprocated equally had significantly higher scores than those who received more than they gave.

SUMMARY AND IMPLICATIONS

This chapter examined exchanges of assistance, activity patterns, and the quality of the relationship existing between rural older parents and their children. The findings were based on a study of 571 older rural adults from a two-county area of the Southwest. Three patterns of assistance were examined through the use of a multiple discriminant analysis: a pattern of giving more than receiving, a reciprocal exchange pattern, and a pattern of receiving more than giving. Results of the analysis indicated that older females and the widowed received more help from children, particularly if health was poor. Joint activities usually reported by rural elderly parents and their children included sharing happy occasions, visiting, and participating in recreational activities in the home. Most parents rated the quality of their relationships with children very highly. Variables critical to assessments of the quality of the relationship were widowhood, sex, race, and joint participation in activities. The highest evaluations of the parent-child relationship were from the married (vs. widowed), whites (vs. blacks), women, and persons who participated in a variety of activities with their children.

Despite the sparseness of the population in the areas where the sample was drawn, older rural parents in the study maintained a rather traditional pattern of interaction with their children. Filial relationships were characterized by close proximity, frequent contact with at least one child, and a two-way exchange of assistance in which a greater amount of help was given to the older generation than was received from them. Thus, rural older adults maintain a style of independence that is supported and undergirded by assistance from offspring. In essence, help from children enables rural older adults to maintain their independence through an *interdependence* with their children.

Based upon the findings presented in this chapter, several implications are offered for those working with and formulating policy for rural families and their older members:

- Target the needs of older women and the widowed. The triple jeopardy of being old, female, and a rural resident predisposes persons to greater dependency on adult children. Interventionists need to be alert to the strains that may be placed on this relationship. Additionally, policymakers must continue to give the special needs of this "at risk" group (i.e., low income, isolation, lack of transportation) consideration when they design programs in rural areas.

- Provide educational programs. Educational programs for adult children that address such topics as processes of aging, psychological and social needs of older parents, bereavement and adjustment to widowhood, financial planning, health care, and availability of community services would help to strengthen the quality of support. More knowledge about these areas might result in greater empathy for parents, improved self-confidence, and reduced feelings of anxiety or helplessness in providing support to elderly parents. Obviously, programs related to aging should be offered for older adults themselves; yet, the adult child should not be overlooked.

- Include significant others of older clients in intervention. Because children are a major source of support to the rural elderly their input about services to older family members needs to be considered in program planning. Input from adult children about programs that would make their care-giving roles less burdensome is important. A family-oriented approach to service delivery would help in accomplishing this goal through the development of programs that include significant others and provide incentives and economic reimbursement for families who assume the major care-giving responsibilities for older family members (Coward & Kerckhoff, 1978; see also discussion of incentives and policy analysis provided in Chapters 9 and 14).

- Offset overbenefited assistance patterns. The differential effects of assistance patterns on morale have important implications for interventionists. Even when the effects of other variables were controlled (e.g., health, income) the pattern of receiving more than giving had a negative impact on morale (Scott, 1982). The nature of dependency, therefore, does not influence the quality of the relationship with the child, but it does have consequences for the psychological well-being of older rural parents. The rural elderly may view caregiving from children as fair or as overly generous; however, the negative feelings about self and declining personal resources can seriously affect morale.

Although assistance from children is important to many older parents' ability to maintain independence, companionship through activities with children is important to the quality of the parent-child relationship. It seems clear that involvement in the lives of older rural parents through mutual participation in activities is a valued aspect of parent-child relations. This important dimension of kin support is often overlooked because assistance is usually of greater concern to professionals in service provision roles.

Programs designed to restore more equitable exchanges between the elderly and their support networks is a strategy that has not been fully explored; yet, it would seem to have great potential. Activities that utilize the talent and the abilities of older persons at various levels of physical functioning should be explored. Such activities as telephone reassurance, friendly visiting, and child care could be taken on by an older person in exchange for some other support.

- Support family relationships and care-giving. The independence of the rural elderly can be protected by supportive networks that complement each other. The findings provide empirical evidence that older adults in rural areas have family supports available to them and that these supports are utilized by those persons who have been identified as being among the most disadvantaged of the older rural population (i.e., females, the widowed). Because natural supports are available to most of the rural elderly, the implication for interventionists and those who provide formal services is to strengthen the functioning of existing supports, rather than replacing or disrupting them. Undergirding naturally occurring helping networks is a strategy being voiced by many professionals who are involved in planning services for the elderly (Coward, 1980; Coward & Kerckhoff, 1978; Shanas & Sussman, 1977). Empirical data from the present study support this strategy for rural areas.

FUTURE DIRECTIONS

Future research needs to address the support exchanged between adult children and rural older parents from the perspective of the adult child. Information, from the child's perspective, about problems and strains in the care-giving role and the advantages of exchange between the elderly and adult children would shed further light in this area. Another area for further examination is the identification of strategies to assist older persons in maintaining their sense of usefulness and importance in the family when they find themselves on the receiving end of support. Adult children and parents alike need to know what to anticipate as their relationships change and how to respond appropriately to the change. Additionally, we need more information about the combined functioning of kin and friend support to the rural elderly. Can friendship networks or other natural helping networks adequately fill the void when children and other kin are not available to provide support? Perhaps our attitudes about independence and dependence need some alteration. Independence that is balanced with a recognition that some dependence is acceptable, at any age, may be a more realistic assumption for families as they experience change and growth over time.

REFERENCES

Atchley, R.C. (Ed.). (1975). *Rural environments and aging*. Washington, DC: Gerontological Society.

Auerbach, A. (1976). The elderly in rural areas: Differences in urban areas and implications for practice. In L. Ginsberg (Ed.), *Social work in rural communities* (pp. 99–107). New York: Council on Social Work Education.

Britton, J., & Britton, J. (1967). The middleaged and older rural person and his family. In E.G. Youmans (Ed.), *Older rural Americans* (pp. 44–74). Lexington, KY: University of Kentucky Press.

Coward, R. (1980). Research-based programs for the rural elderly. In W.R. Lassey, M.L. Lassey, G.R. Lee, and N. Lee (Eds.), *Research and public service with the rural elderly* (pp. 39–56). Corvallis, OR: Western Rural Development Center, Oregon State University.

Coward, R.T., & Kerckhoff, R.K. (1978). *The rural elderly: Program planning guidelines*. Ames, IA: North Central Regional Center for Rural Development Center, Iowa State University.

Hooyman, N. (1980). Mutual help organizations for rural older women. *Educational Gerontology, 4*, 429–447.

Hynson, L.M. (1975). Rural-urban differences in satisfaction among the elderly. *Rural Sociology, 40*, 64–66.

Jackson, J.J. (1971). Sex and social class variations in black aged parent-adult child relationships. *Aging and Human Development, 2*, 96–107.

Kivett, V.R. (1978). Loneliness and the rural widow. *The Family Coordinator, 27*, 389–394.

Kivett, V.R. (1979). Discriminators of loneliness among the rural elderly: Implications for intervention. *The Gerontologist, 19*, 108–115.

Kivett, V.R., & Scott, J.P. (1979). *The rural by-passed elderly: Perspectives on status and needs* (Tech. Bul. No. 260). Raleigh, NC: North Carolina Agricultural Research Service and The University of North Carolina at Greensboro.

Lassey, M.L., Lassey, W.R., & Lee, G.R. (1980). Elderly people in rural America. In W.R. Lassey, M.L. Lassey, G.R. Lee, and N. Lee (Eds.), *Research and public service with the rural elderly* (pp. 21–38). Corvallis, OR: Western Rural Development Center, Oregon State University.

Liang, J. (1982). Sex differences in life satisfaction among the elderly. *Journal of Gerontology, 37*, 100–108.

Patton, C. (1975). Age groupings and travel in a rural area. *Rural Sociology, 40*, 55–63.

Powers, E., Keith, P., & Goudy, W.J. (1975). Family relationships and friendships. In R. Atchley (Ed.), *Rural environments and aging* (pp. 67–90). Washington, DC: Gerontological Society.

Rosencranz, H., Philblad, C., & McNevin, T. (1968). Social participation of older people in the small town. Columbia, MO: University of Missouri.

Scott, J. (1982). *Older rural adults: Perspectives on status and needs*. Final Report to NRTA-AARP Andrus Foundation.

Scott, J.P., & Kivett, V.R. (in press). Differences in the morale of older, rural widows and widowers. *International Journal of Aging and Human Development.*

Shanas, E., & Sussman, M. (1977). *Family bureaucracy and the elderly.* Durham, NC: Duke University Press.

Shanas, E., Townsend, P., Wedderburn, D., Friis, H., Milhoj, P., & Stehouwer, J. (1968). *Old people in three industrial societies.* New York: Atherton.

Sussman, M. (1976). The family life of old people. In R.H. Binstock & E. Shanas (Eds.), *Handbook of aging and the social sciences* (pp. 218–243). New York: Van Nostrand Reinhold.

U.S. Bureau of the Census. (1979). *Social and economic characteristics of the older population: 1978* (Current population reports, Series P-23, No. 85). Washington, DC: U.S. Government Printing Office.

U.S. Bureau of the Census. (1981). *1980 Census of population* (Vol. 1, Characteristics of the population, PC80-1). Washington, DC: U.S. Government Printing Office.

U.S. Senate, Special Committee on Aging. (1976). *Developments in aging: 1975 and January–May, 1976* (Report No. 94-998). Washington, DC: U.S. Government Printing Office.

White House Conference on Aging. (1981). *Rural mini-conference report.* Washington, DC: Author.

White House Conference on Aging. (1982). *Final report* (Vols. 1, 2, 3). Washington, DC: Author.

Youmans, E. (Ed.). (1967). *Older rural Americans.* Lexington, KY: University of Kentucky Press.

Chapter 13

Old Men Living Alone: Social Networks and Informal Supports

Robert L. Rubinstein

INDEPENDENT AGING

The topic of independent aging concerns all elderly persons, regardless of living arrangements and social circumstances. To those older people who live alone, it is a special concern. In 1980, some 7 million persons aged 65 years or older—about 30 percent of the 25.5 million elderly in the United States—lived alone (U.S. Senate, 1982).

Successful independent aging for elderly persons who live alone is tied directly to the viability of each person's social networks and informal supports. In this chapter one aspect of independent aging is discussed: specifically, changes in the lives of a sample of older men who live alone and the effects of these changes on social networks.

Persons may live alone for a variety of reasons and may have a variety of feelings about living alone. For older persons who live alone by choice, the notion of independence may have two contrasting meanings. On the one hand, a person may maintain an independent lifestyle, with all the positive and beneficial elements this phrase connotes. Such a lifestyle, regardless of the actual level of contact one has with others, is itself dependent on the day-to-day workings of the social network a person has established. The commonplace exchanges and interactions, so much a part of everyday life, are the substance of an independent lifestyle and a medium for its facilitation.

On the other hand, a person may be independent of support at certain key moments. Under normal social circumstances one's social network—the group of people each person knows and with whom she or he exchanges words, ideas, feelings or material goods, often on a day-to-day basis—represents an operating social environment. Optimally, this social network should evolve into a "natural helping network" in times of crisis and need so that persons are enabled to continue living as independently as they can. Yet, for some elderly living alone, a

194

natural social network is not likely to be mobilized. A variety of factors may account for this.

Life Changes

The focus here is on life changes because it is not merely the onset of age-related deficits that necessitates concern for a person's network. Rather, that network responds to any changes in roles or transitions in the life course that occur in old age (or at any age). Thus, changes such as retirement, widowhood, or eldership lead to significant network changes that have profound implications for independent aging.

Moreover, the focus is on men—a minority of the elderly—because they have received relatively little attention in the social gerontological writings. About 15 million American elderly are women, and about 40 percent of these live alone (U.S. Senate, 1982). Only about 15 percent of the 10 million elderly men live alone.

A majority of the older women who live alone are widows because all but about 5 percent of the older population of both sexes have never married (U.S. Senate, 1982, p. 13). In contrast, there are relatively few widowed men; men, as a group, do not live as long as women. At all ages, men who survive a spouse have a significantly higher incidence of mortality after the loss than do either women survivors or men who continue to be married (Helsing, Szklo, & Comstock, 1981). Although most surviving spouses over 65 years old do not remarry, elderly widowers tend to remarry at a higher frequency than do widows; about 25 percent of older men who lose a spouse after they are 65 years old remarry (Cleveland & Gianturco, 1976). All in all, about 75 percent of men aged 65 to 74 years and about 67 percent of men aged 75 years or older live with a spouse (U.S. Senate, p. 14).

After the death of their wives, some men may live with children or in some other familial or communal setting. About 6.5 percent of men aged 65 to 74 years and about 10 percent of men aged 75 years or older live with a child or sibling. The percentages of women who enter into similar arrangements are 14.5 percent and 16 percent, respectively (U.S. Senate, 1982, p. 14). However, some 20 percent of all persons age 65 years or older do not have living children (Johnson & Catalano, 1981); so for many, such options are nonexistent.

Social Network

Between 1.5 million and 2 million elderly men live alone; regardless of their relative proportion of the total population, they constitute a large number of persons. Like other elderly, older men living alone are predominantly urban and relatively poor. These men may further suffer from the effects of physical and social isolation (Bennett, 1980; Rathbone-McCuan & Hashimi, 1982), both of which may be significant attributes of living alone. In any situation, successful independent aging depends on the inner resources and the social networks of the older person. In the face of increasing deficits, the strength and the resilience (Sherwood, Morris, & Gutkin, 1981) of a person's general social network as it evolves into a "natural helping network " is of significance in a person's continuing ability to live independently, in the positive sense.

Living alone does not, in and of itself, mean that one is socially disconnected. Any type of living arrangement may subsume a variety of lifestyles. One may live alone and have closely supportive and warmly reliant relationships with others, or one may live alone and have few supportive contacts.

Intuitively, however, one would expect that living alone may not bring about optimal well-being. Further, research has shown that living alone is correlated with increased mortality for widowers (Helsing, Szklo, & Comstock, 1981). Nevertheless, it is the degree of social connectedness and the focus of one's social activity, rather than the fact of living alone, that contribute to satisfaction or dissociation in life.

The experience of living alone and the accompanying feelings of satisfaction or dissociation must be placed in the context of important life changes that occur. Based on a study of 47 men who live alone, this chapter considers aspects of changes such as retirement, widowhood, becoming an older parent of middle-aged children, gender-related concerns, loss of friends, entering the senior milieu and living alone. The study describes, in a general way, the influence of these changes on ongoing social networks and on natural helping networks.

RESEARCH

The data described herein were gathered by the author and others in 1981 during extensive open-ended interviews conducted with 47 older men living alone in the Philadelphia metropolitan area. The purpose of the interviews was twofold: First, to learn how these men spent their time and the activities they engaged in; and, second, to gain some understanding of each person's subjective system of meaning that led him to select or to reject activities.

The interviews were conducted in the spirit of anthropological participant observation. Most men were seen at home for approximately two hours a week for five or six weeks. The interviews relied on fixed questions for obtaining background information and for inquiring about specific areas of interest to the interviewers (activities, social relations, loneliness). The bulk of the interview time, however, consisted of open-ended questions and directed conversations that sought to elicit the "natural" categories, concerns, and ideas of the men interviewed. Topics were not limited.

About half the sample was drawn from participants in senior centers in various city neighborhoods (funded through the local area agencies on aging) or from senior-only housing units. The remainder were not connected to such centers or units and lived relatively independently, although a few were receiving or had received services (mostly minor) from formal service programs. The split sample was designed to permit examination of formal, as opposed to informal, supports.

The average age of subjects was about 78 years; the range was from 65 to 99 years of age. The average monthly income was about $626. The group consisted of 30 widowers (including one who had been widowed in excess of 50 years), 6 divorced men, and 11 men who had never married.

Concept of Network

The idea of a network serves not only as an important analytical tool in the social sciences but also as a construct that is used naturally by social actors. In the latter use, a network is most commonly thought of as "people I know or can get in touch with who can do things for me, such as providing me with love or friendship or with material entities." Other naturalistic definitions of social-network membership are "people who are important to me" or "people with whom I habitually interact." In the social sciences the notion of network has received considerable attention, both generally and in social gerontology (for bibliographies, see Sokolovsky, 1980; Mitchell & Trickett, 1980). Numerous operational definitions have been offered (Mitchell & Trickett, p. 29). The most inclusive definition sees a network as all personal linkages surrounding a focal individual. Although some researchers distinguish ego-oriented networks from those that are not ego-oriented, the notions of personal and social networks appear to be used interchangeably. Another point of confusion is that social networks are often viewed as stable; but, in reality, they fluctuate in membership and evolve in form.

Several underlying assumptions inform the technical concept of a network. Each person is viewed as part of a web of affiliations and ties—a central node of interconnectedness. Each person is also viewed as a social virtuoso, one who can "operate," "manage," or "mobilize" a network; in so doing, he can keep behavior within the bounds of amity and normative constraints or perhaps bend these at times to obtain what is needed. Obviously, the notions of exchange equivalence and reciprocity are important here. In this regard, social-exchange theory may provide an adequate theoretical underpinning for network analysis, inasmuch as a major premise underlying exchange theory is that individuals attempt to maximize material and nonmaterial rewards while reducing the costs of such interactions and exchanges (Dowd, 1975). From this view, networks form a balance between what can be offered by a person and what can be obtained.

Another significant attribute of networks is that they are "naturalistic." They exist as part of natural social life—that is, they are in place as part of the everyday operating environment of most people. Most everyone has one. Stereotypes suggest that there are people without networks ("transients," "loners"), but some very good research has shown these images to be incorrect (Cohen & Sokolovsky, 1980).

Concept of Social Support System

Although a network is part of natural social life, it is closely associated with the notion of a social support system because at some time it may evolve into that.

Rundall and Evashwick (1982) note that social networks are inappropriately equated with support networks. More often than not, the two notions are used similarly, although they, in fact, refer to different things. A social (personal) network is the more inclusive general term, subsuming the "nonspecial" course of social relations mediated through the exchange of intangibles (such as feelings, concerns, and trusts) and tangibles (such as words and material goods and services). A support system, or "natural helping network" (Gottlieb, 1981), relates generally to situations in which a person needs instrumental or emotional aid of some kind during a "special" period of time, such as a relatively short-term crisis or during a long-term decline of certain abilities. As such, it implies that the supportiveness of persons varies with the situation. Normal exchange relations are altered as the needy person calls on or is offered love, trust, honor, duty, or devotion—all intangibles—and the more tangible forms of help or care-giving. Although certain "task forces" of network members are mobilized at times of crisis at any age, profound changes in the composition of networks occur in late life in response to role transitions and situations of need, as the generalized personal network evolves into a natural helping network.

For most elderly who need help (or who do not need but take some help) it is this informal support system that is operative. The use of formal support (government- or agency-supplied help) as the primary means of support is rare. In one study, family and friends provided 80 percent of the care for the impaired elderly (U.S. General Accounting Office, 1977; Lawton, 1980). Other researchers have characterized the informal network as consisting of helpers who "at least occasionally have a common purpose (at least implicitly)" of supporting or being available to support an older person (Sherwood et al., 1981, pp. 1–3).

Process of Network Change

Networks fit with a person's ongoing social life and needs and evolve as these change. The process of change from a general personal network to a natural helping network in old age may be expressed through changes in several areas:

- Because shifts occur in the attributes of linkages with each network contact, the context of network recruitment; the frequency of interaction; and the content, directionality, magnitude, and intensity of each linkage between ego and other may alter (Sokolovsky, 1980; Mitchell & Trickett, 1980).
- The personal attributes of network members may change, favoring close kin ties and geographically proximate contacts.
- Changes in size of overall networks may occur through attrition of same-generation members and their nonreplacement.
- The ideology of a network may change, especially when the recipient of help feels herself or himself to be a burden or "not to be contributing," or when the helpers feel that they are "overtaxed" by the burden of help.

The process through which network change occurs is of importance for the ability of an older person to continue independence. Analogously to a "rite of passage" that takes place within the context of community life, significant transitions in a person's life may occur within the context of an evolving network, the elder's "personal community" (Hirsch, 1981).

Life transitions may be described as social, cultural or personal in character. These may occur in patterns of relationships as new network configurations are worked out.

FINDINGS

Social Transitions

From Worker to Retiree

The end of regular work brings about profound changes in the relationships with persons with whom one associates outside the home. The men interviewed reacted in several ways to retirement. First, few (if any) felt negatively about retirement, except in regard to loss of income and sociality. Most men said that they had been ready for retirement, but several indicated strongly that they missed the "comradeship" of work. About half the men remained in contact with former co-workers after retirement, although in most cases contact was cursory (e.g., infrequent meetings, exchanges of greeting cards). There were few planned get-togethers. For the most part, former co-workers, even the most intimate (such as business partners or "mates"), passed out of these men's lives.

Only 3 of the 47 men were working for income, although several were interested in finding part-time paid work. Eight men were involved at the time of the interviews in unpaid volunteer work of some sort. This work consisted of such occupations as the self-defined career of doing odd jobs for "elderly" neighbors or spending several days a week as a hospital volunteer with specific duties. Volunteer work was often viewed as an extension or replacement of one's earlier career. For example, one man referred to his volunteer work as "my second career." Another man was still working when he went into a hospital for surgery. The condition of his health convinced him to retire. While he was in the hospital, he happened to learn of the hospital volunteer program and signed up. When he left the hospital to go home he had quite literally moved from one career to another. For most of the volunteers, the personal relationships created through volunteer work were considered an important attribute of the work, and many such friendships were considered to be "close" and "friendly." The volunteer situations and friendships were considered to be replacements for work relationships lost through retirement. In such instances, not merely the relationships but the *context* of relationship-formation were being replaced. The context bred an aura of purposefulness and camaraderie that, for many, were satisfactions equal to or greater than the work.

For many men, then, friendships are context-derived and contextualized, and friendships do not generally carry over from one specific context (e.g., work or volunteer work) to another. A specific person is seen in the context, but only occasionally outside of it, and rarely at home.

For the retired men who did not get involved in paid or volunteer work, the senior center acted in some ways as the work context. It supplied a stage and a formally sanctioned reason to meet others. It seems, however, that the communal camaraderie, the regularity, and the context—the purposefulness—that characterize paid and volunteer work may be absent from many center environments. Unless a center acts to facilitate ethnic, age-grade or cultural identity (some centers are primarily the province of one ethnic group), the communal purposefulness that is so much a part of volunteer work (and to a certain degree, of paid work) is missing. Center personnel seem to acknowledge this need by trying to ensure that camaraderie and a degree of purposefulness are present by stressing common themes ("old is beautiful," "we are here for a purpose"). The center friendships of the men interviewed may be close but they are mostly *ad hoc*; some center-attenders referred directly to "my center acquaintances" as a group, isolating them from "real" friends. For some of the center men, however—especially the never-married men—center friendships were peripheral. Few center friends saw each other much outside of the setting of the center.

Finally, for those men who could not reproduce a purposeful context similar to that of work there was a clear diminution of active social contacts and network size in late life.

Men As Parents

Although a man who has children may add the role of grandparent as he ages, he usually remains a parent. Several studies have demonstrated that a spouse (where present) and children, by and large, form the core of an older person's natural helping network, and that a daughter or daughter-in-law most often takes over the position of primary care-giver for a widowed older person in need of help (Brody, 1981; Shanas, 1979a, 1979b).

Of the 36 formerly married men (widowed or divorced) who were interviewed, 29 had living children. Seventeen of these had fairly close relationships with some or all of their children; 7 others had children (all of whom lived more than 100 miles away) with whom the relationship might be close or strained; and 5 men were estranged from all or most of their children, although they lived in the same general area.

Among the 17 men who had had generally close relations with their children, one could see the incipient development of a process in which a daughter or other child became a primary care-giver. Because relationships evolve continually, it is helpful to conceptualize a point at which a relationship of relative equivalence— what Brody (1981) refers to as "the garden-variety of reciprocal services"— becomes one of dependence and a social network becomes a "natural helping network." Gradually, a once-a-week meal became a meal with leftovers for the older man to take back home. Several men had had standing invitations to live with their children. Although men interviewed tended to decline such invitations, preferring to remain "independent" and "not be a burden," there was little doubt that such offers provided a degree of comfort and security.

In the process of conversion—by which a social network becomes a helping network—several elements are put in place. First, a parent-child relationship must contain a potential for dependency support. This potential is present in most relationships, and it is clearly evidenced by the well-documented propensity of children to care for dependent elders. The *process* of support-in-dependency may be gradual, however. It may be triggered and rehearsed when an illness occurs in the older person; but, typically among these men, it was the terminal illness of the children's mother and the widowhood of their father that encouraged the children to make offers of support. Several men reported a common pattern: as each lost his spouse, he began to receive actual services or promises of help in the form of supportive statements such as "If you need anything . . . ," from the children. Most men were reticent to request or to take help, however; they preferred to live as independently as possible, recognizing that a child has her or his "own life." Offers of help—substantial and insubstantial—were reiterated, while minor services continued or increased.

Such common services for older widowers living alone serve two purposes. They assure the older person that he will be helped in time of need, but, at the same time, they permit the continuation of an independent lifestyle.

The process of support-in-dependency was not equally smooth among all 17 of these men who were close to their children. One man, who normally had cordial day-to-day relations with his stepchildren, was worried about the extent of their support for him in old age. He had married their mother when they were of high-school age, and he was insecure about the strength of his tie to them. He noted that his children had made no overtures that indicated they would look after him if he should need it; also, they had grown apart from him since their mother's death—about ten years ago. Because of this uncertainty he had a growing curiosity about nursing homes and life-care communities. He also kept an interest in a family homestead in his native country; there (he had learned) the government had made greater provisions for helping needy elderly than the American government had.

For these men, then, relationships with their children were cordial. In general, children—individually or as a group—had made offers of services. These had been stated in terms of specific needs (offers of money, transportation, help with shopping) or in general terms. Children insisted on helping, and offers of help might be accepted. Most of these men felt that if there were anything they needed, they could turn to their children for help. Most realized they would not remarry and would continue to live alone. However, these men wished to maintain an active reciprocal relationship with their children. They felt they could do this by rejecting offers of help, by continuing to contribute money and labor to their children and grandchildren and by continuing to *live independently*. Of these 17 men, 8 had children who actually had helped them perform instrumental tasks in the past three months (providing transportation, preparing meals, or helping with shopping). Most of the others had relationships with their children that contained the potential for the performance of such tasks on a continuing basis.

A structure is in place, then, for the expansion of these tasks in case they are needed. In that event, the "balance" or "equivalence" of intergenerational reciprocity can be thrown off as a more general network evolves into a "helping network" centered around the performance of instrumental activities. To what extent the altered balance is perceived as a dependence rather than independence is itself dependent on the personalities and the relationships of the persons involved.

Among the seven older live-alones whose children live more than 100 miles away from them, direct day-to-day instrumental aid could not be given by the children. Four of these seven men neither needed nor received regular or irregular help. One has received instrumental help from a sister, another from friends, and one especially needy man has been the recipient of formal services. Interestingly, there appears to be an outward acceptance of this situation by these men—a recognition that children have "lives of their own"—as well as a continued desire to maintain themselves independently.

For the five men whose relationships with their children are strained, a strong question exists about what can be expected, now and in the future, from these adult children in the way of support. In two of the five cases, the issue of what can be expected from children is fully resolved: either the children are completely outside the active network of the elderly man or no reconciliation can be foreseen. Three other men recognize that things are bad now, but they hold out hope that relationships with their children will improve. Although these men take charge of meeting their own needs, each receives some instrumental help from neighbors and friends.

In general, it is known that the typical recipient of care is an elderly woman and that care-giving activity is performed by middle-aged daughters. Yet, one is struck, even in this small sample, by the particular characteristics of the families of the older live-alones who have disrupted or strained relations with their children.

Four of these five men have a son or sons but no daughters. The presence of a daughter-in-law in three of these four instances does not, apparently, alter the relationship between father and son. In contrast, all the men with generally good, usually supportive relations with their children have *at least* one daughter. When intergenerational strains do involve the men with generally good relations with their children, they appear to be the strains between father and son.

Men As Grandparents

Only 6 of the 26 men with grandchildren have relationships with individual grandchildren that are sufficiently close to single out for special recognition. Grandchildren may provide considerable numerical membership to a social network, but, in most cases, they seem to provide relatively little in the form of aid.

Men with No Children

Eighteen of the 47 men have no living children. Of these men, eleven have never married, and seven are widowed (one for more than 50 years). Most of them could get along without much help, if necessary, but having help makes life easier for some. Each of these men has a social network in which he is involved, but many of these networks are less extensive than those of the men with children. In most cases the members of the social networks of these men provide help of various sorts, either on a day-to-day or a week-to-week basis or in times of crisis. Ten of the 18 men receive virtually no instrumental help from others, however, either because they do not need or want it or because there is no one to help them. The remainder do receive instrumental help, ranging from help with shopping to meal preparation.

Twelve of the 18 men with no children have no other family to support them. Two of the remainder have strained family relationships (with siblings, nieces, or nephews), but 4 have generally warm family relations.

Of the 12 men with no family matrix, 5 have constructed social networks that are oriented primarily to the performance of activities with others and mutual emotional support; these networks have yielded instrumental support and will probably yield more, if there is need. Indeed, in several cases, these supports are phrased in terms of quasi-kinship. A friend, supporter, landlady or other is said to be "like a sister," "like a daughter," or "like a nephew." The greatest difficulties with the helping networks and the key network personnel of these men is that (1) they often consist of same-generation personnel who may be equally sensitive to age-related deficits; (2) the helping functions of the networks are generally minor and revolve around one helper; (3) they are not bound together by the "moral glue" of kinship; and so there is some question about how far support will go. Although these networks are brittle and lack resilience, one is overwhelmed by some stories of support—for example, the neighbor who came twice a day, seven days a week, for several months to put medicinal drops into one man's eyes, or the "lady down the hall" who provides hot meals unannounced.

Seven men of the 12 with no children and no family matrix have social networks that are limited in scope. These men may be the most vulnerable to social isolation; but, at the same time, they may be the most resistant to help. They have little or none of what could be described as affectively supportive ties, although most men report participating in minor material exchanges—lending and receiving. These men are fairly isolated, and because of their peculiar style of masculine ideology, some resist the idea of formal help—preferring, no doubt, to continue on their own to the bitter end. For such men, with few (if any) close or supportive ties and with no potential natural helping network in place (if needed) the neighborhood per se may be viewed as supportive. Most of these men have lived in one particular neighborhood for a long time and have an extensive knowledge of it and its instrumental potential. These men tend to draw what might be called peripheral support from co-residents of their neighborhoods. Discounts on meals, special deals on purchases, and ad hoc aid are characteristic ways of exploiting the neighborhood econiche. Although the chance that such ties can evolve into satisfactory and enduring natural helping networks is quite slim, they deserve further recognition as acceptable means of helping such isolated men (Leutz, 1976; Mitchell & Trickett, 1980).

The remainder of the men with no children (six men) do have some family ties to use. Four men have generally warm ties with family, and there is little doubt that these men will be able to call on family members for some degree of help in the future, although the degree of help is unclear. Further, two of these men have other active social ties that are numerous and extensive, as well as a close relationship with a woman.

Worse off are the two childless men who have conflicts with family members. In the case of these men, the likelihood of unmet needs is high; at the least, they are unable to find out if they can count on family ties until the moment they need them. The potential for dependency support may be present, but the process of working it out is accomplished ad hoc.

Men in Widowhood

Widowhood is usually an event of late life, and it is frequently experienced by women. There is little doubt that many widowers face a hard time, although the nature of the difficulties is under debate (Adams, 1968; Atchley, 1975; George, 1980; Glick, Weiss, & Parkes, 1974; Heyman & Gianturco, 1973; Morgan, 1976). Basically, widowers face two sorts of related problems. First they must overcome the grief they experience at the passing of a long-time spouse. If this can be done, they must reconstruct old ties and build new, enduring relationships, if they can.

The tremendous impact of widowhood on the survivor has been pointed out in terms of the profound social changes (Berardo, 1970; Glick et al., 1974; Lopata, 1969, 1973); the psychological alterations (Bowlby, 1980; Parkes, 1972); and the health problems (Parkes, Benjamin, & Fitzgerald, 1969) that may occur. In our view, the difficulties of elderly widowers have been underresearched. Most studies deal with bereavement as experienced by women or persons of both sexes under 60 years old. The most complete study of adult bereavement—that of Glick and associates—deals primarily with experiences of women, and all persons studied were *under* the age of 45 years at the time of bereavement. The classic study by Townsend (1968), however, singled out age-related problems in recovery from widowhood by noting that time "heals" the wounds of loss for younger persons, in the sense that there is a greater chance they will be able to replace that which has been lost; for older persons, healing occurs less rapidly and replacements tend to be less satisfactory than that which has been lost.

Research is inconclusive about levels of social interaction after the death of a spouse. For example, research by Bock and Webber (1972) and Pihlblad and Adams (1972) about the amount of family contact shows declining family contacts for men in widowhood, but other studies have noted little decline in family contact after one to four years of widowhood (Ferraro & Barresi, 1982) and relatively stable social supports during the postbereavement period (Heyman & Gianturco, 1973).

It is common in the case of a mature couple with a traditional division of labor by sex, for the wife to be the person who is most responsible for establishing and maintaining the social ties of the couple. The loss of a wife will often contribute to the loss of social instrumentality. Of the 25 widowers (out of a total of 29 interviewed) 14 men were judged to have failed to reorganize their lives after the death of their long-time spouse, and only eleven men were judged to have successfully reorganized their lives. The study determined that one major criterion for successful reorganization was the ability of the older man to establish a relationship of intimate companionship (friend, confidante, lover) with a woman after his wife had died. Other equally important criteria included working through most of the grief and an ability to be engaged in projects and activities.

By achieving anew a relationship of intimate companionship, a man did not necessarily enlarge his social network substantially; rather, he recreated a vital relationship that could help restore an exchange value and could serve as a focus for other social relationships. Characteristic of men who were not successful in reorganizing their lives was an inability to form such relationships and a continuing predisposition to be ''locked into'' older, declining social networks. Saddest to see were those men who had managed to establish a new relationship, only to have the new loved one die. One fear expressed by the men—and by some women friends about these men—was the fear that they would have to go through yet another period of nursing a sick person before his or her death. In some cases, this fear was said to prevent further involvement to the point of remarriage.

Senior centers and age-segregated housing can have positive roles in reorganization in later life after the death of a long-time spouse. Environments such as senior centers provide a context for persons of similar or complementary social equivalence to meet (same age, ethnicity, and interest; opposite sex). In fact, several profound friendships were made in centers by the men interviewed. Men may feel overwhelmed, however, by the number of women at centers and by the intense pressure some men claim is put on them by women to become ''friends.'' Indeed, no group is more aware of the over-65 sex imbalance than the men interviewed.

Although support from family and friends persists after bereavement, those men who have not successfully reorganized their lives gradually begin to perceive that contact with friends and family decreases, that ''people don't come around anymore,'' or that ''most people I know have died off.'' Whether this is real or not is difficult to say. Among at least a half-dozen men who had not successfully reorganized their lives in widowhood, deep mourning lasted in excess of a year and extra-familial contacts were described as atrophying. Several men claimed that they refused to see anyone except immediate family for at least a year and could not act socially at all. One man, a diabetic, was so distraught that he stopped taking medication, an action that eventually led to the amputation of one leg at the knee. Although such persons are undoubtedly a minority, the unhappiness of this group is profound, and the effects of bereavement on social ties are as profound.

Cultural Transitions

Notions of what constitutes gender-appropriate behavior—both in specific situations and in less-consciously stated areas—are significant influences on adaptibility and sociality, and therefore on the particular form of networks in late life. Gender-derived roles and role patterns determine to some degree a person's desire and perceived ability to create contacts, as well as the style of contacts created. Some support exists for the idea of ''sex-role convergence'' in late life and for the association of life-span variation in sex roles and successful aging (Sinnott, 1977, 1980). Kline (1975) suggests that the social roles of women over the life span are characterized by flexibility and inconstancy, and that these are a key to resilience in old age. By implication, traditional male roles are viewed as being less flexible, and adherence to such a role structure is viewed as engendering deleterious rigidity.

What happens to the sociality of widowers after the death of their spouses? (The average elapsed time since the death of a spouse for this group was about six years.) Those men who had not developed a new relationship with a woman noted that they less frequently did things with married couples (with the exception of relatives). Those men who developed close relationships with women after their wives died more often than not reverted to a pattern in which the woman tended to "take care" of social engagements. Most widowers, however, could not take upon themselves the full social organizing ability of their deceased wives, and the general orientation of their lives as couples—going out, doing things with other couples—was often lost. Many turned to noncouple contexts, such as volunteer work and senior centers, to meet and be with others.

The division between men with a primary intimate relationship with a woman and those without was also pertinent to the social networks of the never-married men. The two never-married men with extensive social networks both had "girl-friends." Both noted that the girlfriends had been instrumental in bringing about social activities and further contacts. The remainder of the never-married men had no socially instrumental help in this sense, and some, by their own admission, lacked the social skills and the desire to meet people and to make enduring connections. Despite the assertion of Gurbium (1975) that the never-married elderly have resolved personal questions about marriage, many of the never-married older men interviewed had not fully resolved the issue of marriage. Even in old age it was still, conflictually, on their minds.

Gender-related roles—indeed, all roles—are socially and culturally informed, but for each person there is a great deal of "play" in the way a role is used. A substantial difference exists between making ties and forming networks as an individual man and doing so as a paired man. Most unattached men interviewed were not able to develop the same quality or quantity of ties as those who had formed a relationship with a woman.

Personal Transitions

Loss of Network Personnel

It is well known that widowhood can have a devastating effect on social networks. In old age, the experience of loss may become a permanent feature; as one man put it, "I've gone to a lot of funerals in recent years." As a result, networks—whether general personal networks or natural helping networks—may suffer, particularly if the membership is primarily of one's own generation.

Twelve men with no children are themselves the last living members of a localized family (i.e., some have distant relatives in distant places) and they have seen key family members die or move away and die. The feeling of devastation and desolation, so much a part of the experience of loss for the widowers, was not exclusive to them, however. Several never-married men related tales of devastation and desolation upon the loss of a close relative—especially a mother. As one never-married man put it, "When my mother died, the world went bad." Some never-married men mentioned that they felt they had an inability to connect with others after such a loss.

In some cases, close friends and associates drop off so fast that one has no hope of ever replacing them. One man, in a very distressing situation, had lived through the death of two middle-aged sons, a close step-sibling, close in-laws and two daughters-in-law—all in the space of about four years. In the fifth year, his wife died. This man, in his fifth year of widowhood at the time of the interviews, was still distraught. It is difficult to see how the notion of replacement has much currency here.

In an opposite way, however, the experience of replacement can be powerful. Four widowers who had reorganized their lives successfully—all of whom had high levels of activity and large and involved social networks—had achieved a degree of replacement by forming relationships of confidential intimacy with women they had known or known about either before marriage (three cases) or before the spouse's death. In the three former cases, the lives of these men had achieved a kind of full-circle quality: the marriage, now over, was bracketed through the experience of bringing premarital and postmarital history together.

Entering the Senior Milieu

The personal transition to the "all-senior" environment of a center can be difficult for men because it may occur along with changes in self-perceptions and social roles (Jacobs, 1974). Many of the men who attended senior centers volunteered that they entered center life very gradually, months or even years after first hearing about a center, and moved toward complete participation over a period of many months. In the early period of feeling one's way into center life, social contact may be friendly but restrained. Although chatting and card playing are ongoing, men consistently noted that they knew little of others at the center and often did not know the names of people with whom they associated (this information came from men who did not usually stint on details about other people).

Once men pass through an initial stage and become more complete participants, the center can become an important context of friendship and interest. Nevertheless, the overwhelming majority of center men tend to keep their center and noncenter lives separate. Although meetings with other center friends do occur outside of the center context, most are unplanned and informal. The center usually comes to represent a concentrated area of social contacts and a contextualized enrichment of a social network. Nevertheless, the extent to which this center network could ever become part of a natural helping network is unclear. There is little doubt that, for many men, center staff and center peers become emotionally and instrumentally supportive, that there is considerable material and nonmaterial interchange with staff and other seniors, and that some close friendships and many acquaintances are formed. Nevertheless, in general, center relationships are contextualized within the center milieu, and that contact is lost if center attendance is stopped.

Onset of Living Alone

A majority of the men interviewed had not lived alone until recently. Living alone therefore represented a recent, late-life personal transition for widowers and a middle-age or late-life transition for the divorced or never-married. In a *de facto* way, living alone connotes the absence of immediate personal intimacy, which has implicit ramifications for social networks. Nevertheless, for many of these men, living alone was directly related to independent living. When asked what they liked about living alone, those who had anything positive to say about it (the majority) offered independence and the ability to be one's own boss, to set one's own hours, and to determine one's own doings as significant attributes.

An emphasis on independence, to be successful, must be balanced against an emphasis on support for independent aging. Ongoing social networks are supportive. They are the mainstay of a positive support to an older person's social identity—particularly in a sociocultural milieu that places a negative value on aging and the aged. As ongoing social networks evolve into helping networks, they are important in providing instrumental supports for old men living alone.

CONCLUSIONS

This study has examined some important life transitions for a group of older men who live alone; in so doing, it has also examined the influence of those transitions on general personal networks and natural helping networks. Significant differences were seen in late life between ever-married and never-married men, between men with children and men with no children, and between men whose children are sons and those with at least one daughter. For men, the contextualization and segregation of areas of social networks (paid work, volunteer work, senior center) was common; other contacts were enduring.

The majority of older men interviewed were located within active social networks. For those without familial supports but in need of help, greater reliance on whatever network exists becomes necessary. Because the need for supportive services is increasing and the pool of available helpers is shrinking, family- or community-based social networks will probably assume greater importance for the elderly in general and may become the major modalities of help and support for older men. In view of their potential importance, it is important to understand the process by which general social networks are transformed into natural helping networks. As the number of the elderly—particularly those without children—increases, one can expect two types of change to occur. One probable change involves increased reliance on neighborhood supports (perhaps in the form of seniors-helping-seniors if an "elder-consciousness" continues to develop). Another change involves the increasing efficacy of helping networks when the tasks are more evenly shared by men and women helpers. Nonelderly men probably form the largest untapped pool of helping potential for the elderly.

REFERENCES

Adams, B.N. (1968). *Kinship in an urban setting*. Chicago: Markham.

Atchley, R.C. (1975). Dimensions of widowhood in later life. *Gerontologist, 15*(2), 175–178.

Bennett, R. (Ed.). (1980). *Aging, isolation and resocialization*. New York: Van Nostrand Reinhold.

Berardo, F.M. (1970). Survivorship and socialization: The case of the aged widower. *Family Coordinator, 19*, 11–25.

Bock, E.W., & Webber, I.L. (1972). Suicide among the elderly: Iso-widowhood and mitigating alternatives. *Journal of Marriage and the Family, 34*(1), 24–31.

Bowlby, J. (1980). *Loss: Sadness and depression* (Vol. 3 of *Attachment and loss*). New York: Basic Books.

Brody, E.M. (1981). "Women in the middle" and family help to older people. *Gerontologist, 21*(5), 471–480.

Cleveland, W.P., & Gianturco, D.T. (1976). Remarriage probability after widowhood: A retrospective method. *Journal of Gerontology, 31*(1), 99–103.

Cohen, C., & Sokolovsky, J. (1980). Social engagement versus isolation: The case of the aged in SRO hotels. *Gerontologist, 20*(1), 36–44.

Dowd, J.J. (1975). Aging as exchange: A preface to theory. *Journal of Gerontology, 30*(4), 584–594.

Ferraro, K.F., & Barresi, C.M. (1982). The impact of widowhood on social relations of older persons. *Research on Aging, 4*(2), 227–247.

George, L.K. (1980). *Role transitions in later life*. Belmont, CA: Wadsworth.

Glick, I.O., Weiss, R.D., & Parkes, C.M. (1974). *The first year of bereavement*. New York: John Wiley.

Gottlieb, B.H. (1981). Social networks and social support in community mental health. In B.H. Gottlieb (Ed.), *Social networks and social support* (Vol. 4, Sage Studies in Community Mental Health). Beverly Hills, CA: Sage.

Gurbium, J. (1975). Being single in old age. *International Journal of Aging and Human Development, 6*(1), 29–41.

Helsing, K.J., Szklo, M., & Comstock, G.W. (1981). Factors associated with mortality after widowhood. *American Journal of Public Health, 71*, 802–809.

Heyman, D.K., & Gianturco, D.T. (1973). Long-term adaptation by the elderly to bereavement. *Journal of Gerontology, 28*(3), 359–362.

Hirsch, B.J. (1981). Social networks and the coping process: Creating personal communities. In B.H. Gottlieb (Ed.), *Social networks and social support*. (Vol. 4, Sage Studies in Community Mental Health). Beverly Hills, CA: Sage.

Jacobs, B. (1974). *Involving men: A challenge for senior centers.* Washington, DC: National Institute of Senior Centers (The National Council on the Aging).

Johnson, C.L., & Catalano, D.J. (1981). Childless elderly and their family supports. *Gerontologist, 21*(6), 610–618.

Kline, C. (1975). The socialization process of women. *Gerontologist, 15*(6), 486–492.

Lawton, M.P. (1980). *Environment and aging.* Belmont, CA: Wadsworth.

Leutz, W.N. (1976). The informal community caregiver: A link between the health care system and local residents. *American Journal of Orthopsychiatry, 46*(4), 678–688.

Lopata, H.Z. (1969). Loneliness: Forms and components. *Social Problems, 17*, 248–262.

Lopata, H.Z. (1973). *Widowhood in an American city.* Cambridge, MA: Schenkman.

Mitchell, R.E., & Trickett, E.J. (1980). Task force report: Social networks as mediators of social support. *Community Mental Health Journal, 16*(1), 27–44.

Morgan, L.A. (1976). A re-examination of widowhood and morale. *Journal of Gerontology, 31*(6), 678–695.

Parkes, C.M. (1972). *Bereavement: Studies of grief in adult life.* New York: International Universities Press.

Parkes, C.M., Benjamin, B., & Fitzgerald, R.G. (1969). Broken heart: A statistical study of increased mortality among widowers. *British Medical Journal, 1*, 740–743.

Pihlblad, C.T., & Adams, D.L. (1972). Widowhood, social participation and life satisfaction. *International Journal of Aging and Human Development, 3*(4), 323–330.

Rathbone-McCuan, E., & Hashimi, J. (1982). *Isolated elders: Health and social intervention.* Rockville, MD: Aspen Systems.

Rundall, T.G., & Evashwick, C. (1982). Social networks and help-seeking among the elderly. *Research on Aging, 4*(2), 205–226.

Shanas, E. (1979a). The family as a social support system in old age. *Gerontologist, 19*(2), 169–175.

Shanas, E. (1979b). Social myth as hypothesis: The case of family relations of old people. *Gerontologist, 19*(1), 3–9.

Sherwood, S., Morris, J.N., & Gutkin, C.E. (1981). *Meeting the needs of the impaired elderly: The power and resiliency of the informal support system* (Final Report HHS/AoA Grant #90–A–1294). Boston: Hebrew Rehabilitation Center for the Aged.

Sinnott, J.D. (1977). Sex-role inconstancy, biology, and successful aging: A dialectical model. *Gerontologist, 17*(5), 459–463.

Sinnott, J.D. et al. (1980). *Sex roles in mature adults: Antecedents and correlates* (Center on Aging, Technical Report NIA 80–1). College Park, MD: University of Maryland.

Sokolovsky, J. (1980). Interaction dimensions of the aged: Social network mapping. In C. Fry & J. Keith (Eds.). *New methods for old age research.* Chicago: Loyola University Center for Urban Policy.

Townsend, P. (1968). Isolation, desolation and loneliness. In E. Shanas et al. (Eds.), *Old people in three industrial societies.* New York: Atherton.

U.S. General Accounting Office. (1977). *Home health—the need for a national policy to better provide for the elderly.* Washington, DC: U.S. General Accounting Office.

United States Senate, Special Committee on Aging. (1982). *Developments in aging: 1981. A report . . . pursuant to . . . [a] resolution authorizing a study of the problems of the aged and aging* (Vol. 1, Report 97–314). Washington, DC: U.S. Government Printing Office.

Part IV

New Directions for Independence of the Aged

Preservation of Independence through Nonformal Support Systems: Implications and Promise

William H. Quinn, George A. Hughston, and David J. Hubler

Two specific kinds of natural support systems are central to this study. The first, an in-depth examination of the family kinship structure, provides necessary information that, directly or indirectly, helps older persons use available family support systems to assist them with the preservation and the maintenance of functional abilities. The family has not only served the purpose of filling a gap in providing services that the formal support system does not but has also offered unique and significant contributions in qualitative dimensions for the support of the aged. *Qualitative dimensions* consist of the emotional and the psychological issues that comprise human relationships. Inherent characteristics of natural support systems are informality and spontaneity. These characteristics are associated with support system effectiveness and complement formal systems that are sometimes unable to regard vociferously elderly needs because of their cumbersome structure or dearth of resources.

The second kind of natural support system to be examined is that of friends and neighbors. Friends and neighbors function to provide support based on similar characteristics and naturalness. Furthermore, friends and neighbors offer additional advantages because they often provide peer support and role models that are useful in helping older persons achieve a sense of belonging. Care will be taken throughout this chapter to refrain from using the terms friend and neighbor interchangeably when they do not apply together to specific issues. Friend and neighbor are quite distinct as they apply to the lives of older persons and to their corresponding status and social class. Often, however, a friend and a neighbor are the same person. Many older persons find similar kinds of supports: their friends are their neighbors, and their neighbors are their friends. This is particularly the case for the working class (Rosow, 1967; Wood & Robertson, 1978).

Note: The research for this chapter was partially supported by the Virginia Center on Aging and the Administration on Aging, DHHS, Washington, D.C.

The selection of these two support systems of focus is not intended to imply that other natural support systems (i.e., social organizations, religious organizations) are not important for older persons; rather, the implication is that the two selected systems deserve close scrutiny. Also, the accessibility of family, friends, and neighbors for most of the elderly makes them meaningful for examination.

RATIONALE

Both the family and friends and neighbors have demonstrated significant influence upon the status and the well-being of older persons. Prior writings about the value of family, friends, and neighbors for the elderly support the need for additional examination (Larson, 1978; Lee, 1980; Hess & Waring, 1978; Stephens, Blau, Oser, & Miller, 1978; Streib & Beck, 1980; Ward, 1978; Weeks & Cuellar, 1981).

Review of the research on supportive services for older persons indicates the need for identification of specific variables within the family structure, as well as the influences of neighbors and friends. These variables affect the psychological and the social adjustment of the aged. The following reasons demonstrate the need for the examination of natural supports and their effects upon elderly people:

- Families, friends, and neighbors have the potential to unleash vast amounts of energy and strength to assist the aged.
- Shortages of professional and para-professional personnel trained to work with the elderly will continue to exist.
- Skyrocketing costs of building formal support networks, training and hiring staff, and hospitalization continue.
- Family and social networks may produce invaluable support in the care of the impaired eldery (see Chapters 8 and 9).

The family as an institution has historically demonstrated itself to be a viable and natural organization for establishing personal maintenance and adjustment for older family members (Shorter, 1975; Streib & Beck, 1980; Weeks & Cuellar, 1981).

The importance of family responsibility and involvement with the elderly has not diminished. Furthermore, the affectional and supportive functions of the family have emerged as crucial integrative mechanisms for the elderly in American society. These ties are often the only remaining social supports to which the elderly attach (Lee, 1980; Shanas, 1979; Troll, 1971).

Sussman and Burchinal (1962) found that people as they age become more involved with their families than with non-kin. The extended kin network has served as a link between age groups that functions in a process of mutual exchange of economic and social ways (i.e., services, gifts, advice). As Parsons (1965) wrote, the family may be viewed as having two primary functions: First, the family is a primary agent of socialization for the child. Second, the family is a primary basis of security for the adult throughout life.

Neighbors and friends have been, and continue to be, considered assets for the aged. Arling (1976) found that friendship-neighboring was clearly related to less loneliness and worry. Furthermore, these relationships provided a feeling of usefulness and respect. It would be reasonable, then, to assume that enhancing a person's ability to contribute can increase independence. The morale of older persons has been found to be positively related to the amount of involvement the elderly person has with friends (Carp, 1966; Wood & Robertson, 1978).

A reciprocity is built in friendships that can be significant in social interaction (Blau, 1961, 1973). Establishment of interdependence in friendships and with neighbors can build trust and honesty, which allows persons to feel more confident and secure and to become more self-reliant. Friendship building may also diminish anxiety about facing certain life situations because of reduced feelings of aloneness and isolation. Adams (1967) wrote that relationships with friends are characterized by value consensus desirable at the moment; whereas, kinship ties are dominated by intimacy and "positive concern." Characteristics of kinship relations often lead to feelings of obligation and tend to persist over time. Thus, it seems appropriate to study how more long-lasting friendship patterns could be sustained and how family kinship ties could moderate obligation with affection and esteem. Friendship characteristics and patterns as they relate to the aged warrant further examination.

Finally, maintenance of continuity and preservation of independence for the aged is not simply an ideal wished for by society to relieve its guilt about the plight and the neglect of the elderly or to recover from the burden of supporting them. The striving to prolong independence and to maintain a lifestyle they are accustomed to is, for most elderly persons, a heartfelt desire of lasting importance. Study samples and investigative surveys of Clark and Anderson's work (1967) clearly show the importance of independence for the elderly. The theme of independence was found to be a matter of top priority to the aged. Identified were six major cluster areas the aged used as a system of personal goals to judge themselves. The foremost priority and goal in the expression of self-esteem for the elderly was independence (Clark & Anderson). Healthy elderly people view independence to be a way of showing pride. Loss of independence, or even the threat of it, ranks as a primary source of dissatisfaction with life. The possibility exists that independence is internalized to the extent that the aged concern themselves less with the social consequences and more with the avoidance of loss that cannot be tolerated. The value of independence is a powerful force that is used to encourage persons to do more for themselves.

There is evidence to indicate that needs of the elderly are best met through the utilization of family and social networks. Powers and Bultena (1974) found that earlier statements made by old people expressing personal need and the willingness to use public programs were not good indicators of later behavior. Persons who reported a greater desire to participate in formal programs did not subsequently become more involved in the programs than those who reported less desire. Many aged persons, including those with interest in public programs, continue to emphasize relationships of an informal nature. In addition, most existing nonfinancial needs are being met through established friend and family networks. An Executive Summary of the Technical Committee on Research in Aging from the 1981 White House Conference on Aging underlines this need and verifies its importance.

> Social factors in aging are powerful. The ways in which older people live, and the social supports and institutions they have access to will determine the nature of their lives and the quality of their survival, yet these factors are poorly understood. We need new knowledge on the variations in social, economic, ethnic, and environmental contexts of aging. (p. 2)

FAMILY STRUCTURE AND CHANGE

Cross-cultural studies have demonstrated that kinship structures confronted with advanced industrialization and technology do not dissolve; they evolve and adjust (Keefe, Padilla, & Carlos, 1979; Lee, 1980; Murdock, 1949). Kinship structures assume new activities and functions, usually in harmony with a changing social system. In a study of several western societies, Shanas and associates (1968) found that the old are not physically or socially isolated from other generations or from siblings or other relatives. A major source of assistance for the elderly was the family network. This assistance included social contacts, care during illness, help in emergencies, and protection in old age. For those never married or having no children, siblings were especially important (Bachrach, 1980). Men were more likely than women to have few contacts, but the vast majority of both groups wanted to live independently. Principles of compensation and replacement of members (Townsend, 1964) in the family network are most crucial for the aged and often their presence is required in order to provide available supports.

The presence of an extended-family form for elders is common. Nuclear units have been found to be linked together within and across generations (Hill, 1965; Kerckhoff, 1965). Kerckhoff (1966a) reported on three norm-clusters he found to be 20 percent truly extended, 20 percent nuclear, and 60 percent modified extended. This finding supported the assertions made by Litwack (1965) and Sussman and Burchinal (1962) about the presence of a modified extended family in our society. Johnson (1978), Quinn (1982, 1983), Quinn and Keller (1983), and Streib and Beck (1980) maintained that the majority of urban aged were found to be immersed in social networks that offered frequent and satisfying relationships with at least some of their adult children and siblings. Troll (1971) and Streib and Beck reinforced this proclamation that the modified extended family does exist and does include the older member. Troll further wrote that it was a mistaken assumption that bonds of families were broken at marriage and so created an absence of intergenerational relationships. Troll suggested that there have been four dimensions useful in studying kin structure. Streib and Beck address nurturant functions, economic functions, and legal and cultural functions. These issues (the first two only briefly, because they have been satisfactorily expounded on in other reports of studies) are examined in this chapter under the following categories:

- residential proximity
- interaction frequency and type
- economic interdependence and mutual aid
- qualitative measures: familism, value transmission, and strength of affectional bonds
- cultural and social class differences

A cross-cultural focus on the availability of the kin network in western societies has added additional evidence that family life for all family members is significant. Lefroy (1977) found that the extended kin network, not the nuclear unit, was the relevant structure for the majority of persons, including the elderly. The older person gained substantial support during the aging process by being included in the family. The studies also alluded to the view that institutional care need not be the only alternative for care of the elderly (see also Sussman, 1976).

The Spanish-American elderly use the family, as well as social activities, as a strong support system in periods of high emotional stress (Bastida, 1977; Keefe et al., 1979). The connectedness of most elderly members with their family and kin remains binding even within industrialized societies (Lee, 1980; Munnicks, 1977; Paillat, 1977; Piotrowski, 1977; Rosenmayr, 1977). A "pull" factor to restore ties remains for aged persons with substantial family involvement over the life span; a "push" factor by which families reconstitute nuclear family relationships that tend to exclude older family members also remains. The elderly become committed to exchange relationships (P.M. Blau, 1964; Z. Blau, 1973) as they experience the forces of family change.

Evidence has appeared to support strongly the viability of an extended family structure for older persons. Atchley (1972) believed that there was much evidence that the more extended family system was typical and functional and included a network of services and activities linking nuclear families. There was less evidence to support those proposing a cessation to the examination of extended relationships because the family was isolated. Thus, an assessment of the functions and the nature of the system network may facilitate the prolongation of independence for the elderly.

It is quite possible that a study that examines only the nuclear-extended debate is a narrow conception of family structure. Concepts of status, ascription, achievement, class and kinship demand exploration of age and social stratification. Problems of intergenerational transfer (such as occupational position, devaluation of status, and negative sanctions) potentially play a part in the quality of family life. For example, the middle class, because of its nuclear family structure, is likely to demonstrate greater family rejection than the lower class, because rejection is more culturally sanctioned (Karcher & Linden, 1974). Greater life expectancy in this half-century does present greater problems in kin systems in which no systematic provision for older persons on the basis of parental and grandparental roles exist.

Changing family forms for the elderly are evident. An example of community living that demonstrates a warm and caring atmosphere is the Share-a-Home Association in Orange County, Florida. This group, aged 61–94 years, thus far has successfully defended itself from critics opposed to variant family forms. Sussman (1976) described this home arrangement as an alternative for elderly persons to nursing homes and to dependency relationships with young family members in which the elderly have formed a family of their own.

There are three types of functions families can perform more effectively to prepare and to serve individual needs than the uniform handling by formal supports can do. In the family context—

1. contributions are more highly prized when they lead to reciprocal exchange;
2. capability of family members to reallocate roles of responsibility is demonstrated;
3. opportunities for the expression of intimacy develop.

Yet, the family as we conceive of it in our culture may be distinctly different from the variant social organizations that some describe as families. If these functions are expected to hold for family, communal households, group marriages, and social networks that differ from traditional nuclear and kinship structures, they may not provide resources for handling the crises, the dependencies, the disabilities, or the deviance of its members. These divergent forms expect contributions from all persons. They further expect group goals that consist of equal reciprocities in which costs and rewards are somewhat balanced. Group goals and age composition could significantly influence the probability for success within variant family forms. The aged in some cases may not be able to perform functions at levels equal with others or to establish a balance of cost and reward in relationships.

FAMILY INTERACTION PATTERNS

The dramatic numerical and proportional increase in the elderly population has important implications for family dynamics throughout the life cycle. There are presently over 25 million persons living in the United States who are over 65 years of age, and it is predicted that by the year 2000, there will be approximately 32 million older persons (U.S. Senate, 1982).

This trend will have a significant impact on the social structure and the social-psychological changes of the elderly in society. If zero population growth is, indeed, achieved and maintained, the dependency ratio will be affected by the decreasing size of younger age cohorts. Implications from these demographic facts show support for a perceived strengthening of a welfare society for old people (Shanas & Hauser, 1974). Demographic change will have direct impact on all generations as it affects dynamics of interaction and development over the family life cycle.

Brody (1974) presented a developmental theory of aging and personality by viewing aging as a normal developmental phase of life, with its own tasks to be mastered. Developmental tasks of the aging family (Duvall, 1971) demonstrate the importance of interaction in late adulthood as older persons maintain marital stability, develop relationships with friends, and adapt to changing familial patterns. Central themes of the developmental theory are individuality, hetero-geneity, and continuity. Brody contended that older persons were more hetero-geneous and had more numerous and varied experiences than younger people. The entire family experiences a developmental phase affecting all persons involved, which can promote easy transitions or difficult adjustments. Outcomes are de-pendent upon previous interactional patterns, level of maturity, nature of goals, and the paths to achieve them (Robinson & Thurnher, 1979). In Chapter 1, Kuy-pers and Bengtson expound on this process in later-life families.

Residential Proximity

Most surveys show that older persons favor living in their own homes, not in the homes of children or other relatives (Troll, 1971). Sussman (1976) found that 76 percent of the elderly favor an independent residence—particularly when the older person is married. This desire of the aged to maintain living arrangements independently can be seen in other societies as well. In a study of actual living arrangements, preferred living arrangements, and financial status in Japan, Kii (1977) found that when actual living arrangements were controlled as financial status increased, endorsement of separate living increased. Most elderly who live with offspring do so out of economic necessity.

Data indicate that a more nucleated family with autonomous intergenerational patterns is most favorable for the maintenance of high levels of morale in retirement (Kerckhoff, 1966a; Wood & Robertson, 1978). Building on this finding, researchers might be able to discover whether, conversely, high morale leads to a greater possibility of maintaining a nuclear family structure—assuming that the older person with greater life satisfaction has less psychosocial dependency for living in close proximity to extended-family members.

Patterns of residence among family members are affected by the type of environment and socioeconomic status. Urban areas more predominately lend themselves to providing greater family support. The movement from rural to urban living gives rise to a buildup of generations over an extended time (Bultena, 1969; Streib & Beck, 1980). A trend could develop in which small towns and rural areas develop an increasing number of aged persons more vulnerable than those in cities (Scott and Kivett, 1980)—particularly when residents in rural areas have little or no extended family nearby (see Chapter 12).

Physical distance among family members varies by social class, particularly among the middle and the working class. This pattern is especially true for norms, value sets, and intergenerational continuity and strain. Indications are that blue-collar workers expect an extended-family form as a family structure (Kerckhoff, 1966b). Although they tend to reside closer together, their greater expectations can more often go unfulfilled and produce rifts among family members. Middle-class people generally provide financial aid, whereas the working class support their aged with services (Troll, 1971). Moving farther away geographically could mean for the working class the loss of support services and potential anxiety at not meeting family needs. Working-class families can be further jeopardized when economic aid is not readily available.

Overall, older persons want to consider themselves capable of taking care of themselves. At the same time, they want to be comforted by the assurance that others are close enough to provide support, if necessary. Many live within walking distance of their family or a short ride away; others—84 percent, according to Shanas and associates (1968)—live less than an hour away from some family member. Studies have consistently shown that elderly parents and adult children are important to each other (Arling, 1976; Atchley, Pignatiello, & Shaw, 1979; Bultena, 1969; Lee & Ellithorpe, 1982), and so they establish a proximity that allows them easy contact.

Frequency of Interaction

The study of interaction has included the measurement of frequency in contexts in which the older person has separate residence, is in an institution, or within the family household. Frequency of interaction has been measured in varying relationships, including older parent-adult child, grandparent-grandchild, sibling, and other relatives (Lee, 1980).

No association has been found to exist between frequency of activity with the family and well-being (Pihlblad & Adams, 1972; Lopata, 1978; Lee & Ellithorpe, 1982). Unless it is demonstrated that greater frequency of interaction is desirable and worthwhile for the elderly, encouraging older persons to have frequent contact is a questionable strategy that has only limited relevance and implication.

Frequency of interaction between older persons and family members is a function of motivation, expectations, values, and needs inherent within the dynamics of human contact. Persons with high motivation and expectations of familial interaction are more likely to display more interest in family involvement than persons with little desire to interact. Certainly, the attitudes of persons about family relationships, life cycle stages of the family, family values, and residential proximity are factors in determining the extent of importance in interaction and, subsequently, the frequency of interaction (Streib and Beck, 1980).

Family interaction that is treasured by older persons may affect the extent of life fulfillment (Wood & Robertson, 1978). Aged persons who want greater interaction but do not get their social needs met have a greater chance of being disappointed. Two key variables in social interaction may be the amount of interaction desired by older persons and the degree of willingness on the part of other family members to interact with elderly relatives. In conjunction with interaction frequency, these two influences determine the actual support and the psychological well-being of the aged. A measure used to determine social distance in relationships with older persons has been developed that can identify family members who may be most useful in the support of elderly relatives (Kidwell and Booth, 1977). Those persons with the least social distance may hold positive attitudes toward the aging and may have greater interest in interaction that would be conducive to effective social relationships. Overall, there are many variables of family life that determine the frequency of interaction and, most importantly, the actual level that is expected and applied. Variation in personality, family form and values, family history, age, sex, and race are variables that suggest the need to consider persons and families in a single context.

Economic Interdependence

One critical variable in determining extended family status is that of aid between and among generations. Economic aid can exist in one of two forms: services or financial. Some evidence indicates a straight-line flow of support from the middle generation to the older (Aldous & Hill, 1965; Adams, 1964). Additional research has demonstrated a two-way flow of aid (Atchley et al., 1979; Lee & Ellithorpe, 1982; Lopata, 1978; Riley, Foner, Moore, Hess, & Roth, 1968; Shanas et al., 1968). Interestingly, this exchange of aid can include support by aged parents of widowed children (Bankoff, 1983), particularly as four and five generations survive and the children become old. It appears that individual research is necessary for a clear definition of interdependence in the provision of aid. A general pattern, however, is that parents continue to give to children throughout the life span if they are able.

Concern that the family is in the position of having limited assets, and the accessibility and understanding needed to involve elderly family members, is evident. Assertions have been made that many families are involved in an unequal exchange process with an imbalance in reward or cost ratios. Some families are unable and unwilling to accept heavy responsibility for the support of elderly members. Whether the family can be utilized and, if so, how it can be supplied with sufficient financial and service incentives to establish itself as the primary group able to fulfill tasks of helping aged family members becomes a key question (Weeks & Cuellar, 1981). Government policy favors paying strangers to care for the aged but no comparable provision has been made to assist family members in providing care for aged relatives (Kamerman and Kahn, 1976). Family systems competent to help their own members will continue to be a necessity (Waldman, 1976; Sussman, 1977; Brody, Poulshock, & Masciocchi, 1978).

To achieve this goal would require incentives for use as catalysts in families to help develop interpersonal relationships based on an equal balance of cost and reward. Greater reciprocity would help to diminish resentment in relationships and to discourage bitterness and discontent. Significance of life conditions, aspirations, composition of family members, and current social and economic status are factors to explore as they affect the incentives and the final outcome of family cohesiveness.

There is some disagreement that the lack of income is the most significant factor in the dissolution of the extended family. Sussman (1977) hypothesized that lack of income is a crucial factor. He examined the viability of the theory that financial support can motivate families to help elderly members:

- Would incentives increase the desire to provide an acceptable environment to elderly members?
- Would elderly members desire living with kin if economic burdens were unshackled?
- What is the "power" of certain incentives for encouraging families to provide healthy environments for the elderly members?

In the results of Sussman's Cleveland sample of 936 people compiled of two elderly samples (n = 101; n = 479; mean age = 74 years) and a family sample (n = 356), several findings relevant to this report were identified:

- The greatest preference expressed concerning a financial incentive was a monthly check ($200–$400) as reimbursement to the family for caring for older persons. In fact, six times as many subjects stated this option over the second most frequent responses (tax deductions and food stamps).
- The greatest preference expressed concerning a service incentive was for medical care. Seven times as many subjects chose this option over any other.
- In response to the question concerning what should be done with old people, most subjects indicated that they did not believe institutionalization was a desirable alternative for the aged who did not want to live alone. Over 58 percent believed that older persons should not have to go to a home for the aged. Among this 58 percent, over 75 percent believed the family should care for an older member.
- In response to the question concerning the willingness of persons to accept older people into their homes, a majority (59 percent) indicated that they would consider it favorably; 33 percent said no, but out of that percent, 30 percent stated that under certain conditions they would consider it favorably.
- In response to the question concerning the responsibility for making sure older people had a place to live, a majority (53 percent) expressed a belief that the family should accept that responsibility; others (39 percent) expressed the belief that the role was the responsibility of government.
- If incentives were a reality, a majority of families indicated the willingness to accept older persons into the household.

In a multiple classification analysis of variables related to the willingness of families to accept an elderly member, the respondent's age, past experience in caring for older people, and attitudes toward caring for older people were significantly related to the willingness of the family to support an aged member. It appeared that financial support alone would not facilitate the support by families of their aging members; attitude and experiential factors were also important. What must be noted, however, is the preference expressed: the majority (76 percent) of the elderly in the sample preferred to live in their own homes. Only when they could not provide for themselves would they consider living with family.

The data just described indicate the serious attention that needs to be given to the utilization of the family network. Most families demonstrate a concern for meeting the needs of elderly members, provided the incentives are present and forthcoming. Incentives helped the support process, but they were not the sole determinants in making decisions. Demonstrations and model projects will determine whether family structure, family and individual life-cycle stage, lifestyle, and health status affect the willingness of persons to participate in the supportive network. They will also determine the types of incentives that are most effective.

The affective, as well as the financial, element is of primary importance in establishing functional and rewarding familial relationships. One major cost-benefit advantage of the Sussman study (1977) was the avoidance of institutionalization. Thus, the utilization of natural support systems like the family has been brought to the forefront.

Quality of Relationships

Unprecedented demands for intimacy and affection have emerged within families (Burgess, Locke, & Thomas, 1963). This "companionate" family form implies change in family patterns that has a direct effect on older persons. Treas (1977) discussed historical changes that have created new constraints on families, consequently altering patterns in the care of aged kin. The lessening importance of economic transfers within families—although their importance is sometimes overlooked (Nydegger, 1983)—has been replaced by emotional ties upon which family members trade in exchange with one another (Shorter, 1975). Furthermore, governmental programs, rather than undermining family responsibilities for the care of the aged, could create a new role for kin as mediators between the institutional bureaucracy and elderly relatives (Sussman, 1976). Shanas (1980) suggests that older people and their families are challenged to work as a team to utilize the bureaucratic structure in a way that is functional for the elderly member and the family. This role relieves some care-taking pressures, which, consequently, provides more familial opportunities for satisfying affective and emotional needs (Sanders and Seelbach, 1981). Thus, structural and conceptual changes in the contemporary family suggest the necessity for evaluation of qualitative dimensions that exist in families with aged members.

The quality of family relations varies according to the type of society, the family values, and the bureaucratic structure in existence. Societies in which the family is directly responsible for support of the aged differ from those in which the responsibility is accepted by the state or external formal structures. Historically, family patterns of reciprocity and social exchange (both in affection and task execution) determine, to a great extent, the quality of the existing relationship with older family members. That most older persons prefer to maintain separate living arrangements and the possibility that more frequent contact may not be more beneficial and likely to sustain a relationship suggest that separate housing may contribute to a relationship of high quality.

The analyses of frequency of contact, residential proximity, and closeness of the relationship indicate contradictory results. Some evidence does indicate that a close relationship exists when there is easy visiting distance and frequent contacts (Rosenberg, 1970; Rosow, 1967; Ward, 1978). Shanas (1973) supported this view and demonstrated that the elderly were not isolated from children or siblings and often received their psychological and social supports from these sources. This relationship has been more common for persons having a higher socioeconomic status (Riley & Foner, 1968), which demonstrates that social class affects the correlation between the frequency of interaction and the closeness of relationship.

The results of other research indicate little or no effect of geographical proximity upon closeness between adult children and older parents (Britton, Mather, & Lansing, 1961; Shanas et al., 1968). They found that satisfying relationships were dependent, not upon proximity, but on *communication*. Residential proximity was not a factor in the achievement of greater closeness, possibly because relationships were strictly obligatory. Adams, in 1968, found no relation between affection and consensus and frequency of interaction. Thus, it is important not to assume that greater interaction builds a closer relationship. The summary of the research regarding this issue (Lee, 1980; Streib & Beck, 1980; Troll, 1971) cautioned that residential proximity and frequency of interaction were not necessarily factors in greater closeness but a result of a sense of obligation. What many older persons desired was autonomy, independent living, and emotional involvement with their family. Rosenmayr and Kockeis (1965), years ago, labeled this "intimacy at a distance."

There are differences in desired interaction frequency and style between older men and older women. The examination of filial responsibility show that women tend to expect more filial support than men (Seelbach, 1977). Mother-daughter ties appear to be the strongest intergenerational bonds (Adams, 1968; Brody, 1981; Johnson, 1978; Crossman, London, & Barry, 1981). Relationships to older mothers are based on their status as persons with more intense involvement with kin; relationships with older fathers are based on value consensus and occupational status. Vocational responsibilities over the years often prevent men from establishing and maintaining close ties and building confidence in their ability to establish social relationships. As a result, retirement or loss of a companion can be particularly traumatic for males and can lead to isolation or ineffective social relationships. The relationships of men are more obligatory and more distant than are those of women (Lowenthal, Thurnher, & Chiriboga, 1975), who may disagree in values but share activities and affection (Adams, 1968; Johnson & Catalano, 1981).

The strong mother-daughter relationship has been closely scrutinized to determine the dynamics that develop and maintain the strength of family bonds. Johnson (1978) found that mothers (47 percent) and daughters (38 percent) reported that the biggest reason for good family relationships was the other person's ability to meet family role expectations. The nature of the relationship that developed over many years and through many crises was interpreted to be the relevant factor in determining the quality of the relationship. There was also speculation that when community supports intervened to minimize family dependency, they resulted in higher quality interactions. Smith and Bengtson (1979) suggest this same idea and apply it to the institutionalized elderly as well. Institutional support is particularly helpful to the intergenerational relationship when the adult child is required to meet the demands of the nuclear family. Effective social services for the aged parents help to relieve the pressure from adult children, which then allows the children to focus on the affective dimensions of family relationships (Hess & Waring, 1978; Shanas, 1979).

Clearly, health and formal support systems influence these intergenerational relations. Results of the Johnson and Bursk (1977) study showed, for example, a significant correlation between health and the attitude held toward aging factors of the elderly parent. On the one hand, poor health exacerbated family relationships because of the extreme burden placed upon family members. On the other hand, services for the elderly, such as day care and respite, provided greater family independence by allowing other members time and energy to devote to other responsibilities and interests (Archbold, 1980; Brody et al., 1978; Wan & Weissert, 1981).

Some persons who desire and experience greater distance can be supported in other ways (i.e., home repair maintenance, financial support to telephone their family). Creativity and recognition of greater potential are most important in facilitating helpful relationships for the elderly with their families. Thus, the affective bonds within families continue and often grow stronger for the aged (Brody, 1970; Cottrell, 1974; Lebowitz, 1978; Stern and Ross, 1965; Treas, 1977).

Marriage for Older Persons

The desire of persons to achieve and to maintain intimate relationships with other human beings does not subside in late adulthood. The wish to share, to support, to rely upon, and to be needed continues to be important for older persons (see Chapter 5). In later life, marriage, for example, brings increased satisfaction that differs from that of the immediately preceding stages (Gurin, Veroff, & Teld, 1960; Stinnett, Carter, & Montgomery, 1972; Stinnett, Collins, & Montgomery, 1970; Rollins & Feldman, 1970; Cleveland & Gianturco, 1976; Ferraro & Barresi, 1982). The advantages of married life include companionship, intimacy, and the opportunity for expression of feelings. Although intimacy has been shown to be a vital need throughout the life span (Erikson, 1963; Lowenthal & Haven, 1968; Lowenthal et al., 1975), myths regarding intimacy in old age can be pervasive. When Traupman, Eckels, and Hatfield (1982) examined intimacy as a multidimensional concept relevant to the lives of older women, they found that life satisfaction and well-being were strongly related to satisfaction in an intimate relationship. Further, both passionate and companionate love, as well as sexual satisfaction, influenced contentment within the relationships. Of particular importance was the confirmation that the passionate and sexual dimensions of these relationships were very important.

Older persons experience problems that are both typical and unique in a marital relationship. The lack of consensus or common interests, philosophy of life, and conflicting values (Stinnett et al., 1972) have always been central issues in marital conflict. The husband's dissatisfaction with personal lack of respect from the wife and the wife's dissatisfaction with spousal communication have been serious problems for older couples (Thompson & Chen, 1966).

The qualitative aspect of marriage over extended time has been assumed to be more central for women, which may explain women's expectation of adequate communication. Implied in Blau's studies (1961, 1973) is the presence of a flexibility in women as they are forced to move from close relationships in marriage to same-sex relationships in old age, because they often outlive their husbands (U.S. Senate, 1982). It is apparent that marriage or remarriage is not available to many older women. For some, however, the opportunity does exist; but the motivation varies, depending on the view and the appeal of remarriage as an alternative life style.

Remarriage for men is often crucial. They may need help in fulfilling household tasks because of deficits in anticipatory socialization; the earlier stages of marriage normally may not require the fulfillment of such tasks. Steps that facilitate successful remarriage for interested men might include societal and familial support to seek remarriage, training in interpersonal skill development, and acceptance in taking on a new role of intimacy expression earlier in life. Hill and Dorfman (1982) propose four key dimensions in marital adjustment at retirement: (1) husbands learning to participate in household tasks, (2) joint participation in financial planning, (3) collective decision making in fostering companionship, and (4) strategies to provide privacy for spouses. Certainly the intimacy level need varies among persons and each couple is challenged to discover and maintain appropriate emotional closeness and personal autonomy.

The postparental period of marriage in contemporary society could last over 40 years or more (Troll, 1971). McKain (1969) contends that approximately 75 percent of marriages at this stage are successful (although the term *successful* has varied definitions). Success is often determined by the ability to adjust to varying circumstances. A key adjustment stage in marriage occurs at retirement. A sharing of household tasks which increases morale (Kerckhoff, 1966b) and role differentiation toward more expressive behavior (Lipman, 1962) can ease such a transition. Marital success can hinge on the amount of work done, as each spouse accomplishes tasks on a "do-what-one-can agreement" (Clark & Anderson, 1967).

Now that more couples are surviving jointly as mortality rates decline (Shanas & Streib, 1965), there is a need to identify the unique problems of the aged and to formulate adjustments. Medley (1977) has presented a theoretical framework for analyzing marital adjustment in the postretirement years. He identifies three ideal-typical conjugal relationships: (1) husband-wife (both partners fulfill traditional roles and support each other), (2) parent-child (one spouse assumes a protective role over the other), and (3) associates (partners are friends but seek their greatest rewards outside the marriage). Family therapists report what couples themselves eventually realize: a marriage with strong emotional bonds can handle the postretirement crises as well (or as poorly) as the crises of the past (Silverstone & Hyman, 1976; Kirschner, 1979).

Adjusted couples achieve a more egalitarian relationship (McKain, 1972). Key elements in marital adjustment involve the response to retirement, the sharing of household tasks, and affection with sharing and cooperation. Success of marriage hinges on—

- desire for companionship and affection,
- familiarity with spouse,
- approval by children and friends,
- financial stability,
- individual well-adjusted behaviors.

Longevity, greater numbers of older people, and greater opportunities for personal choice have not produced an upsurge in the marriage rate for older people during the last decades (Treas & Van Hilst, 1976; Streib & Beck, 1980). Reasons for this leveling rate include the ratio of men to women (there are three or more single women for every single man), the demands of courtship (adequate health, mobility, and income), and cultural attitudes (there is little impetus within the culture to encourage marriage and remarriage). Older persons as parents desire to protect estates for offspring and as a hedge against an uncertain future. One functional cultural shift might be changes that emphasize companionship and a satisfying life to the end. In addition, more support to the less mobile, to those with lower income, and to persons with inadequate health, as well as to engage persons in the social network of persons of the other sex, may contribute to opportunity for companionship and, possibly, remarriage.

FRIENDS AND NEIGHBORS

The value of social networks to the elderly cannot be lightly regarded. Friends and neighbors are important to the well-being of older persons, just as they are for persons in earlier life stages. A friend offers the greatest source of companionship next to that of spouse. The role of friend remains longer than that of worker or organization member (Atchley, 1972).

It would not be realistic to consider others in the social network as replacements for family members. The relationships of each are categorized differently by variations in expectations, affection, and interpersonal behavior. Rosow (1967) has written that neighbors, in particular, do not substitute for children in providing the same kind of support. In old age, involvement with children and relationships with friends compose two independent systems. They each have different role sets that do not match in a reciprocal way. Friends serve as alternative activity partners. There is no general principle whereby older parents visit friends to specifically counteract limited contact with children, although certain groups do develop compensatory association.

There is a wide difference between kin, friends, and neighbors in the nature of their emotional dependence. Relationships with friends have been more temporal than with kin and have consisted of value consensus; relationships with kin involve intimacy and positive concern that lead to obligation and permanence (Adams, 1968). Friends have sometimes been more valued than family because the nature of the relationship with friends has been more voluntary (Adams, 1967). Opportunity for selection prevents forced bonding, which allows more flexibility in responses between two persons. Relationships between kin and friends are not competitive, however, because those with kin have been more affectional or emotional and those with friends have been built on reciprocity. Complementarity has sometimes been the theme of interaction among friends, because friendships serve to relieve some of the caretaking from the family.

Persons have interest in and attraction toward other persons of a similar age. This phenomenon is characteristic of many age groups: as younger persons join with other young persons, middle-age persons seek out persons of similar age, and older persons, when accessibility is adequate, initiate or maintain relationships with other older persons. Bultena (1976) reported that older men had the majority of daily and weekly contacts with older persons; 67 percent of daily contacts and 59 percent of weekly contacts were with persons over 60 years of age. Friendships varied in significance by life events; those undergoing similar experiences or crises find solidarity (Hess, 1972). Hess wrote that this is a universal phenomenon also seen in the nature of adolescent groups and in women in the "empty nest" life stage. Age is not likely to be the only factor that affects attraction to others. Interests, values, common history, and educational level have played a significant part as each group is perceived as having characteristics unique to its life cycle stage.

Persons with similar interests and activities, value alignments, and common historical experiences tend to seek out and to receive support from each other. This tendency is as true for the elderly as it is for adolescents or any other group, although the strengths and the reasons for attraction to peers may vary for each age group. Older persons with similar characteristics of socioeconomic status, marital status, and value orientation have more integrated and supportive friendship networks (Bultena & Wood, 1969; Rosenberg, 1970). The commonalities older persons possess among themselves facilitate greater social interaction.

The elderly seek out age-peers for a variety of reasons distinctly separate from family. Friendship ties result in a network of complementarity. Friendships have been built to obtain role models to emulate, to guide, or to serve as some reference point for the person and the lifestyle (Rosow, 1970). In a society that has encouraged rolelessness in old age, the role model achieves significance as a guide for acceptable or expected roles.

In a study by Moss, Gottesman, and Kleban (1976) of three informal support groups (neighbors, friends, and confidants), one-third of the elderly actually gave to each other. Help was provided in a variety of ways, with much of the assistance on the affective level. Their findings demonstrated that there was an extensive array of supports within the environment of the aged. Older persons who had the fewest resources tended to hold the fewest number of informal supports. For instance, those who did not have a neighbor to rely upon in an emergency were those who also had more serious health problems and less independent functioning in daily tasks. Measures of social interaction (having friends, neighbors, and confidants) demonstrated a significant correlation. When applied to several variables of the older person's situation, it became clear that those who reported more extensive informal relationships with friends and neighbors were in a more satisfying position than those not reporting informal social interaction. This study of informal social relationships has advocated the need to utilize the resources of the elderly in helping their peers and in demonstrating that social interaction significantly affects the welfare of the aged.

The importance of peer relationships for older persons varies according to need, opportunity, family relationships, and desire. Availing older persons of the options present for peer support is conducive to meeting perceived needs in social relationships and the opportunity to enter exchange assistance patterns.

This importance of peer relationships for the elderly has led to the creation of social support programs. The realization that friendship ties are important to elderly people and the awareness that social contacts are nonexistent or rarely identifiable for some has led to the development of friendly visitor programs throughout the nation. These volunteers have been used in an attempt to take the place of family supports. They were originally organized by church-related groups and then public agencies in the 1950s. Friendly visitors have been helpful in establishing therapeutic support and socialization networks to help the aged.

Friendly visitors are conceived of in a variety of ways with a range of functions. Beattie (1976) views the friendly visitor as fulfilling the role of a "listener" who has the task of recognizing problems and alerting others who may be in a position to offer assistance. Often, volunteers are of a similar age and are trained by social workers to be providers of help. These volunteers identify with problems the elderly have experienced and serve as models demonstrating their own ability to adjust to the aging process. Friendly visitors provide companionship to the elderly and alert professionals who can offer needed medical, psychological, and financial services to the welfare of the aged.

Elderly persons may effectively provide this function as friendly visitors. Older persons who desire to remain active are a viable source of volunteers for friendly visitor programs, and training programs have shown these people to be effective in giving support (Gayton, 1978). An analysis of the volunteers showed that they were conformists who needed clear-cut goals. They are more concerned about being treated with kindness and consideration than about attaining a leadership position. Interpersonal communication by utilizing the volunteer helps support the aged in periods of loneliness or grief and in the daily tasks of living. The volunteer can help identify individual problems that aged persons have. This role of the volunteer serves as an interface between agencies and older persons.

CONCLUSIONS AND IMPLICATIONS

The analysis of research and the description of ways in which informal support structures can be used comprise the core of this study. The following policy and community service implications have been developed and proposed in outline form for brevity. These are based on the results of this study and a review of previous studies on the topic (Quinn, 1980).

Policy Implications

- Consideration should be given in future study of the well-being of older persons in society to the presence of family members and to the nature of relationships older persons have with these members. These family members may, or may not, be providing support and care, attending to the emotional and psychological needs of the elderly, adding a social link to their lives, and serving as a secure human bond available to them throughout the aging process. This evaluation would facilitate the harnessing of family resources as a support system for the aged.

- There are a significant number of adult children who are willing and able to meet some of the needs of their parents. They need to receive some kinds of encouragement for accepting these responsibilities and a portion of what may be a considerable burden through monetary, social, and/or service rewards. Specifically, rewards might include financial support to visit, telephone, or transport aged parents and monthly inducements for care, home repair services, moving expenses, travel expenses, tax write-offs, low-cost loans to renovate or build additions to homes, and property tax waivers.

- Some attention might be given to studies directed at the barriers that restrict or prevent family members from support of aged parents. One objective might be directed at helping adult children alleviate life stressors and obstacles (i.e., work considerations to facilitate the aged family support system).

- The ability to maintain good health in old age and to make appropriate compensations when confronting aspects of health appears to be crucial for many in successful aging. Emphasis on medical knowledge, physical illness, and health education are keys to allowing the aged to reach this goal and to facilitate living during health deterioration.

- One potential vehicle for the achievement of this health goal is the utilization of the family. One way to engage the family system might be the formulation and the implementation of methods in which medical facilities can inform and support the family in the care of the ill aged (i.e., day hospitals and day-care programs) and facilitate transfers from institutions to home care. Medical facilities could also serve as resources to families in providing information and direction on health in old age.

- Emphasis should be given to the designation of service agency changes to support home care programs for the aged (i.e., human services, friendly visitors, and alternative care to help the family). More effective ways need to be developed, implemented, and evaluated that bring health care and social services into the home at the rate of client need and request and to coordinate with family support system efforts.

- Little attention or exposure has been given to older persons who contribute to the lives of other age cohorts. Adult children repeatedly confirm the enormous strength they have received from parents through their knowledge, wisdom, guidance, and experience. This potential needs to be harnessed by providing opportunities for older persons to make contributions through adult education, helping family members and peers, and by other means. This opportunity to be contributory members of society can enrich their own lives and society.

- Family members and society would do well to accept marriage or remarriage of older persons and to remove some of the cultural constraints that impose standards to reinforce singlehood or widowhood. This attempt should involve the designation of creative programs that would allow the less mobile and the lower income persons this opportunity. Advantages of marriage may include financial stability, companionship, greater psychological well-being, and success at meeting the task of daily living. Methods to foster this objective would include the removal of tax barriers that make it more economically feasible to remain nonmarried, interventions that confront family attitudes that restrict marriage or remarriage for older family members because of sexual values, financial considerations, individual expectations of standards of behavior, and living arrangements for older persons which restrict social involvement and intimacy.

- The recent knowledge that family life remains important to its aged members could lead us into a determination of specific factors or aspects of family life that foster or prevent its supportive function. A next step might be to examine specific issues of family life most integral to the maintenance or enhancement of family health. Some possible more narrowly defined directions might include the abuse of the aged by family members, the processes and the consequences of disinheritance by older parents of their family members, interventions of a proven scientific nature that remediate problems in family relationships of these generations and foster growth, the short- and long-term effects of group structures for the elderly and their children to build harmony (i.e., a consideration of filial attitudes), and the effects of a dual-career marriage on relationships with aged parents.

- More emphasis might be placed on the refinement and the redirection of research on family life of the aged (see Chapter 17). Development of theoretical frameworks for utilizing the family support system to help the aged should include interactional patterns, interfaces of formal and informal support structures, and developmental and exchange patterns of the elderly.

- The development of structural designs to help family members understand and support the elderly in dealing with the bureaucracy would provide linkages between formal and informal support systems that provide balance and would minimize the responsibilities of formal support systems for the aged, which require enormous sacrifices and resources from society. Possible methods to achieve this objective might be to formulate groups comprised of family members and bureaucratic officials, and to provide written materials to help the family increase their knowledge of services for the aged.

- Although engaging the resources of the family is well founded, consideration of its limited resources and energy is equally important. Searching for alternatives to family support is a fruitful, yet barely explored area of investigation. Social support networks (i.e., friends and neighbors) alternative living arrangements, and intergenerational nonfamily contact (i.e., Foster Grandparent Program) are among some of these under-utilized resources.

Community Service Implications

- A most direct implication from studies on family life of old age is the need for investigating interventions of a scientific nature that help prevent or remediate problems in family relationships. Because there is some evidence that good relationships enhance the well-being of the aged, the success and the expectation of it through therapeutic, community, and service interventions may benefit the older person, the family, and society by provision of supports that lessen the burden of bureaucratic structures or reverse the attitude of neglect or denial that family problems do exist.

- Recent writings on the topic of the family life of old age indicate the pathological nature of some family members and relationships that divide instead of coordinate family needs, responsibilities, and support. Outcome research on therapeutic interventions that attend to family health and remediate relationships of disharmony is necessary. Although a contemporary emphasis has been placed on the family system that may include older members as a unit, there also are human phenomena that distinguish these relationships from others of different family life cycle stages. Cognitive, social, and psychological aspects of aging play an important part in the determination of relationships, as well as to the changing life conditions of middle age. Presently there is little research in this area, which severely hampers service providers and mental health practitioners from determining successful intervention.

- The establishment of models focused on educating adult children groups to understand older parents and the aging process and their use of self in interactions may enhance the quality of such relationships (Otten & Shelley, 1976; Silverstone & Hyman, 1976; Silverman & Brahee, 1979).

- Older parent groups within an educational model designed to develop their understanding of children and other family members may foster the development of a broader social support network for the aged and enhance intergenerational relationships.

- Service providers who attend to the elderly population in their communities need to be acutely aware of the potential family impact on the life conditions and the aging process of their clients. They would do well to use creative methods and strategies to involve the social system of the elderly—particularly family members, peers, and other non-kin, who may be accessible to, willing to, or even respectfully persuaded into involvement with older persons. Therapy groups, education programs, and service linkages may be some potential models worthy of exploration; they facilitate transitional stages in the family life cycle and remediate pathological interactional patterns.

- At the same time that extraordinary family resources are harnessed to support older family members, aged persons put great value on maintaining independence. Some way must be established that facilitates the aged's quest to achieve, to be useful, and to have confidence in successfully confronting life tasks. Programs that utilize their resources for contributions in the community; that carefully plan and execute the necessary requirements for them to reach their goals; and that develop food, home-maintenance, and transportation services to help them will allow many to remain independent. These programs may potentially modify financial burdens the elderly face and for which agencies take responsibility; they may also enhance psychological well-being.

- Service agencies may be effective in liaison work between medical facilities and the resources responsible for the health of the aged, and to the families who accept responsibility for home care. Creative provisions of support might include friendly visitors and human services (such as transportation) as case management orientations and strategies are developed. Some attention must be given to helping the family of the ill aged meet financial, social, and psychological needs.

- Additional and more sophisticated staff training for the helping professions would help service-providers working with the elderly and their families to identify, define, sustain or modify qualitative dimensions of interaction in order to enhance healthy family relationships and personal growth and well-being. Furthermore, this staff training is needed for formal support caregivers who must consider the association of psychosocial dimensions with biomedical needs.

SUMMARY

The premise used to examine these specific support systems was based on the assumption that primary groups were significant in the lives of older persons. The absence of primary groups creates for older people a confrontation with their own destiny without the connection of other human beings. High morale and well-being often suffer as family, friend, and neighbor availability narrow. Separation sometimes becomes a threat to the person's satisfaction, including cognitive, physical, and emotional functioning.

Each natural supportive network does not serve as a reinforcement or safety valve for the others. Different types of relationships make different provisions and all may be required for some persons, at least under certain conditions (Weiss, 1977). Underlying assumptions for specific sets of provisions vary; consequently, relationships become specialized in these provisions. This specialization may require persons to maintain a number of different relationships to establish conditions necessary for satisfaction. Weiss wrote that kin relationships may be based upon a sense of alliance used to provide sources of help when needed. Friendship and neighbors offer provisions relating to community interests, and marital relationships involve a sense of attachment and intimacy. It is quite possible that the absence of certain relational provisions might be indicated by distress.

This review of the available knowledge of older persons and their family and friendship-neighboring patterns was importantly extended to outline some effective informal support mechanisms for allowing the elderly to maintain continuity in their lives. Needed areas of emphasis and creativity in developing alternatives and variations in supportive ways were presented. An analysis of the factors important in the assessment of informal support systems can help to clarify such needs.

Certainly none of these informal support systems can be the end-all or be-all for the elderly, because demographic trends and family structure and value changes indicate that collective effort is vital for preserving the independence of the aged. The desire for emotional attachments may frequently replace economic functions of the family, but the need for subsidies to families participating in the daily care of aged relatives is deserving of additional emphasis. Families and social networks do not uniformly seek identical degrees of emotional involvement. They cannot separately be expected to execute tasks supportive of the aged in total. Service and professional support of a formal nature by society at large will continue to be necessary. The interface of formal and informal systems is a primary focal point for study.

Caution must be used to refrain from being overwhelmed by the plight of the older person or from feeling guilty because of neglect of the elderly. The facts have shown that the older person is an individual basically living within himself in a rapidly changing world and coping with the aging process and the forthcoming problems whenever they are presented. Natural support systems function to help bolster this adjustment to the aging process and prevent, minimize, and remediate the problems of human life in old age.

REFERENCES

Adams, B. (1964). Structural factors affecting parental aid to married children. *Journal of Marriage and the Family, 26,* 327–331.

Adams, B.N. (1967). Interaction theory and the social network. *Sociometry, 30,* 64–78.

Adams, B.N. (1968). *Kinship in an urban setting.* Chicago: Markham.

Aldous, J., & Hill, R. (1965). Social cohesion, lineage type, and intergenerational transmission. *Social Forces, 43,* 471–482.

Archbold, P.G. (1980). Impact of parent caring on middle-aged offspring. *Journal of Gerontological Nursing, 6*(2), 78–85.

Arling, G. (1976). The elderly widow and her family, neighbors, and friends. *Journal of Marriage and the Family, 38*(4), 757–768.

Atchley, R.C. (1972). *The social forces in later life: An introduction to social gerontology.* Belmont, CA: Wadsworth Publishing Co.

Atchley, R.C., Pignatiello, L., & Shaw, E.C. (1979). Interactions with family and friends: marital status and occupational differences among older women. *Research on Aging, 1*, 83–95.

Bachrach, C.A. (1980). Childlessness and social isolation among the elderly. *Journal of Marriage and the Family, 42*(3), 627–637.

Bankoff, E.A. (1983). Aged parents and their widowed daughters: A support relationship. *Journal of Gerontology, 38*, 226–230.

Bastida, E. (1977). Family support systems for the Spanish-American elderly. A paper presented at the Annual Meeting of the Midwest Sociological Society, Minneapolis, MN.

Beattie, W.M. (1976). Aging and the social services. In R.H. Binstock & E. Shanas (Eds.), *Handbook of aging and the social services*. New York: Van Nostrand Reinhold.

Blau, P.M. (1964). *Exchange and power in social life*. New York: John Wiley & Sons.

Blau, Z. (1961). Structural constraints and friendships in old age. *American Sociological Review, 26*(3), 429–439.

Blau, Z. (1973). *Old age in a changing society*. New York: New Viewpoints.

Britton, J.H., Mather, W.G., & Lansing, A.K. (1961). Expectations for older persons in a rural community: Living arrangements and family relationships. *Journal of Gerontology, 16*, 156–162.

Brody, E. (1970). The etiquette of filial behavior. *Aging and Human Development, 1*, 87–94.

Brody, E. (1974). Aging and family personality: A developmental view. *Family Process, 13*(1), 23–37.

Brody, E.M. (1981). "Women in the middle" and the family help to older people. *The Gerontologist, 21*(5), 471–480.

Brody, S., Poulshock, S.W., & Masciocchi, C.F. (1978). The family caring unit: A major consideration in the long term support system. *The Gerontologist, 18*(6), 556–561.

Bultena, G.L. (1969). Rural-urban differences in the familial interaction of the aged. *Rural Sociology, 34*(1), 5–15.

Bultena, G.L. (1976). Age-grading in the social interaction in a male population. In B. Bell (Ed.), *Contemporary social gerontology*. Springfield, IL: Charles C Thomas.

Bultena, G.L., & Wood, V. (1969). The American retirement community: bane or blessing? *Journal of Gerontology, 24*, 209–217.

Burgess, E., Locke, H., & Thomas, H. (1963). *The family: From institution to companionship*. New York: American Book Company.

Carp. F. (1966). *The future of the aged: Victoria plaza and its residents*. Austin, TX: University of Texas Press.

Clark, M., & Anderson, B.G. (1967). *Culture and aging: An anthropological study of older Americans*. Springfield, IL: Charles C Thomas.

Cleveland, W., & Gianturco, D. (1976). Remarriage probability after widowhood: A retrospective method. *Journal of Gerontology, 31*(1), 99–103.

Cottrell, F. (1974). *Aging and the aged*. Dubuque, IA: William Brown.

Crossman, L., London, C., & Barry, C. (1981). Older women caring for disabled spouses: A model for supportive services. *The Gerontologist, 21*(5), 471–480.

Duvall, E.M. (1971). *Family Development* (4th ed.). New York: J.B. Lippincott.

Edwards, J.N., & Klemmack, D. (1973). Correlates of life-satisfaction: A re-examination. *Journal of Gerontology, 28*, 497–502.

Erikson, E. (1963). *Childhood and Society* (2nd ed.). New York: Norton.

Ferraro, K., & Barresi, C. (1982). The impact of widowhood on social relations of older persons. *Research on Aging, 4*(2), 227–247.

Gayton, H.J. (1978). Organizational policies for the utilization of volunteers: A social scientific approach. Paper presented at the 53rd Southwestern Sociological Meeting.

Gurin, G., Veroff, I., & Teld, S. (1960). *Americans view their mental health.* New York: Basic Books.

Hess, B.B. (1972). Friendship. In M.W. Riley, M. Johnson, & A. Foner (Eds.), *Aging and society: A sociology of age stratification* (Vol. 3). New York: Russell Sage.

Hess, B.P. and Waring, J.W. (1978). Changing patterns of aging and family bonds in later life. *Family Coordinator, 27*(4), 303–314.

Hill, E.A. and Dorfman, L.T. (1982). Reaction of housewives to the retirement of their husbands. *Family Relations, 31,* 195–200.

Hill, R. (1965). Decision making and the family life cycle. In E. Shanas & G. Streib (Eds.), *Social structure and the family: Generational relations.* Englewood Cliffs, NJ: Prentice-Hall.

Johnson, C.L., & Catalano, D.J. (1981). Childless elderly and their family supports. *The Gerontologist, 21*(6), 610–618.

Johnson, E.S. (1978). "Good" relationships between older mothers and their daughters: A causal model. *The Gerontologist, 18*(3), 301–306.

Johnson, E.S., & Bursk, B.J. (1977). Relationships between the elderly and their adult children. *The Gerontologist, 17*(1), 90–96.

Kamerman, S., & Kahn, A. (1976). Explorations in family policy. *Social Work, 21,* 181–187.

Karcher, C.J., & Linden, L.L. (1974). Family rejection of the aged and nursing home utilization. *International Journal of Aging and Human Development, 5*(3), 239–244.

Keefe, S.E., Padilla, A.M., & Carlos, M.L. (1979). The Mexican-American family as an emotional support system. *Human Organization, 38*(2), 144–151.

Kerckhoff, A.C. (1965). Nuclear and extended family relationships: Normative and behavioral analysis. In E. Shanas & G. Streib (Eds.), *Social structure and the family: Generational relations.* Englewood Cliffs, NJ: Prentice-Hall.

Kerckhoff, A.C. (1966a). Norm-value clusters and the strain toward consistency among older married couples. In I.H. Simpson and J.C. McKinney (Eds.), *Social aspects of aging.* Durham, NC: Duke University Press.

Kerckhoff, A.C. (1966b). Family patterns and morale in retirement. In I.H. Simpson & J.C. McKinney (Eds.), *Social aspects of aging.* Durham, NC: Duke University Press.

Kidwell, I.J., & Booth, A. (1977). Social distance and intergenerational relations. *The Gerontologist, 17*(5), 412–420.

Kii, T. (1977). Attitudes of the Japanese elderly toward living with offspring. A paper presented at the Annual Meeting of the Midwest Sociological Society, Minneapolis, MN.

Kirschner, C. (1979). The aging family in crisis: A problem in living. *Social Casework, 60*(4), 209–216.

Larson, R. (1978). Thirty years of research on the subjective well-being of older Americans. *Journal of Gerontology, 33*(1), 109–125.

Lebowitz, B.D. (1978). Old age and family functioning. *Journal of Gerontological Social Work, 1*(2), 111–118.

Lee, G.R. (1980). Kinship in the seventies: A decade review of research and theory. *Journal of Marriage and the Family, 42*(4), 193–204.

Lee, G.R., & Ellithorpe, E. (1982). Intergenerational exchange and subjective well-being among the elderly. *Journal of Marriage and the Family, 44,* 217–224.

Lefroy, R.B. (1977). Elderly persons and family life. *Australian Journal of Social Issues, 12*(1), 33–51.

Lipman, A. (1962). Role conceptions of couples in retirement. In C. Tibbitts & W. Donahue (Eds.), *Social and psychological aspects of aging.* New York: Columbia University Press.

Litwack, E. (1965). Extended kin relations in an industrial democratic society. In E. Shanas & G. Streib (Eds.), *Social structure and the family: Generational relations.* Englewood Cliffs, NJ: Prentice-Hall.

Lopata, H.Z. (1978). Contributions of extended families to the support systems of metropolitan area widows: Limitations of the modified kin network. *Journal of Marriage and the Family, 40*(2), 355–364.

Lowenthal, M.F., & Haven, C. (1968). Interaction and adaptation: Intimacy as a critical variable. *American Society Review, 33*(1), 20–30.

Lowenthal, M.F., Thurnher, M., & Chiriboga, D. (1975). *Four stages of life: A comparative study of women and men facing transitions.* San Francisco, CA: Jossey-Bass.

McKain, W.C. (1969). *Retirement marriage.* Storrs, CT: University of Connecticut Press.

McKain, W.C. (1972). A new look at older marriages. *Family Coordinator, 21*(1), 61–69.

Medley, M.L. (1977). Marital adjustment in the post-retirement years. *Family Coordinator, 26*(1), 5–11.

Moss, M.S., Gottesman, L.E., & Kleban, M.H. (1976). Informal social relationships among community aged. Paper presented at the 29th Gerontological Society Meeting, New York.

Munnicks, J. (1977). Linkages of older people with their families and bureaucracy in the Netherlands. In E. Shanas and M.B. Sussman (Eds.), *Older people, family, and bureaucracy.* Durham, NC: Duke University Press.

Murdock, G.P. (1949). *Social structure.* New York: Macmillan.

Nydegger, C.N. (1983). Family ties of the aged in cross-cultural perspective. *The Gerontologist, 23,* 26–32.

Otten, J., & Shelley, F.N. (1976). *When your parents grow old.* New York: Funk and Wagnall.

Paillat, P. (1977). Bureaucratization of old age: Determinants of the process possible safe-guards and reorientations. In E. Shanas and M.B. Sussman (Eds.), *Older people, family and bureaucracy.* Durham, NC: Duke University Press.

Parsons, T. (1965). The normal American family. In S. Farber, F. Mustacchi, & R.H. Wilson (Eds.), *Man and civilization: The family's search for survival.* New York: McGraw-Hill.

Pihlblad, C., & Adams, D.L. (1972). Widowhood, social participation, and life satisfaction. *Aging and Human Development, 3,* 323–330.

Pihlblad, C., & McNamara, R. (1965). Social adjustment of elderly people in three small towns. In A. Rose & W. Peterson (Eds.), *Older people and their social world.* Philadelphia: F.A. Davis.

Piotrowski, J. (1977). Old people in Poland: Family and bureaucracy. In E. Shanas and M.B. Sussman (Eds.), *Older people: Family and bureaucracy.* Durham, NC: Duke University Press.

Powers, E.A., & Bultena, G.L. (1974). Correspondence between anticipated and actual uses of public services by the aged. *Social Service Review, 48*(2), 245–254.

Puner, M. (1974). To the good long life: What we know about growing old. New York: Universe Books.

Quinn, W.H. (1980). Policy and community service implications for families of later life (Grant No. 90 AT–2012/01). Washington, DC: Department of Health, Education and Welfare.

Quinn. W.H. (1982). Older parent and adult child interaction: Qualitative dimensions in building family strengths. In N. Stinnett, J. DeFrain, K. King, H. Lingren, G. Rowe, S. Van Zandt, &

R. Williams (Eds.), *Family strengths 4: Positive support systems* (pp. 235–250). Lincoln: NE: University of Nebraska Press.

Quinn, W.H. (1983). Personal and family adjustment in later life. *Journal of Marriage and the Family, 45*, 57–73.

Quinn, W.H., & Keller, J.F. (1983). Older generations of the family: Relational dimensions and quality. *American Journal of Family Therapy, 11*, 23–34.

Riley, M., & Foner, A. in association with Moore, M., Hess, B., & Roth, B. (1968). *Aging and Society* (Vol. 1). New York: Russell Sage Foundation, 1968.

Robinson, B., & Thurnher, M. (1979). Taking care of aged parents: A family cycle transition. *The Gerontologist, 19*(4), 586–593.

Rollins, B.L., & Feldman, H. (1970). Marital satisfaction over the family life cycle. *Journal of Marriage and the Family, 32*, 20–28.

Rosenberg, G.S. (1970). *The worker grows old*. San Francisco, CA: Jossey-Bass.

Rosenmayr, L. (1977). The family—source of hope for the elderly of the future. In E. Shanas & M.B. Sussman (Eds.), *Older people, family, and bureaucracy*. Durham, NC: Duke University Press.

Rosenmayr, L., & Kockeis, E. (1965). *Unwelt and familie alter menschen*. Berline: Luchterland-Veglag.

Rosow, I. (1967). *Social integration of the aged*. New York: The Free Press.

Rosow, I. (1970). Old people: Their friends and neighbors. *American Behavioral Scientist, 14*, 59–70.

Sanders, L.T., & Seelbach, W.C. (1981). Variations in preferred care alternatives for the elderly: Family versus nonfamily sources. *Family Relations, 30*, 447–451.

Scott, J.P., & Kivett, V.R. (1980). The widowed black, older adult in the rural south. *Family Relations, 29*, 83–90.

Seelbach, W.C. (1977). Gender differences in expectations for filial responsibility. *The Gerontologist, 17*(5), 421–425.

Shanas, E. (1973). Factors affecting care of the patient: Government policy, role of the family, and social attitudes. *Journal of the American Geriatrics Society, 21*(9), 394–397.

Shanas, E., & Hauser, P.M. (1974). Zero population growth and the family life of older people. *Journal of Social Issues, 30*(4), 79–92.

Shanas, E. (1979). Social myth as hypothesis: The case of the family relations of older people. *The Gerontologist, 19*(1), 3–9.

Shanas, E. (1980). Older people and their families: The new pioneers. *Journal of Marriage and the Family, 42*, 9–14.

Shanas, E., & Streib, G. (Eds.). (1965). *Social structure and the family: Generational relations*. Englewood Cliffs, NJ: Prentice-Hall.

Shanas, E., Townsend, P., Wedderburn, D., Friis, H., Milhoj, P., & Stehouwer, J. (1968). *Old people in three industrial societies*. New York: Atherton Press.

Shorter, E. (1975). *The making of the modern family*. New York: Basic Books.

Silverman, A.G., & Brahee, C.I. (1979). As parents grow older: An intervention model. *Journal of Gerontological Social Work, 2*(1), 77–85.

Silverstone, B., & Hyman, H.K. (1976). *You and your aging parents*. New York: Pantheon Books.

Smith, K.F., & Bengtson, V.L. (1979). Positive consequences of institutionalization: Solidarity between elderly parents and their middle-aged children. *The Gerontologist, 19*, 438–447.

Stephens, R.C., Blau, Z.S., Oser, G.T., & Miller, M.D. (1978). Aging, social support systems, and social policy. *Journal of Gerontological Social Work, 1*(1), 111–118.

Smith, K.F., & Bengtson, V.L. (1979). Positive consequences of institutionalization: Solidarity between elderly parents and their middle-aged children. *The Gerontologist, 19,* 438–447.

Stephens, R.C., Blau, Z.S., Oser, G.T., & Miller, M.D. (1978). Aging, social support systems, and social policy. *Journal of Gerontological Social Work, 1*(1), 111–118.

Stern, E.M., & Ross, M. (1965). *You and your aging parents.* New York: Harper and Row.

Stinnett, N., Carter, L.M., & Montgomery, J.E. (1972). Older persons' perceptions of their marriages. *Journal of Marriage and the Family, 34*(4), 665–670.

Stinnett, N., Collins, J., & Montgomery, J.E. (1970). Marital need satisfaction of older husbands and wives. *Journal of Marriage and the Family, 32*(3), 428–434.

Streib, G.F., & Beck, R.W. (1980). Older families: A decade review. *Journal of Marriage and the Family, 42,* 205–221.

Sussman, M.B. (1976). Family life of older people. In R.H. Binstock and E. Shanas (Eds.), *Handbook of aging and the social sciences.* New York: Van Nostrand Reinhold.

Sussman, M.B., & Burchinal, L. (1962). Kin family network: Unheralded structure in current conceptualizations of family functioning. *Marriage and Family Living, 24,* 231–240.

Sussman, M.B. (1977). *Incentives and family environments for the elderly.* Final Report to Administration on Aging (Grant #90-A-316).

Thompson, P., & Chen, R. (1966). Experiences with older psychiatric patients and spouses together in a residential treatment setting. *Bulletin of the Menninger Clinic, 30*(1), 23–31.

Townsend, P. (1964). Family and kinship in industrial society. [Monograph] *The Sociological Review, 8,* 89–96.

Traupman, J., Eckels, E., & Hatfield, E. (1982). Intimacy in older women's lives. *The Gerontologist, 22*(6), 493–498.

Treas, J. (1977). Family support systems for the aged: Some social and demographic considerations. *The Gerontologist, 17*(6), 386–491.

Treas, J., & Van Hilst, A. (1976). Marriage and remarriage rates among older Americans. *The Gerontologist, 16*(2), 132–136.

Troll, L.E. (1971). The family of later life: A decade review. *Journal of Marriage and the Family, 33,* 263–390.

United States Senate, Special Committee on Aging. (1982). *Developments in aging: 1981. A report . . . pursuant to . . . (a) resolution authorizing a study of the problems of the aged and aging* (Report 97-314, Vol. 1). Washington, DC: U.S. Government Printing Office.

Waldman, S. (1976). *National health insurance proposals: provisions of bills introduced in the 94th Congress as of February 1976.* Washington, D.C.: U.S. Government Printing Office.

Wan, T., & Weissert, W. (1981). Social support networks, patient status and institutionalization. *Research on Aging, 3,* 240–256.

Ward, R.A. (1978). Limitations of the family as a supportive institution in the lives of the aged. *The Family Coordinator, 27*(4), 365–373.

Weeks, J.R., & Cuellar, J.B. (1981). The role of family members in the helping network of older people. *The Gerontologist, 21*(4), 388–394.

Weiss, R. (1977). The provisions of social relations. In Z. Rubin (Ed.), *Doing unto others.* Englewood Cliffs, NJ: Prentice-Hall.

White House Conference on Aging. (1981). *Executive Summary of Technical Committee on Research in Aging.*

Wood, V., & Robertson, J.F. (1978). Friendship and kinship interaction: Differential affect on the morale of the elderly. *Journal of Marriage and the Family, 40*(2), 367–374.

Chapter 15

Role of Children and Childhood in Independence of the Aged

Thomas R. Chibucos

A chapter that emphasizes a role for children in independence of the elderly is warranted in a book on social gerontology for four reasons. First, there are data indicating that old persons have a substantial amount of contact with their families, including their grandchildren (e.g., Butler & Lewis, 1973; Hill, 1970; Shanas et al., 1968; Sussman, 1963). More generally, children are an undeniable "element" of the total social network of old people (Lewis, 1982). The extent to which children, alone or in combination with others, influence the independence of older adults cannot be clearly delineated at the present time; however, there are indications of the kinds of impact that are possible (e.g., Mead, 1974; Powell & Arquitt, 1978; Streitfeld, 1976). The second reason concerns a historical-cultural belief regarding the concept of independence. A belief in the desirability of "independent aging" derives from a value system whose impact in this domain is felt in the earliest years of life and whose pervasiveness across the rest of the life span is undeniable (cf. Kagan, Kearsley, & Zelazo, 1978; Garbarino, 1982). Third, having this chapter in this book contributes to a view of human development that emphasizes intergenerational and human continuity. Not to have this emphasis or not to act in accordance with it is to violate the continuity and the consistency of human experience that has brought our species to the current day. The practice of intergenerational contact has worked for a large period in human history. Its benefits are discussed at length by Mead. Finally, theoretical conceptualizations of young humans as active participants in their own development have achieved at least equal status with those emphasizing a "passive" child (cf. Bell, 1968; Hartup, 1978; Overton & Reese, 1973; Parsons & Bales, 1955). It is logical to extend the analysis of putative child influences beyond their effects on parents and siblings (Lerner & Spanier, 1978) to include aged persons. It is also logical to take a perspective of reciprocal intergenerational influences as in other facets of the study of social relationships (Aldous, 1978; Lerner, 1978).

PERSPECTIVE

The term *independence* is defined to mean self-perceived and actual behavioral and psychological individuality, a definition that can be applied throughout the life span with the exception of the prenatal period and early infancy. This use of the term expands the meaning of Quinn and Keller (1981) who defined independence as "psychological and emotional individuality." *Self-perceived* and *actual* are used because equating independence with individuality seems to trivialize one of the facets of human existence that (as far as we know) makes humans unique— self-awareness. *Psychological* includes *emotional* also. Independence is not all-or-none, nor is it forever. Also, it does not imply social or physical distancing. In fact, it is a central thesis of this chapter that social distancing is antithetical to independence and physical distancing is largely irrelevant to it.

Interconnectedness refers to social relationships, for example, relationships with other people. Following Lewis (1982), social relationships are considered to be of three types: love, friendship, acquaintance. Any of these relationships can be intra- or extra-familial; also, the relationships can exist and be long-lasting, even without extended interactions. In this regard, it is instructive to realize that there is a distinction between interactions and relationships (Lewis). The latter are usually derived from the former. It is important to keep in mind that what is observed is interactions, what is implied is relationships. The focus on people in the definition of interconnectedness and the exclusion of *things* like health-care systems is intentional because the important mediating factor is always people—even in systems.

A passionate ideology of individualism is one of the things that has made America the haven for political and religious freedom that it is. Further, it made achievement of enormous material, technological, and intellectual progress possible. It seems not an overstatement to assert that "our culture denigrates interdependence and sees it as a form of weakness" (Garbarino, 1982, p. 49). Although this deep-seated commitment to personal independence must be carefully guarded, it must be moderated in the context of family and individual development (Bronfenbrenner, 1979; Garbarino, 1982; Kenniston, 1977), because families and individual persons need to be interconnected with other human beings if they are to survive. In fact, in our culture, it might be said that the essential "tension" developmentally is between the need for independence and the need for interconnectedness.

THEORY AND RESEARCH

Suggested Analytical Framework

A preliminary framework for analyzing independence in the aged, and the role of children in that independence, is presented below. It includes two important features: ecological relevance (Bronfenbrenner, 1979) or social objects and social functions (Lewis, 1982) and developmental perspective (Wohlwill, 1973). It may be useful to conceive of the development of independence through interconnectedness as a process that is negotiated many times throughout development. One does not achieve a final status; one moves toward independence during each of several major periods of life, and then, as situational contexts and other changes take place, one goes at it again. Table 15–1 is a gross and incomplete picture of the process.

Social Objectives and Functions

The first column in the table is self-explanatory. The second column contains the social objects—people—that are associated with interconnectedness *and* with independence at each age period. Several points must be noted. First, the same social object, because it is serving different social functions simultaneously, may be involved in both interconnectedness and independence. For example, the mother serves social functions in the area of feeding (e.g., eye contact, tactile

Table 15–1 Overview of Life Stages, Salient Events, Interconnectedness, and Independence

Time Period	Interconnectedness/ Independence	Examples of Salient Life Events
Prenatal (0–birth)	Mother/mother	Feeding, contact, birth
Infancy/toddlerhood (birth–30 mos.)	Family origin/mother	Attachment, maturation of cognitive & motor skills
Childhood (31 mos.–12 years)	Peers & teachers/parents	Peers, school
Adolescence (puberty–19 years)	Friends/parents & advisers/ teachers	Sexual maturation, more peers
Early adulthood (20–45)	Mate & children/parents	Education, work, moving
Middle adulthood (40–65)	Fellow workers/children	Early reminiscence (reevaluation), career changes, growth of children
Late adulthood/old age (60–death)	Friends & family of procreation/family of origin, family of procreation	Approach of death, children in adulthood, renewal through grandchildren

stimulation), which promulgate interconnectedness. She also serves other social functions such as being the secure base for infant exploration and prompting skill development that are likely to lead to independence. For example, the family of procreation serves both interconnectedness and independence for old people. By offering the hope of renewal through the third generation and by providing a series of ages with which to compare themselves, they provide a concrete framework for ultimate separateness or independence. Second, the listing of social objects in the independence half of the second column is meant to emphasize the point that at all periods in the life span, people serve as reference points for persons in determining their state of independence. Independence as it is defined here, however, may, or may not, involve distancing from the social object. Finally, the salient-life-events column contains a suggested listing of situations or occurrences that prompt and result from both interconnectedness and independence. The second and third columns also serve to emphasize the assumption that at all points in the life span, an intimate connection exists between independence and interconnectedness. For example, infants with no identifiable organic problem can deteriorate physically and psychologically until they die. This failure to thrive results from the lack of a nurturing, loving relationship with a primary care-giver (Vaughan, McKay, & Behrman, 1979). Similarly, in old age, observational impressions (Egerton, 1972; Norman & Smith, 1975) and other data collected in scientifically rigorous ways support the idea that physical and psychological health are promoted by the existence of human social relationships (Pilisuk & Minkler, 1980).

Developmental Perspectives

Figure 15–1 illustrates the assumption that the development of independence is a life-long process in which the social objects of interconnectedness are redefined at different time points. One way to use Figure 15–1 is to start at the lower end and, pretending you are the target person, move through the various time periods. In this way the simultaneous pulls and pushes toward independence and interconnectedness can be seen as can the fact that given social objects serve both social functions concurrently.

Several other points about Figure 15–1 need to be highlighted. First, a clear place for children in the lives of old people is asserted. Although the data reviewed later support this theoretical position, there are few research data that specify the kinds of interactions and relationships existing between old and young. Second, it is best to think in terms of various levels of influence; for example, the interaction between a child and an old person is likely to be different depending on whether there is another person in the situation (both in the short-term and in the long-term). This assumption is supported by data indicating that mothers treat children

Figure 15–1 Life-Span Perspective on Independence and
Interconnectedness

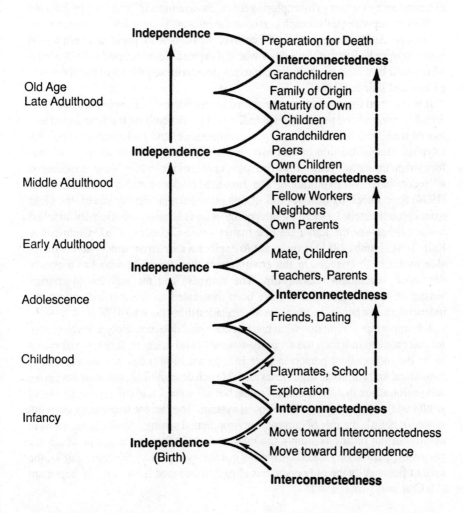

differently when fathers are present (Parke, 1981). Common experience also
supports this proposition.

Third, the model in Figure 15–1 makes most questions about the relative
importance of independence at different age levels somewhat irrelevant. For

example, an answer to the question, "Is independence in old age (by serving as a care-giver for a handicapped child) more important or more meaningful than independence in infancy (by exploring a new environment)?" can only be guessed at. We can suppose that for each person at the relevant point in life, the meaning of the independence is comparable. Of course, the framework presented here would lead to the prediction that the toddler who *did* explore would *become* the old person who would be a care-giver, given the requisite interim sequences of interconnectedness and independence.

It is assumed that healthy and healthful independence (i.e., self-perceived and actual behavioral and psychological individuality) depends on interconnectedness (social relationships) for its existence, maintenance, and prolongation. The prototypical exemplification of this assumption, familiar to those whose work has focused on the earlier years of the life span, concerns the toddler's use of mother as a "secure base" for exploration. The interested reader should consult Ainsworth (1974) for compelling descriptions of this phenomenon. Briefly stated, the child from approximately 10 to 36 months of age who is securely emotionally attached to the mother—or the father for that matter—(see Chibucos, 1982; Chibucos & Kail, 1981; Lamb, 1981) is more apt to explore a new environment and is better able to adjust to changes in the environment than the child who has a poorly developed attachment relationship. The wariness and the withdrawal characteristic of young children who have been mistreated are another indication that independence depends on prior positive relationships (Lewis, 1980).

It is important to note that what has just been said does not imply a developmental determinism in which the securely attached child has been forever guaranteed to be the independent person in later life. Lewis (1982) has articulated several theoretical and empirical arguments against such determinism; the most pervasive and profound are that the causes of social behavior are found (to varying degrees I would add) in the structure of the social system. The current framework does not ignore or belittle the role of current "environmental setting" for the aged. Current environmental setting is simply the most recent situational context in which the person happens to be located. Although context is important (Kahana, 1982), the kind of personality the old person has already developed is also clearly important (McCrae and Costa, 1982).

Selective Review of Relevant Research

There is considerable evidence to support the view that normal aging is characterized by behavioral and psychological individuality and that children are a meaningful part of the social interconnectedness of the elderly. Before a selective review of the relevant studies can be presented, several points need to be made about the data base in this area. First, the quantity and the quality of studies that pertain to the independence of old persons as they interact with young children is far from desirable. Also, research on other relevant aspects of human aging is largely descriptive; when it is not, it is based on a very select population—the institutionalized aged. The difference between institutionalized and noninstitutionalized old people must be emphasized. Only 5 percent of all people 65 years of age and older are institutionalized, while 20 percent of all households are headed by someone 65 years of age or older (Allan, 1979). The data for institutionalized old persons indicate that 14 percent are married, 20 percent were never married, and about 50 percent have at least one surviving adult child; the corresponding figures for the noninstitutionalized aged are 56 percent, 5.6 percent and 80 percent respectively (Brody, 1979). Of the 5 percent of the aged in institutional care, 1 percent are 65 to 69 years of age, and 26 percent are ≥ 80 years of age (Brody 1979).

This situation is analogous to the knowledge base pertaining to the effects of nonparental care on children ≤ 6 years of age. In this case, virtually all the information has been gained from children in very high quality, mostly university-based, day-care centers (Belsky & Steinberg, 1978). In the real world (National Childcare Consumer Study, 1975), center care of *all* qualities accounts for no more than 3 percent of nonparental care; the bulk of nonparental care is home care by relatives (43%), or by care-givers (babysitters) in the child's own home (26%) or someone else's home (16%). The discrepancy between the real world of child care and child development, and where the research has been done is substantial.

Although the case can be made that the day-care center for children or the institution for old people is one element of the social ecology for these age groups, it would be misleading to maintain or to act in our interpretation of research as though it were a major ecological niche. Clearly, the implication is not that the behavior of individuals in these circumstances should be ignored. Rather, it means that researchers using such atypical populations should be clear about the limits of what is known and should be careful about how that which is known is communicated to the lay public and the media.

There are substantial numbers of sick, decrepit, and psychologically or physically damaged old persons (Butler, 1975); but rigidity, "disengagement," senility, and dependency are not typical. For example, when Kahana, Kahana, and McLenigan (1980) did a study of the "adventurous" aged, they found that new careers, major moves, and other voluntary major life changes were not atypical. In another study, Erlich (1980) presented information citing the usefulness of elderly neighbors in a comprehensive neighborhood demonstration program. Old persons living in the community are resources and providers of assistance to children, family, and friends (Kahana, 1982). More specifically, Kahana (1974) discovered that the elderly living independently in an urban setting provide more home services than they receive.

Kahana and associates (1980) reported that 80 percent of 483 residents of a Florida retirement community indicated that their status had recently improved. Further, in a review of self-help among the aged, Hess (1976, p. 61) concluded that "a common theme is old people helping old people, informally or in an organized manner, with or without the help of social service professionals." She also notes that in New Jersey alone, there are estimated to be several thousand organized senior groups.

McCrae and Costa (1982), viewing personality as an independent variable, concluded that the number of physical complaints, the degree of psychological well-being, and the extent of death anxiety depend more on life-long personality patterns than on age.

These authors have paid particular attention to "openness to experience" as a major personality construct (McCrae & Costa, 1980) in determining the behavior and attitudes of old people. Their emphasis has been on continuity rather than on change. For example, men who had changed careers in the previous ten years exhibited greater openness to experience than those who had not (Costa & McCrae, 1978). The authors acknowledge that because the data were correlational, the job change could have caused greater openness rather than the reverse. What is important for this review, however, is the fact that the theoretical conceptualization results in a view of behavior and attitudes in the aged that allows for the reasonable expectation of continued independence in those who are predisposed to be independent. From a different vantage point, Maas and Kuypers (1974, p. 203) assert that "old age does not . . . introduce decremental psychological processes. Rather, old age may demonstrate . . . problems that have long-term antecedents."

Empirical research on developmental "plasticity" in old age employing operant learning methodology indicates that independence can be established in such areas as self-care, locomotion, and communication skills (Baltes & Barton, 1979). Cogent analysis by Baltes and Baltes (1982) indicates the likely impact of social-role demands that require dependent-like behavior in the institutionalized aged— that is, ". . . in an institutional system, like nursing homes, dependency of the elderly and the dependence-supportive behavior *by others* may be role congruent for both actors" (p. 531, emphasis added). The common and erroneous view that age and independency are negatively correlated derives from an overemphasis of this kind of role performance in an atypical ecological niche, the nursing institution. It must be remembered that only 5 percent of people $\geq$ 65 years of age are in institutional care (Allan, 1979).

The emphasis on the institutionalized aged by gerontologists and the lay public alike provides an ironic note: 5 percent of households headed by an old person contain at least one grandchild (Atchley, 1977). Further, of the 75 to 80 percent of the elderly ($\geq$ 65 years old) who have grandchildren, 75 percent live within 30 minutes or in the same household with their grandchild(ren), 50 percent see their grandchild(ren) every day, and 75 percent have contact with their grand-child(ren) every week or two (Harris & Associates, 1975). It is clearly the case that close ties are maintained between the elderly and their families of procreation (Kahana, 1982; Lowenthal, 1964; Troll, 1979). Troll (1980) has justifiably noted the caution necessary in the area of grandparent research because of the scarce quantity and the questionable quality of the basic data. (This author agrees.) The facts seem pretty clear, however, that a sizeable minority, possibly even a majority of elderly do spend considerable time with young children. What they do when they are together is unclear; though, Hagestad, Cohler, and Newgarten (cited in Troll, 1980) were told by the vast majority of grandchildren and grandparents (over 80% in both cases) that they try to *influence* each other. ''In spite of widespread beliefs that old people are isolated from—or even deserted—by their families, almost all surveys find that the oldest generation is an integral and active part of the family structure'' (Troll & Bengtson, 1982, p. 903).

The activity does not stop there—with family interconnectedness. Whether it is in terms of mass political involvement (e.g., the Gray Panthers) or on local levels, the independent functioning of interconnected aged persons is plain to see. Some examples of self-help have already been given. The Foster Grandparents Program is a national example in which the real action takes place locally; the degree of involvement and commitment by old people to this program is extensive (Mitchell & Schachel, 1979; Norman & Smith, 1975; Egerton, 1972). This program is a stunning example of an area in which children are a key element in the social network of the aged. The reciprocal benefits (Egerton, 1972) are diverse, but one benefit that needs to be highlighted here is the positive influence on the independ-ence of the elderly that creative interconnectedness with children produces. As noted previously, empirical data about the specific role(s) of children in independ-ence of the aged are badly needed. Nonetheless, that children do play a significant role seems indisputable· they are a significant part of the social reality for a large number of the aged.

DISCUSSION AND CONCLUSIONS

Several major conclusions are listed below.

- It is suggested that independence in old age be thought of as the logical result of successful sequences and patterns of interconnectedness and independence at preceding times throughout life.
- Independence and age are not negatively correlated. Independence in the aged is not atypical. In fact, it seems to be normative.
- Children and old people apparently spend a good deal of time together. To assume they do not have reciprocal influences seems ludicrous. On the other

hand, what they do together and the mechanisms and patterns of influence are largely not known.

- Nonetheless, the preliminary analytical framework and the available data suggest that children make a contribution to the interconnectedness and independence of old people.

Based on these conclusions, the proposed analytical framework, and the selective review of research, the most obvious need for information is in the area of direct interaction between children and the elderly. This is really but one instance of the need to expand research on the social networks that comprise reality for both age groups. Additionally, although the cost and effort needed will be great, it is imperative that research on the non-institutionalized aged be increased significantly. This need applies not only to research involving children and the aged, of course. It is also necessary that researchers focus on the personal, situational, and life-history variables that influence independence and interconnectedness developmentally so that a more valid assessment of these social functions can be made in the elderly.

What emerges from the perspective provided by the analytical framework and from the available data is the conclusion that old people not only *can* be independent but, more importantly, *are* independent to a much greater extent than is usually assumed. Further, children and old people seem to spend a good deal of time together so that the interconnectedness of the aged includes, as one component, social relationships with children. It should not be overlooked, therefore, that children can be influential in the independence of the elderly. Further, children benefit in personal ways by their contact with old people, and one can argue that society as a whole benefits as well. Although the benefits to children have only been alluded to in this chapter, it seems clear that ultimately "mutual trust, kindness, cooperation . . . and social responsibility . . . are learned from other human beings" (Bronfenbrenner, 1970, p. 117). To decry a lack of status accorded to human aging in our culture, to point out the myths about and the biases in language toward the aged needs restating. Nevertheless, we must also realize the fact of independence for most old people, and the fact of a high degree of generational interconnectedness.

This is not to minimize the wide range of problems of the elderly; but the language of bias, the language of despair and gloom are self-fulfilling prophecies when they are not balanced by an alternative view. "Ultimately, it is the belief that the individual psyche can achieve mastery over both negative biological and societal influences which gives us the most potentially positive view of old age" (Kahana, 1982, p. 886).

A prescription for life-long independence is difficult to write. Even so, it surely must include the fostering of interconnectedness from the very beginnings of life. It would seem also to include a developmental emphasis on diversity or pluralism.

The analytical framework presented in this chapter followed Garbarino's (1982) view of pluralism and focused on multiple possible paths to the same developmental outcome. Indeed, many alternative social arrangements are sound, and families and their members must have access to support from within and also from the rest of society. What Garbarino calls competence—the ability to succeed in social contexts—depends on communication skills and (most germane to the present discussion) positive self-confidence in mastering the world. As nothing succeeds like success, so it is that competence develops as a result of people in one's social network reinforcing, directing, correcting, and so on. If it is the case that competence and interconnectedness, fostered by a pluralistic conception of human development, produce independence, then the reciprocal benefits of old people and children together are likely to be great indeed.

REFERENCES

Aldous, J. (1978). Family careers: Development change in families. New York: Wiley.

Allan, Carole, B. (1979). The older consumer: The time is now. *National Journal*, Nov. 24, 1998–2003.

Ainsworth, M. (1974). Infant-mother attachment and social development: Socialization as a product of reciprocal responsiveness to signals. In M. Richards (Ed.), *The integration of the child into the social world*. Cambridge: Cambridge University Press.

Atchley, R. (1977). *Social forces in later life* (2nd ed.). Belmont, CA: Wadsworth.

Baltes, M.M., & Baltes, P.B. (1982). Microanalytical research on environmental factors and plasticity in psychological aging. In T.M. Field, A. Huston, H.C. Quay, L. Troll, & G.E. Finley (Eds.), *Review of human development*. New York: John Wiley & Sons.

Baltes, M.M., & Barton, E.M. (1979). Behavioral analysis of aging: A review of the operant model and research. *International Journal of Behavior Development*, 2, 297–320.

Bell, R.D. (1968). A reinterpretation of the direction of effects in the study of socialization. *Psychological Review*, 75, 81–95.

Belsky, J., & Steinberg, L.D. (1978). The effects of day care: A critical review. *Child Development*, 49(4), 929–949.

Brody, E.M. (1979). Women's changing roles, the aging family and long-term care of older people. *National Journal*, Oct. 27, 1828–1833.

Bronfenbrenner, U. (1970). *Two worlds of childhood: U.S. and USSR*. New York: Russell Sage Foundation.

Bronfenbrenner, U. (1979). *The ecology of human development*. Cambridge, MA: Harvard University Press.

Butler, R.N. (1975). *Why survive?* New York: Harper & Row.

Butler, R., & Lewis, M. (1973). *Aging and mental health*. St. Louis: C.V. Mosby.

Chibucos, T.R. (1982). Adjustment to infant day care: The importance of infant-parent attachment. Unpublished manuscript.

Chibucos, T.R., & Kail, P.R. (1981). Longitudinal examination of father-infant interaction and infant-father attachment. *Merrill-Palmer Quarterly*, 27(2), 81–96.

Costa, P.T. Jr., & McCrae, R.R. (1978). Objective personality assessment. In M. Storandt, J.C. Siegler, & M.F. Elias (Eds.), *The clinical psychology of aging*. New York: Plenum.

Egerton, J. (1972). Foster grandparents at work here. *American Education, 8*, 25–28.

Ehrlich, P. (1980, October). *Mutual help for community elderly: A demonstration and research project*. Paper presented at the Institute of Gerontology, Wayne State University, Detroit, MI.

Garbarino, J. (1982). *Children and families in the social environment*. New York: Aldine.

Harris, L., & Associates. (1975). *The myth and reality of aging in America*. New York: National Council on Aging.

Hartup, W.W. (1978). Perspectives on child and family interaction: Past, present, and future. In R.M. Lerner and G.B. Spanier (Eds.), *Child influences on marital and family interaction*. New York: Academic Press.

Hess, B.B. (1976). Self-help among the aged. *Social Policy, 7*(3), 55–62.

Hill, R. (1970). Family development in three generations. Cambridge, MA: Schenkman.

Kagan, J., Kearsley, R.B., & Zelazo, P.R. (1978). *Infancy: Its place in human development*. Cambridge, MA: Harvard University Press.

Kahana, B. (1982). Social behavior and aging. In B. Wolman (Ed.), *Handbook of developmental psychology*. Englewood Cliffs, NJ: Prentice-Hall.

Kahana, B., Kahana, E., and McLenigan, P. (1980, November). *The adventurous aged: Voluntary relocation in the later years*. Paper presented at the 33rd annual scientific meeting of the Gerontological Society, San Diego, CA.

Kahana, E. (1974). The role of homes for the aged in meeting community needs (Final Report). Detroit, MI: Elderly Care Research Center, Wayne State University.

Kenniston, K. (1977). *All our children: The American family under pressure*. New York: Harcourt Brace Jovanovich.

Lamb, M.E. (Ed.). (1981). *The role of the father in child development* (2nd ed.). New York: John Wiley & Sons.

Lerner, R.M. (1978). Nature, nurture, and dynamic interactionism. *Human Development, 21*, 1–20.

Lerner, R.M., & Spanier, G.B. (Eds.). (1978). *Child influences on marital and family interaction*. New York: Academic Press.

Lewis, M. (1980). Peer interaction and maltreated children: Social network and epigenetic models. In T.R. Chibucos (Ed.), Toward broader conceptualization of child mistreatment. *Infant Mental Health Journal, 1*(4), 224–231.

Lewis, M. (1982). The social network systems model: Toward a theory of social development. In T.M. Field, A. Huston, H.C. Quay, L. Troll, & G.E. Finley (Eds.), *Review of Human Development*. New York: John Wiley & Sons.

Lowenthal, M. (1964). Social isolation and mental illness in old age. *American Sociological Review, 29*, 54–70.

Maas, H.S., & Kuypers, J.A. (1974). *From thirty to seventy*. San Francisco: Jossey-Bass.

McCrae, R.R., & Costa, P.T. Jr. (1982). Aging, the life course, and models of personality. In T.M. Field, A. Huston, H.C. Quay, L. Troll, & G.E. Finley (Eds.), *Review of human development*. New York: John Wiley & Sons.

McCrae, R.R., & Costa, P.T. Jr. (1980). Openness to experience and ego level in Loevinger's Sentence Completion Test: Dispositional contributions to developmental model of personality. *Journal of Personality and Social Psychology, 38*, 1179–1190.

Mead, M. (1974). Grandparents as educators. *Teachers College Record, 76*(2), 240–249.

Mitchell, A., & Schachel, C. (1979). Journey in time: A foster grandparent program. *Young Children,* March, 30–32.

National Childcare Consumer Study (1975). (Contract 105–74–1107). Washington, D.C.: Department of Health, Education, and Welfare.

Norman, R.E., & Smith, R. (1975). Companion to the elderly. *Journal of Home Economics,* March, 35–37.

Overton, W.F., & Reese, H.W. (1973). Models of development: Methodological implications. In J.R. Nesselroade & H.W. Reese (Eds.), *Lifespan developmental psychology: Methodological issues.* New York: Academic Press.

Parke, R.D. (1981). *Fathers.* Cambridge, MA: Harvard University Press.

Parsons, T., & Bales, R.F. (1955). *Family, socialization and interaction process.* Glencoe, IL: Free Press.

Pilisuk, M., & Minkler, M. (1980). Supportive networks: Life ties for the elderly. *Journal of Social Issues, 36*(2), 95–116.

Powell, J.A., & Arquitt, G.E. (1978). Getting the generations back together: A rationale for development of community-based intergenerational interaction programs. *The Family Coordinator,* October, 421–425.

Quinn, W.H., & Keller, J.F. (1981). A family therapy model for preserving independence in older persons: Utilization of the family of procreation. *The American Journal of Family Therapy, 9*(1), 79–84.

Shanas, E., Townsend, P., Wedderturn, D., Friis, H., Milhoj, P., & Stehouwer. (1968). *Old people in three industrial societies.* New York: Atherton.

Streitfeld, E. (1976). Young and old together. *Social Policy.* Nov.-Dec., 100–102.

Sussman, M.B. (1963). Relationships of adult children with their parents in the United States. In E. Shanas and G. Streib (Eds.), *Social structure and the family: Generational relations.* Englewood Cliffs, NJ: Prentice-Hall.

Troll, L.E. (1980). Grandparenting. In L.W. Poon (Ed.), *Aging in the 1980s.* Washington, DC: American Psychological Association.

Troll, L.E. (1979). *Families in later life.* Belmont, CA: Wadsworth.

Troll, L.E., & Bengtson, V.L. (1982). Intergenerational relations throughout the life span. In B.B. Wolman (Ed.), *Handbook of developmental psychology.* Englewood Cliffs, NJ: Prentice-Hall.

Vaughan, V.C., III, McKay, R.J. Jr., & Behrman, R.E. (Eds.). (1979). *Nelson textbook on pediatrics* (11th ed.). Philadelphia: W.B. Saunders.

Wohlwill, J. (1973). *The study of behavioral development.* New York: Academic Press.

Chapter 16

Career Impact on Independence of the Elderly

Terri A. Eisler

The preservation of independence in old age is a goal sought by the elderly and by society. Independence can enhance the functioning and well-being of the elderly person, and it can lessen the burden on the formal and informal support systems of society.

The concept of independence has been defined in various ways throughout the studies on aging. Some researchers, like Lawton (1971), view independence as the means by which elderly persons can perform some basic self-maintenance functions—dressing themselves, cooking, handling their finances, and shopping; others (Kalish, 1975; Hughston & Quinn, 1979) view independence as the ability of persons to master their environment and to maintain a familiar lifestyle. Of course, it may be argued that the ability to master one's environment is merely an extension of the ability to perform certain basic daily tasks. The term independence as used in this chapter, however, is designed to convey this mastery in a broader sense—the sense that one still has some control over one's life, one's friends, actions, needs, and self-esteem. Thus, the term *independence* is actually a composite of several concepts that describe personality, interpersonal relationships, actions, or specific situations or conditions (Kalish, 1975).

Independence in old age can be lost as a result of physical deterioration, which forces persons to depend on others for care. It can be lost as a result of mental deterioration, which produces changes in memory, judgment, and orientation and again forces persons into dependent positions. Blenkner (1969) describes another source of dependency—the loss of meaningful others, which reduces a person's social roles and power. Finally, the loss of wages owing to retirement or other causes may force a person to become economically dependent on pensions and Social Security programs, as well as welfare and family gifts (Kalish, 1975).

It is this latter dependency, economic dependency caused by the loss of a career, that provides the central focus of this chapter. It is the author's contention that the continuation of a career in old age reduces economic dependency and influences other areas of independence as well. Furthermore, careers are positively related to the preservation of independence in old age.

KEY CONCEPTS

Independence

Because independence is of primary concern to the elderly, its loss, or the threat of its loss, ranks as a major source of dissatisfaction with life. To healthy elderly persons, their independence is a source of pride and a means by which they can avoid inconveniencing others. Clearly, then, the preservation of independence in old age is not just society's goal, so that children and social service agencies can be relieved of the burden of caring for the elderly; it is a primary goal of the elderly themselves. The need for independence and the ability to maintain it in old age, the need to preserve a familiar life style and to continue to function in an autonomous manner is of utmost importance. This need for independence and the maintenance of self-esteem does not suddenly disappear, however, when one reaches 65 years of age or retires. It continues throughout the life span (Clark & Anderson, 1967; Kalish, 1969; Hughston & Quinn, 1979).

Independence can be maintained through various means. Social service agencies can offer programs, families and friends can act as nonformal support systems, other organizations can offer services and equipment, and the elderly person can be given the opportunity to continue in, or to reenter, a career of one's choice. The maintenance of a career—along with the financial security it provides—yields other intrinsic and extrinsic rewards. Careers are a major source of self-esteem, identity, independence and life-satisfaction (Troll, 1982; Super, 1953). These aspects are just as important in later life as they are during the earlier phases of the life cycle.

Career

A career is a sequence of occupations in which one engages (Tolbert, 1974). These jobs or occupations are usually related to prior jobs and training, as well as to future anticipated jobs (Troll, 1982). Usually, some degree of planning and commitment is associated with these jobs. A career can be distinguished from a job by several factors. Most adult men and over half of the adult women in America have *jobs*; that is, they participate in the labor force by performing specific activities at regular time schedules for money (Troll). Only 30 percent of all workers, however, move systematically up the status hierarchy in an orderly progression to form what is known as an "orderly career" (Troll). In addition, careers appear to be largely a phenomenon of the middle and upper classes. Most labor force participants have jobs. When these jobs demand commitment, planning, and time and provide both intrinsic and extrinsic rewards, they become *careers*—the province of a small portion of our society.

Career exploration, choice, entry, continuation, maintenance, and decline are the major stages associated with the occupational aspect of human development. Stages of career development roughly coincide with the stages of childhood, adolescence, adulthood, and late adulthood (Super, 1953; Ginzberg, 1952). For Super, however, career maintenance lasts only from age 45–64 years; the final stage, decline, continues from 65 years of age onward. This final stage is characterized by a decline in physical and mental powers, as well as in activity levels. Apparently, theories of career development assume that career related activities (entry, exploration, maintenance) do not exist in old age, but end at 65 years of age or retirement. Today, there is evidence that challenges this assumption; increasing numbers of old people either are remaining in their present positions or are entering new career areas (Gilmer, 1982; "Inflation Forces," 1979). If we accept the premise that the choice of a career is intertwined with almost all aspects of our daily lives (Troll, 1982), it follows that the loss of this career and its accompanying financial and social losses can have dramatic and often deleterious effects on our lives. The central tenet of this chapter is that the ability to maintain one's career or to pursue a new one is intricately related to the ability to preserve one's independence in old age.

This chapter briefly reviews career development and the differences in career patterns between men and women. Changes in career patterns during mid-life are discussed, as well as the implications of career maintenance throughout the life span.

THEORETICAL APPROACHES TO CAREER DEVELOPMENT

Theories of career development can be divided into several types; among these are the developmental, needs, and social learning theories. Super (1953), Ginzberg (1952), and Tiedeman and O'Hara (1963) are most closely associated with the developmental approach. Roe (1957), Holland (1966), and Hoppock (1967) are generally associated with the psychological need theories; and Krumboltz and Thoresen (1969) and Goodstein (1972), with social learning theory.

Career development is a life-long, continuous process. It is influenced by experiences throughout the life cycle—social learning factors, family environment factors, economic factors, personality factors, psychological needs, developmental factors, the trait and factor approach—which predict career development and eventual career choice. Clearly, career development does not end with adolescence or with college graduation; it continues into mid-life and even retirement. It is appropriate, then, to discuss it in the context of the aging person.

Careers furnish more than a daily routine and a means for earning money, they also provide meaning to life, an identity, and a source of self-esteem. Although the extrinsic rewards of income, security, and fringe benefits are not to be denied, many careers provide intrinsic rewards as well. Work may be a source of prestige, social recognition, a basis of self-respect, autonomy, and independence (Troll, 1982). More than just a source of financial independence, a career may provide the opportunity to function independently within one's discipline, to conduct the type of research one chooses, to start new programs, and to experiment with new designs and concepts. Studies have shown that older men differ from younger men in their desire to control and to manage more aspects of their work; older men express a strong need to be independent (Veroff & Feld, 1970; Friedmann & Havighurst, 1954; Strong, 1959). Independence appears to be a component or an intrinsic reward of having a career.

Women, too, are recognizing this aspect of working as more and more women enter and stay in the labor force. Along with the financial security of having one's own money, the desire to make one's own decisions, to assert oneself, and to control one's own destiny arises, and the need and desire for social, economic, and personal independence emerge.

Jobs and careers are influenced by and influence all aspects of a person's life. Family background, education, socioeconomic level, national economic conditions, personal experiences, and often serendipitous circumstances can influence the types of occupations we choose. Furthermore, the type of work we do can influence where we live, who our friends are, our family life, our self-esteem, our identity, our mental and physical health, and the amount of control we have over our destinies.

Men and women have different patterns of career development, owing largely to societal constraints and expectations. Child-rearing practices (Kacerguis & Adams, 1979), educational practices, and occupational opportunities differ for men and women (Troll, 1982; Hansen & Rapoza, 1978). Males are expected to work (Troll, 1982). Women are still socialized into the dichotomy of work or not working (Eisler, 1981), and their careers are often considered transient and of less importance that those of men (Vetter, 1978).

Although society has always expected its men to work, women, too, have always worked (Troll, 1982). The phenomenon is not new, just its recognition. With the increased labor force participation of women (Vetter, Sechler, Lowry, & Canora, 1979), employers, government, and educators have been obliged to take the phenomenon of women's employment more seriously and to study it.

LIFE SPAN CAREER CHANGES

In keeping with the concept of career development as a continuous life-long process, it is appropriate next to consider mid-life career development and change.

Along with the recognition of the existence and importance of this phenomenon, this section also examines the relevance of mid-life careers to the preservation of independence.

Life expectancy is increasing, retirement age is dropping, and improvements in the treatment of cancer and heart disease are adding years to the life span (Entine, 1977). Entine estimates that by the year 2000, the average retirement age will have dropped to 55 years and that at least 57 million persons will be over retirement age.

The increased number of retired middle-agers with longer life spans and better health makes the prospect of mid-life career change more of a reality today than ever before. There are many sources of this change. Entine divides them into four types: unanticipated and anticipated, internal and external. Unanticipated internal causes include serious illness that may prevent a worker from performing job tasks, and the death or divorce of a spouse—which has forced many women back into the labor market. External examples of unanticipated causes are unemployment (the layoff of workers or plant closings because of economic conditions), obsolescence (specific jobs become obsolete owing to advances in technology), and dissatisfaction (the worker becomes bored or dissatisfied with the job).

A signal example of anticipated internal sources of mid-life career changes is the empty nest syndrome, when many middle-aged women enter or reenter the work force after their children have grown and left home. Sixty percent of all women 45 to 54 years old were in the work force in 1978 (Troll, 1982). Other sources are the reentry of women—and men—into higher education. Adult education or career retraining often enables the middle-aged worker to develop new job skills for advancement or career change. At mid-life many persons reevaluate their priorities and values; this process often causes a voluntary career change (Schlossberg, 1977).

External anticipated sources of mid-life career change include planned retirement; anticipating the changes in life style and loss of income, persons may reevaluate their present positions and change careers to insure themselves of financial security and basic need fulfillment. Promotions and advancements that require moving, that cause significant changes in life style and friends, or that interfere with a spouse's career may also be the impetus to seek a career change in mid-life.

During middle age persons appear also to be reevaluating their lives—reassessing their priorities and sensing that their lives and options are finite (Heald, 1977). This process often provides the impetus to seek fulfillment of their unrealized dreams. Personal independence may often be one of these unrealized goals. Humans want some control over their lives, some sense of autonomy or independence (Schlossberg, 1977). This desire for autonomy has become apparent in the middle management positions of large and small organizations. Many of these persons feel locked into their jobs, with little chance for change, flexibility, advancement, or autonomy. In short, they are not in control of their careers, and because their occupations permeate all aspects of their lives, these people often feel a lack of control or autonomy over their personal lives.

This feeling of depression, despair, restlessness and rebellion (Heald, 1977) characterizes the mid-life crisis and is commonly described as a male phenomenon. However, for females previously locked into dissatisfying or unfulfilling careers in the home or outside, this phenomenon is just as real. Persons at this stage often make drastic changes in their lives. Incidences of suicide, accidents, extra-marital affairs and divorce burgeon in middle age (Heald, 1977). Career change is another aspect of this development. It is the person's final quest for meaning, identity, self-esteem, fulfillment, and autonomy in life.

PRACTICAL IMPLICATIONS FOR THE ELDERLY

Successful aging requires adequate health and adequate income. Sources of income for the elderly in 1976 (Kart, 1981) included Social Security, 39 percent; earnings, 23 percent; asset income, 18 percent; private pension, government employee pensions, and other, 18 percent. The current uncertainty about Social Security, inflation, and the fact that individuals are living longer and retiring earlier (Entine, 1977) have an obvious implication: other sources of income must be found.

In addition, the independence of the elderly must be maintained. Independence has many forms: social, financial, emotional, and conditional or situational (Kalish, 1975). Adequate income can provide a great deal of independence because it allows a person to maintain a style of life he has chosen or become accustomed to and to maintain or terminate relationships by choice, not because financial situations have forced him to do so. In addition, with adequate income, an elderly person can obtain medical care and advice to meet needs and to make use of the public and private services that exist. All this does not deny the importance of good health and the other aspects of life; however, it should be obvious that old age is more comfortable with adequate income.

There are various sources of income; some have been mentioned before. Because of the increased life span, however, a recent development is gaining in popularity—the return of retirees to the work force. Although the return is not a large movement now, its beginnings can be seen in many of the larger companies that are providing job-training and placement for their retirees.

Many of these second or third careers involve new fields of interest—areas the retirees might not have previously considered as a career. Now they can afford to risk the time and the effort to experiment with something new ("Inflation Forces," 1979). Some retirees have made use of skills developed in their prior careers, and have allowed themselves the freedom to expand their career horizons. These second careers normally require fewer hours of work, less interference in family life, and provide the intrinsic rewards as well as the supplemental income so necessary for maintaining one's independence in old age.

In reality, few of our career development theories or services focus on the needs of the elderly. Additional training in the provision of these services is a necessity.

Some of the larger corporations are providing courses and career counseling for their retirees, and national counselor organizations have recently recognized the need. Needed now is an increased awareness that career development and choice is truly a life-long process and a commitment on the part of training institutions to teach their students how to provide this source to elderly career oriented persons. Until the elderly can actually attend career development sessions geared to their cohort group and needs and until placement services recognize its legitimacy, careers for the elderly may remain another unfulfilled need.

There is little in the research reports on careers in old age, and even less on its relationship to the maintenance of independence. Independence in old age, for the most part, is seen simply as the ability to perform certain daily functions—grooming activities, handling money (Lawton, 1971). It does not describe the composite of needs for autonomy, mastery over one's environment, and self-esteem that comprise independence. The desire for the freedom to choose one's companions, housing, food, medical care-givers, and activities are all part of that independence. Independence for the elderly is closely related to adequate health and adequate income. One source of income is earnings; and careers—first, second, or third—can provide economic independence for persons throughout the life span.

Why has the concept of careers in old age been ignored? Is it that we have misperceived the situation and have viewed all people over 65 years of age as retirees? Recent research (Gilmer, 1982; "Inflation Forces," 1979) has shown that persons with careers do not retire; very often, they continue to work. Some may lessen their pace or enter new professions, but they do not retire or stop working. Thus, for that 30 percent of the population involved in a career, the concept of a career in old age is quite relevant, and the relationship of that career to self-esteem, self-concept, identity, autonomy, and independence cannot be denied.

Several major conclusions can be drawn from this study. Careers provide both intrinsic and extrinsic rewards; they affect personal, private, and professional lives (Troll, 1982). Moreover, they involve thoughtful planning and movement along a continuum (Troll, 1982; Tolbert, 1974). Vocational development is also often seen as being synonymous with the development of self-concept (Super, 1953). Above all, it is clear that career development and choice are life-long and continuous (Krumboltz, 1976). Just as the development of self-concept and self-esteem does not terminate in adulthood or at retirement, neither does the desire to continue to engage in meaningful work, the desire to maintain an adequate income and style of life, and the need for independence. Using a broader perspective in their study of career development, educators and researchers should examine the relationship of careers and independence more closely as they look at the elderly.

REFERENCES

Blenkner, M. (1969). The normal dependencies of aging. In R.A. Kalish (Ed.), *Dependencies of old people.* In *Occasional papers in gerontology* (Vol. 6). Ann Arbor & Detroit: Institute of Gerontology, University of Michigan & Wayne State University.

Clark, M., & Anderson, B.G. (1967). *Culture and aging: An anthropological study of older Americans.* Springfield, IL: Charles C Thomas.

Eisler, T.A. (1981). *Parental influence on the career choices of women: Some cohort differences.* Unpublished Dissertation.

Entine, A.D. (1977). Counseling for mid-life and beyond. *The Vocational Guidance Quarterly, 25,* 332–336.

Friedmann, E.A., & Havighurst, R. (1954). *The meaning of work and retirement.* Chicago: University of Chicago Press.

Gilmer, B.V. (1982). *Personal communique.*

Ginzberg, E. (1952). Toward a theory of occupational choice. *Personnel and Guidance Journal, 30*(8).

Goodstein, L.D. (1972). Behavioral views of counseling. In B. Stefflre and W.H. Grand (Eds.), *Theories of counseling.* New York: McGraw-Hill.

Hansen, S.L., & Rapoza, R.S. (1978). *Career development and counseling of women.* Springfield, IL: Charles C Thomas.

Heald, J.E. (1977). Mid-life career influence. *The Vocational Guidance Quarterly, 25,* 309–312.

Holland, J.L. (1966). *The psychology of vocational choice.* Waltham, MA: Blaisedell.

Hoppock, R. (1967). *Occupational information* (3rd ed.). New York: McGraw-Hill.

Hughston, G.A., & Quinn, W. (1979). *The family as a natural support system for the aged.* Paper presented at the 32nd Annual Scientific Meeting of the Gerontological Society, Washington, DC.

Inflation forces retirees into new careers. (1979, August 20). *Business Week,* pp. 119–120.

Kacerguis, M., & Adams, G. (1979). Implications of sex typed child-rearing practices, toys, and mass media materials in restricting occupational choices of women. *Family Coordinator, 28,* 369–375.

Kalish, R.A. (1969). Introduction. In R.A. Kalish (Ed.) *Dependencies of old people. Occasional papers in gerontology* (Vol. 6). Ann Arbor & Detroit: Institute of Gerontology, University of Michigan & Wayne State University.

Kart, C.S. (1981). *The realities of aging.* Boston: Allyn & Bacon.

Kalish, R.A. (1975). *Late adulthood: Perspectives on human development.* Monterey, CA: Brooks-Cole Publishing Company.

Krumboltz, J.D. (1976). A social learning theory of career selection. *The Counseling Psychologist, 6,* 71–80.

Krumboltz, J.D., & Thoresen, C.E. (Eds.). (1969). *Behavioral counseling: Cases and techniques.* New York: Holt, Rinehart & Winston.

Lawton, M.P. (1971). The functional assessment of elderly people. *Journal of the American Geriatric Society, 19,* 465–481.

Roe, A. (1957). Early determinants of vocational choice. *Journal of Counseling Psychology, 4,* 212–217.

Schlossberg, N.K. (1977). Breaking out of the box: Organizational options for adults. *The Vocational Guidance Quarterly, 25,* 313–319.

Strong, E., Jr. (1959). *Change of interests with age.* Stanford, CA: Stanford University Press.

Super, D. (1953). A theory of vocational development. *American Psychologist, 8,* 185–195.

Tiedeman, D.V., & O'Hara, P.P. (1963). *Career development: Choice and adjustment.* New York: College Entrance Examination Board.

Tolbert, E.L. (1974). *Counseling for career development.* Boston: Houghton Mifflin.

Troll, L.E. (1982). *Continuations: Adult development and aging.* Monterey, CA: Brooks-Cole Publishing Co.

Veroff, J., & Feld, S. (1970). *Marriage and work in America: A study of motives and roles.* New York: Van Nostrand Reinhold.

Vetter, L. (1978). Career counseling for women. In S.L. Hansen and R.S. Rapoza (Eds.), *Career development and counseling of women.* Springfield, IL: Charles C Thomas.

Vetter, L., Sechler, J., Lowry, C.M., & Canora, V. (1979). *Factors influencing non-traditional vocational education enrollments: A literature review.* National Center Publications, Columbus, OH: Ohio State University.

Chapter 17

Research on Family Life in Old Age: Exploring the Frontiers

Jay A. Mancini

Older people, their families, and those who investigate them have been identified as *pioneers*. In her Ernest W. Burgess Award address, Ethel Shanas suggested: "Old people and their families are the new pioneers of our era. They have ventured into uncharted areas of human relationships, and developed systems of exchange and interaction without help or guidance from the so-called helping agencies in our industrial society" (1980, p. 14). Previously, in discussing the status of research on family gerontology, Troll, Miller, and Atchley (1979) noted: "Current investigators of families in later life are pioneers. They are often operating in uncharted territory . . :" (p. 37). If Shanas and Troll are accurate in their pioneer designations, it would seem appropriate to describe the frontier in which older families and investigators find themselves. The primary objective of this review is to summarize what has been written about needed research on the family life of older adults and to suggest new directions for investigators. Before delineating these new directions, several research or professional issues are discussed that have a bearing on the development of an accurate, meaningful knowledge base for family gerontology. The issues pertain to—

- research designs and family myths,
- theory development,
- quantitative and qualitative research,
- the criterion of well-being,
- the importance of family life in old age,
- a cumulative body of knowledge.

EXPLORING THE RESEARCH ISSUES

Several of the issues to be reviewed are endemic to an emerging field of study (part of its growing pain); others are particular to family gerontology. Each sheds some light on the directions taken by professionals in their attempts to understand family influences on successful aging, and partially illuminates the research frontier. In short, much of the significant research to date has addressed the enrichment, alienation, and empty nest myths of aging; that currently there is an unfortunate lack of theory development; that studies have not been sufficiently qualitative; that too many investigations have focused on well-being as the significant criterion variable; that the importance of family for successful aging may have been overestimated; and that the family gerontology field suffers from a lack of cumulative knowledge.

Family and Aging Myths

Widespread misconceptions about older people and their families concern *alienation, enrichment,* and the *empty nest.* A substantial number of research papers have addressed (fully or partially) these questions: Do families neglect their elderly? Do family relations enhance successful aging? Are there deleterious effects on parents when children establish separate residence?

The amount of contact that typically occurs between older parents and their adult children has been examined because it was once thought that one artifact of a modern, industrial American society was greater separation between kin and because it was assumed that contact was directly related to the mental health of the old. Instead, research has shown conclusively that older people are not alienated from their families, at least not because of contact patterns (Shanas, 1979). Related to the alienation myth is the enrichment myth (Mancini, 1980). This notion assumes that the lives of older people are necessarily improved when they are in regular contact with family members; however, research has failed to demonstrate such a relationship. A third hypothesis that has motivated research has involved the so-called "empty nest syndrome." This term signifies the point when a couple's last (or only) child leaves the home and so provides the opportunity for the couple relationship to reemerge in importance. Though the term may be functional as a life cycle benchmark, research data on the whole do not suggest that parents, especially mothers, are adversely affected (Troll et al., 1979). In the course of reviewing the research reports of the 1960s, Troll (1971, p. 198) concludes, "There is little evidence of the empty nest crisis accompanied by great distress and massive readjustment. . . ."

By now, investigations have repeatedly shown that generations in the family do have contact and are not alienated, that the lives of older people are not necessarily enriched by contact, and that the negative effects of children departing the parental home are negligible. Yet, researchers persist in examining these issues in conventional ways and, predictably, fail to increase the body of knowledge on the family in later life. Social gerontologists appear to approach the study of older families with little creativity and tend not to stray beyond testing the alienation, enrichment, and empty nest hypotheses.

Theory Development

A noteworthy omission in the research reports on family gerontology is the development of testable theory. This gap, though recognized at least ten years ago (Troll, 1971), has not been filled by the recent efforts of those who study family life in the later years (Streib & Beck, 1980). In an emerging area of study, such as family gerontology, there is a tendency to generate descriptive information while assuming that at some point this descriptive approach will shift to a greater focus on proposition development and theory testing. Theorizing can be premature, but it is not unusual for a content domain to remain at the descriptive level long after it is useful. An example is family sociology in its general theoretical frameworks. For many years, professionals couched their research in "conceptual frameworks," which appeared to be a series of loosely connected concepts (Hill & Hansen, 1960); only recently has family sociology progressed from conceptualizing to theorizing. Enough studies are now extant on the family life of older adults to support increased theory development efforts. For example, a recent bibliography of such research catalogued more than 500 papers, articles, and books (Lewis, 1978); and in 1981 alone, there were at least 100 publications on family gerontology (Olson & Markoff, 1982).

Ryff (1982) has said that "a priori theoretical accounts of why certain variables are likely to be correlated with life satisfaction are missing, and obtained findings are left in a sort of explanatory ambiguity" (p. 210). Her comments can equally be applied to family gerontology. A major limitation in the field is its potpourri approach to meaningful knowledge about older people and their families. Greater efforts at theory development tend to introduce more focus to future research; but at the present time, there is inadequate theoretical guidance for research initiatives. (Some attention has been given to this realm by Quinn, 1983, in his model-building of intergenerational relationships.)

Quantitative and Qualitative Research

It is not uncommon for social scientists to ask that more attention be directed toward the qualitative aspects of family life (Troll et al., 1979), usually in response to research findings that show little or no relationship between contact with family and successful aging (Lee, 1979; Mancini, 1979). Nevertheless, accurate assessment of relationship quality has been elusive and has not yet captured the dynamics of family life. Troll and her colleagues have used the phrase "ebb and flow" to explain the necessity of new research arenas. *Ebb and flow* suggests the ups and downs and the negative and positive aspects of relationships—whether they be feelings of affection, communication patterns, intimacy-sharing or instrumental and affective exchange. Conventional research designs are insensitive to the ebb and flow of life; they are typically oriented to capturing a momentary—perhaps transitory—slice of everyday life in the hope that something more stable is reflected.

Observational and case-study approaches to the family life of old people are practically nonexistent (Quinn, 1982, offers one exception). Social survey methods are not without merit, but they may not be particularly appropriate for assessing the qualitative aspects of family life that researchers feel are important to successful aging. Asking attitudinal questions about relationship quality may be too far removed from the real essence of relationship dynamics. One example may be found in a recent report by Lee and Ellithorpe (1982) on the impact of intergenerational exchange on well-being. These researchers expected—consistent with widely held presumptions—that the positive or negative aspects of such exchange would be significantly related to a measure of well-being because intergenerational exchange is a dimension of relationship quality. Because they found no relationship they questioned the notion that suggests well-being and family life ought to influence one another. Several years earlier, Mancini (1979) had examined the way perceived competence in the older parent role varied with well-being. The findings selectively supported the expected positive relationship, but the actual amount of variance accounted for in well-being was modest. In both of these inquiries, the goal was to demonstrate how qualitative aspects of family life were important for successful aging but the social survey methods employed were limited in their ability to tap the qualitative dynamics of relationships. A current need in the study of family life in old age is twofold: to continue to identify the various qualitative aspects of family relationships, and to utilize research methods that themselves are more qualitative.

The Criterion for Well-Being

For many years well-being (also called life satisfaction, morale, and happiness) has been the dependent variable of choice in social gerontology research focusing on the family. Maddox and Wiley (1976, p. 15) suggest it is "perhaps the oldest, most persistently investigated issue in the social scientific study of aging." George and Bearon (1980) have advised caution in blindly focusing on a measure of well-being as the "bottom line" of one's research. One aspect of their concern is the global nature of well-being, and its failure to pinpoint the exact nature of satisfaction. Researchers traditionally expect a global measure to vary substantially with specific aspects of everyday life (e.g., spending time with family or exchanging instrumental and affective commodities); however, the *linkages* between the highly specific and the ambiguously global are often not specified. One example from family gerontology involves well-being and contact patterns with family. Studies concur that the amount of contact is unrelated to well-being (Troll et al., 1979). What is not known are the conditions under which family contact may be important, such as whether contact is desired and whether spending time together is perceived as satisfying. Studies also suggest that the meaningful outcomes of events and experiences in older people's lives may not find their way into global measures but may be related to specific aspects of well-being. For example, intergenerational exchange may have a substantial impact on parent-child satisfaction, not on global well-being. Greater attention should be given toward reevaluating the usefulness of global measures of well-being and to specifying the linkages between well-being and particular aspects of everyday life.

How Important Is the Family?

Part of the drive to study family life in old age originates in the belief that family involvement is germane to being satisfied with life. Over 20 years ago, Thompson and Streib (1961) suggested that relationships with family are among the more significant social relationships for older people, and social science writers since that time have generally agreed. The question of how important, though, has not yet been answered.

Research results have consistently documented that health and socioeconomic factors have the most pronounced influence on successful aging (Mancini & Quinn, 1981). Those older adults who remain physically active, who are not debilitated by disease or accidents, and who have access to economic resources that more than meet their needs are more likely to thrive in the later years. Compared with these factors, what is the contribution of family life to well-being? Most of the studies that have included a wide array of health and social factors have used information about the amount of contact to represent the family domain (Edwards & Klemmack, 1973; Martin, 1973; Mancini, Quinn, Gavigan, & Franklin, 1980); needless to say, the family did not fare well in these investigations. It should be noted, however, that the amount of contact is an inadequate indicator and lacks meaning. For example, not having face-to-face contact during a particular period of time could simply be evidence of any of the following: family members are on vacation; the weather is exceedingly bad; the older adult does not especially like the children or grandchildren; or family members are not in close enough proximity for regular visiting to occur. Still, even though contact is a poor indicator of family life, investigators have not ventured much beyond it when comparing the importance of family with health, socioeconomic status, and other independent variables. Research that examines the relative contribution of family variables within the context of other factors said to be important for successful aging is needed for an accurate understanding of the role families play in the lives of their older members.

Cumulative Knowledge (The "Very Little" Report)

In their review of investigations on the family life of older adults, which was conducted during the 1970s, Streib and Beck (1980) argued the need for cumulative research. Their point is perhaps supported by the number of articles in which the author reports that "very little" has been done previously on the subject of the research. It is less surprising that topics out of the mainstream have been neglected, such as the mediation role middle-aged parents may assume between the first and third generations (Robertson, 1975). Nevertheless, professionals should be concerned that marriage relationships in old age (Keith & Brubaker, 1979), the effects of a husband's retirement on his wife (Keating & Cole, 1980), the effects of a child's divorce on older parents (Johnson, 1981), and the dynamics of family relationships (Troll et al., 1979) are said to be grossly underresearched. That very little is known about the above areas is striking in light of the fact that Lewis (1978) included more than 500 citations in his bibliography on family gerontology. When reputable social researchers contend that knowledge about some core dimensions of family relationships is lacking while hundreds of professional publications are extant, it raises the question of what has been studied, why it has been studied, and, as a result what is really known about family life in old age. Apparently, social science has taken a whimsical approach to the family gerontology content domain—which has resulted in a disproportionate focus on several areas—and so it has not resulted in a cumulative body of knowledge.

The issues just posited and discussed partially explain the current state of affairs in the study of family life in old age. In general, the research has been marred by a lack of systematic conceptualization and investigative creativity. As a result, theory development has been retarded and qualitative aspects of family life have been underresearched. The next section of this chapter, a review of reviews on the family in later life, demonstrates the need for new directions in gerontological research on the family.

REVIEWING THE REVIEWS

There is no shortage of review articles on the family life of old people. Therefore, individual studies are not reviewed; rather, future directions for research suggested by these extant sources are summarized: Troll (1971), Troll and associates (1979), Bengtson & DeTerre (1980), Mancini (1980), Streib & Beck (1980). Each review makes a distinctive contribution to identifying needed research (see Table 17–1).

Troll's (1971) review of research conducted during the 1960s reflected initial efforts to examine the qualitative aspects of family life in old age. In her own words, qualitative aspects of interaction were "introduced but not pursued extensively" (p. 269). During the 1960s, a number of family theorists and researchers were exploring the utility of the developmental framework in order to explain the normative transitions that occur in family life. Troll discussed the application of the framework to the later stages of the family life cycle—especially as it pertained to the "empirical determination of stages and critical transition points" (p. 206). She also noted the need for an investigation of the period of time that begins after children are "launched" and ends before the onset of old age—what is now typically called the *middle years*. There also existed at that time the need to contrast and to compare varying components (such as family and friends) in the informal support network. The living arrangements of older people, especially cohabitation, were also cited as worthwhile avenues of research. Finally, marital sexuality and the sexual adjustment of older couples were identified as having had received minimal attention up to that point, especially as individual changes occur from the middle to later years. In general, Troll repeatedly develops the theme that research is needed that incorporates a wide range of the adulthood years in the course of tracking developmental continuity and change.

Toward the latter part of the 1970s, Troll and her colleagues (1979) expanded her earlier work into a detailed examination of the family in later life. In addition to discussing general issues in this area of study, they reviewed the research on older couples, the unmarried older person, parents and their middle-aged children, grandparenthood, and relationships with siblings and other kin. The book concluded with drawing implications for the general public, counselors, academicians, and policymakers.

Their list of research needs is expansive and reflects each of the major sections in the book. Among the more unusual suggestions for future research are increased focus on dyads; changes and continuities in marital quality over the middle and later adult years; male roles in the older family; and the effects of older parents' divorce upon the relationship with middle-aged children and on the well-being of those adult children.

Researchers who study various periods in the family life cycle have been calling for investigations of the conjoint reality of relationships—that is, from a couple rather than an individual perspective. This need is particularly evident for the family in later life because of the interest in informal support. Though many contend that family support is crucial to successful aging, research designs rarely capture the dynamics of a particular relationship. All too often individual-supplied information is accepted as reflective of a dyadic relationship. The understanding of marital quality over an extended time is largely the result of cross-sectional research designs—approaches that attach developmental significance to fleeting glimpses of married life. Because these studies, for the most part, have not provided adequate control for the limitations of cross-sectional study, one must seriously question what is known about the influences of family development on the marital relationship.

Table 17–1 Future Directions for Gerontological Research on the Family: A Review of the Reviews

Reviewer	Review
1. Troll (1971)	Qualitative aspects of kin interaction ("introduced but not pursued extensively" in the 1960s); delineation of family developmental processes in adulthood and old age; grandparenting role, attitudes toward grandparents; differences between middle and late adulthood stages; qualitative differences in relationships both in and out of the family; longitudinal research, accurate calibration of ages and stages when developmental change occurs, broader sampling, and more complex indices; marital sexuality and sexual adjustment; value similarity and family interaction; extralegal cohabitation; parent-child relationships after the launching stage and before old age; transmission of values across multiple generations; sibling, in-law, and other extended kin relations
2. Troll, Miller, & Atchley (1979)	Longitudinal and cross-sequential methodologies; family dynamics of conflict, negotiation, and cooperation; changes in marital quality and interaction over the middle and later adult years; male attitudes toward marriage and housework, especially cohort differences; sexuality; age, social class, racial, and ethnic variations in the impact of widowhood on older men; male-female differences in experiencing widowhood; impact of older adult separation or divorce upon middle-aged children; complex nature of older parent–adult child relations; return migration in order to be closer to family; adult child–older parent relationships over the life course; greater focus on qualitative studies; dyadic perspectives, rather than relying on individual reports; diverse effects of divorce on older parent–adult child relationship; grandfatherhood; four generational inquiries; sibling, in-law, and other extended kin relationships; function of grandparent role for widows in comparison to those with spouse
3. Bengtson & DeTerre (1980)	Ways in which older family members spend time with, assist, feel about, and agree with other kin members; specific financial information regarding intergenerational financial assistance; parent-child relationships over the whole life cycle, especially after adolescence; mediating role of family on behalf of older members; conditions under which cash allowances paid to relatives caring for older adults are mutually beneficial for all generations; positive dynamics of family life; characteristics of healthy families; models for optimal functioning of all generations in the family; relationship between personal well-being in old age and one's history as a child, a spouse, and a parent

4. Mancini (1980)   Expectations for older family members held by those who are younger; use of discretionary time in a family context; manner in which requirements for personal dependence and independence are reconciled in a family; family size influence on well-being; determinants of older parent–adult child contact; effects of instrumental exchange on well-being, especially when exchange is not equitable; importance of affective-emotional exchange for successful aging; family's role in facilitating coming to terms with impending death of an older member; examination of dynamics of parent-child relationship over time; content of communication during older parent–adult child contact; family rituals; process of redefining parental and child roles

5. Streib & Beck (1980)   Economics of aging and family life; legal underpinnings of services for the elderly; legal rights of elders, including civil rights as they pertain to competence, guardianship, and power of attorney; cultural identity; study of social change and the older family; restudying communities; intergenerational relations between launching of last child and entrance into old age; longitudinal research; theory development; inferential research; studies on sibling, in-law, and other kin relationships; demographic base on which all research on the older family must be grounded; manner in which health and economic factors shape structure and function of older families, especially how the old relate to their children; interface between family life and the health and welfare system; knowledge that is cumulative, study of macroenvironment and how it impacts on older families' microenvironment

In general, older males are becoming more common targets of research efforts, especially their grandfather role and their role in everyday household tasks. Though the effects of retirement on men has been addressed repeatedly, studies are less likely to explore the more affective dimensions of adulthood. For example, most of the grandparent studies have been conducted on grandmothers. The impact of divorce on the family, especially on young children, has been investigated over a number of years but few researchers have applied that line of inquiry to older couples and their adult children. Yet, it seems reasonable that such a change in family structure is felt by the second and third generations, if for no other reason than the presumption that long-standing marriages remain standing. Aside from these areas of needed research, Troll and associates (1979) call for methodologies that support dyadic research and that concern relationship continuity.

Bengtson and DeTerre (1980) have discussed the need for both microsociological and macrosociological research. In particular, they wonder about the financial aspects of support between the generations, which includes actual monetary contributions from children to older parents and the effects of cash allowances to families providing care for their elderly members. These questions represent one aspect of the larger issue of the family's mediating role in the relationships older people have with institutions and bureaucracies. Bengtson and DeTerre (1980) have also noted the necessity of identifying the characteristics of healthy families, the positive aspects of family dynamics, and the optimal functioning models for both older and younger generations in the family.

A 1980 review by Mancini largely focused on microsociological research issues. Included in the discussion was the need to examine the nature of how time is jointly used by older people and their families, as well as determinants of contact with the family. A particular aspect of family time-use involves family rituals and traditional events, which may serve to provide the family with a sense of history and the older person with an opportunity to participate in the creation of that history. Mancini also felt that the redefinition of parent and child roles over an extended time was an important domain for researchers because of its potential explanatory power about current relationship quality. The redefinition of these roles may be related to the issue of dependence-independence. Moreover, Mancini asked how the family supports the older member's concurrent needs for remaining as independent as possible and for increased reliance on family in the case of frail health and limited financial resources. Finally, he discussed a microsociological component of the family's mediating function that pertains to the role children and others may play in assisting an old person in coping with impending death.

The last review summarized in Table 17-1 is an overview of research conducted during the 1970s (Streib & Beck, 1980). These authors believed that the more promising areas of future research concerned the interface between the macrosociological and microsociological domains. As an example, they cited the potential significant relationships between the family and the health and welfare systems. Streib and Beck also discussed the issue of social change and family life, and suggest the need for restudying communities (such as that already accomplished in Middletown). The legal rights of elders were also said to be underresearched. In general, these authors expressed disappointment over the lack of cumulative knowledge of the family in later life. When they compared their assessment with that of the previous decade (Troll, 1971), it was noted that the state of knowledge and of research had not changed substantially.

The various reviews appear to indicate that the frontier of research on the family in later life is wide open, a fact that bodes well for contemporary researchers but does not speak well for work already completed. What is really known about family relationships in old age remains unclear. The concluding remarks on new directions for gerontological research on the family complement the contents of these reviews, and focus around family relationships; marriage relations; the family's mediating role; life cycle issues; intergenerational exchange; and, methodology issues. Each of the following contributes significantly to an understanding of the core experiences of family life in the later years.

RESEARCH FRONTIERS AND FUTURE DIRECTIONS

During the 1970s, Jerome Kaplan suggested that "we have only begun our knowledge search on the family in aging" (1975, p. 385). Though scores of professionals have engaged in research on family life in old age, the complexity of this domain of study warrants continued investigation. There appears to be sound reason to continue examining the relationship between old people and their kin, to capture the significance of marriage for older couples, to identify the family's mediating role in the successful aging of their older members, to understand the interface between life in the middle and later years, to understand the importance of intergenerational exchange, and to elaborate new methodologies for studying family interaction (see Table 17–2).

Family Relationships

Earlier in this chapter the preponderance of research on contact with the family was noted, as well as the failure of research to link contact with well-being. Although the tendency has been to conclude that family contact and well-being, in reality, are unrelated, few studies have attempted to identify the range of potential intervening variables. Among these conditional factors are the following:

- whether contact is due to choice, rather than to obligation
- whether family members serve as confidants

Table 17-2 Future Directions for Gerontological Research on the Family

Family relationships	Conditions under which contact with family promotes well-being; effects of discretionary and obligatory activity on quality of life; confidant role of family members; influence of family structure on family relationship quality; how older adults influence the well-being of other family members.
Marriage relationships	Affectional dimensions of older marriages; comparisons of "her" marriage and "his" marriage; retirement adjustment of older women
Family's mediating role	Transition to institutionalization; manner in which family promotes good health
Life-cycle issues	Family life in the middle years
Intergenerational exchange	Nature of exchange and intimacy at a distance; generational differences in viewpoints on exchange; meaning behind exchange
Methodological issues	Specification of marital adjustment components; creative approaches to contact research; partitioning of exchange domain; matching relationships with specific aspects of well-being

- the shape of the family structure
- the impact of the older adult upon the family

The spirit in which generations in the family spend time together may be the linchpin in determining whether the well-being of either old people or their kin is influenced. Both research and common sense suggest that one's satisfaction is enhanced when time-use preferences and actual behavior correspond (Mancini & Orthner, 1982). If the contact one has with kin is largely due to societal or family expectations, then what occurs during contact may be obviously perfunctory; however, if the contact is due to genuine concern and interest in the activities of others, then the time spent together is more likely to be rewarding. Part of this sense of worth may be attributable to the confidant function a family member may provide. Some years ago Lowenthal and Haven (1968) demonstrated the importance of having someone in whom one can confide. Though a friend is usually considered to be a logical confidant, a family member could also be such an intimate. The importance of a confidant has also been researched by Weiss (1969), who maintains that a fully functioning person probably has one or more people with whom to share innermost concerns. Whether contact and well-being interrelate may depend on the nature of the relationship function—that is, if relationships with kin provide the older adult a comfortable forum in which to express thoughts and feelings.

Most studies of family contact are ambiguous because they typically get a measure of how often the older adult sees, talks with, or corresponds with kin. The reader, though, rarely knows the circumstances under which the contact occurred, or whether the contact was with a sibling (one child) or with four or more different children. Recent research has examined the relationship between family size (number of children) and well-being and has reported an inverse relationship, even after socioeconomic status controls were applied (Watson & Kivett, 1976). This result raises the question of how family structure influences successful aging. Larger families may concurrently provide a broader informal support network and a greater range of kin who are sources of concern. Furthermore, in selected cases, disagreements among adult children about who should provide particular types of support for aged parents may have an adverse impact.

Usually relationship effects are conceptualized and researched unidirectionally. Studies of intergenerational relationships do not typically examine the impact on the well-being of an older person's adult child; yet, this impact may be the primary predictor of the older adult's own well-being. For example, the adult child's satisfaction with the relationship with an aged parent is likely to determine partially how much time is spent together and what occurs during that time. The personal constraints associated with providing care for an older parent no doubt influence the level of vitality an adult child may possess. In general, researchers need to examine the impact that an older adult may have on the lifestyle and well-being of kin and employ that knowledge to explain successful aging.

Marriage Relationships

Researchers have been allocating more of their time to the study of the family, rather than to marriage relationships in old age. It is difficult to know whether this preference is due to greater importance being attached to parent-child relations or to the decreasing number of available older couples. After 75 years of age, 70 percent of men and only 23 percent of women have a living spouse (Troll and associates, 1979). It appears that for these older adults with a living spouse, marriage can be critical to well-being—especially when the relationship is a satisfying one (Mancini, 1979).

The affectional dimensions of older marriages warrant further investigation, especially as they relate to informal support. In particular, the nature and role of companionship in these long-standing relationships may be instrumental in gaining a clear understanding of marital quality. Earlier, it was suggested that satisfaction with time-use is important to the meaningfulness of family contact. Likewise, the manner in which older husbands and wives spend time with one another ought to provide insight into how they communicate, the extent to which they share important feelings and thoughts, and the impact the relationship has on the quality of life. An interesting question to address concerns the function of marriage among those who are not satisfied with the relationship. Although it is obvious that marriage satisfaction relates substantially to well-being, other dimensions of the marriage (aside from its happiness level) may be equally important for successful aging; for example, the equity of affective and instrumental exchange in the marriage may be a primary indicator of personal well-being.

Several years ago, Jessie Bernard (1973) discussed the sometimes differing worlds of marital life, and spoke of "his" marriage and "her" marriage. There appears to be reason to explore further the separate realities that older husbands and wives may experience. In 1978, Lee found that marital satisfaction contributed relatively more to the morale of wives; health, however, was more important for morale among the husbands. These findings probably reflect average differences in the health levels and concerns of older women and men, as well as traditional differences about the role of the family. Too often, however, people who do not fit normative expectations of what wives and husbands should do are ignored. One such instance involves the retirement adjustment of older working wives and their husbands. Studies of retirement are largely based on men; women are included only as the husband's retirement affects the housewife role (Troll and associates, 1979; Keating & Cole, 1980). What is the nature of retirement adjustment for women who have combined work-career and family, and does it parallel that of men? Does role diversity among women mitigate the negative effects of leaving the work role? An important aspect of "her" marriage and "his" marriage may be found in contrasting the manner in which retirement is experienced and managed.

Family's Mediating Role

Families can act on behalf of their older members in several significant ways, especially in regard to legal and health issues (Bengtson & DeTerre, 1980; Streib & Beck, 1980). Change in residence can be a source of trauma for many older people, particularly if it results from increased frailty or economic constraints. A special case of relocation has been noted by Wells and Macdonald (1981)—the move of an older person from one institution to another. Areas of future study should include the process whereby families and their elders arrive at a decision concerning relocation, the function of visiting the old person in the new environment, and the types of exchange that occur with the older adult. For example, patterns of exchange may alter because the institution provides various services, and the discontinuity may have an adverse impact on family interaction.

Investigators consistently find that successful aging is profoundly influenced by health (Larsen, 1978), which is a domain that includes the presence of chronic and acute disease, mobility level, medication usage, and preventive health behavior. All too often, older adults are frustrated by what appears to be uncontrollable health difficulties. Family members can have substantial input into elders' successful aging simply by easing their entrance into the health care system, by supporting them in effective health behavior, and by being a resource for information and understanding when health problems arise. Perhaps the most important service a family member can provide is to encourage the older adult to fully get into health care programs. These potential advocacy roles that younger generations can fill have yet to be adequately addressed by research.

Life Cycle Issues

Over the last 30 years considerably more attention has been given to the examination of the family relationships of later life rather than those of middle age. The lack of emphasis on mid-life is reflected in the research needs discussed by Troll (1971), Troll and associates (1979), Bengtson and DeTerre (1980), and Streib and Beck (1980). Recent comprehensive bibliographies on research on families in mid-life also demonstrate the necessity for increased efforts (Olson & Markoff, 1982; Olson, 1979, 1980, 1981).

That middle age is underresearched is partially due to the period often being seen as not especially critical. Children have already been launched, and retirement is in the future. Yet, it would seem that a great deal of retirement adjustment and successful aging occurs during middle age. Certainly, the modes of interaction between parents and adult children are developed and solidified over the postlaunching, pre-retirement years; grandparenthood also begins. It is in the mid-life period, too, that important physical and health changes occur—changes that prove to be significant for later life (Troll, 1975). Because these events are potential precursors of lifestyle patterns in retirement, researchers should account for them in their models of successful aging.

Intergenerational Exchange

Several researchers have suggested that a core aspect of intergenerational relations involves the exchanges that may occur, which include reciprocal emotional support, as well as actual services and goods (Lee & Ellithorpe, 1982; Mancini, 1980). There have not been many investigations, however, that have explored intergenerational exchange. Moreover, research completed thus far has been inconclusive about the manner in which exchange has an impact on older adults or their kin.

Several important aspects of exchange may link it with relationship quality and with successful aging. First, inasmuch as a number of families are separated because of contemporary mobility patterns, exchange and intimacy must occur, of necessity, at a distance. Specific types of instrumental exchange (care in time of illness, child care or aid in running errands) are prohibited; yet, exchange probably still occurs and may be made at an affective or emotional level. Most research designs have assumed that older people and their kin live in fairly close proximity and are eligible to exchange a wide range of services, but they have not adequately accounted for the effects of distance. Another dimension worthy of study pertains to generational differences in viewpoints on exchange, because most researchers have only examined it from the perspectives of older adults (Lee & Ellithorpe, 1982; Mancini & Simon, 1982). The generations may differ in what they think is being exchanged, how often exchange occurs, and whether exchange is perceived as equitable or exploitive. There may also be important perceptual differences in the value of what is being exchanged; such differences may then be the key to whether or not relationships are enhanced or damaged. Finally, the meaning attached to exchange behavior by the generations may play a role in successful aging. For example, if the exchange of goods, services, and understanding is one-sided, a person might be placed in an undesirable dependent position. In spite of good intentions, the overall outcome may be feelings of incompetence that detract from one's quality of life. Generally, a great deal of research is still needed on this aspect of intergenerational relationships, a domain that is rich in information on family dynamics.

Methodological Issues

Family gerontology shares several concerns with the general family studies field. One of these concerns is the specification of marital adjustment components. Very frequently, adjustment measures are global and treated as unidimensional; however, a recent study by Lee (1978) indirectly suggests the importance of focusing upon the many dimensions of marital quality. In that study, it was discovered that morale and marriage adjustment were more strongly associated among women, which pointed to the differing marital worlds of husbands and wives. The exact origin of those differences is unclear, but although they may be due to variation in the value placed on marriage, they may be attributable more directly to differences in satisfaction with specific aspects of the marriage. These specifics might involve companionship, sexual intimacy and affection, communication, or task-sharing.

Throughout this chapter (as well as in Chapter 4), research on family interaction has been repeatedly discussed. Interaction may be significant for understanding intergenerational relationships but researchers have been provincial in their approaches. New methodologies for assessing and analyzing contact and interaction are necessary if the role that spending time together plays in personal or relationship satisfaction is to be understood. One direction that may be fruitful involves identifying the meaning behind contact and the motivation behind spending time together.

A methodological aspect of intergenerational exchange also requires further work. Researchers typically summarize a wide range of exchange attitudes and behaviors into a single global indicator of this aspect of relationship dynamics (Lee & Ellithorpe, 1982; Mancini & Simon, 1982). Yet, why should it be assumed that all exchanges are of equal importance to older people or to their families? Providing care during time of illness, providing transportation, providing child care, performing household repairs, listening to problems, giving money and gifts, and assisting in decision making do not appear to be similarly relevant to relationship quality. They each require a different level of personal investment and interest, and represent needs of unequal seriousness. As in the case of the study of marital quality, researchers need to focus upon particular exchange behaviors and expectations—both emotional and practical.

Finally, a shift in the way relationships are contrasted with well-being may provide a more accurate assessment of the contribution family life makes to successful aging. Earlier, the lack of theoretical direction in family gerontology was discussed, and a central point was made that there was frequently no rationale for the associations among variables. There is a critical need also to match relationships and their functions with particular dimensions of well-being. If, for example, one aspect of well-being is defined as feeling positive about growing older, then it should be asked whether relationships function to promote that positive feeling. If research demonstrates that they do not function in that manner, it does not indicate that well-being per se is not influenced by family relationships. All one actually knows is that the relationship does not influence *that* aspect of well-being. Other, as yet undefined, dimensions of successful aging may be markedly influenced by intergenerational relationships.

SUMMARY

The goal of this review has been to elaborate needed research areas in family gerontology and to cite some of the larger issues relevant to this domain of study. It has been suggested that the importance of family life may be overestimated; that the criterion *well-being* is not always the appropriate choice; that research has tended to address the alienation, enrichment, and empty nest hypotheses; that qualitative approaches are underutilized; that concerted theory development efforts are advised; and that the field still lacks a cumulative body of knowledge. Extant reviews on research are expansive and suggest that few areas exist in which additional efforts are not required. Both microsociological and macrosociological phenomena remain to be explored and involve family relations, marriage relations, the family's mediating role, life-cycle issues, and intergenerational exchange. These efforts at understanding the content of family life in old age will be enhanced by improved research methodologies. In conclusion, the research frontier about families in later life is broad and multidimensional. For the researcher this situation is advantageous because there are few definitive answers to the important questions on generational relationships; however, it is equally disadvantageous because explorations of a frontier often lack the guideposts needed for fruitful discovery.

REFERENCES

Bengtson, V., & DeTerre, E. (1980). Aging and family relations. *Marriage and Family Review, 3,* 51–76.

Bernard, J. (1973). *The future of marriage.* New York: Bantam.

Edwards, J.N., & Klemmack, D.L. (1973). Correlates of life satisfaction: A reexamination. *Journal of Gerontology, 28,* 497–502.

George, L.K., & Bearon, L.B. (1980). *Quality of life in older persons: Meaning and measurement.* New York: Human Sciences Press.

Hill, R., & Hansen, D.A. (1960). The identification of conceptual frameworks utilized in family study. *Marriage and Family Living, 22,* 299–311.

Johnson, E.S. (1981). Older mothers' perceptions of their child's divorce. *The Gerontologist, 21,* 395–401.

Kaplan, Jerome. (1975). The family in aging. *The Gerontologist, 15,* 385.

Keating, N.C., & Cole, P. (1980). What do I do with him 24 hours a day? Changes in the housewife role after retirement. *The Gerontologist, 20,* 84–89.

Keith, P.M., & Brubaker, T.H. (1979). Male household roles in later life: A look at masculinity and marital relationships. *The Family Coordinator, 28,* 497–502.

Larsen, R. (1978). Thirty years of research on the subjective well-being of older Americans. *Journal of Gerontology, 33,* 109–124.

Lee, G.R. (1978). Marriage and morale in later life. *Journal of Marriage and the Family, 40,* 131–139.

Lee, G.R. (1979). Children and the elderly: Interaction and morale. *Research on Aging, 1,* 335–360.

Lee, G.R., & Ellithorpe, E. (1982). Intergenerational exchange and subjective well-being among the elderly. *Journal of Marriage and the Family, 44,* 217–224.

Lewis, R.A. (1978). Transitions in middle-age and aging families: A bibliography from 1940 to 1977. *The Family Coordinator, 27,* 457–476.

Lowenthal, M.F., & Haven, C. (1968). Interaction and adaptation: Intimacy as a critical variable. *American Sociological Review, 33,* 20–31.

Maddox, G.L., & Wiley, J. (1976). Scope, concepts, and methods in the study of aging. In R.H. Binstock and & E. Shanas (Eds.), *Handbook of aging and the social sciences* (pp. 3–34). New York: Van Nostrand Reinhold.

Mancini, J.A. (1979). Family relationships and morale among people 65 years of age and older. *American Journal of Orthopsychiatry, 49,* 292–300.

Mancini, J.A. (1980). Strengthening the family life of older adults: Myth-conceptions and investigative needs. In N. Stinnett (Ed.), *Family strengths: Positive models for family life* (pp. 333–343). Lincoln, NE: University of Nebraska Press.

Mancini, J.A., & Orthner, D.K. (1982). Leisure time, activities, preferences, and competence: Implications for the morale of older adults. *Journal of Applied Gerontology, 1,* 95–103.

Mancini, J.A., & Quinn, W.H. (1981). Dimensions of health and their importance for morale in old age. *Journal of Community Health, 7,* 118–128.

Mancini, J.A., Quinn, W., Gavigan, M., & Franklin, H. (1980). Social network interaction among older adults: Implications for life satisfaction. *Human Relations, 33,* 543–554.

Mancini, J.A., & Simon, J. (1982, June). When push comes to shove: Older adults' expectations of support from family and friends. Paper presented at the annual meeting of the Southern Gerontological Society, Orlando, FL.

Martin, W.C. (1973). Activity and disengagement: Life satisfaction of in-movers into a retirement community. *The Gerontologist, 13,* 224–227.

Olson, D.H. (1979). *Inventory of marriage and family literature* (Vol. 5). Beverly Hills, CA: Sage.

Olson, D.H. (1980). *Inventory of marriage and family literature* (Vol. 6). Beverly Hills, CA: Sage.

Olson, D.H. (1981). *Inventory of marriage and family literature* (Vol. 7). Beverly Hills, CA: Sage.

Olson, D.H., & Markoff, R. (Eds.). (1982). *Inventory of marriage and family literature* (Vol. 8). Beverly Hills, CA: Sage.

Quinn, W.H. (1982). Older parent and adult child interaction: Qualitative dimensions in building family strengths. In N. Stinnett (Ed.), *Building family strengths* (Vol. 4). Lincoln, NE: University of Nebraska Press.

Quinn, W.H. (1983). Personal and family adjustment in later life. *Journal of Marriage and the Family, 44.*

Robertson, J.F. (1975). Interaction in three generation families, parents as mediators: Toward a theoretical perspective. *International Journal of Aging and Human Development, 6,* 103–110.

Ryff, C.D. (1982). Successful aging: A developmental approach. *The Gerontologist, 22,* 209–214.

Shanas, E. (1979). Social myth as hypothesis: The case of the family relations of old people. *The Gerontologist, 19,* 3–9.

Shanas, E. (1980). Older people and their families: The new pioneers. *Journal of Marriage and the Family, 42,* 9–15.

Streib, G.F., & Beck, R.W. (1980). Older families: A decade review. *Journal of Marriage and the Family, 42,* 937–956.

Thompson, W.E., & Streib, G. (1961). Meaningful activity in a family context. In R.W. Kleemeier (Ed.), *Aging and leisure: A research perspective into the meaningful use of time* (pp. 177–211). New York: Oxford University Press.

Troll, L.E. (1971). The family of later life: A decade review. *Journal of Marriage and the Family, 33,* 163–290.

Troll, L.E. (1975). *Early and middle adulthood.* Monterey, CA: Brooks-Cole.

Troll, L.E., Miller, S.J., Atchley, R.C. (1979). *Families in Later Life.* Belmont, CA: Wadsworth.

Watson, J.A., & Kivett, V.R. (1976). Influences on the life satisfaction of older fathers. *The Family Coordinator, 25,* 482–488.

Weiss, R.S. (1969). The fund of sociability. *Trans-Action, 6,* 36–43.

Wells, L., & Macdonald, G. (1981). Interpersonal networks and post-relocation adjustment of the institutionalized elderly. *The Gerontologist, 21,* 177–183.

Index

About the Editors

William H. Quinn, Ph.D., is an assistant professor and the director of the marriage and family therapy program in the department of human development and family studies at Texas Tech University, as well as an assistant clinical professor in the department of family medicine at Texas Tech University's Health Sciences Center. Dr. Quinn's research interests include intergenerational family relationships, family systems interventions and outcomes, family systems and physical illness, and family therapy and drug abuse.

George A. Hughston, Ph.D., is the chairperson for the department of home economics at Arizona State University, Tempe. He received his doctorate at The Pennsylvania State University and participated in an adult development and aging traineeship sponsored by the National Institute of Child and Human Development, U.S. Department of Health, Education and Welfare.

About the Contributors

Greg Arling, Ph.D., is the director of the Virginia Center on Aging in Richmond. He is also an associate professor of gerontology at the Medical College of Virginia, Virginia Commonwealth University.

Vern L. Bengtson, Ph.D., is currently professor of sociology at the University of Southern California, as well as director of the Research Institute of the Andrus Gerontology Center in Los Angeles. He received his Ph.D. from the University of Chicago and has held research or teaching appointments at Cal Tech, the University of Stockholm, and the University of Chicago, in addition to U.S.C. Dr. Bengtson is a member of the National Institutes of Aging's review panel for research and training in aging, as well as a consultant to the Social Security Administration's extramural research program. He was also a technical consultant to the 1981 White House Conference on Aging (Committee on the Family).

Ellie Brubaker, Ph.D., A.C.S.W., is currently an assistant professor in the department of sociology at Miami University, Oxford, Ohio.

Timothy H. Brubaker, Ph.D., is presently a professor in the department of home economics and consumer sciences as well as an associate of the family and child study center at Miami University, Oxford, Ohio.

Rodney Cate, Ph.D., received his doctorate from The Pennsylvania State University. Currently, Dr. Cate is an associate professor of human development and family studies and is the assistant dean of the graduate school at Oregon State University.

Thomas R. Chibucos, Ph.D., is an associate professor and coordinator of family and child studies at Northern Illinois University. He has published in the areas of human infancy, child mistreatment, and research methodology, and has been a consultant for local, state, and federal governments, as well as the private sector.

Charles Lee Cole, Ph.D., is an associate professor of family studies and director of the marital and family therapy training program in the department of family environment at Iowa State University, Ames, Iowa.

Terri A. Eisler, Ph.D., is the coordinator of women's services at Northeastern Illinois University. She received her doctorate from Virginia Polytechnic Institute in family development.

Beth Emery, is a doctoral candidate in human development and family studies at Oregon State University.

June Henton, Ph.D., received her doctorate from the University of Minnesota, and currently is the head of the department of human development and family studies at Oregon State University.

David J. Hubler is a master's degree candidate in family studies at Northern Illinois University.

Helen Q. Kivnick, Ph.D., is a clinical and research psychologist trained at the University of Michigan, and now in private practice in California. She currently holds visiting appointments in the department of psychiatry, University of Pennsylvania, and the Institute of Human Development, University of California, Berkeley, and is an adjunct faculty member at the California School of Professional Psychology, Berkeley. Dr. Kivnick has written numerous articles and papers on grandparenthood and mental health across the life cycle.

Joseph A. Kuypers, Ph.D., is currently an associate professor in the school of social work at the University of Manitoba, Winnipeg. His research and writing has focused on aging across the life cycle, with special emphasis given to the older family and adaptation to crisis situations.

Shirley A. Lockery, Ph.D., received her doctorate in social work from the University of Southern California. Currently, she is the associate director of planning and operations at the University Center on Aging (UCOA) at San Diego State University.

William J. McAuley, Ph.D., is the director of the Virginia Tech Center of Gerontology in Blacksburg, Virginia.

Jay A. Mancini, Ph.D., is associate director for program development at the Virginia Tech Center of Gerontology, and associate professor of family development at Virginia Tech. He was formerly a senior associate with the human resources research and development center of the SRA Corporation, Washington, D.C.

Carla Masciocchi is the project coordinator of the Rehabilitation Research and Training Center in Aging at the University of Pennsylvania. She has directed a number of research projects on chronic illness, long-term care, and the psychosocial status of families who care for impaired aged members. In addition, she has developed patient evaluation systems for several rehabilitation centers, and lectures at the University of Pennsylvania.

Tamerra Moeller, Ph.D., is the director of training at the Rehabilitation Research and Training Center in Aging, University of Pennsylvania. She teaches at the university and the medical school and coordinates the center's training activities throughout the university and offers seminars and programs to personnel in rehabilitation, aging, and mental health. A licensed psychologist, Dr. Moeller has counseled families for several years.

Karen A. Roberto, Ph.D., is an assistant professor and coordinator of the gerontology program in the department of human services, University of Northern Colorado. Her research interests include informal support networks in later life, friendships of older adults, and life-span development.

Robert L. Rubinstein, Ph.D., received his doctorate from Bryn Mawr College and is currently a research anthropologist with the Philadelphia Geriatric Center.

Jean Pearson Scott, Ph.D., completed her doctorate at the University of North Carolina, Greensboro. Currently, she is an assistant professor in the department of human development and family studies at Texas Tech University. Her research interests include support networks of older persons, relationships of families in later life, coping strategies of older families with chronic illness, and rural aging.

Wayne C. Seelbach, Ph.D., is associate professor of sociology and gerontology and head of the department of sociology, social work, and criminal justice at Lamar University, Beaumont, Texas.

E. Percil Stanford, Ph.D., received his doctorate in sociology from Iowa State University with an emphasis in gerontology. He is currently a professor and director of the University Center on Aging (UCOA) at San Diego State University.

Adria Thomas, M.A., is research coordinator of the Rehabilitation Research and Training Center in Aging at the University of Pennsylvania. Ms. Thomas has conducted research in the areas of mental health, substance abuse, long-term care demonstration projects, and the effects on families who provide care for impaired elderly.